THE THIRTY-YEAR WAR

THE THIRTY-YEAR WAR

A HISTORY OF DETROIT'S STREETCARS, 1892–1922

NEIL J. LEHTO

Michigan State University Press | East Lansing

Michigan State University Press
East Lansing, Michigan 48823-5245

Printed and bound in the United States of America.

26 25 24 23 22 21 20 19 18 17 1 2 3 4 5 6 7 8 9 10

LIBRARY OF CONGRESS CATALOGING-IN-PUBLICATION DATA AVAILABLE
Cloth: 978-1-61186-230-0
PDF: 978-1-60917-515-3

Book design by Charlie Sharp, Sharp Des!gns, East Lansing, MI
Cover design by Erin Kirk New
Cover image looking up Woodward Ave., Detroit, Mich. was taken circa 1910–20. Detroit Publishing Company Collection, Prints and Photographs Division, Library of Congress, LC-DIG-det-4a24908.

Michigan State University Press is a member of the Green Press Initiative and is committed to developing and encouraging ecologically responsible publishing practices. For more information about the Green Press Initiative and the use of recycled paper in book publishing, please visit *www.greenpressinitiative.org*.

Visit Michigan State University Press at *www.msupress.org*

One is fairly lost in the moves and counter moves that have been made in the Detroit situation. For thirty years, railway matters there have been in the public eye. Some day no doubt a historian will arise who will set down the record of events for posterity, but unless that historian is a disciple of the romantic school that product will be dull reading. If the time is not too remote when this work is begun then a story ought to result that would be enthralling. The man who does the task, however, will need to get back of the facts to the persons who directed the various moves and disclose if he can the actuating motives.

"Thirty-Year Controversy Brought to an End,"
Street Railway Journal, May 20, 1922

Contents

Introduction

This is the story of the Thirty-Year War waged by the City of Detroit against its street railway companies between 1892 and 1922. It is based on first-hand accounts, biographies, and contemporary newspaper and magazine articles, as well as state corporate, Detroit common council, and other historical records. All of the characters are real, and all of their dialogue with each other is drawn from these sources.

The horse-drawn street railway system built by attorney Eben Willcox and his investors on Jefferson Avenue in 1863 to carry passengers between Detroit's two railroad stations soon spread onto the other spoke-like streets drawn by Augustus B. Woodward in 1806 named Woodward, Jefferson, Michigan, Grand River, and Gratiot Avenues and Fort Street. By 1890, when Detroit voters elected one of their greatest mayors, Hazen S. Pingree, the new owners of the city's private street railway companies led by George Hendrie and U.S. Senator James McMillan were laying plans and arranging the necessary financing to replace their horses with overhead electric-powered streetcars while their many thousands of daily passengers were clamoring for lower fares. A few months following a violent, four-day strike in 1891 by street railway drivers and conductors, joined by disgruntled daily riders, Detroit's corrupt Common Council gave Hendrie and McMillan new thirty-year street railway franchises, getting nothing in return but an empty promise of new electric-powered streetcars. Mayor Pingree stepped in with a startling veto, and he followed with a politically powerful demand for citywide three-cent fares.

For years, state and federal courtrooms in Detroit filled with lawyers arguing streetcar cases. Politicians who had always campaigned for three-cent fares against the company's succession of owners finally and quietly gave up and, instead, shifted to demanding municipal ownership of the street railways on which the city would itself offer three-cent fares. They failed repeatedly. It was not until 1922 that Ford gasoline millionaire Mayor James J. Couzens was able to claim victory, having conceded citywide six-cent fares.

The Thirty-Year War was a remarkable period in Detroit history, filled with amazing characters, as the two sides fought before the Common Council, in the state legislature, at a state constitutional convention, and in both the state and federal trial courts, with numerous cases reaching the Michigan and U.S. Supreme Courts. They argued over everything imaginable, paying a legion of lawyers to represent them, mostly notably over franchises, internal improvements, and municipal home rule, the subjects with which the story begins.

CHAPTER 1

Before the Thirty-Year War

Ferries and Franchises

Nine years after the Pilgrims landed at Plymouth Rock, thousands of Puritans came from England to settle along the Charles River at Massachusetts Bay. On the south side of the river, on a three-mile-long peninsula less than a mile wide, they built homes and farms in today's Boston. Others settled on the north side of the marshy river in Charlestown and two miles west in Newton. Together, they became a national port of foreign trade, bound together by religious, cultural, social, and political ties.

On November 9, 1630, leaders of the Boston, Charlestown, and Newton settlements gathered over a problem they shared—the lack of a ferry between them across the Charles River. Together, they agreed that anyone building a ferryboat regularly crossing the river could charge one penny per passenger and one penny for every hundred pounds of goods transported. In June of the following year, Edward Converse offered to do so, and they granted him the first colonial adaptation of the franchise. Anyone wanting to operate a ferry in old England needed a franchise granted in the form of a charter from the monarchy, exercising its sovereign power over the private use of the public land and water, granting consent for a term of years, regulating fares and means of operation, and requiring equal service to all passengers and shippers. Transporting crops and goods on ferries, canals, bridges, and toll roads or selling them at fairs and wharves came to be valuable prerogatives of the monarchy for which the need of a franchise was accepted. These kinds of activities, later described as public utilities or, in some cases, common carriers, were natural monopolies occupying a market in which the more they carried the lower their unit cost. The only expense of a ferry after its building is operating the boat. A single vessel that satisfies existing demand, if large enough, made negligible the expense of adding new riders so that hiring a single vessel was more efficient than using two or more competing ferries. A natural monopoly, however, tended to charge a premium price unless regulated. Together, these economic conclusions, right or wrong, and experience with them produced what the common law called a public utility franchise, described by the U.S. Supreme Court in 1888 as "a right, privilege or power of public concern, which ought not to be exercised by private individuals at their mere will and pleasure, but should be reserved for public control and administration, either by the government directly, or by public agents, acting under such conditions and regulations as the government may impose in the public interest, and for the public security."[1]

The U.S. Constitution divided the English monarchy's sovereign power over public lands and waters between the state and federal governments, resulting in frequent and often fierce jurisdictional disagreements. Each jealously guards its own power. The clash of local, state, and federal interest is the daily debate of legislators and judges in the shaping of local, state, and national policy over not only ferryboats but also streetcars in Detroit during the Thirty-Year War. The common law of England had broadly distinguished between the natural monopolies created by public utilities and the ordinary trades in which there was effective competition, barring the monarchy from creating and protecting monopolies among them. These principles are embodied in the Fourteenth Amendment of the U.S. Constitution, which protects the common law privileges and immunities of individuals. So, for example, the butchering of livestock cannot be prohibited by creating a state-protected monopoly.[2] Anyone wanting to operate ferries, roads, bridges, lighthouses, and harbors in colonial times, and railroads, natural gas, electricity, telegraph, street railways, telephone, cable television, and fiber-optic broadband Internet services today, however, can be denied a public utility franchise without any right to complain under the Fourteenth Amendment.[3]

From time to time, competing ferries came along until 1640, when Massachusetts legislators granted exclusive ferry rights between Boston and Charlestown to Harvard College in a gesture of support to the new school. A year later, they declared, "there shall be no monopolies granted or allowed amongst us—but if such new inventions that are profitable to the country—and that for a short time."[4] In 1701, Harvard leased its Charles River ferryboat to private managers. Harvard's exclusive public utility franchise set the stage for the U.S. Supreme Court's landmark ruling in the *Charles River Bridge* case.

In April 1713, Harvard College sent a delegation to the Massachusetts General Court, the state's legislative body, to protest plans by a Boston investor to build a bridge over the Charles River. Harvard successfully objected that a new bridge would drive its private ferry operator out of business.[5] Seven years later, on April 27, 1720, Boston again directed its legislative representatives to promote the building of a bridge over the Charles River "at the place where the ferry hath been usually kept."[6] Legislative leaders refused, urging the physician who had applied to work out a deal with Harvard. Nothing further came of his proposal. By the end of the Revolutionary War, in anticipation of revived commerce, Harvard had spent £300 repairing the ferryboat and, by 1781, was receiving annual rent of £200 with profits assured to grow for years to come in the absence of a competitor.

Several groups of investors petitioned the Massachusetts legislature in 1785 for charters to build toll bridges across the Charles River. The winners of a forty-year franchise were eighty-seven of Charlestown's most highly regarded businessmen, including among them John Hancock. They won by agreeing to pay Harvard £200 per year for forty years, after which the bridge would revert to Massachusetts. The state charter incorporating the Proprietors of the Charles River Bridge set forth specific details of construction, including the minimum width, the building of a draw, and installation of lamps, and an elaborate schedule of tolls. The opening of the new Charles River Bridge in Boston to public traffic on June 17, 1786, marked Bunker Hill Day. The bridge—the first connecting Boston to the mainland—was built on seventy-five piers of oak. It was 1,470 feet long and 42 feet wide. As many as twenty thousand people attended the celebration. Four days after the opening, bridge traffic included 20 coaches, 150 chaises, 137 carts, and 103 horses. In 1792, the Massachusetts legislature extended the Charles River Bridge charter for another thirty years following protests from the owners that a proposed new West Boston Bridge would cut their profits in half. They argued that if state allowed further competition it would "give a stab to all enterprise . . . founded on public grants needed . . . in raising other most useful bridges in this state."[7]

During the next two decades, the U.S. Supreme Court decided two landmark cases strengthening its role as the judicial branch of government, *Marbury v. Madison* and *Trustees of Dartmouth College v. Woodward*.[8] The first case established the Supreme Court's power under the Constitution to review laws adopted by the U.S. Congress. The second added the review of laws passed by state legislatures.

A group of Charlestown merchants, led by Isaac Warren and John Skinner, presented a petition to Massachusetts for a charter to build another bridge across the Charles River in 1823. Owners of the Charles River Bridge protested, denying any need for a new bridge and calling attention to the threat posed to their property, then valued at $300,000. Wharf owners along the river also objected, arguing that a new bridge so close to theirs would further obstruct navigation. Harvard, too, expressed concern for its ferry, its ownership of two shares of stock in the existing bridge company, and its annual £200 payment. Opponents blamed Charlestown real estate speculators whose property would be enhanced in value by the building of a new bridge. Warren's supporters introduced a bill in the legislature, which took no action.

Two years later, Warren's group again petitioned. Renewed pressure evoked public objections by owners of the Charles River Bridge, who now claimed a vested property right to operate unimpeded by a second bridge. Corporations building bridges, they argued, sink their entire capital into construction. Once invested, their capital expenditure is sunk. There is nothing more for them to do except to maintain the bridge and collect tolls, without which their sunk capital is worthless. On the other hand, they argued, a bank retains its capital in many different and active income-producing liquid assets. Consequently, they urged the Massachusetts legislature to follow principles of justice, equity, and good faith. Meanwhile, even as their stock rose from $333 in 1792 to $1,650 in 1805 to $2,080 by 1814, they refused to reduce tolls and neglected bridge repairs.

In January 1826, a joint legislative committee took up Warren's then more elaborate petition, arguing that the Charles River Bridge obstructed river travel, its access avenues were too narrow, over-crowded, and dangerous, a new bridge would equalize land prices in Charlestown and Boston, and it would serve the growing western part of Boston. It would also accommodate a naval base at Charlestown and benefit users of the new Middlesex canal. They claimed the tolls charged by the Charles River Bridge were "burdensome, vexatious, and odious." The Charles River Bridge Company protested that the legislature could not grant the request without providing compensation for its loss of tolls.[9]

A legislative committee rejected all of the arguments made by the Warren petition. Instead, it suggested that the owners of the Charles River Bridge construct an additional drawbridge to keep water vessels traveling continuously. Citing Chief Justice John Marshall's decision in *Fletcher v. Peck*,[10] the committee said the legislature had to construe the original franchise as a contract according to its plain meaning and original understanding as granting a right to receive tolls for its entire duration.

Two years later, nonetheless, the Massachusetts legislature bowed to mounting public pressure and granted a franchise for the Warren Bridge. The new company could charge only the same tolls as the Charles River Bridge with a six-year term expiring in 1834 when the bridge would revert to the commonwealth and become a free crossing. Finally defeated in the legislature, the owners of the Charles River Bridge sought protection from the state courts. U.S. Senator Daniel Webster, Warren Dutton, and Lemuel Shaw, who would later become the Massachusetts Supreme Court's chief justice, argued that the Charles River Bridge charter could only be construed as granting exclusive privileges and, therefore, the legislative act of 1828 impaired the obligation of contract in violation of the federal Constitution. John Davis, a Yale Law School graduate and prominent state legislator, along with Simon Greenleaf, a good friend of U.S. Supreme Court Justice Joseph Story, represented the Warren Bridge. The Massachusetts Supreme Court split, 2-2, thereby denying injunctive relief, primarily because it concluded that the claim to exclusive rights was, at best, ambiguous.[11]

Before the case was argued in the U.S. Supreme Court, the Warren Bridge had already been built and opened, 262 feet from the Charles River Bridge in Charlestown and 825 feet away in Boston. Oral arguments lasted four full days, March 7–11, 1831, with Chief Justice John Marshall presiding. Justice Gabriel Duvall was absent. Despite a determined effort by Justice Joseph Story to secure a judgment for the Charles River Bridge, the Supreme Court was unable to agree on a majority opinion. Intentional indifference, subsequent absences, and vacancies stalled a decision by the Marshall court before his death four years later in 1835. Consequently, the case was reargued from January 19 to 26, 1837.[12] By then, the Warren Bridge was free to public use, and the Charles River Bridge was out of business. Webster argued that the original franchise of 1785 embodied an implied contract, granting an exclusive right to operate a bridge against competing bridges between Boston and Charlestown, which the Supreme Court rejected, 4-3.[13]

New Chief Justice Roger Taney's majority opinion emphasized that Massachusetts had a legitimate interest in guaranteeing the public had convenient means of transportation. Through their elected officials, the people of Massachusetts had granted the franchise, and "in grants by the public, *nothing passes by implication*" (emphasis added).[14]

While Massachusetts was obliged to uphold the terms outlined, he said, the Charles River Bridge could not infer any privileges not specifically granted. The franchise itself said nothing about competing bridges unlike the exclusive grant to operate a ferry made to Harvard College. Section 10 of Article I of the U.S. Constitution says, in part, that no state shall pass any law "impairing the Obligation of contracts." Although not the best-known constitutional passage, the contract clause has entered into more Supreme Court decisions than has any other. During the tenure of Chief Justice Marshall, the court tended to side with the interest of corporations. Marshall defined the contract clause more broadly and wrote a series of important decisions reflecting his interpretation. For example, in *Fletcher v. Peck*, Marshall had ruled that a state could not revoke even a corruptly obtained land grant because it was a contract.

In *Proprietors of the Charles River Bridge v. Proprietors of the Warren Bridge*, Taney wrote,

> Borrowing, as we have done, our system of jurisprudence from the English law, and having adopted, in every other case, civil and criminal, its rules for the construction of statutes, is there anything in our local situation or in the nature of our political institutions which should lead us to depart from the principle where corporations are concerned? Are we to apply to acts of incorporation a rule of construction differing from that of the English law, and, by implication, make the terms of a charter in one of the states more unfavorable to the public than upon an act of Parliament framed in the same words would be sanctioned in an English court? Can any good reason be assigned for excepting this particular class of cases from the operation of the general principle and for introducing a new and adverse rule of construction in favor of corporations while we adopt and adhere to the rules of construction known to the English common law in every other case, without exception? We think not, and it would present a singular spectacle, if, while the courts in England are restraining, within the strictest limits, the spirit of monopoly, and exclusive privileges in nature of monopolies, and confining corporations to the privileges plainly given to them in their charter, the courts of this country should be found enlarging these privileges by implication and construing a statute more unfavorably to the public and to the rights of community than would be done in a like case in an English court of justice.[15]

Three dissenting justices—Story, John McLean, and Smith Thompson—wrote separate opinions. Story's dissent, written in a sweeping and majestic style, is among the most often cited in the history of the Supreme Court. Story interpreted the original grant as giving an exclusive right for the Charles River Bridge Company to the unimpaired collection of tolls for the duration of its grant. Story said,

> To sum up, then, the present grant carries with it a *necessary implication* that the legislature should do no act to destroy or essentially to impair the franchise; that (as one of the learned judges of the State court expressed it) there is an implied agreement of the State to grant the undisturbed use of the bridge and its tolls, so far as respects any acts of its own, or of any persons acting under its authority. In other words, the State impliedly contracts not to resume its grant, or to do any act to the prejudice or destruction of its grant. I maintain that there is no authority or principle established in relation to the construction of crown grants, or legislative grants, which does not concede and justify this doctrine. (emphasis added)[16]

Story was greatly troubled by Taney's opinion. He argued:

> For my own part, I can conceive of no surer plan to arrest all public improvements founded on private capital and enterprise than to make the outlay of that capital uncertain and questionable, both as to security and as to productiveness. No man will hazard his capital in any enterprise in which, if there be a loss, it must be borne exclusively by himself, and if there be success, he has not the slightest security of enjoying the rewards of that success for a single moment. If the government means to invite its citizens to enlarge the public comforts and conveniences, to establish bridges, or turnpikes, or canals, or railroads, there must be some pledge that the property will be safe, that the enjoyment will be coextensive with the grant, and that success will not be the signal of a general combination to overthrow its rights and to take away its profits. The very agitation of a question of this sort is sufficient to alarm every stockholder in every public enterprise of this sort throughout the whole country.

> Already, in my native State, the Legislature has found it necessary expressly to concede the exclusive privilege here contended against in order to insure the accomplishment of a railroad for the benefit of the public. And yet we are told that all such exclusive grants are to the detriment of the public.[17]

The Strait of Lake Erie

In July 1701, Antoine de le Mothe Cadillac came to secure the French fur trade in the Great Lakes by building a fort to guard what he called *le detroit du Lac Erie*, meaning "the strait of Lake Erie." Ever since, the straight story of Detroit has been about the constant struggle between the genius of its people and the folly of its leaders. Cadillac and his party of fifty soldiers, two priests, and twenty voyageurs, artisans, and farmers, and their wives and children, built Fort Pontchartrain on the strategic higher ground rising between today's Griswold and Shelby Streets on the north bank of the Detroit River along its narrowest stretch between Lake St. Clair and Lake Erie. They dug a moat surrounding the fort's sixteen-foot-high wooden stockade and constructed tall bastions at each corner. Within the fort, they first built the Ste. Anne de Detroit Catholic Church.

Three wilderness waterways emptied into the Detroit River from above Cadillac's fort: the Campau River, later called May Creek, on the west; Parent's Creek on the east; and the particularly beautiful Savoyard Creek on the north, which originated in a willow swamp not far from the intersection of Congress and Riopelle Streets in the middle of today's Lafayette Park. The Savoyard Creek's deep and strongly flowing current kept a gristmill turning throughout the year, passing through today's Cadillac Square before emptying into the Detroit River near Third Street.

"Above the banks of the river are so many vast meadows where the freshness of those beautiful streams keeps the grass always green," Cadillac wrote in a report to his superior officers in Montreal on October 5, 1701.

> These same meadows are fringed with long and broad avenues of fruit trees, which have never felt the careful hand of the watchful gardener; and fruit trees, young and old, droop under the weight and multitude of their fruit, and bend their branches toward the fertile soil which has produced them. On both sides of this strait lie fine, open plains where the deer roam in graceful herds, where bears, by no means fierce, and exceedingly good to eat, are to be found, as are also the savory wild duck and other varieties of game. The islands are covered with trees, chestnuts, walnuts, apples and plums abound, and, in season, the wild vines are heavy with grapes of which the forest rangers say they have made a wine that, considering its newness, was not bad at all.[18]

Cadillac wisely sent a few privileged families up and down the Detroit River to settle farms just two hundred to six hundred feet wide but up to several miles deep, separated by narrow ditches.[19] They built log houses on their riverfront property with stone chimneys and ovens, and planted gardens and pear tree orchards. On the fields to the rear, they kept herds of cattle, horses, and sheep and raised crops of wheat and corn, ground at a public mill. While these pioneer French farmers are remembered today only by their names given to Detroit streets—St. Antoine, St. Aubin, Beaubien, Brush, Chene, Joseph Campau, Dequindre, Livernois, and Riopelle among many, many others more and less well known—their farms, connected by a riverside cart path called the Old River

Road, had a powerful, lasting impact on shaping Detroit. The Old River Road became known as Water Street and finally Atwater Street. Cadillac and the French government granted more ribbon farms as far as twelve miles north to St. Clair Shores and forty miles south to Monroe and along both sides of the Rouge, Huron, and Raisin Rivers.

During the French and Indian War of 1760, British troops captured Fort Pontchartrain, causing the flight of many French families, some of whom resettled across the river. Others moved farther north and south along the river to land near already established ribbon farms. Many honest French settlers and some dishonest land grabbers made claims against the federal government along all of the inland rivers throughout southeastern Michigan after the Michigan Territory passed to the United States under the Jay Treaty in 1796. The federal government spent many years sorting out the genuine among more than eight hundred claims before formally recognizing those properly derived from French legal authority with dutiful regard for the protection of private property guaranteed by the U.S. Constitution adopted in 1788.

In 1800, the U.S. Congress divided the Northwest Territory. The western part became the Indiana Territory, consisting of Indiana, Illinois, Wisconsin, and Minnesota lying east of the Mississippi River, the western half of Michigan's Lower Peninsula, and all of the Upper Peninsula lying west of Mackinac Island. Three years later, when Ohio was granted statehood in 1803, the U.S. Congress added Detroit and eastern Michigan to the Indiana Territory, whose capital was faraway Vincennes, Indiana, on the lower Wabash River. Detroit protested, and on January 11, 1805, the U.S. Congress adopted an act creating the Michigan Territory. By 1805, Detroit townsfolk had built what they called the King's Wharf and another called the Merchant's Wharf. Inside the stockade were three hundred buildings including a public warehouse, five taverns, stores, barns, and one hundred houses jammed together across just two acres of land bounded by today's Jefferson Avenue and Griswold, Shelby, and Larned Streets with five hundred mostly French-speaking residents. The stockade had two gates opening onto the river and one each on the east and west sides, protected by blockhouses. The main east-to-west streets of St. Louis, St. Anne, St. James, and St. Joseph were but twelve feet wide with precarious two-foot-wide wooden sidewalks. Two streets, named L'Erneau and St. Honore, and two narrow alleys, called McDougall and Campau, provided north-to-south travel.

British commanders had worried that the cramped Detroit stockade was both indefensible and a tinderbox where precautionary rooftop ladders traditionally lay between many of the houses and every residence kept water casks equipped with poles for carrying to the frequent fires. Therefore, British troops built Fort Lernoult several hundred yards north of the old town. The American military renamed it Fort Shelby and brought in four six-pound cannons that artillery soldiers mounted in its corner bastions. Spreading northeast of Fort Shelby was what the French settlers had long recognized as a public common, already cleared of brush and trees as a place of safety in the event of a fire and as a safeguard against attacking native Indians, who had then aligned themselves with the British still in control of Canada across the river. Described as an area of two thousand acres extending as far back as three miles from the Detroit River, the public commons was cultivated by French families with crops grown on family plots and used to pasture their livestock. Detroit was otherwise surrounded by vast swamps and wetlands seasonally drained by the Huron and Rouge Rivers to the southwest and the more distant Clinton River to the northeast as well as scores of streams, ponds, and lakes.[20] Today's Detroit was shaped not only by its natural geography,

Cadillac's settlement, the public commons, Fort Shelby, and the French ribbon farms but by the radical design of its major roads conceived in 1805 by an eccentric young bachelor lawyer from Washington, D.C., with a passion for Caesar Augustus. Detroit has ever since been described as a city planned to death.

Woodward Avenue

When the U.S. Congress created the Michigan Territory in 1805, President Thomas Jefferson's choice for territorial governor was William Hull, a lazy and overweight fifty-one-year-old lawyer from Newton, Massachusetts, who had been a distinguished officer of the Revolutionary War. Jefferson chose an ambitious and thin thirty-year-old attorney, Augustus Brevoort Woodward, as one of three judges of the territorial court.[21] In the utter fiasco of the city's next generation, only Woodward's political career survived because, during the War of 1812, it was Hull who surrendered Detroit, was taken prisoner by the British, released in New York, charged with treason, and sentenced to hang but reprieved by President James Madison in recognition of his Revolutionary War record. Hull spent the remaining years of his life in Newton, Massachusetts, trying to clear his name before he died in 1825. Woodward was regarded as something of a hero in the distant federal government, if not locally, because he was the only territorial officer who stayed in occupied Detroit before the British commander expelled him as more trouble than he was worth, something Hull and everybody else in Detroit had known for years.

"Had the other territorial officers yielded Hull the deference and respect which was due to his character and station, their example would, in all probability, have been followed by the general public, and his administration might have had a fair measure of success," said Michigan Supreme Court Judge Thomas M. Cooley in his excellent 1885 book, *Michigan: A History of Governments*. "But the governor was peculiarly unfortunate in having in one of the judges a person of characteristics much more pronounced than his own, and with not only the power but the will, as subsequently appeared, to embarrass and embitter his whole official life."[22]

The U.S. Senate confirmed Woodward's appointment on March 1, 1805. A few weeks later, he began the long journey to Detroit, likely boarding a stagecoach to Baltimore, Philadelphia, and Pittsburgh, from which a keelboat could have taken him down the Ohio River to Marietta, Ohio, where the stockade was named for Campus Martius or "Field of Mars" in ancient Rome. The trip from there was mostly wilderness travel by wagon to Lake Erie where he could board a ship. When Woodward reached Detroit on June 29, the city was gone. For him, it was the opportunity of a lifetime, but his dream of building a city in the wilderness was a nightmare for Detroit's residents who had lost everything on June 11 in a fire started at the bakery of John Harvey. While hitching up a pony in his barn at Ste. Anne and Ste. Honore Streets, a careless laborer knocked a smoldering ash from his pipe into the straw.[23] The embers slowly grew, flames erupted and spread, and in little more than four hours, from eight thirty in the morning until half past noon, the Ste. Anne de Detroit Catholic Church and all houses and buildings within Detroit's stockade were burned to the ground. A few stone chimneys and a stone warehouse were all that remained.[24]

On July 1, Woodward stood by listening as leaders among the devastated five hundred townsfolk gathered under early-fruited pear trees in the public gardens east of the stockade. They agreed on a simple plan of immediate rebuilding of tightly packed homes on narrow streets just as before the fire, while extending the north wall of the stockade into the public commons. Stepping forward, Justice Woodward objected. Joining him in urging patience was Frederick Bates, then Detroit's federal postmaster, whom President Jefferson had appointed the second territorial judge. Woodward and Bates prevailed on the gathering to await arrival of their new governor. Hull, who had traveled with the new territorial secretary, the Rev. Stanley Griswold of Connecticut, on the Hudson River through Albany, north across Lake Champlain to the St. Lawrence River, Lake Ontario, and Lake Erie, arrived with his family later that same evening.[25] Hull spent a few days finding lodging and settling his family in the small house of a farmer a mile away before he could meet with Woodward and Bates on July 4 when he agreed with them against immediate rebuilding of the old town.

The third judge originally appointed by Jefferson, Samuel Huntington, had refused to take the dangerous wilderness post. William Sprigg of Ohio likewise declined before Jefferson found an agreeable replacement whose confirmation, however, was delayed by the U.S. Senate until March 29, 1806. The appointee, John Griffin, did not find his way to Detroit from Indiana, where he had been a territorial judge, until September 26, 1806. Griffin spent much of his next eighteen years in Detroit seeking appointment anywhere else. Griffin came under Woodward's reassuring thumb, where he loyally stayed until 1824 when they both lost reappointment by President James Madison.

Woodward convinced Bates and Hull to make use of the opportunity they had to enlarge and beautify Detroit by laying out much larger five-thousand-square-foot lots on much wider roads, spreading out all of the dwellings, stables, and shops. The governor and two judges agreed on the need to set aside prime land within the old town for a courthouse and jail. They agreed on the need to preserve open spaces for public use both large and small although doing so would require much more land than was available to them as Michigan's new territorial government, consisting solely of themselves, even before resolving private claims by the old town's property owners and inhabitants.[26]

In the remaining days of July 1805, Woodward eagerly took up the task of preparing a new layout for Detroit. He presented his first plan on July 20, which was unacceptable to all but a few of those who suffered losses in the fire. Woodward returned to his drawing board. He hired Thomas Smith, a British-trained surveyor, who was living across the Detroit River in Sandwich, Ontario.[27] In a letter to then secretary of state Madison on August 3, 1805, Hull explained:

> We immediately fixed on a plan, and employed the best surveyor we could find in the Country to lay out the Streets, Squares, and lots. If possible, the plan shall be transmitted by this conveyance. The principal part of the grounds embraced by the plan belong to the U.S. without any question. Many of the lots in the old Town are cut up by the Streets, which has reduced us to the necessity of exchanging them for lots on the Domain or Commons—we have likewise from the necessity of the case, concluded to sell as many lots on the commons as will be necessary to the accommodation of those citizens who wish to build this town, and did not own lots in the Town. This rule, however, we make, expressly subject to the ratification of Congress.[28]

Woodward's ambition for Detroit was grand. He wrote:

> Nature has destined the City of Detroit to a great interior emporium, equal, if not superior, to any other on the surface of the terraqueous globe. The commerce of seven immense Mediterraneans—Ontario, Erie, Huron, Michigan, Superior, Cuinissique, Arabasca—connected by noble rivers with the Atlantic ocean at two points, New York and Quebec, and stretching on the other side to the Pacific and even to the hyperborean ocean, must glide along its borders. In such a case the art of man should aid the benevolence of the Creator, and no restricted attachment to the present day or the present interests, should induce a permanent sacrifice of ulterior and brilliant prospects.[29]

John Gentle, keeper of a general store burned in the fire, wrote a series of satirical columns published anonymously by Pennsylvania newspapers in 1807. They included a description of what happened during Detroit's hot and muggy late July and August, as everyone waited upon Woodward's plan for the rebuilding of Detroit.[30] Gentle wrote:

> After a few days spent in preparing their apparatus, the judge began his operations on a height contiguous to the fort. There he placed his instruments, astronomical and astrological, on the summit of a huge stone, which stone shall ever remain a monument of his indefatigable perseverance.[31]
>
> For the space of thirty days and thirty nights he viewed the diurnal evolutions of the planets, visible and invisible, and calculated the course and rapidity of the blazing meteors. To his profound observations of the heavenly regions, the world is indebted for the discovery of the streets, alleys, circles, angles, and squares of this magnificent city, in theory equal in magnitude and splendor to any on the earth. But the most arduous and tedious performance was the laying out and measuring the marshes a mile back from the town into streets, lots, circles, and grand squares, measuring and un-measuring them, arranging and deranging them, for the space of two full months more.[32]

Having completed his measurements and calculations, Woodward realized that his layout needed much more of the surrounding federal land. Therefore, he proposed to travel back to Washington, D.C., where he would persuade the U.S. Congress to donate the entire two-thousand-acre public commons northeast of the old town for what he called park lots. In addition, he wanted an additional eight-thousand-acre wilderness tract beyond his park lots. He argued that the territorial government could sell all ten thousand acres, raising all of the cash needed to finance the construction of the roads, government buildings, and public places envisioned in his plan.

Woodward may have had some lofty ideas worthy of the extreme patience his delay in rebuilding demanded from Detroit's residents as autumn's colors spread, leaves fell, and winter's cold and snow approached, but it could also be said that the grandiose scheme he formulated lived up to what became the bold new city's motto: "We hope for better days. It will rise again from the ashes."[33] For Detroit's old town residents, from the beginning, as it unfolded, his was an impractical, if not grotesque, plan they wished would itself would go up in flames. Against the unbridled power of the governor and judges, the territorial legislature that Woodward dominated, they harbored such hopes in vain.

Hull and Woodward's departure for Washington, D.C., was delayed by their duty to research local property ownership, some immediate rebuilding, establishing a skeleton government, and sheer hubris.[34] Subject to congressional approval of Woodward's plan, the governor and judges had allowed some owners in the old town to rebuild. Most construction ended by September 4, 1805, however, when Governor Hull was warned by the federal government against the cutting of timber in the federally owned white pine forest along Lake Huron, the St. Clair River, and Lake St. Clair, the only practical places of supply from which logs could be floated downstream to Detroit.[35] Woodward and Hull posted a report to President Jefferson on October 10, 1805, describing the perilous condition of Detroit and the problems they faced perfecting land titles in the two-acre old town, the public commons, and the French ribbon farms, for which surviving records of only eight they found to be regular. They wrote:

> It is now nearly a century and half since the first settlement was made in this country under the French government, and in the reign of Louis XIVth. The few titles granted by the Government of France were of three French acres in front, on the banks of the river, by forty in depth. . . . However defective, therefore, the class of original proprietors may be with respect to the evidence of title according to the American forms, it is conceived their rights are extremely strong.
>
> From this state of things some consequences have resulted, which are not, indeed, difficult to foresee, but which it is difficult to remedy. One of these consequences, and, perhaps, not the least important, is the effect it has had on the destiny and moral character of the progeny of the original colonists. When it is remembered that the troops of Louis XIVth came without women, the description of persons constituting the second generation will not be difficult to conceive. When it is considered, at the same time, that, destitute of titles to land, they were precluded from the means of acquiring them, it will be obvious that an entrance into the savage societies, or, at most, employments in the commerce carried on with them, were their only resources.[36] While, therefore, the American colonization of the same and of subsequent dates has grown into regular agriculture, and opulent States, these countries have been destined to anarchy, to ignorance, to poverty.[37]

Not until October 11, 1805, did Hull and Woodward depart on what appeared to be a rather relaxed winter-long visit to Boston and Washington, D.C., Hull taking along his wife and one of their daughters. Over the next three months, Woodward expended at least $300 from the territorial treasury wining and dining members of Congress seeking their favorable vote on legislation for rebuilding Detroit. On the last day of its session, April 21, 1806, the U.S. Congress approved a broad outline of Woodward's plan for dealing with losses suffered in the fire by the owners and inhabitants of Detroit. The federal legislation adopted was deceptively simple:

> An act of congress of the United States of America, entitled, "An act to provide for the adjustment of titles of land in the Town of Detroit and Territory of Michigan, and for other purposes."
>
> Section 1. Be it enacted by the Senate and the House of Representatives of the United States of America, in congress assembled, that the governor and the judges of the Territory of Michigan shall be, and they *or any three of them* are hereby authorized to layout a town, including the whole of the old Town of Detroit, and ten thousand acres adjacent, excepting such parts as the president of the United States shall direct to be reserved for the use of the military department, and shall hear, examine and finally adjust all claims to lots therein, and give deeds for the same. And to every person or the legal representative or representatives of every person, who not owing or professing allegiance to any foreign

> power, and being above the age of seventeen years, did, on the eleventh day of June, one thousand eight hundred and five, when the old town of Detroit was burned, *own or inhabit* a house in the same, there shall be granted by the governor and the judges aforesaid, *or any three of them*, and where they shall judge most proper, a lot, not exceeding the quantity of *five thousand square feet*.
>
> Section 2. And be it further enacted, that the land remaining of the said ten thousand acres, after satisfying claims provided for by the preceding section, shall be disposed of by the governor and the judges aforesaid, at their discretion, to the best advantage, who are hereby authorized to make deeds to purchasers thereof, and the proceeds of the land so disposed of shall be applied by the governor and the judges aforesaid, toward building a court house and jail in the Town of Detroit. And the said governor and judges are required to make a report to congress, in writing, of their proceedings under this act. (emphasis added)[38]

However, almost five more months passed before anything was accomplished in Detroit. Although Hull had returned on June 7, he and Bates could do nothing without *three votes*, which required the presence of either Woodward or Griffin. Woodward finally returned to Detroit on September 3. A few more days later, on September 6, excited and determined, Woodward laid out his neobaroque plan for rebuilding Detroit. It was at least inspired by Pierre Charles L'Enfant's design for the District of Columbia that L'Enfant had taken from French Versailles.[39] Later historical researchers discovered a copy of L'Enfant's plan pasted into the private memorandum book Woodward carried everywhere.[40]

The geometric layout he proposed started with a 4,000-foot equilateral triangle with its three angles bisected by lines he proposed as 200-foot-wide main avenues extending like spokes from the hub of a wheel in all directions, connected by diagonal 120-foot-wide avenues, interspersed with 600-foot by 400-foot hexagonal public squares. At the apex of each triangle was a 1,000-foot-diameter circular public space he called a "circus," reserved for parks, public buildings, churches, and schools. These he envisioned as fully landscaped, adorned with sculptures and fountains. The basic design would be repeated as Detroit grew outward like a great spider web, but scaled as it was for fifty thousand people living and working within just its first triangle, the cost of building Woodward's roads overwhelmed the public treasury for many years.[41]

Woodward's first triangle was fixed along Washington Boulevard, pointing true north with its base generally along Ste. Anne Street that he renamed Jefferson Avenue. Otherwise, his plan disregarded the names and locations of Detroit's existing roads, and the astronomical accuracy of its geometric layout yielded nothing to the city's greatest natural resource, the Detroit River and its three inland creeks, in an obsession with imposing mathematical order on untidy nature and its human inhabitants. The beautiful and bountiful Savoyard Creek was reduced to drainage and, worse, sewage, later completely enclosed and lost with the building of the Grand Sewer in 1936.

Woodward's scheme of roads, parks, squares, and building lots ignored the location of all the existing roads, Fort Shelby, the homes and businesses that the governor and judges had already allowed to be built, and the Ste. Anne Church burial ground. The question of what to do with the graves gave rise to much argument and hard feelings, and for nearly a dozen years Father Gabriel Richard struggled against vacating the grounds. For many more years, from time to time, excavators digging sewers or cellars near the old church along Jefferson Avenue, between Griswold and Shelby Streets, uncovered decayed body parts. The question was not settled until 1818 when a new bishop

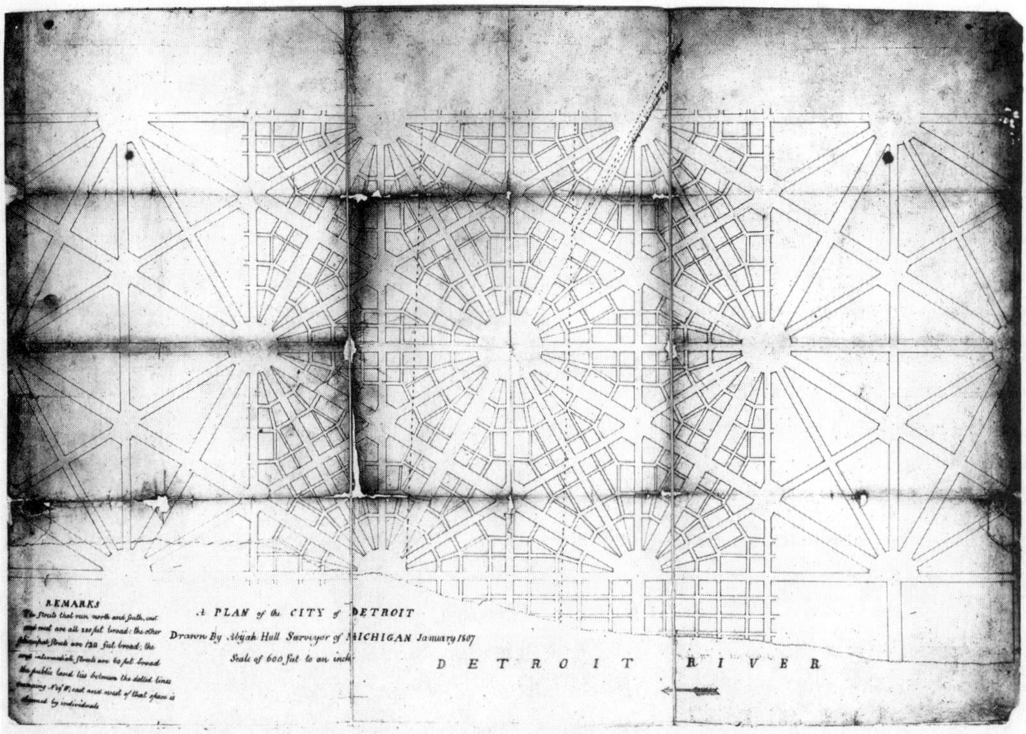

The first official plan of Detroit after the 1805 fire that was found in U.S. Department of State archives in 1909. Courtesy of the Burton Historical Collection, Detroit Public Library.

disinterred and reburied on land granted for a Catholic burial ground on Larned Street east of Bates Street a "certain quantity of bones from the middle of the main street, where were formerly the old burying grounds and old Church of St. Anne."[42]

Where Woodward's roads and public places crossed over private ownership claims in the old town, he proposed to offer other land elsewhere in foot-for-foot exchange, raising a ruckus. Old town property owners naturally wanted their more valuable land considered as their so-called donation lots, giving up only so much as was covered by the new streets and public places, while Woodward, in particular, thought that the entire old town should go to public auction because not enough land remained after his proposed wider roads and planned public places to satisfy everyone with a valid claim. With five hundred inhabitants and built-up expectations, other details of Woodward's plan for parceling out lots were out of whack with the reconstruction some had done over the past fourteen months, so more trouble arose.

Moreover, Woodward's plan protected from his roads, parks, and squares all of the land south of the old town's Ste. Anne Street, all owned by Bates and leading French families. The same was true of scattered lots along the north side of Ste. Anne Street. Hull's large fifty-by-fifty-foot brick house was at the southeast corner of Jefferson Avenue and Randolph Street, just outside old town boundaries. The governor and judges appointed themselves as sole members of a land board to survey lots and dispose of the old town's land by sale according to Woodward's layout.[43] On October 6, the land board set aside a parcel upon which Father Gabriel Richard could rebuild, and they granted additional land for the building of two schools for the teaching of Catholic boys and girls. It was not until July 26, 1819, that the governor and judges granted to the Rev. John Monteith a corner lot at Larned Street and Woodward Avenue for the building of a Presbyterian church.

On October 9, John Gentle, Robert Abbott, John Harvey, Hugh R. Martin, and John R. Williams formally protested Woodward's layout, and many others threatened violence.[44] The governor and judges answered by inviting them to elect a committee to devise a better scheme. They did so, and when their compromise plan was taken up on November 5, Judge Woodward threatened his resignation and stormed away from the meeting. Hull, Bates, and Griffin disagreed among themselves and, lacking the three votes required by Congress, nothing could be accomplished. On November 10, Hull proposed the following resolution:

> Three members not being agreed with respect to the location of donation lots granted by Congress to the inhabitants of the Town of Detroit and that Act requiring the concurrence of three members to carry it into effect, and further attempts under the present state of things must apparently be fruitless, no other course but a suspension of our duties of law seem to present itself, however it may impede the progress of the City, whatever inconvenience it may produce to the inhabitants or embarrassment to the government, it seems to be dictated by imperious necessity.[45]

Neither Bates nor Griffin supported putting the resolution to a vote. The next day, imperious Woodward came back. He had decided to accept the committee scheme. By November 29, 1806, further meetings produced a workable compromise that divided all inhabitants of the old town at the time of the fire into several classes, solving the problem of donating five thousand square feet of land in the old town and public commons to each of them. The four principal classes consisted of all property owners and then inhabitants of the old town, giving priority within each class to heads of households.[46] The governor and judges agreed on November 15 to protect the thirty or so persons who had already erected homes on lots in the old town by requiring that they pay two cents per square foot to the territorial government for land exceeding five thousand square feet.[47] Persons with improved land in the old town subject to a higher claim would be required to pay two cents per square foot to the person with a higher claim. By January, Governor Hull, acting alone by agreement of Woodward and Griffin, decided claims from all 251 persons for five thousand-square-foot donation lots. Land along Woodward and Jefferson Avenues ended up in the hands of the wealthier among the first-class inhabitants. Three weeks later, Hull wrecked his accomplishment by asking Woodward and Griffin whether those persons who had not taken the U.S. citizenship oath of allegiance before the fire should have received donation lots. He delivered a lengthy speech in their favor. Judges Woodward and Griffin wavered but decided against doing so, reversing 170 grants Hull had made.[48]

"So, the farce went on, the people being alternately threatened and cajoled until many of them became almost ready to yield their old holdings and leave the Territory," historian Silas Farmer concluded.[49] Hull responded generously, construing the act of 1806 to make grants not only to individual owners and to occupants but also, in some cases, to their wives and even to their slaves.

Farmer was one of Detroit's earliest historiographers, an honorary appointive office first created by Detroit's Common Council in 1843 and mostly ignored ever since but still on the books today. He took the job very seriously.[50] In 1884, Farmer published a truly remarkable book to which he gave a title almost as long and ambitious as what he did. He called it *The History of Detroit and Michigan or, The Metropolis Illustrated: A Chronological Cyclopaedia of the Past and Present Including a Full Record of Territorial Days in Michigan and the Annals of Wayne County.* Farmer and his father worked as land surveyors and mapmakers. Both were highly skilled at penmanship and drawing. Exquisitely illustrated with pen-and-ink drawings of many early Detroit homes and buildings, numerous charts, maps, and diagrams, Farmer's book aspired to retell not just the city's past but everything else about the city and nearly accomplished doing so.

Detroit's already devastated residents, having survived two Michigan winters scattered across the territory in cramped farmhouses, bark shacks, tents, and temporary buildings, fell into angry acceptance of Woodward's layout. The land board continued to meet two or three times a week for many years. Almost everyone else in Detroit, led by Governor Hull, resisted any expansion of Woodward's plan beyond the old town. The development of Woodward's layout of lots along today's Washington Boulevard was stymied by the continued presence of the federal government's Fort Shelby. The military commander and his cannon practice discouraged any building within his field of fire south to the Detroit River until 1827 when the fort was abandoned and demolished by the city. Instead, Court House Avenue came to serve as downtown Detroit's main thoroughfare. It happened to line up fairly well with an ancient Indian trail leading to Pontiac on the Clinton River and still farther to Saginaw on Lake Huron. The governor and judges had envisioned building a courthouse and jail in Grand Circus Park on the west side of Court House Avenue, but they never had enough cash in the territory treasury to do so. Consequently, among all of the names he gave to his downtown streets, Court House Avenue was the least satisfying of Woodward's choices, probably a last-minute toss-off in his original drawing because in the final plan of 1806, it was renamed Woodward Avenue, he explained, not for himself but rather because it ran "toward the wood."[51] In 1818, the governor and judges tried to change its name to Congress Avenue between Campus Martius and Adams Street. North of Adams, Woodward Avenue was platted only half of its originally planned 120-foot width and renamed Witherell Street. "The Street was rightly named Witherell, 'for it withered all his plans,'" Woodward quipped.[52] Neither change overcame popular usage.

At its meeting of June 1, 1807, the governor and judges appointed Woodward to act for the land board. President Jefferson had not found anyone capable and willing to fill the vacancy left by Bates, leaving neither Woodward nor Hull with three votes. A fierce political battle had erupted between Hull and Griswold, who was ambitious to replace him as governor.[53] In order to avoid the "enmity of either," historian Clarence M. Burton said, Woodward packed up and took his sole authority away to a 490-acre French ribbon farm on the River Raisin in Monroe County's Frenchtown that he had purchased for $600 in 1807 from Samuel and George Egrew.[54] He stayed there until news came of James Witherell's appointment to replace Bates a few days before September 5, 1808.[55] One thing is clear from the long episode. Woodward had no patience with anyone who opposed his plan for building Detroit, and he had no reluctance to use all of the procedural weapons available to him in bringing the business of territorial government to a halt if he was not getting his way. On July 18, 1807, he had written to Madison from his Frenchtown farm:

> The town titles will be definitely arranged as soon as the military reservation is made. We gave great dissatisfaction in the distribution of the donations. Mr. Bates and myself were dearly of the opinion that the donations should not be suffered to run afoul of the adjustments of the ancient titles. The governor gave way to the public storm. As their wish was, however, impracticable in its own nature, not from the mere reluctance of those who were to make the distribution, we have been constantly obliged painfully to tread back upon our steps, and none of us have given satisfaction to the people. Perhaps none could have done it under the jealousies and dissensions prevailing among them. But they would have been more respectful toward their government if it had been steady and firm; on one side desiring nothing wrong, and not to be driven from what they knew to be right on the other.[56]

On October 24, 1808, when the land board resumed meeting, it did so without Woodward's attendance. In 1915, Burton gathered together and published minutes of the land board from October 24, 1808, to November 22, 1820.[57] Indicative of Woodward's stubborn indifference, he was absent from all land board meetings until November 8, 1815, after Lewis B. Cass was appointed territorial governor. During those seven years, Judge Griffin loyally defeated all efforts by Governor Hull and Judge Witherell to revise Woodward's plan. The prolonged absence from land board meetings of the architect of Detroit is astonishing. Having had his plan adopted, the myriad tasks of sorting out the dirty details and the often messy, personal disputes between friends and neighbors were somehow beneath his dignity. Those once harboring mere doubts about his layout of Detroit would grow in their opposition during his long years of demonstrated contempt.

In his absence, the so-called park lots were surveyed and laid out along Woodward Avenue rather than Washington Avenue as originally conceived. Land board records disclose no explanation for the change. The federal surveyor laid out forty-six lots on the east side and forty lots on the west side of Woodward Avenue. The lots closest to Grand Circus Park were no larger than five acres and increased in size northward for two and a half miles. They were sold at auction in 1808 and 1809. Otherwise, the land board accomplished little else until Cass arrived.

A down-to-earth man of action with a strong will, Governor Cass sized up Woodward as a pompous fob and Woodward's plan as an obstacle not only to the growth of Detroit but also to his personal real estate holdings. At the first meeting presided over by Governor Cass on November 6, 1815, moving quickly, the land board appointed Solomon Sibley, U.S. attorney, to investigate all still pending land claims, asked the federal government to survey the still remaining eight-thousand-acre wilderness tract, and gave Cass full power for its sale. The wilderness tract was divided into forty-eight lots of 160 acres and twelve lots of 80 acres, evenly divided across Woodward Avenue.[58]

Almost a year later, on October 15, 1816, Woodward offered a resolution intended to preserve his plan. Henceforth, he proposed, all property sold exceeding five thousand square feet would remain subject to the roads, public squares, circuses, and other public spaces he had designed. He drew no support. A few days later, on October 21, 1816, Woodward offered a vaguely worded resolution joined by Governor Cass and Judge Griffin. Henceforth, compliance with his layout of roads, building lots, and open spaces would be confined to the old town area between Grand Circus Park and the Detroit River according to the "original plan as devised and adopted by the Governor and Judges in one thousand eight hundred and five, one thousand eight hundred and six, and one thousand eight hundred and seven, as reported to congress."[59] The drawings prepared by Woodward and Smith in 1805 and the 1806 and 1807 plans prepared by Abijah Hull, to which the resolution referred, did not encompass the French ribbon farms west of Cass Avenue or east of Brush Avenue, now owned, not coincidentally, by Governor Cass and Elijah Brush, respectively.[60] In Woodward's absence, seven years before, acting governor Reuben Atwater and Judges Griffin and Witherell had set the groundwork by sending a report to Congress on May 9, 1809, advising that they had "laid out a town, including the whole of the *old town of Detroit*, a plan of which has heretofore been forwarded to the general government" (emphasis added).[61]

This final, official demise of Woodward's plan was a severe personal blow. Political opposition had crystallized around Governor Cass, who rapidly became the dominant man in Michigan. He had purchased the Macomb family farm soon after his appointment by President Madison in 1813. Cass and the owners of other larger parcels wanted to subdivide and sell lots to the growing population of Detroit. Cass did not want to be hamstrung by platted boulevards and grand avenues cutting across his property at angles, slicing it into odd-sized and odd-shaped parcels. What remained unaccomplished of Woodward's plan was abandoned so that Governor Cass and other private property owners could lay out streets to their individual preferences. By agreeing to this face-saving measure proposed by Woodward, Cass ended his stranglehold on Detroit's development, which was an exceptionally dull place to live. Woodward vainly but eloquently objected.

> Are cities built in a day? Can you throw them down when your ground plan is found contracted and inconvenient and erect new ones on a better ground, among the ruins of the old? . . .
>
> No, cities are the work of time, of a generation, of a succession of generations; their original plan must remain, and cannot be changed without the heights of inconvenience, trouble, and expense. A proper and prudent foresight can alone give to a great city its fair development. Order, regularity, beauty, must characterize its original ground plan. It must have a capacious grasp; no petty interests ought to be permitted to enter into collision with its permanent welfare. Uniformity of plan, amplitude of avenue, of square, of space, of circus,[62] free circulation of air and a variety of decoration and embellishment are not to be hoped for, if one age shall determine on its limited and contracted view of things that a city can never reach beyond a certain limit, enough and more than enough ought to be allowed to give it a full expansion of growth.[63]

Many years later, Farmer expressed regret at the discarding of Woodward's plan. "No one who studies the original plan can avoid wishing that it could have been adhered to," he said. "The portions of the City of which we are most proud and which are most admired by strangers, our main avenues, the Campus Martius, the Grand Circus, and the smaller public squares, are all parts of Judge Woodward's plan. His diagonal streets and avenues have produced several locations of special prominence, which afford exceptional opportunities for architectural display. Peculiar and pleasing vistas result in many places from the triangular intersection of streets arranged for in his plan."[64]

Burton, however, expressing what most everyone else thought, breathed a sigh of relief. "Imagine the present city with eleven miles of river frontage, constructed on this plan," he wrote. "A Grand Circus Park every 4,000 feet of that distance and twice as many semi-circular parks and hundreds of triangular parks like Capitol Square and the downtown public library. There would be as many squares like the Campus Martius as there were Grand Circus Parks. Even the natives would get bewildered in this labyrinth."[65]

The 120-foot-wide avenues that became Detroit's main thoroughfares until the building of its freeways in 1950—Fort Street and Woodward, Michigan, Gratiot, Grand River, and Jefferson Avenues—were ever since used for daily travel and, therefore, inevitably served to direct future development. Bare remnants of Woodward's design can be seen today in the many short one-way streets in central downtown. The main road on Woodward's plan, Washington Boulevard, never was extended beyond Grand Circus Park or south to the Detroit River when Fort Shelby was demolished in 1827. Grand Circus Park, a swamp in those days, was not drained, filled, and raised until 1844 and today remains but a half circle divided down its center by Adams Street and Woodward Avenue.

The north-tilted large rectangular open area planned for the junction of Woodward, Michigan, and Monroe Avenues and Fort Street named Campus Martius survives only in smaller scale today overlooked by Compuware Corporation's world headquarters. Mostly sold away to improve downtown traffic in the 1900s, Campus Martius was partially reestablished in 2004 with two outdoor stages, sculptures, public spaces, and an ice skating rink. A fuller restoration would have required demolishing several buildings.

The spacious lots created by Woodward's aristocratic Roman plan for a frontier trading post of no more than one hundred households, living at bare subsistence levels, did establish a legacy, only ending now two hundred years later. Joined as it was to the French ribbon farms, Detroit became a city deeply invested in single-family home ownership on maple- and elm-tree-lined sixty-foot-wide streets for which it led all other major cities in the United States until the 1950s. The lack of downtown land suitable for otherwise inexpensive tenement housing discouraged early migrant and immigrant settlers and the concentration of ready customers they would have provided for downtown merchants and craftsmen. Instead, early migrants and later immigrants who came to Detroit from across Europe, New England, and the South found a city of established residents jealously guarding all of the real estate. Most of them quickly passed through its port and train stations on their way to the federal land office looking for cheaper and more readily available property, ultimately producing a variety of problems from which southeastern Michigan still suffers, including its sprawling neighborhoods and lack of mass transportation.

Detroit's ribbon farms, as they continue to be called in property title records, otherwise shaped the laying out of metropolitan Detroit's roads and a significant part of its history. Cadillac's ribbon farms reserved to the government no roads. Therefore, later roads followed the dividing lines between these private claims, running parallel to the Detroit River and Lake St. Clair, with secondary roads running perpendicular from them, evident today east of mostly buried Connor Creek in the wealthy neighborhoods of Grosse Pointe along Lakeshore Boulevard. Farther from the water, traditional mile roads running east-to-west were eventually surveyed. They became so named beginning at Five Mile Road (Fenkell Road) with Six Mile Road (McNichols Road), Seven Mile Road, and Eight Mile Road (Baseline Road),[66] and continuing north as far as Thirty-Six Mile Road with some exceptions. Roads north of Fifteen Mile Road generally have local names as do as all of the north-south roads.

Internal Improvements

Detroit remained little more than a military and fur-trading post until the opening of the Erie Canal on October 26, 1825. "We can now go from Detroit to New York in five and a half days," the *Detroit Gazette* reported. "Before the war, it took at least two months or more."[67] Suddenly, migrants from upper New York could bring their families, livestock, and farm equipment to Michigan. It was cheaper and faster to ship wheat from Detroit across Lake Erie and down the Erie Canal to New York City than it was transporting wheat by land from farms in upper New York State.

Before then, the sale of federal land in Michigan had favored speculators over farmers. The minimum parcel for sale was a quarter section—160 acres for $320 payable with interest over four years. That was so much in the hard economic times that the U.S. Congress ordered a moratorium on federal foreclosures, which was renewed until 1823 when it decided to sell eighty-acre parcels for $100. Settlers from all over New England came to Michigan by the thousands, establishing farms and building towns where the rivers could power mills and the land was fertile. Northville, Plymouth, Birmingham, Royal Oak, Rochester, Utica, and Romeo carry the names of places from which they came across New England. The sale of public land in Michigan reached nearly 1.5 million acres by 1836.[68]

Because water was the easier mode of travel across long distances, Michigan's first railroad connected Lake Erie at the Maumee River to the Kalamazoo River at Lake Michigan. Construction started in 1835, but Michigan's bid for statehood and the Toledo War intervened. The area at the mouth of the Maumee River was part of a forty-six-square-mile strip including Port Lawrence, which had been part of the Michigan Territory. Its residents voted in Michigan elections and were served by Michigan courts. Port Lawrence had merged with neighboring Vistula in 1833 to compete for selection as the site of a connection from the Wabash River to the Erie Canal underway by the State of Ohio. When Ohio was admitted to the Union in 1803, federal surveyors had included this strip of land within its boundaries. Michigan's petition for statehood to the U.S. Congress sought to get it back, and newly appointed twenty-three-year-old Territorial Governor Stevens T. Mason backed up his demand boldly, sending a one-thousand-man force of the Michigan Militia to the contested area. After two years of wrangling, the U.S. Congress worked out a compromise, and Michigan voters approved trading the Toledo strip for the entire Upper Peninsula. Under Mason's leadership and eager for the building of railroads and canals, the delegates who drafted Michigan's Constitution of 1835 included a remarkably enthusiastic requirement:

> Internal improvement shall be encouraged by the government of this state; and it shall be the duty of the legislature, as soon as may be, to make provision by law for ascertaining the proper objects of improvement, in relation to roads, canals and navigable waters; and it shall also be their duty to provide by law for an equal, systematic, economical application of the funds which may be appropriated to these objects.[69]

"Internal improvements" was a phrase first loosely applied beginning in the 1780s to the roads, canals, and navigable waters,[70] which were needed outside the original thirteen colonial states—all of which enjoyed ports on the Atlantic Ocean—to transport goods to and from the new inland states.

Ever since the appropriation of federal money on March 28, 1806, for construction of the Cumberland Road, the first national highway eventually stretching between the Potomac and Mississippi Rivers, the president and U.S. Congress have argued over the making of internal improvements, a debate littered with political and constitutional law questions that have never been completely resolved.

Political issues arose between the older and newer states, sharpened between those favoring and those opposing an active federal government, and continued between others who disagreed whether taxpayer-supported internal improvements led to public corruption and wrongly displaced private capital. Constitutional issues arose from the fact that the framers said nothing specific about the authority of the federal government to build roads—or make any other internal improvement—except as justified by the needs of the post office, for which section 8 of Article I specifically authorized the U.S. Congress to establish post roads.[71] Not without heated disagreement was the building of military roads justified as a necessary and proper exercise of an implied power granted to Congress under section 8 of Article I to provide for the common defense, make war, regulate an army and navy, suppress insurrections, and repel invasions.

Justice Story wrote the first comprehensive legal treatise on the U.S. Constitution, *Commentaries on the Constitution of the United States*, in 1833 while serving on the U.S. Supreme Court from 1811 to 1845. A fourth edition included notes and additions by Michigan Supreme Court judge Thomas M. Cooley.[72] Justice Story's elegant public answer to the question of federal authority to make internal improvements quieted constitutional debate only somewhat.

"Congress may appropriate money, not only to clear obstructions to navigable rivers; to improve harbours; to build breakwaters; to assist navigation; to erect forts, light-houses, and piers; and to other purposes allied to some of the enumerated powers; but may also appropriate it in aid of canals, roads, and other institutions of a similar nature, existing under state authority," he said. The only constitutional limitation on federal taxation to finance internal improvements under the general welfare clause of section 8 of Article I, Story said, was whether the project was of local or national character. "If it be purely local, congress cannot constitutionally appropriate money for the object. But, if the benefit be general, it matters not, whether in point of locality it be in one state, or several; whether it be of large, or of small extent. Its nature and character determine the right, and Congress may appropriate money in aid of it; for it is then in a just sense for the general welfare."[73]

Story elaborated that the federal government was confined by the framers of the Constitution to the appropriation of money for the general welfare and could not itself undertake internal improvements under the commerce clause found in section 8 of Article I of the U.S. Constitution. "The power to regulate commerce cannot include a power to construct roads and canals, and improve the navigation of water-courses in order to facilitate, promote, and secure such commerce, without latitude of construction departing from the ordinary import of the terms, and incompatible with the nature of the constitution," Story concluded. "The liberal interpretation has been very uniformly asserted by Congress; the strict interpretation has not uniformly, but has upon several important occasions been insisted upon by the executive."[74]

So, when, on May 4, 1822, President Monroe vetoed a bill appropriating money to continue work on the Cumberland Road, his veto was accompanied by a fifty-two-page treatise on the constitutional issues that arise in the making of such an internal improvement. He sent copies to all of the judges on the U.S. Supreme Court. Chief Justice Marshall and Justice Story politely acknowledged receipt. Justice William Johnson, however, who had a long political record favoring the federal government's building of roads, canals, and improved navigation, sent a letter that is sometimes described as the only advisory opinion ever issued by the U.S. Supreme Court.[75] Justice Johnson wrote:

> Judge Johnson has had the honour to submit the President's argument on the subject of internal improvements to his brother judges and *is instructed* to make the following report. The judges are deeply sensible of the mark of confidence bestowed on them in this instance and should be unworthy of that confidence did they attempt to conceal their real opinions. Indeed to conceal or disavow it would be now impossible as they are all of the opinion that the decision on the Bank question completely commits them on the subject of internal improvements as applied to post roads and military roads.[76] On the other points, it is impossible to resist the lucid and conclusive reasoning contained in the argument. The principle assumed in the case of the Bank is that the grant of the principle power carried with it the grant of all adequate and appropriate means of executing it. That the selection of those means must rest with the general government and as to that power and those means the Constitution makes the government . . . supreme. (emphasis added)[77]

The drawing of such fuzzy lines between the specific and general power of the government and between the national and the local general welfare provided a rationale basis for applying constitutional limits to the building of big, expensive transportation projects, and these lines have ever since shaped how the presidents and U.S. Congress debate among themselves and eventually decide upon making internal improvements.[78]

States having seaports can make internal improvements financed by levying duties on shippers at the cost of inland state consumers while the inland states can do so only at their own expense. Consequently, until the remarkable success of New York's Erie Canal, the building of internal improvements by state governments was rare. After achieving statehood in 1835, the Michigan state government got into the business of building internal improvements as demanded by its new constitution. The Erie Canal, said Judge Cooley, "was striking evidence of what improved means for the transportation of persons and property might do for a state." Cooley offered the unique perspective of a judge who had lived through most of early state constitutional and railroad history. "The proof that the people were awake to its importance is seen in the fact that in forming their constitution . . . they took pains to impose upon the legislature the duty of following the example of New York."[79]

Governor Mason and the state legislature envisioned profits from tolls and fares flowing into the treasury and a market bonanza for the state's farmers, loggers, and iron and copper miners. They created a Board of Internal Improvements, which was financed with a $5.2 million bond issue and was directed to build two canals—one from Mount Clemens to Kalamazoo and another at Sault Saint Marie—and three railroads: the "Southern," "Central," and "Northern," all running east-to-west across the southern half of the Lower Peninsula. The sale of the bonds and the construction projects were both colossal failures due, in part, to Governor Mason's financial naïveté, the Panic of 1837, and the consequent lingering national economic depression that continued through the mid-1840s. Since the 1830s, land speculation had flourished in the

United States and Michigan, accompanied by large increases in public and private debt.[80] New York banks, which were central to the country's infant national banking system, strained to meet ever-increasing demands for gold and silver coin. President Jackson's "Specie Circular," which required payment for public lands to be made in hard money, caused many banks to collapse in what was called the Panic of 1837, resulting in the closing of hundreds of banks and businesses and soaring unemployment.[81]

Only sixteen miles of the Mount Clemens–Kalamazoo canal were completed from Lake St. Clair to Rochester before it was abandoned in 1845. The federal government took over building the Sault Saint Marie canal. Two railroad lines were partially completed. They were sold at a loss to private investors in 1846 and became the Michigan Central and the Michigan Southern Railroads. Construction had never gotten underway on the "Northern" line from Port Huron to Grand Haven. So deep and widespread was public anger over these failed internal improvements that delegates who drafted the State Constitution of 1850 adopted an even more remarkable prohibition:

> The state shall not be a party to, nor interested in, any work of internal improvement, nor engaged in carrying on any such work, except in the improvement of or aiding in the improvement of the public wagon roads[82] and in the expenditure of grants to the state of land or other property.[83]

Cooley wrote,

> Having all their bitter experience with internal improvements fresh in mind, when they formed a new Constitution in 1850, the people resolved to put it out of the power of the legislature again to involve them in extravagant projects. And here we reach another landmark, significant in itself, but especially notable when contrasted with the provision respecting internal improvements which has already been quoted, from the Constitution of 1835. In 1850, the people deemed it necessary to prohibit what in 1835 they commended. . . . These were very positive provisions, and by adopting them the people believed they had rendered it impossible that projects of doubtful wisdom and utility should be engaged in at the public cost.[84]

Detroit's First Exclusive Franchise

Bethuel Farrand said he walked the south shore of Lake Erie from Aurelius, New York, to Detroit in early 1825 carrying with him little more than an idea for supplying the city's water. Detroit's few water wells were inferior because the city rested on stiff impervious clay so that the water they produced was not naturally filtered and those wells dried up early in the summer. There were no convenient natural springs. Peter Berthelet had erected a wharf on the river at the foot of Randolph Street under an agreement with the territorial government adopted on August 5, 1824:

> Peter Berthelet, his heirs and assigns, shall at all times during the existence of the above grant, at his own or their own expense, erect and make and keep in repair, at some convenient place, at or near the end of said wharf, next the channel of the river, a good and sufficient pump, at which all persons who may reside in the City of Detroit shall be, at all times, free of wharfage or other expenses, entitled to take

> and draw water for their use and convenience, and for that purpose a free use of said wharf shall be given, for carts, wagons, sleighs, or other machinery to be used in drawing and carrying away the water.[85]

Berthelet's pump was hardly an improvement for Detroit's 2,200 residents, many of whom still came to the river with buckets hung across their shoulders on a wooden yoke. A few men earned a living by filling and hauling water in barrels carried by two-wheeled French carts. Word of Detroit's difficulty reached Farrand, a civil engineer, and his partner, Rufus Wells, an experienced pump manufacturer. Farrand explained his plan to three public meetings in February 1825. He proposed building a twenty-square-foot pump house on Berthelet's Wharf with two horse-powered, five-inch pumps forcing water into a forty-gallon cask located in the cupola, which would stand almost fifty feet tall. From there water would flow by forty-one-inch tamarack logs to a reservoir at the rear of the Firemen's Hall on the corner of Randolph Street and East Jefferson Avenue. The 9,580-gallon reservoir would be sixteen feet square, built of white oak plank, two inches thick and six feet long, caulked with oakum, and mounted on a timber frame sixteen feet high covered with a shingle roof. Smaller wood pipes would carry water to users along East Jefferson Avenue and Larned and Congress Streets. Farrand would put in service pipes and basement penstocks.[86] Families would pay $10 per year in quarterly installments. Farrand's plan met with approval, and on February 22, 1825, the Common Council granted him "the sole and *exclusive* right of watering the City of Detroit and for other purposes" (emphasis added). The ordinance specifically provided that

> if the common council shall at any time desire to resume the privileges to be granted him by such agreement, they shall have the right to do so, upon paying him a full and fair compensation, to be agreed upon between the said council and the said Bethuel Farrand; and in the event of their not agreeing, the said compensation to be ascertained by twelve disinterested persons, to be chosen mutually by the parties aforesaid.

Farrand and Wells spent the summer on the Clinton River cutting and rafting tamarack logs down Lake St. Clair and the Detroit River to Berthelet's Wharf. Before winter, Farrand quit and moved his family to Ann Arbor, where he settled and was elected Washtenaw County's first probate judge in 1827. His son, Jacob S. Farrand, would be appointed to serve on Detroit's Board of Water Commissioners in 1864. Wells purchased all of Farrand's rights, confirmed by an ordinance passed on March 30, 1827 "granting to Rufus Wells, or his legal representatives, the *exclusive* right of supplying the City of Detroit with water" (emphasis added).

Extending the gravity-fed water system demanded building a much larger reservoir on the highest ground in Detroit at a natural spring on the site of the original Fort Shelby where the Common Council proposed boring a well. So, on July 3, 1829, the Common Council granted to Rufus Wells, Phineas Davis Jr., Lucius Lyon, and Anson Earl Hathon part of the second lot from the southeast corner of Wayne and Fort Streets and the *exclusive* right to supply Detroit's water until 1850.[87] Upon expiration, the ordinance required surrender of the entire water system to the city. They spent months drilling a four-inch hole to a depth of 260 feet before the pipe clogged with pebbles and quicksand. The chief engineer on the $6,000 water well scheme was a man known today only as Mr. Failing.

Wells and his partners went back to a skeptical Common Council with a plan to draw water from the river using a ten-horsepower rotary pump owned by the Detroit Iron Works located at West Jefferson and Cass Avenues. They would build an eighteen-square-foot, nine-foot-deep brick reservoir with a capacity of 21,811 gallons enclosed in wood. In view of their losses and new expenses, they demanded and got significant financial concessions beginning with an extension of their exclusive rights to 1865, repeal of the surrender requirement on expiration, and relief from the expense of providing and maintaining service leads and penstocks to each customer. The Common Council argued over the matter at seven meetings until it passed on June 30, 1830. The four owners then went to the Legislative Council of the Michigan Territory, which adopted special legislation on March 2, 1831, incorporating the Detroit Hydraulic Company with two hundred shares of common stock at $100 each.[88] They erected a new pumping station, installed a twenty-horsepower pumping engine, and constructed a new 120,000-gallon reservoir allowing them to serve many more customers over the next five years using three-inch wooden water mains. Customers never ceased complaining. The shallow water mains froze during the winters of 1830 and 1831. They never achieved an adequate supply of good water, and they never earned enough money to encourage themselves to make any improvements. On March 30, 1835, Detroit voters approved the sale of $50,000 in bonds to purchase and improve the water system. In 1836, a special committee of investigation appointed by the Common Council declared that the company had forfeited all of its rights and privileges and exchanged $20,500 bonds paying 6 percent interest due on June 1, 1856, for the entire waterworks plant.

CHAPTER 2

The Hendrie Streetcar Era

Detroit's First Street Railway Company

On November 20, 1862, during the War of the Rebellion,[1] with the population of Detroit reaching fifty thousand, almost all of whom lived and worked south of Grand Circus Park between Livernois on the west and Mount Elliott on the east,[2] Detroit's Common Council adopted an ordinance consenting to the construction of street railway tracks in the middle of all city streets.[3] Attorney Eben N. Willcox and three Detroit businessmen, Cornelius S. Bushnell, John A. Griswold, and Nehemiah D. Sperry,[4] sought consent on behalf of a corporation they planned to form under a new Michigan law allowing private individuals to organize street railway corporations. The state's Tram-Railway Act adopted by the legislature in 1855 had been amended in 1861 to specifically authorize individuals to form street railway companies, and delegate to municipalities a measure of the state's sovereign power by requiring street railway corporations to obtain municipal consent before laying railway tracks on city streets.[5] The state legislature did so because faster horse-drawn streetcars disrupted other, slower, horse-drawn traffic and drew pedestrians into the streets, and their railways slowed and added to the cost of building and maintaining roads and the water and drainage pipes underneath. The main advantage of street railways was that, for the horses, drivers, shippers, and passengers, iron rails and iron wheels enabled faster, safer, and more comfortable travel upon even the best-maintained roads of which Detroit had none. Cobblestones paved a short stretch along Jefferson Avenue. All the other streets were dirt, interrupted by mud and puddles in the rain and snow.

This was Willcox's second bid at building of a street railway in Detroit. On May 22, 1862, he had persuaded Henry K. Sanger and R. N. Rice, both railroad executives, and several others to petition Common Council for permission to operate street railways.[6] The ordinance granted gave them a first option to build on all streets but allowed the city to buy all or part of their railways and streetcars after ten years at no more than the $100 par value of each share of stock. Unable to attract others investors or lenders on these terms and lacking the funds or confidence in the venture themselves, they walked away, and the Common Council repealed the ordinance on

August 26. The Common Council then advertised for new bidders, adding sweeteners attorney Willcox considered critical to the success of street railway companies then just beginning to operate all across the country.

As suggested by the *Charles River Bridge* case, Willcox asked the Common Council to expressly give his streetcars *exclusive* use of the streets upon which they installed tracks together with the first option to build on all other streets in Detroit and elimination of any municipal purchase option. This was the grant of a thirty-year citywide monopoly. He asked that consent be assignable to new owners without the Common Council's further permission. Section 1 of the ordinance said, "That consent, permission and authority is hereby given, granted and duly vested in Eben N. Willcox, and his associates, who may be approved by the Council, *their successors and assigns*, organized into a corporation, under the laws of the State of Michigan" (emphasis added). This made Detroit's consent or franchise, as it most often would be described, a valuable asset in and of itself owned by the street railway company that could be borrowed against or sold. Finally, as required by street railway legislation, the franchise was given not to the Willcox investors individually but rather to a *corporation*. This would allow Willcox and his investors to buy and sell their individual stock on the open market, spreading among themselves the risks of failure as well as the rewards of success and the further ability to sell majority control to new owners without permission from the Common Council.

Throughout the early 1800s, wary state legislators in Michigan and across the country closely regulated corporations by special legislation creating them one at a time. After gaining experience and seeing their many successes and failures, state legislators began adopting laws under which could be formed only certain kinds of corporations, principal among them those using public land for railroads, electric, telegraph, and telephone poles and lines, natural gas pipes, and street railways. Only years later did the Michigan Legislature adopt general-purpose laws for creating any kind of profit and nonprofit corporation. While Michigan had not always done so when creating them one-by-one by special act, the State Constitution of 1850 erected hurdles against corporations existing longer than thirty years. Section 10 of article 15 of the State Constitution of 1850 said:

> No corporation except for municipal purposes or for the construction of railroads, plank roads and canals, shall be created for a longer time than thirty years; but the Legislature may provide by general laws applicable to any corporations, for one or more extensions of the term of such corporation while such term is running, not exceeding thirty years for each extension.

In Michigan, the state legislature originally chose, for example, sixty years for plank road companies but thirty years for street railways. Upon expiration of their corporate life, by simple operation of law, street railway companies would be forced to cease operating and to wind up their financial affairs with stockholders, bondholders, and other creditors.

The granting of public utility franchises by statute or ordinance incorporating regulations was the characteristic manner by which state or local governments regulated corporations using the public land to do business affecting the public interest under the common law since precolonial days as illustrated by the corporate charter at issue in the *Charles River Bridge* case. City governments were also first created by special acts of state legislation. Such legislation frequently regulated how cities granted franchises for street railways and other public utilities. The granting of franchises was considered so important that many states required cities to follow the same public notice, hearing, and other formal procedures used in adopting ordinances as opposed to the simpler requirements for making other decisions by resolution. Such was the case in Michigan.

Detroit's ordinance granting a franchise to operate a street railway company explicitly embodied a bilateral contract itself expiring in thirty years. Consequently, even if a new street railway company bought the railways, streetcars, and horse barns of the company before its thirty-year corporate life was ending, the new company could not continue to operate after the ordinance expired. Detroit also incorporated into its ordinance detailed operating regulations and reserved the right to adopt others for the protection of the public health, safety, and welfare under its police power. For example, the ordinance set the maximum fare at five cents and specified the roads upon which streetcars could be operated, ideally spreading out from downtown as envisioned by Judge Woodward in 1805. The specifically named streets included Fort Street and Michigan, Gratiot, Grand River, Jefferson, and Woodward Avenues on which the ordinance established deadlines for construction.

"The convenience of the system is due primarily to the manner in which Judge Woodward in 1805 was moved to lay out the new city after the total destruction by fire of the century-old French town of Detroit," explained historian Charles Moore.[7] "Using L'Enfant's plan of Washington as a model, Judge Woodward platted broad avenues radiating from a common centre and extending to various points of the compass. As a result, all the main lines pass a given point; and by combining the routes on two thoroughfares, as, for example, Grand River and Jefferson Avenues, a passenger living in the extreme north-western portion of the city can be conveyed to the extreme south-east section without change of cars."[8]

The ordinance specifically required tracks of the "Philadelphia" pattern.[9] The company could use only horse-drawn streetcars traveling no faster than six miles per hour providing service every twenty minutes, fifteen hours a day from April 15 to October 15 and twelve hours a day for the remainder of the year. Streetcars operating after sunset were required to carry a red light in the front and green light in the rear.

Upon formally accepting the ordinance on January 10, 1863, Willcox and an entirely new crop of investors from Syracuse, New York, deposited a refundable construction guarantee in the form of $5,000 in treasury bonds. Significantly, by express terms of the ordinance, the company was exempt from any other fees or taxes to Detroit except an annual payment of fifteen dollars per streetcar that would not begin until 1868. Several months later, on May 12, 1863, the new Willcox investors filed articles of association with the secretary of state formally incorporating what they called "The Detroit City Railway" to which they assigned all of their rights, privileges, and obligations under the ordinance.[10] The Street-Railway Act required each share of stock to have a par value of $100. The articles provided for the issuance of up to one thousand shares providing $100,000 in capital stock. Willcox and his Syracuse partners said they personally invested $14,000, sold the other $86,000 in stock, and issued $100,000 in bonds to pay for the needed railways, offices, barns, horses, and streetcars.[11] Construction of a single-track railway in the middle of Jefferson Avenue got underway a few weeks later on the two-mile stretch between Third Street and Mount Elliott Avenue to serve passengers arriving and departing from the city's two railroad depots—the westside Michigan Central and the eastside Detroit and Milwaukee.

Beginning on August 4, 1863, riders swarmed aboard the eight fast-moving, two-horse streetcars built in Troy, New York. Next offering services were the Woodward, Gratiot, and Michigan Avenue lines. Railway tracks on Woodward reached just north of Grand Circus Park to Alexandrine Avenue, financed by a $21,000 increase in capital stock in 1864.[12] By then, the company was operating eleven streetcars from 6 A.M. to 10 P.M. daily over eight miles of track using ninety-two horses with five-cent fares. Congressional legislation adopted on March 3, 1865, allowed street railway companies to increase fares by up to one cent, passing along to passengers a duty on gross receipts the U.S. Congress had imposed as a Civil War revenue measure. The Detroit City Railway did so, raising its fare to six cents from November 1865 through April 1866.[13]

Management of the Jefferson Avenue line between the two train stations was turned over to George M. Hendrie. He owned a large stable of horses, wagons, and carriages that he used supplying general trucking, passenger, and freight transfer service between the railroad depots. He could operate streetcars more economically than anyone else. The Gratiot Avenue street railway line was extended north to Russell Street, and the Michigan Avenue line reached Thompson Street. In October, the company built a horse barn at the rear of the Cass Hotel on Third Street. All routes started at Woodward and Jefferson Avenues.

Opposition from neighboring residents persuaded the shortsighted company against building the five-and-half mile Fort Street line. The Detroit City Railway Company also decided against building the three-mile Grand River Avenue line because the company believed it would not attract enough riders. As construction deadlines set by the ordinance expired, the Common Council formally forfeited its exclusive right to operate on those streets.[14]

Along came a more insightful and aggressive competitor. On January 31, 1865, eager investors obtained a franchise to operate a five-cent line on Fort Street. The public stock offering of $100,000 sold out in a few hours, and articles of association were filed for the maximum thirty years on February 9, 1865. The new Fort Street and Elmwood Avenue Railway Company operated on Fort Street from the western city limit near Livernois Avenue running eastward through Campus Martius and along Crogan (now Monroe) Avenue to the Elmwood Cemetery. The street railway line was extended west the following year to River Road (Jefferson Avenue) and Clark Street in Springwells Township where the car barn, blacksmith shop, and dock serving the ferry to Sandwich, Ontario, were located. The new company eventually operated four cars built by Gould & Company of Albany, New York, and seven cars from Worchester, Massachusetts, and Troy, New York. The company extended the Fort Street line to Fort Wayne and added a new barn near the Elmwood Cemetery with a waiting room and offices. By 1869, the successful company had retired its entire debt and increased its capitalization to $130,000. The Common Council amended its ordinance on June 30, 1880, changing the name to the Fort Wayne and Elmwood Railway Company with capital stock of $156,000. More important, the Common Council extended the franchise to operate for thirty years from that date to 1910.[15]

Meanwhile, on May 1, 1866, the hapless original owners of the Detroit City Railway Company, who were still losing money, hired Hendrie and his new partner, industrialist James H. McMillan, to manage all day-to-day operations. Altogether, they put 1,123 shares of the company's 1,210 shares into a stock trust naming as co-trustees Hendrie and McMillan.[16]

Hendrie then personally leased the entire street railway system from the trust under a seven-year agreement. This arrangement effectively put Hendrie and McMillan on both sides of the deal,

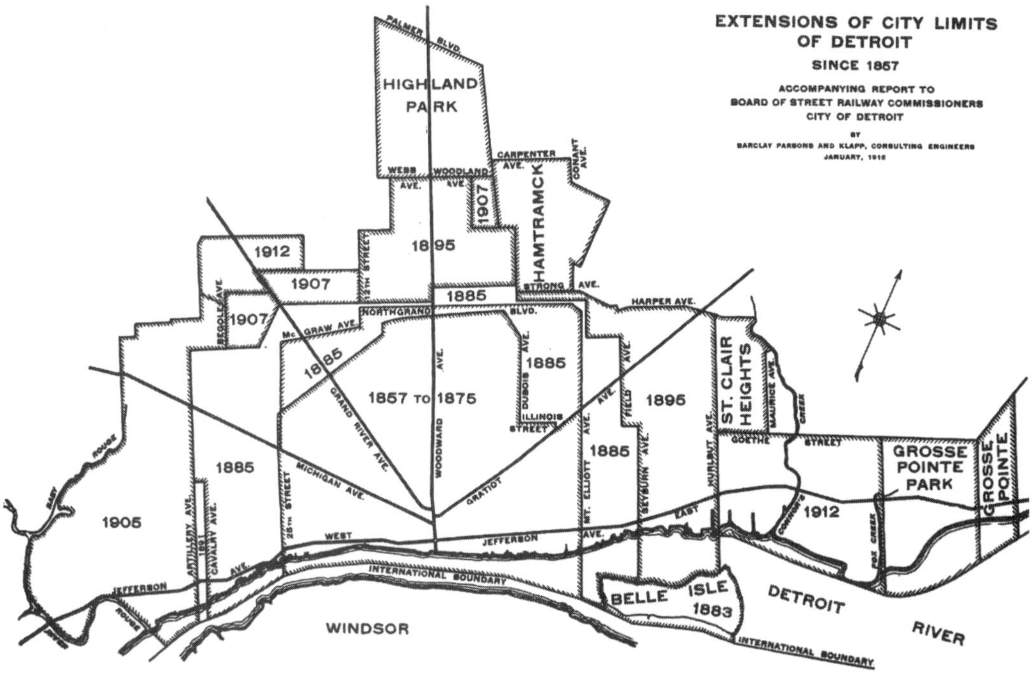

Map of annexations by the City of Detroit since 1867 prepared by Barclay Parsons & Klapp, *Report on Detroit Street Railway Traffic and Proposed Subway Made to the Board of Street Railway Commissioners City of Detroit* (January 1915), 34.

protected McMillan from any personal financial liability, vested Hendrie with full management authority over its railways, streetcars, and employees, and illustrated their legal sophistication.[17] Joining Hendrie and McMillan's unique deal with the Detroit City Railway Company were three junior investors who bought five shares each. The new shareholders were attorneys Sidney Davy Miller, Elijah W. Meddaugh, and Frederick E. Driggs. Miller was Hendrie's brother-in-law, an enterprising, aggressive, and brilliant thirty-six-year-old Harvard lawyer with offices at fashionable 168 East Jefferson Avenue.[18] The Detroit Savings Bank would appoint him its general counsel in 1871. George Hendrie and James McMillan joined the bank's board of directors in 1877. Miller would go on to the presidency of the Detroit Bank and Trust and to establish one of today's leading Detroit law firms, Miller Canfield Paddock & Stone.

Hendrie put his trucking business manager, Thomas Cox, in charge as superintendent, and Cox set about replacing the balky flat bars originally used with T-rails. Cox extended double lines on Woodward Avenue to Farnsworth Street and, by 1869, constructed a single line running as far as Baltimore Avenue with a turntable upon which streetcars could reverse direction. He constructed double lines eastward along Jefferson Avenue, and he installed another turntable at its Woodward Avenue intersection. The company erected streetcar barns on Erskine Street and later at St. Antoine and Woodbridge Streets. The three-story barn was a block long and 150 feet wide with railway tracks out to East Jefferson Avenue.

By 1870, Detroit's growth prompted extension of the Michigan Avenue line into Springwells Township, requiring a franchise from the township's board of trustees and an agreement for use of the Detroit and Saline Plank Road Company's right-of-way. Hendrie used the opportunity to demand that passengers traveling across Detroit's legal boundary buy a second ticket. In the years ahead, as the city's population moved farther out, his demand for a second ticket at the municipal boundary caused township residents to anxiously seek legal annexation to Detroit for the sole purpose of paying a single fare. Once annexed, while the township government's ordinance remained fully operative until it expired, as a political and business matter, street railway companies complied with Detroit's five-cent fare requirements. It was an undecided legal issue that street railway companies never contested until 1910. Their successors eventually won in the U.S. Supreme Court in 1916.[19]

The *Detroit Daily Post* summed up the situation on June 12, 1872, as Detroit's population was reaching one hundred thousand. "The road as at present equipped and run is no credit to the City and is not calculated to secure the goodwill and patronage which it might."[20] Nevertheless, a few years later on May 2, 1876, a report to the Common Council commented favorably: "Street railways have of late years contributed greatly in the development of a city's prosperity; they have enabled the man of small income to live far away from his employment or business, at a cheap rent or in a cheap home, and for a nominal fare be carried to and from his business or occupation at all hours of the day and night. They are at present, as they have been in the past, the means of building up and improving the outer portions of all cities, and thus of converting farm lands into valuable property, in many cases more valuable and more desirable as residence property than that which is more centrally located." By then, Hendrie managed about fourteen miles of railways and employed 150 men using 450 horses and 65 streetcars. Hendrie added no new railway lines, and over the years, he let railway maintenance and streetcar services suffer. Riders complained that drivers made poor time, stopping for ten minutes at switches waiting for other streetcars to pass. Streetcars were unheated in winter, although straw was strewn about the floor to warm the feet of riders, who objected they were often unsanitary. In summer, riders complained that conductors paid little attention to ventilation. Newspaper columnists continued to raise a stink about the lack of street cleaning of horse manure. Horses produced at least ten pounds each day on each railway line they traveled.

Every passing decade saw a doubling of Detroit's population. New residences steadily spread outward from today's downtown along Fort Street and Woodward, Jefferson, Michigan, Grand River, and Gratiot Avenues, where real estate developers were busy building working-class single-family homes, tightly packed onto narrow lots, twenty to thirty feet wide and lacking the front-yard driveways and backyard garages common in suburban southeastern Michigan today but, instead, always within walking distance of a street railway line. The dependence of Detroit's neighborhoods on streetcars for their day-to-day transportation would grow tremendously in significance over the next hundred years. An insightful 1985 book by Kenneth T. Jackson, professor of history at Columbia University, explained:

> The central business districts of large cities thrived during the time of the trolley. There were many centralizing forces unrelated to the electrification of public transport. The steel-frame skyscraper,

> developed in the last two decades of the nineteenth century, was the perfect embodiment of the heavily centralized city. The telephone and the elevator made life in tall buildings bearable and possible, as did the electric light bulb. But the extraordinary prosperity and vitality of most urban cores between 1890 and 1950 cannot be understood without reference to the street systems. Unlike the railroads, the streetcars penetrated to the very heart of the city. The tracks radiated out from the center like spokes on the wheel, tying residential areas far distant to the heart of the metropolis. Because the routes invariably led downtown, with only an occasional crosstown or lateral line, the practical effect was to force almost anyone using public transit to rely on the central business district.[21]

A popular horseracing track at Burns and Jefferson Avenues in Hamtramck Township in today's Indian Village attracted investors to seek township consent to operate five-cent streetcars for two miles along Jefferson Avenue from the end of the Detroit City Railway Company line at Mount Elliott. The exclusive consent granted by the township board of trustees on August 29, 1868, lacked a specific expiration date.[22] It was assigned to the Detroit City Railway Company on November 1, 1881, which replaced the railways at the four-foot, seven-inch gauge. For the first time, a streetcar could operate all the way from the Michigan Central station to Grosse Pointe.

On June 13, 1873, the Common Council granted thirty-year consent over a mayoral veto for a new street railway company, the Detroit and Grand Trunk Junction Street Railway, operating from Mount Elliot Avenue to the western city limits using Congress, Joseph Campau, Larned, Randolph, Seventh, Baker (Bagley), Twenty-Fourth, and Dix Streets (Vernor Highway). Mayor Hugh Moffat said he opposed building a line so close to the double-tracked Detroit City Railway lines on East Jefferson Avenue.

Another competitor emerged seeking consent from Detroit to operate the city's first crosstown line running from Grand River Avenue to Larned Street and across to Gratiot Avenue. The Detroit City Railway Company, asserting its exclusive rights, offered to immediately construct the line itself. The Common Council went ahead anyway, and on a Saturday night, October 28, 1876, beginning at midnight, when all danger of Hendrie getting a court injunction had passed, several hundred laborers from the Polish neighborhood installed six blocks of railway tracks along Larned Street from Griswold Avenue to Third Street. The nightlong drama drew a large crowd of spectators.[23]

Early the following year, Mayor Alexander Lewis announced to the Common Council that he would block any further construction, and in May 1877 bondholders foreclosed. Hendrie swooped in and gained control of the Central Market, Cass Avenue and Third Street Railway Company as surety for its foreclosure receiver, a favored position from which, three months later, he bought all of its streetcars, three miles of railway track, and franchise at the distressed judicial foreclosure auction price of $25,000. He abbreviated the company named to the Cass Avenue Railway Company.

Hendrie filed amended articles of association for the Detroit City Railway Company on July 17, 1877, that increased capital stock to $500,000 with no immediately evident business purpose. At the time, Hendrie, McMillan, and their three junior partners controlled 1,138 shares. To keep two-thirds majority control, Hendrie and McMillan would need at least 3,334 shares, which an increase in capital stock to 5,000 shares made possible regardless of whatever rights the original stockholders retained under the 1866 stock trust. Terms of neither the stock trust nor the lease agreement were ever shared publicly. Subsequent events suggest that Hendrie and McMillan wanted to end their management arrangement and obtain full personal ownership of the Detroit City Railway Company because they were cultivating an agreeable second-term alderman on the Common Council.[24]

The Thirty-Year Franchise Extension of 1879

John Christian Jacob would play a key role on the Common Council doing Hendrie's bidding for the next twelve years. Jacob was first elected as a Republican to fill a vacancy in 1877 and reelected to a full two-year term in 1878. He was defeated in 1880 and again in 1882. Jacob switched to the Democratic ticket in 1884 and never again lost at the ballot box. Following the 1898 election, the Republican-controlled Common Council tossed out the results of one key precinct based on alleged voter fraud and ballot counting irregularities, neatly reversing the outcome, 1,105-1,019, in favor of his opponent, Republican Peter Knauss.

Jacob was a powerfully built man who wore a stiff three-inch beard and spoke with a thick German accent. His grocery, dry goods, and wet goods store in the tough German fifth ward on Rivard Street south of East Jefferson Avenue became the center of Detroit's Democratic ward politics. More than one early Detroit historian described him as a saloonkeeper. Common Council minutes verify his posting of annual indemnity bonds for trafficking in liquor.[25] Jacob's parents emigrated from Bavaria, Germany, in 1850, settling on a farm in the Warren Township area when he was fifteen years old. He sometimes drove an oxcart into Detroit selling produce. Eventually, Jacob bought a flat and storefront on Rivard Street, where he and his wife, Margaret, raised nine children. Jacob was indicted, along with three other Democratic members of the Common Council, for soliciting a 10 percent kickback from a paving contractor in 1889. Among other things, the grand jury also heard testimony against Hendrie's street railway companies but returned no criminal indictment. The grand jury said:

> Positive and conclusive evidence was given that wealthy and powerful corporations, having contracts and valuable franchises from the City, which they were seeking to renew, contributed largely to the election expenses of aldermanic candidates, known by them to be friendly to their interests, some of which candidates were seeking re-election. The busiest portion of Woodward Avenue is occupied by four street car tracks, to the detriment and inconvenience of the public, under the representation that the said tracks are used by two competing lines, when, as a matter of fact, the four tracks are owned and operated by the same body of men. We recommend that this abuse be corrected by the Common Council, and that one of the corporations be compelled to surrender the rights they now hold under such false pretensions.[26]

Following long delays, all criminal charges against Jacob were dismissed in 1891. In 1896, he was again charged with soliciting a bribe from a firm of architects in connection with plans for a new county building.[27] These charges, too, were dismissed when a critical witness failed to appear in court.[28] Jacob spent most of the last few years of his life on his Grosse Pointe farm.[29] When he died on May 4, 1901, Detroit newspapers speculated that Jacob left an estate estimated at $1 million.[30]

Detroit's street railway ordinances required companies "to keep the surface of the streets, inside rails, and for two feet, four inches outside thereof, in good order and repair, and all snow, ice, dirt

Detroit Alderman John Christian Jacob. The drawing originally appeared in the *Detroit Free Press* on April 3, 1896.

and filth cleared and removed from the same. . . . Provided, however, that upon the paved portions of said streets the materials for repaving shall be supplied at the expense of the City." In the early years, if they were enforced, these roadway maintenance requirements cost Hendrie very little. By 1879, however, as Detroit's population was reaching 115,000, the Board of Public Works, responsible for keeping Detroit's streets in good repair, complained that Hendrie's companies were refusing to furnish labor in paving two feet, four inches outside the rails. The dispute prompted the Common Council to seek a ruling from the Michigan Supreme Court, which had no trouble disposing of Hendrie's quibbling argument that the ordinance required that he repair only one foot, two inches on each side. "We think the language of the ordinance can only be made sensible by construing it as compelling the company to care for so much of the street as lies within two feet and four inches of their track, wherever it may be, and on each side to the full distance," the court said.[31]

A few months later, Common Council minutes of October 31, 1879, record Jacob's introduction and referral to a committee he headed of an ordinance repealing the troublesome and costly paving requirement. The ordinance proposed by Jacob required that Hendrie pave and maintain only between the railways. He added language reversing an increase from 1 to 3 percent in the annual fee Hendrie would have to start paying on gross receipts of the Detroit and Grand Trunk Junction Street Railway Company and the Cass Avenue Railway Company beginning in 1881.[32] Hendrie also complained, "It cannot be intelligently expected that large additional investments will be readily made with a view only to the creation of a future traffic when more than half the period of the original grant has expired, and there is no other guaranty of its renewal than that arising from the growing demand of the people for inexpensive transportation."

Therefore, Jacob proposed extending for thirty years the consent to use public streets obtained by the Detroit City Railway Company.[33] The new expiration date would be November 14, 1909.[34]

These audacious changes would enrich Hendrie by thousands of dollars over the years as roadway improvements grew steadily more sophisticated and street railway service extended further outward along Jefferson, Woodward, Michigan, and Gratiot Avenues to serve Detroit's rapidly growing population, most of which enjoyed no other means of transportation. Only the very rich could afford to keep a horse and carriage. Detroit's agreement to this sweetheart deal in 1879 proved to be a financial bonanza to Hendrie and an awful mistake by the Common Council when the original 1892 expiration date approached.

Detroit levied a personal property tax on the Detroit City Railway Company under a new Michigan General Property Tax Act passed by the state legislature in 1882. Hendrie refused to pay the $4,597 tax bill claiming an exemption under the Street-Railway Act.[35] Nonetheless, a tax collector dutifully seized sixty-one of his horses at the Antoine Street barn in September 1884, and Hendrie paid under angry protest. Two months later, he struck back, stripping uniformed police officers and firefighters of the free streetcar rides they had enjoyed for years. Meanwhile, Hendrie sued to block future personal property tax assessments. Neither the Wayne County Circuit Court nor the Michigan Supreme Court agreed, and Hendrie filed the first of many street railway company appeals to the U.S. Supreme Court over the next four decades. It promptly dismissed for lack of a federal question.[36] In 1887, after an attempt by Detroit to collect personal property taxes upon repeal of a section of the amended Street-Railway Act imposing a 0.5 percent tax on capital stock, Hendrie sought a compromise. He would increase the street railway franchise fee to 1.5 percent of gross receipts from 1882 to 1896 with a boost to 2 percent in later years, in lieu of all other taxes. The City of Detroit agreed but, nonetheless, reneged and again levied a personal property tax, which was struck down by the Michigan Supreme Court.[37]

A Most Valuable Franchise

On May 1, 1868, the Common Council granted five investors consent to operate streetcars for thirty years on the west side of Woodward Avenue from the Detroit River turning onto Grand River Avenue. The new line was eventually extended to the Grand Trunk Railway crossing west of Sixteenth Street. The Common Council acted despite objections from the Detroit City Railway Company, which unsuccessfully sought an injunction against the laying of any additional tracks on Woodward Avenue from Judge Charles I. Walker of the Wayne County Circuit Court on June 29, 1868.[38]

Today, the State of Michigan has no copy of the corporate filing made by the original investors but notes incorporation of the Grand River Street Railway Company on February 27, 1869.[39] The Common Council amended its ordinance on March 3, 1883, specifically naming the Grand River Street Railway Company. More important, expiration of its franchise was extended until December 31, 1915, as part of a new ordinance awarded on November 10, 1885, under which the company agreed to pay a new street railway fee of 1 percent of gross revenue in lieu of all other taxes.

The company enjoyed considerable success carrying thirty thousand passengers monthly and paying dividends of as much as 15 percent. In mid-1888, its owners agreed to sell all of their stock for $275,000 to Sidney Davy Miller acting as undisclosed agent for McMillan's younger brother, Hugh McMillan, and others.[40] On December 27, 1889, Hugh McMillan signed amended articles increasing capital stock of the Grand River Street Railway Company to $1 million. The December

31, 1915, expiration date of its franchise would prove to be of inestimable valuable. A year later, on December 1, 1890, Hendrie formally organized a new $1 million company he called the Grand River Railway Company. It purchased all of the Grand River Street Railway Company's street railways and streetcars and entered into a lease arrangement to operate under the old company's franchise.[41]

Horseless Streetcars

In late 1872, an epizootic—animal epidemic—interrupted streetcar service across much of the United States. The disease swept through Hendrie's stables, too. The *New York Times* reported on October 22, 1872, that at least seventy-five of Hendrie's horses were sick and that all streetcar service in Detroit had stopped entirely for several days. The influenza epidemic began in Ontario in late September and spread by exportation to the United States, affecting up to 99 percent of all exposed horses with a death rate of up to 10 percent. The terrible episode frightened most street railway companies across the country. They started thinking about a more reliable means of propelling streetcars, replacing horses, which had a useful life in harness of less than five years even when they were healthy. Hendrie, instead, was plowing all of his company's earnings into buying Detroit's other streetcar companies with the intention of regaining a citywide monopoly.

The Fort Wayne and Elmwood Railway Company allowed Aretus Andrew Wilder to test a steam-powered streetcar on December 6, 1872. Wilder had operated a wood planing machine company in Detroit for many years and described himself as a machinist, mechanical engineer, and inventor who collected an impressive list of patents during his lifetime. He boasted in 1852 that his planing machine operated "at the rate of from four to six thousand feet per hour, with the power of four horses, and the attendance of three hands, which may be boys."[42] Wilder's idea was to install a low-pressure steam engine within a streetcar, hiding most of its moving parts and reducing its noise. The popular wisdom was that quieter operation and the more familiar appearance of a passenger coach as compared to a conventional railroad engine would be less frightening to horses. Unfortunately, perhaps, they were called "dummy" steam engines. The *Detroit Union* newspaper reported:

> About five o'clock yesterday an experimental trial run of a dummy steam engine drawing a streetcar made a trip on East Jefferson Avenue. It proceeded about the pace a person could walk until it reached the ascent of the avenue where the twelve passengers had to leave the attached car and assist in pushing it up the hill. It proceeded as far as Shelby Street and returned, the steam having been exhausted. It does seem to be an improvement over the horsepower. The engine was invented by A.A. Wilder of this city and was built by the San Jose and Santa Clara Railway of California.[43]

Charles J. Van Depoele was a pioneer in using electric motors to power streetcars. He was a Detroit furniture manufacturer specializing in church pews and wooden religious artwork. Before he emigrated from Belgium in the summer of 1869, he had studied electricity in France. He put his experience to work installing electric lighting on the front of the Detroit Opera House in 1878 and inside of the Most Holy Trinity Church for Christmas Eve in 1879, the first public building lighting in the United States. In 1880, he moved to Chicago, carrying on experiments with arc lighting, incandescent lamps, dynamo electric generators, reciprocating electric motors, converters, and current controlling apparatus. He received one of the earliest patents for overhead electric railways. He designed an electric railway put into successful operation at the Chicago Inter-State Fair in 1883, in South Bend, Indiana, and Appleton, Wisconsin, in 1885, and in Windsor, Ontario, on June 6, 1886. Converting to electric power required building a power house equipped with dynamos, erecting poles and stringing transmission and support wires, installing heavier rails, and buying new heavier electric-motor streetcars. Not the least of its problems was the widespread fear many people had of suffering deadly electrocution on the streets not only from the wires and rails but also from the streetcars themselves.

It was while the Windsor system was under construction that three real estate developers, George Dorr, Samuel A. Plumer, and Calvin K. Brandon, joined Bethune Duffield, an attorney associated with Hendrie's Detroit City Railway Company, and Henry M. Campbell, lawyer with the Michigan Central Railroad, the majority owner, in building an electric streetcar line in Detroit. The Common Council adopted an ordinance on April 17, 1886, consenting to their operation of Van Depoele–designed electric streetcars equipped with a spring-loaded pole pushing against an overhead wire and center-located third rail as a feeder service running from the Detroit City Railway line at Twenty-Fourth Street along Dix Avenue to Livernois Road. The Dix Avenue Railway Company reassigned its consent almost immediately to the Detroit Electric Railway Company by which Hendrie hid his involvement.[44]

Its operation, beginning on September 1, 1886, was plagued by complaints from residents about arcing electric noise, irregular service, and objections to its T-rails, but the streetcars ran as fast as twenty-seven miles per hour with electric apparatus provided by the Van Depoele Construction Company. Two twenty-horsepower electric motor streetcars operated from six o'clock in the morning until eleven o'clock at night with plans to add two fifteen-horsepower cars. Generators in the Michigan Central Railroad shops supplied electric power. It experimented with adding a ground plate six feet underground every forty feet. This failed. The Common Council responded to resident complaints with formal resolutions of protest and on June 11, 1889, revoked its consent to operate electric streetcars. The Common Council ordered the company to replace the service with horses, which were supplied and the line jointly operated by Hendrie's Detroit City Railway Company. Van Depoele sold his electric streetcar patents to the Thomson-Houston Electric Company, a predecessor of General Electric. He died of heart failure in Lynn, Massachusetts, on March 18, 1892.

Electric storage batteries, soda motor,[45] and compressed air streetcars all failed elsewhere. Cable-drawn streetcars were being used successfully in a few cities that were safe from winter's snow and ice. Grand Rapids had ordered a horse-drawn street railway company to build a cable line on Lyon, Union, and Bridge Streets in 1884, serving the main uphill roads east of the downtown area. The company refused. In 1887, however, a competitor, the Valley City Street and Cable Railway Company, constructed one of the most complicated cable plants ever attempted. The experiment failed. The slot cut into the road by which streetcars connected to a continuously moving underground cable was probably too narrow for the local winters, and excessive friction frequently caused the cable to break. Consequently, the Valley City Street and Cable Railway, a system of almost seven miles costing $1 million, spent $105 a day on cable replacement, well more than four

Cameron Currie. The photograph originally appeared in Robert B. Ross and George B. Catlin, *Landmarks of Detroit: A History of the City*, rev. Clarence M. Burton (Detroit: Evening News Association, 1898).

times its gross receipts. On July 1, 1891, the company merged with its competitor and converted to electric cars. No other cable-drawn streetcars ever again operated in Michigan.

In 1890, a reporter for the *Grand Rapids Eagle* interviewed Cameron Currie, secretary of the Detroit City Railway Company. Currie said he had a low opinion of cable, partly on safety grounds and partly because he expected to operate and maintain an overhead electric system for a quarter of the cost of cable, sheaves, and pulleys. Currie explained that Detroit was a city of single-family houses with low population density. Ridership was simply not large enough to pay for cable traction in Detroit, a conclusion also reached by the well-managed Fort Wayne and Elmwood Railway Company after it conducted a cost comparison in 1889.[46] While experimentation here and across the country continued, more than anything else, Hendrie was squeezing every penny he could from his horses.

Hendrie's long-term plan for gaining a citywide monopoly was made evident when construction crews spread out busily converting tracks across Detroit from his 4 feet 7 inches to the industry-standard gauge of 4 feet 8½ inches. He finished by June 1, 1889.[47] That summer, he began installing wires on poles to test the operation of an overhead electric system along Mack Avenue from Gratiot Avenue to East Jefferson Avenue in Grosse Pointe. His construction crews drew protests from a few fearful neighboring residents, who staged protests disrupting the workers by sending women crawling into excavations and cutting down already erected poles. Hendrie sued to enjoin the protestors but quit the project before getting a ruling and, instead, installed a slotted third-rail system, the actual electrocution danger of which to passersby was much greater. The Hendrie family was actively involved in other tests of electric operation on Detroit's southwest side. They owned the Detroit Rouge River and Dearborn Railway Company, which began operating an overhead electric street railway line from Woodmere Cemetery across the Rouge River. Company treasurer Lester E. Wise said:

> Our troubles were many and varied. Fort Street at the time was not paved and most of the year a very bad road to travel. The rails we laid were of the old flat iron type, and the farmers who came to Detroit over Fort Street soon discovered that the streetcar tracks made a good wagon road. As a result, we were obliged to instruct the motormen, after giving fair warning to the farmer who refused to turn off the tracks when a car approached, to bump them. In one or two cases, he carried out our instructions so well that the farmers' wagons were turned over into the ditch. It did not take very long to educate the farmers that the streetcar had the right-of-way.[48]

CHAPTER 3

Beginning of the Thirty-Year War

The Five-Cent Case Reaches the Michigan Supreme Court

Trouble over streetcar fares erupted on October 8, 1890, when a conductor ejected John Heffron from a Jefferson Avenue streetcar in an intense argument over the company's transfer policy. Heffron was a real-estate developer who briefly served on the Board of Public Works in the 1880s. Otherwise, there is no indication that his lawsuit was a stunt taken on behalf of any political candidate. He was one of the original incorporators of the Peoples State Bank. He and two partners formed the American Electrical Heater Company in 1894. Heffron sued, and the Michigan Supreme Court decided against him on July 1, 1892, in a court battle that marks the beginning of the Thirty-Year War.[1] Heffron had paid the full five-cent fare upon boarding the Woodward Avenue line for a ride to the Michigan Central depot, requiring a transfer at Jefferson Avenue. Company policy printed on the back of the ticket allowed a free transfer if made "within fifteen minutes of time punched."[2] Heffron said he waited fourteen minutes, briefly visited the post office, came back, and waited eleven more minutes before the Jefferson Avenue streetcar came along. The conductor insisted that he needed to buy a new five-cent ticket. "If no car had passed within that time, and the car from which plaintiff was ejected was the first one to pass after plaintiff had alighted from Woodward Avenue car, the plaintiff may, under proper declaration, have action against defendant, but no such state of facts was averred in the declaration in the case," the supreme court said.[3]

On December 27, 1889, George Hendrie increased the capital stock of the Detroit City Railway Company to $3 million and assigned all of its assets—its franchise expiring on November 14, 1909, railways, streetcars, horses, barns, and equipment—by a deed of trust naming as cotrustees Sidney Davy Miller and their brother-in-law, William K. Muir.[4] Hendrie did so to secure a $1 million bond issue paying 6 percent. A deed of trust is another of the many uses to which the common law trust was put to productive use in securing commercial loans. In this case, ownership of all company assets was transferred into a trust setting forth duties of the trustees for their day-to-day management and for their easy recovery by the lender in the event of default. Subsequent events suggest that at least $750,000 of those bonds went into Hendrie's pocket.

A year later, on December 1, 1890, Hendrie filed articles of incorporation for an entirely new street railway company with a maximum thirty-year corporate life he called the Detroit Street Railway Company to which he assigned all rights of the Detroit City Railway Company under the deed of trust. The new company had a thirty-year corporate life under the Street-Railway Act not expiring until November 30, 1920. Holders of the initial stock offering disclosed in the state filing were James McMillan; Hendrie and his son Strathearn; Miller and his son, Sidney T. Miller; Muir; and John H. Fry, general superintendent of the Detroit City Railway Company.[5] Each bought forty shares. All that remained was getting Jacob reelected as president of the Common Council and a franchise from Detroit for the new company to operate on city streets.

Well-Blended Scotch

William K. Muir quit his job as railway station agent at Ayr, Scotland, and immigrated to Ontario in 1852 when he was twenty-three years old, finding employment with a construction company building what became the Grand Trunk Railroad Company with lines operating between Niagara Falls and Detroit. He rose to division superintendent for the Great Western Railway in Hamilton, Ontario, where he worked with railroad founder, William McMillan. He became acquainted with McMillan's two sons, James and Hugh.

In Hamilton, Muir hired James McMillan as purchasing agent to gather railway and train car building supplies for the Great Western as it extended lines into Michigan from Detroit to Grand Haven. Muir spent his summers at Grosse Pointe for several years before 1882, when he retired to manage a wide portfolio of investments in railroads, manufacturing, and Great Lakes steamships. He bought a lakefront lot on which he built a home he named Otsikita Villa, derived from what the Indians called Lake St. Clair. Muir also did business with a railroad cartage company owned by two brothers, William and George Hendrie. So begins the story of three Scottish families from Canada who earned huge fortunes doing business in Detroit and politics in Lansing from their Grosse Pointe mansions.

George Hendrie

William and George Hendrie made their money breeding, training, and working horses during the last half of the nineteenth century, using them to haul the workers, raw materials, and finished goods from the mines, ports, railroads, and factories of the Industrial Revolution. By the beginning of twentieth century, George Hendrie would often be described as a "capitalist" in the newspapers and many biographical directories that were extremely popular in those days.[6] The term "capitalist" described men whose businesses and investments in real estate, mining, lumbering, transportation, and shipping had generated such large amounts of money that they began reinvesting in banking, insurance, and the many riskier manufacturing businesses that were emerging, remaking the country and earning for them even greater wealth.

The Hendrie brothers had come to southern Ontario with the great wave of Scottish immigrants arriving there in the mid-1800s. George was born in 1835 and educated at the Glasgow High School. At age fifteen, he went to work in the offices of a Glasgow railroad and later a steamship line. In

George Hendrie. The photograph originally appeared in Robert B. Ross and George B. Catlin, *Landmarks of Detroit: A History of the City*, rev. Clarence M. Burton (Detroit: Evening News Association, 1898).

1855, George joined William in operating a Hamilton cartage business. Together, they handled all of the freight deliveries for the busy Great Western Railway of Canada. They expanded into London, Toronto, and Montreal.

No railroad tracks connected Detroit's two railroad depots, so freight in transit from one line to the other had to be trucked from one freight house to the other. Every day, passengers required transportation between stations by coach, hack, carriage, or omnibus. Fifty or more horse-drawn truckers competed for the freight business, all of them using Jefferson Avenue, which suffered miserable condition under the steady wear and tear, needing frequent maintenance and repair by city crews. Muir realized that the railroads would be better served by having all transfer services furnished by one trucking company. Therefore, in 1859, with Muir's help, George Hendrie left his brother and came to Detroit, where he took over the Great Western Railway agency at the Detroit and Milwaukee Railroad station.[7] Hendrie soon opened branch offices in Saginaw, Grand Rapids, and Milwaukee. Hendrie and Company quickly put the independent truckers out of business, and he was left with a monopoly serving all of the freight needs of Detroit's railroad depots and shipping docks. Naturally, Hendrie began operating horse-drawn omnibuses, large carriages seating up to thirty people, carrying railway passengers going to and from the two stations and Detroit's hotels. Two earlier attempts by others to earn a living offering passenger service along Jefferson and Woodward Avenues dated back to 1847. Both had failed. His new monopoly, however, made him a prosperous living.

Four years later, on June 20, 1863, an army of fully loaded horse-drawn carts and twenty-five men with shovels had appeared at the corner of Jefferson Avenue and Bates Street. The laborers started digging and leveling a nine-foot-wide, half-foot-deep trench in the middle of the road, a supervisor out ahead, staking out and barking back orders loudly. As the day progressed, another crew hauled and dumped into the trench cartloads of cinders that they spread and raked two inches deep while others laid 3 inch by 8 inch, 6½-feet-long oak ties across the trench four feet apart. Still more men laid thirty-foot-long, two-inch-square iron strap rails they spiked to four-inch-square wooden stringers fastened to the ties. A following team of workers spilled more cinder around the ties flush with the top of the rails and the surrounding road. The next day, the entire crew was doubled, and the work went forward rapidly. They were using an unusual gauge, measuring but four feet, seven inches between the rails rather than the ordinance-required standard railroad Stephenson gauge, but the city never objected.[8]

The cinders they were spreading would make good footing for horses whether pulling streetcars or not. Hendrie stabled more horses than any other man in Detroit. His well-known expertise in raising, training, and working these mighty animals was evident throughout his life. Nobody outside of the upper end of the city's social and financial circles knew much else about this most private man. On August 1, 1863, curiosity may have driven Hendrie to join some of his socially prominent friends, Detroit politicians, and newspaper representatives, who gathered at the corner of Jefferson Avenue and Randolph Street at half past six in the evening for an inaugural streetcar ride to Elmwood Avenue and back. Hendrie lived along the route at 625 Jefferson Avenue. The Grand Trunk Railroad had just delivered the first two cars from their builder in Troy, New York, and the announcement was rather hasty. Hendrie would have felt jealous awe at the smooth ride of the well-furnished sixteen-foot streetcar. The inside was finished with maple, with beautifully cushioned seating for ten people along each side, stretching its entire length, with a wide aisle in the center. The cars had roomy platforms on both ends with entry made through marvelously engineered sliding doors. Leather straps across the platforms guarded against children falling or passengers jumping onto a streetcar in motion. Attached to signal bells at either end of the streetcar was another leather strap by which riders could signal the driver to stop anywhere. That evening's ride was free. The regular fare would be five cents.

The next morning, laborers moved onto the middle of Woodward Avenue, and their digging progressed toward Campus Martius, where they would soon split up, one crew working three miles westward along Michigan Avenue and another proceeding three-quarters of a mile eastward along Gratiot Avenue. Working steadily through the end of September, other crews extended the Jefferson Avenue line as far as the Marine Hospital at Mount Elliott Avenue. The streetcar company began offering twenty-five tickets for a dollar and transfer privilege for passengers leaving from or going to the railroad depots and hotels on Woodward Avenue. The company opened a transfer station on the second floor of a building at Woodward and Jefferson Avenues in 1864.

At first, Hendrie probably saw no financial threat to his business from horse-drawn streetcars as they passed in front of his fine residence on beautiful tree-lined East Jefferson Avenue, and he did nothing about it. Like many others of his wealth and social status, thirty-year-old Hendrie was troubled by a more personal threat—service in the Union army. The Civil War still raged over the winter of 1863 following the Battle of Gettysburg, and the following year, President Abraham

Lincoln needed more infantry troops gathered and organized by the states, including Michigan. The U.S. Congress had authorized state governments to conduct a military draft if they could not meet their quotas with volunteers. Since 1862, Michigan's support for the war under Governor Austin Blair was as genuinely enthusiastic as was its widespread resistance to the military draft with comparisons to slavery. In the early years, commutation and substitution were legally and socially acceptable means of military service evasion for those able to pay. The going rate for substitutions was upward of $400. Of the 168,649 men drafted into the Union army, 117,986 were substitutes. Detroit's wealthy men like Hendrie uniformly hired substitutes, arranged financial support for their families, or both. According to records in the State Archives of Michigan, an eighteen-year-old named Joseph Gaffele was mustered into Company F of the Twenty-Fourth Infantry in Detroit on December 13, 1864, substituting for a draftee named George Hendrie.[9] Instead, on October 31, 1865, George Hendrie married well. His bride was Sarah Sibley Trowbridge, daughter of Charles C. Trowbridge, a leading banker and railroad investor who had served as Detroit's mayor in 1834. Her mother, Catherine Sibley, was the daughter of Solomon Sibley, chief justice of the Michigan Supreme Court from 1827 to 1837.

George Hendrie's tremendous influence on the history of southeastern Michigan is remembered today only by the tree- and shrub-cloistered one-lane Hendrie Lane in Grosse Pointe Farms, the once elegant Hendrie Avenue a block south of the Ford Freeway at Woodward Avenue,[10] the gentle curves under majestic oaks of Hendrie Boulevard in Huntington Woods and Royal Oak, the unpaved and bumpy Hendrie Road serving the horse farms of Metamora, among them 162 acres once owned by the Hendrie family, the Hendrie River, and a railway settlement called Hendrie in Michigan's Upper Peninsula. Four of his seven children are counted among the early settlers of Bloomfield Hills at Long Lake and Kensington Roads, a half mile east of Woodward Avenue. Sons William and George built country estates there and spinster sisters, Margaret and Sarah, lived on many rolling acres in a nearby farmhouse they called The Covert. Across Long Lake Road was the Bloomfield Hills Open Hunt Club for which the brothers served as the original executive committee. The sisters' farmhouse was sold in 1937 to Carol O. Barton. It has since been donated to the Bloomfield Hills School District, moved about one mile north, and restored for visits by elementary school children. For much of his career, Hendrie kept his home on East Jefferson Avenue, and he built a magnificent Grosse Pointe summer residence near Moross Road that he called Willow Bank, from which he was served by daily yacht service to Detroit, joined by friends and acquaintances. His street railway lines did not reach the neighborhood until 1891. His son Strathearn would build a three-story mansion at 207 Lakeshore Drive. They had downtown offices up the grand staircase's marble treads to the second floor of downtown Detroit's first skyscraper, the ten-story Hammond Building that towered over everything around it for years, as did the Hendrie fortune.[11]

The Hendries organized several interurban street railway companies, including the Hamtramck and Grosse Pointe Railway in 1888, the Wyandotte and Detroit River Railway in 1892, and the Detroit and Pontiac Railway Company in 1895.[12] George Hendrie was a major owner in Eureka Iron and Steel, Wyandotte Savings Bank, and several Upper Peninsula railroad and mining companies. Hendrie owned a 500-acre parcel in Dearborn and a 431-acre horse farm in Royal Oak Township, a large part of which would be donated by his family for the Detroit Zoo. Along with William B. Moran, descendent

James H. McMillan. Prints and Photographs Division, Library of Congress, LC-DIG-det-4a20024.

of Detroit's prominent French family,[13] in 1881 he acquired a half interest in the 2,500-acre Grand Marais marsh lying along the Detroit River between Detroit's Water Works Park and Grosse Pointe. How this came about demonstrates the hard dealing sometimes engaged in by men of wealth and power. In 1872, cousins William G. Moran and William B. Moran purchased a private claim along the Detroit River for $6,000, dividing the land between them. William G. Moran supposedly suffered mental problems. Needing cash to settle divorce proceedings in 1882, he sold his eastern half for $7,500 to George Hendrie, who three days later resold the land to William B. Moran. Exercising their considerable political clout, Hendrie and William B. Moran went on to secure passage of a bill by the state legislature directing the Wayne County drain commissioner to build a series of dykes and ditches throughout this and the surrounding area. They also obtained federal permits for its reclamation and draining into the Detroit River. Hendrie and Moran reaped a considerable financial harvest from a Grosse Pointe neighborhood today called Windmill Pointe. In 1895, William G. Moran's guardian sued to overturn Hendrie's purchase, losing in the Michigan Supreme Court.[14]

Hendrie was a member of the Episcopalian Christ Church on Jefferson Avenue, the Detroit Commandery No. 1, the Knight Templars of Detroit, and the Detroit Country Club. He was treasurer of the Highland Park Club, which operated a horseracing track in Highland Park, later acquired by Henry Ford for his automobile plant there. Hendrie was instrumental in organizing and raising funds for the public purchase of Belle Isle by Detroit. Indeed, George Hendrie commanded the top of Detroit's high society, business, and political circles until Hazen S. Pingree was elected mayor.

Boss McMillan

James H. McMillan was the most influential capitalist and political figure in late nineteenth-century Detroit and Michigan. In 1889, he recognized Hazen S. Pingree as his only effective rival, and ten years later McMillan's Republican Party allies destroyed Pingree.

McMillan was born in Hamilton, Ontario, on May 12, 1838, the oldest son in a family of seven brothers and one sister. After he moved to Detroit, taking the job arranged for him by William Muir, his responsibilities as railroad purchasing agent grew with his ambition and talent. Eventually, he was handling finances and hiring and supervising the one-thousand-man construction crew. In 1860, he married Mary L. Wetmore, daughter of one of Detroit's wealthiest grocers. In 1864, a financially troubled freight car factory for which had been working as credit manager invited him to join in full partnership. McMillan, age twenty-six, persuaded the owners to bring in an older, wealthy friend, a lawyer named John S. Newberry, age thirty-seven. The business was renamed the Michigan Car Company. McMillan and Newberry formed another separate company, the Detroit Car Wheel Company, to build for them quality wrought-iron railroad wheels, which they used to financially squeeze out their partners.

The demand for freight cars soared during the Civil War and boomed with the leasing of freight cars by financially strapped railroads. McMillan and Newberry bought out their partners and opened new production factories in Missouri, Indiana, and Ontario. Meanwhile, they started new heavy industrial plants, the Detroit Iron Furnace Company, Baugh Steam Forge Company, Fulton Iron and Engine Works, Newberry Furnace Company, and Detroit Pipe and Foundry Company.

McMillan was one of the original incorporators of the Michigan Bell Telephone Company in 1881. Together with Newberry, George Hendrie, and others, in exchange for 1,300,000 acres of land, he undertook building the Detroit, Mackinaw and Marquette Railroad across the Upper Peninsula, establishing a freight car ferry at Mackinaw City and constructing an international railroad bridge at Sault Saint Marie. He engaged in Great Lakes shipping. McMillan headed the Detroit & Cleveland Navigation Company and the Detroit Dry Dock Company. He would serve on the board of directors of at least twenty-two other industrial companies. In 1888, following the death in childbirth of his daughter, Mrs. Grace Jarvis, he founded Detroit's Grace Hospital for poor women and children.

McMillan began his political career in 1877, winning election to Detroit's Board of Estimates, which supervised the city budget. The following year, he accepted the post of treasurer of the State Republican Committee. A year later, he was elected Republican Party chairman, serving just a few successful months before the 1879 state election. He returned as party chairman in 1886, reached into his own pocket, reorganized from the county level up, and won a statewide victory in the 1887 election. During his career as state chairman he personally pumped $400,000 into the party. Throughout the 1890s, McMillan and his wealth ruled the Michigan Republican Party with an iron fist, getting himself appointed by the Republican state house of representatives to the U.S. Senate in 1889, reappointed in 1895, and again in 1901.

In the U.S. Senate, McMillan's major accomplishments were to revive L'Enfant's original plans for the District of Columbia, removing the railroad depots and railroad tracks to create the National Mall, to enlarge the White House, to widen the avenues and add new parks, to group new office

The original McMillan Fountain. Courtesy of the American Catholic History Research Center and University Archives, Catholic University of America.

buildings into the Federal Triangle, and to construct the Memorial Bridge and a water filtration plant and reservoir serving the District of Columbia.

McMillan rarely returned to Detroit after his election. His grand four-story home on Jefferson Avenue and his mansion in Grosse Pointe were permanently shuttered after he bought an oceanside home in Eagles Head at Manchester-by-the-Sea, Massachusetts, where he suffered massive heart failure and died on August 10, 1902. McMillan had been the quintessential self-serving Gilded Age plutocrat, exercising his financial and political power almost solely in the service of gaining more wealth for himself and his friends.[15]

Ten years following his death, a fountain dedicated to his memory was erected on the grounds of the renamed McMillan Reservoir in the District of Columbia at a cost of $40,000, mostly raised in Detroit. In preparation for reservoir expansion work, the fountain was dismantled in 1941, put into storage, moved from place to place, and eventually ended up in the Fort Washington National

Park in Maryland. In 1983, the fountain's upper basin and central figures, the Three Graces, were moved back to Crispus Attucks Park and rededicated instead to former mayor Marion S. Berry by the District of Columbia. In 1992, the figures were moved again to their current location at the reservoir site, where they remain inoperable and fenced away from public access. The base of the fountain sits in broken pieces beyond repair forgotten somewhere in Fort Washington.[16]

Mayor Hazen S. Pingree. Prints and Photographs Division, Library of Congress, LC-D4-40050.

CHAPTER 4

The Progressive Era

Mayor Hazen S. Pingree

The military green bronze monument of Hazen S. Pingree on a prominent corner of Grand Circus Park looks directly up Woodward Avenue away from the heart of Detroit. Sculptor Rudolph Schwarz of Indiana, who designed numerous grand Civil War monuments at the turn of the century that were erected across the South and Midwest, depicted Mayor Pingree uncharacteristically relaxed in a fine, upholstered armchair.[1] The finished piece was originally positioned on the lower end of Grand Circus Park from which Pingree was looking south down Woodward Avenue toward the old city hall.[2]

Long after city hall's demolition in the 1890s the monument was moved and his orientation turned so that today he is instead looking north up Woodward Avenue past the fourteen-story Fyfe Building across Adams Street that was the world's largest shoe store when it opened in 1919. The inexplicable reorientation may serve some aesthetic purpose, but Pingree himself would have loudly protested because his heart was in city hall.[3] A bronze panel inscription tells passersby a lot about him in a few words. It says:

The Citizens of Michigan
Erect this Monument to the Cherished Memory of
Hazen S. Pingree
A Gallant Soldier.
An Enterprising and Successful Citizen.
Four Times Elected Mayor of the City of Detroit.
Twice Governor of Michigan.
He Was the First to Warn the People of the Great Danger
Threatened by Powerful Private Corporations, and the First to
Awake to the Great Inequalities in Taxation and
to Initiate Steps for Reform.

The Idol of the People
He died June 18, MDCCCCI, Aged 60 Years

Pingree began his political career as the Republican Party's hopeless candidate in the 1889 mayoral election pitted against the Democratic Party's entrenched ward politics, from which he emerged as the first of the country's great turn-of-the-century Progressive Era politicians. His intuitive grasp of the levers of local power and his exercise of them was simply breathtaking. He won election four times from 1889 to 1895 on a reform agenda ever since mouthed by all campaigning Detroit politicians, even more than a hundred years later, spouting cliché-ridden promises to make city hall work for the people instead of the bureaucrats, clean up public corruption, restrain the power of public utilities, and shift the burden of taxation from the people to the corporations. Pingree and a handful of mayors around the Midwest first conceived such populist promises responding to the needs and aspirations of its industrial and manufacturing plant working-class voters. Pingree was different, however, because he actually tried to do what he promised.

Born in Denmark, Maine, on August 30, 1840, Pingree grew into a broad-shouldered young man with a square jaw and piercing blue eyes who was training as a leather cutter in a Massachusetts shoe factory when he enlisted in 1862 with the First Regiment of the Heavy Artillery, Massachusetts Volunteers, to fight in the Civil War.[4] He was taken prisoner on May 25, 1864, and held at Gordonville and Lynchburg, Virginia, and later at Salisbury, North Carolina, where he met Michigan soldiers, who filled him with tales about lively Detroit and its bustling factories. Pingree was transferred to the notorious Andersonville prison camp and from there to a newly built prison called Camp Lawton outside of Millen, Georgia. He escaped on November 27, 1864, by alertly answering to the name of a comrade too sick to appear at roll call for a prisoner exchange with the Union army. Whether Pingree did so selfishly, leaving behind the rightful soldier, has been debated by other historians, none of whom identified the man whom Pingree rushed to stand in for at the exchange.[5] Any doubts about how he obtained his release might be relaxed because Pingree rejoined his regiment in several battles and personally witnessed the surrender of Confederate General Robert E. Lee at Appomattox Court in 1865. If his prison escape left him with lingering guilt, he never let self-doubt discourage him in his public life.

Before his election, Pingree earned his wealth running a boot and shoe factory in postwar Detroit, where much bigger fortunes had already been generated from the mining, transportation, and processing of Michigan's lumber, copper, and iron by its railroads, steamships, and industrial plants for at least twenty-five years by a few of its well-invested French settlers, shrewd Yankees, and a few early immigrants from Scotland, Ireland, Germany, and Poland. While copper and timber products were the city's chief industries during the Civil War, ready capital and consumer demand had propelled iron refining, steel manufacturing, foundry, and machine products. Manufacturing of railroad freight cars, stoves, cigars, pharmaceuticals, varnish, soda ash, and alkaline and flour millings and meatpacking were booming. Innovation and invention were encouraged. Hard work

OPPOSITE: Richard H. Fyfe seated in the center along with other members of the board of directors of the Dime Savings Bank in 1913. Courtesy of the Detroit Historical Society.

and diligence were rewarded in a city where the promise of opportunity and a good life was being realized. The new money families engaged in industrial manufacturing were joining the old money families invested in real estate, mining, railroads, and shipping in the upper class.

When he first came to Detroit in late 1865, Pingree secured a job cutting leather in a small Woodward Avenue boot and shoe store recently purchased by Richard H. Fyfe, twenty-six-old son of Scottish emigrants, who moved to Michigan from New York in the early 1840s.[6] Years later, Fyfe would become Detroit's leading retail shoe merchant, vice president of the Citizens Savings Bank, and an active business and civic leader whom Mayor Pingree would appoint to the Public Lighting Commission in 1893.[7] Pingree worked a few months for Fyfe before joining Charles H. Smith, an accountant, in buying the used machinery of a boot and shoe factory, H. P. Baldwin & Company, for $1,360.[8] By the end of 1866, they had eight employees and earnings of $20,000 with Pingree acting as the factory's traveling salesman. Thirteen years later, Pingree & Smith was one of Detroit's largest employers with seven hundred workers and earnings of more than $1 million.

Pingree was a stubborn man who learned from experience. When his shoemakers walked out after he rejected their demand for a union shop and a small wage increase in 1885, no settlement was reached for eleven months during which factory production dropped from four thousand to six hundred shoes a day. While some middle-aged shoemakers had trained in the highly respected handcraft, Pingree operated a mechanized shop and most of its workers would have been easy to replace. Instead, he finally agreed to labor arbitration. In 1887, a fire destroyed his entire building. He confidently rebuilt the largest shoe manufacturing plant in the country outside of New England.

Pingree's family, wife Frances, daughters Gertrude and Hazel, son Hazen Jr., and two household servants, lived among the newly wealthy, socially prominent families of Detroit at 1040 Woodward Avenue, near the corner of Warren Avenue, rather than along East Jefferson Avenue, where many of the old money families made their homes. Like other upwardly propelled young men, he was always well dressed with a black silk top hat and full-length black frock coat, and he joined the city's best business associations and social and political clubs, rising to their leadership posts. One of them, the 1,200-member Michigan Club with an office, reading room, and conference hall at 92 West Fort Street, counted among its members all of Detroit's elite Republican Party financiers, overseen with an iron fist by James McMillan, then one of Michigan's U.S. senators. Others included James F. Joy, railroad magnate; Thomas W. Palmer, retired U.S. senator, foreign minister to Spain, and lumber baron; Russell A. Alger, lumber baron and former governor; William G. Thompson, former mayor; James Vernor, druggist and ginger ale inventor;[9] Dexter M. Ferry, insurance and seed farm magnate; and Elder F. A. Blades of the Methodist Episcopal Church.

It was Blades who boldly suggested that the Michigan Club put forward the forty-nine-year-old political novice, who was chairman of the club, as their candidate for mayor in the 1889 election.[10] Elated by Republican Benjamin Harrison's narrow presidential victory over Democrat Grover Cleveland the year before, and feeling a resurgence growing under the political leadership of McMillan, Pingree seemed to be a safe choice to the commercial-class businessmen who, by their large and growing numbers, actually ran Republican Party campaigns in Detroit.

Before municipal home rule was incorporated into the state constitution in 1908, Michigan's rural Republican legislators ruled Detroit's local government structure with a heavy hand. They distrusted Detroit's voting Democratic Party majority and limited its power by innumerable pieces of special

Russell A. Alger. From *A Gallery of Pen Sketches in Black and White of Our Michigan Friends "As We See 'Em,"* ed. C. O. Youngstrand (Detroit: Wm. Graham Printing Company, 1905).

Dexter M. Ferry. From *A Gallery of Pen Sketches in Black and White of Our Michigan Friends "As We See 'Em,"* ed. C. O. Youngstrand (Detroit: Wm. Graham Printing Company, 1905).

legislation enacted hodgepodge over the years.[11] Among many other things, the state legislature had put city government into a multiarmed straitjacket with an unwieldy thirty-two-member Common Council representing sixteen wards elected for two-year terms, half every year.[12] The mayor, who served a two-year term, had veto power over ordinances and resolutions adopted by the Common Council subject to override by a two-thirds majority. He could nominate directors for the public works, water, fire, and health departments, corporation counsel, comptroller, receiver of taxes, tax assessor, parks board, and hundreds of menial patronage appointments, all subject to Common Council confirmation. The clerk and treasurer were separately elected. Detroit's police chief was independent from the mayor. In 1865, the state legislature had established the Metropolitan Police Commission and given it oversight of the newly created Detroit Police Department. The governor appointed the four-member commission. Such structures were common across the United States in the mid-nineteenth century. Their rationale was the perceived need to keep law enforcement out of urban Democratic political hands, which the rural Republican state legislatures considered riddled with corruption.

Hampering Pingree's campaign as candidate of the Republican Party was its long history favoring outstate rural voters and the party's adoption of a solidly dry temperance plank to which Detroit's thirsty wet immigrant population was strongly opposed. They regularly elected saloonkeepers to the Common Council.[13] Pingree arranged an ethically balanced Republican slate calculated to appeal to the city's overlooked and unhappy wet German and Polish voters living east of Woodward Avenue, while keeping in his camp the largely dry native-born American, British, and Canadian Republican voters dominating neighborhoods on Woodward Avenue's west side. Pingree ran a superb grassroots campaign, which he began by publicly drinking redeye whisky at Baltimore Red's saloon.[14] Pingree bought the German-language *Sonntag's Herold* newspaper and installed his own editor who, not surprisingly, endorsed his election. He courted and obtained the vigorous, last-minute support of Father Dominic Kolasinski, the most popular of Detroit's Polish parish priests, who had been ousted by the Catholic Church's Irish-American bishop in 1885.[15] Pingree's direct and personal appeal to voters had avoided issues while benefiting from a chronically corrupt and inefficient city hall. He emerged from the campaign well known as a forceful, coarse, and vulgar orator and a brilliant showman who was a skillful manipulator of public opinion.

Surprising everybody, Pingree won, polling 13,954–11,616 over incumbent mayor John Pridgeon Jr. Even more surprising, the Republicans also won the council elections, carrying nine seats to five for Democrats with two seats taken by independents, resulting in a closely divided Common Council. One big thing did change. John Christian Jacob was denied reelection as president by the independents, angering the Democrats into whose overcoat pockets Cameron Currie boasted he was regularly stuffing money in return for street railway favors.[16] Jacob's loss stalled Hendrie's plan to seek new thirty-year franchises.

"The first Pingree administration attempted to inject large doses of efficiency into the old system," wrote Melvin G. Holli, a professor at the University of Illinois at Chicago in 1999. "Responsible, efficient, and clean and honest government had been the goal of a number of reform mayors, and in this respect, Pingree's crusade for a better Detroit had few features that could not be found within business-inspired reform movements in other cities."[17]

Pingree did not come to the job with a ready progressive agenda to wrestle away the power of corporate interests. His views evolved slowly from his experience in running city hall, shaped by the grassroots demands of Detroit voters that his ambition for higher office propelled him to satisfy. Mayor Pingree's inaugural message on January 14, 1890, only briefly mentioned street railways. "More rapid transit is demanded by the public and should be insisted upon by us, their servants. If a change of motive power is necessary, then it should be made. Better communication between the northeastern and the northwestern portions of the city is also needed. Proposed lines should be fixed by the Common Council and the franchises therefor should never be disposed of except to the highest bidder. There are four street railway tracks on a portion of Woodward Avenue and it is my firm belief that but two should be permitted to remain."[18]

The *Detroit Free Press* sent a reporter to city hall to do a follow-up story. "It looks to me as if the time had come for some change for the better in our streetcar service," he said. "There is no doubt that the transit is too slow, and that Detroit as a city is falling considerably behind the times in respect to several public services."

Pingree was asked what kind of motor he would suggest to take the place of horses: "Those

Woodward Avenue horse and wagon traffic south of Campus Martius in the 1890s.

engaged in that business ought to know best. . . . It might be asking too much to insist upon the cable system as it is very expensive, but I know a good many intelligent men who indorse . . . overhead electric cars."

The *Free Press* questioned Cameron Currie about removing two tracks from Woodward Avenue: "We certainly need all of our tracks and I'm sure the Grand River avenue road needs its tracks." Asked about bringing rapid transit to Detroit, Currie said, "We are studying new methods all the time and as soon as we become satisfied of anything better than horses we will adopt it," he said. "The electric conduit system is a flat failure; the overhead wire objected to by the public, and the cable system is very uncertain."

Currie was asked how long the Detroit City Railway's franchise had yet to run: "Eighteen years." Currie knew very well that the Detroit City Railway's franchise would expire in no more than nine years. He had very likely closely worked with Alderman Jacob on getting the thirty-year extension in 1879 when he came to work with Hendrie and McMillan.

Asked "Is that not sufficiently long to warrant you in making the investment for a cable system?" Currie replied, "If we were sure of a satisfactory system, yes. There is some saving over horses, but not as much as some maintain."[19]

During his first year as mayor, Pingree tackled a problem faced everyday by Detroit's 205,000 residents: paving the city's 150 miles of roads, which put him face-to-face with Hendrie's streetcars. The freight wagons and passenger carriages that shared the roads with streetcars created two constant and costly problems. Wagon and carriage drivers typically rode with a set of wheels along one of the upwardly protruding rails. The other set of wheels would follow a path on the outer side of the opposite rail, causing grooves to form in the roadway along both tracks that filled with water in the summer and ice in the winter, demanding frequent maintenance. Driving over the protruding rail was always a jarring experience for anyone else driving or riding wagons and carriages, giving rise to public demand for level paving not only outside but also between the rails. Pingree eventually won Common Council adoption of competitive bidding requirements and work specifications for street paving that demanded concrete foundations with a cedar, brick, macadam, or asphalt hard surface. He began by paving East Jefferson and Lafayette Avenues, two wealthy neighborhoods.

His annual message to the Common Council beginning his second year again barely mentioned street railway.

> More than a year has passed since the question of rapid transit in Detroit has been agitated. Yet the only step that has been made thereto has been the laying of the girder rail on East Jefferson Avenue. For a time there was a great cry for rapid transit by means of the overhead electric wire. But it has gradually dawned upon the only large cities, where electricity has been used to any great extent—Cleveland, Cincinnati, and Boston—that this device was not the coming motive power for street cars. Meantime other large cities—Chicago, New York, St. Louis—have been going ahead with the cable system, which has been found to give the best service, the greatest satisfaction, with the least danger, Broadway being equipped with the cable system. And the best opinion in the country on rapid transit for surface roads puts it down as the most reliable, serviceable, and, in the long run, economical. A thorough canvas made by one of our local papers less than a year ago showed that the sentiment of a large majority of our citizens was in favor of cable roads. I recommend the appointment of a special committee on rapid transit, whose duty it shall be to continually keep before the street railway companies the urgent necessity of meeting the popular demand for rapid transit.

The Father of Municipal Home Rule

Pingree's approach to managing the City of Detroit was reflected in the more lofty thinking of Michigan's greatest judge, Thomas McIntyre Cooley. The late 1800s, with its sharp rise in the power of men enriched by their exploitation of the nation's real estate and its natural resources and the advance of the industrial worker, drew them both—the Detroit politician and Michigan Supreme Court judge—into recognizing a need to rebalance the rights of ordinary people. Both believed that an arrogant capitalist class cared nothing for the public health, safety, and welfare of the working class from which their growing wealth was drawn.[20]

Most scholars of legal history describe Cooley's hundreds of opinions for the Michigan Supreme Court as obedient to the "original intent" and "plain meaning" of the state constitution. Those catchphrases might conjure up for some an image of him as a reactionary conservative whose

Judge Thomas M. Cooley. Courtesy of the Thomas McIntyre Cooley papers, 1824–98, Bentley Historical Library, University of Michigan.

jurisprudence springs from right-wing politics favoring so-called strict construction of the law and judicial restraint. They would be wrong. Cooley stands among a very few judges, chief among them Justices Oliver Wendell Holmes Jr. and Benjamin N. Cardozo of the U.S. Supreme Court, Judge Learned Hand of the U.S. Second Circuit Court of Appeals, and today's Judge Richard Posner of the U.S. Seventh Circuit Court of Appeals, all great intellectuals and legal scholars, who defied easy political labels and who brought to the bench and their prolific writing dazzling eloquence, great passion for the law, and deep humility for their role as judges.

"The life of the law has not been logic; it has been experience," Justice Holmes famously began his book, *The Common Law*, in 1881.

> The felt necessities of the time, the prevalent moral and political theories, intuitions of public policy, avowed or unconscious, even the prejudices which judges share with their fellow-men, have had a good deal more to do than the syllogism in determining the rules by which men should be governed. The law embodies the story of a nation's development through many centuries, and it cannot be dealt with as if it contained only the axioms and corollaries of a book of mathematics. In order to know what it is, we must know what it has been, and what it tends to become. We must alternately consult history and existing theories of legislation.[21]

Born in 1824 to farmer Thomas Cooley and his wife, Rachel Hubbard, in the "Burned-Over" region of western upper New York at a time of religious revivals and anti-Masonic and Whig political unrest, Cooley attended Attica Academy.[22] In 1842, he studied law with Theron Strong, a former Democratic congressman, in Palmyra, New York. He came to Michigan in 1843 and continued his legal apprenticeship at the law firm of Tiffany & Beaman in Adrian. After he was admitted to the practice of law, Cooley worked as a deputy court clerk. Restless with intellectual curiosity and stirred with ambition, Cooley worked in two law firms while editing the progressive *Adrian Watchtower*, serving as court commissioner and town recorder, raising six children with his wife, Mary Horton, and cultivating a one-hundred-acre farm. Cooley wrote poems attacking war and slavery; he helped organize the Free Soil Party in Michigan in 1848 but became an active Republican in 1856. The state legislature appointed him to compile the state's public acts the following year. In 1859, he joined the University of Michigan as a professor of law. Because of his exceptional work for the legislature, the Michigan Supreme Court appointed Cooley as the reporter of decisions. Based on Cooley's experience working in local, county, and state legislative and judicial branches of government, Governor Austin Blair, a lawyer from Jackson and a Republican Party member himself, appointed Cooley to the state supreme court in 1864. Cooley became chief justice in 1868 under a newly enacted statute assuring his elevation. It stipulated "after December 31, 1867 the office of the chief justice shall devolve upon the judge whose term shall soonest expire by its own limitations."

Before he died in 1898 of pneumonia, complicated by epilepsy and depression, Cooley won a national reputation as a scholar of federal constitutional and of the English common law. He was the inventor of administrative law and the legal father of municipal home rule. Cooley was committed to advancing local self-government as an absolute right of the English common law referred to as "Cooley's Doctrine," in stark contrast to a rival theory prevailing across the country at that time called "Dillon's Rule" that just as firmly asserts to the contrary that cities have no authority independent of state government.

John F. Dillon was born in New York in 1831. He enrolled in the University of Iowa Medical School at the age of nineteen, and while practicing as a physician took up reading the law. He was admitted to the Iowa bar in 1852 and elected prosecutor of Scott County in 1853 and judge of the circuit court in 1858. Dillon was appointed to the Iowa Supreme Court in 1862 where he wrote opinions in *Clark v. City of Des Moines* and *City of Clinton v. Cedar Rapids and Missouri River Railroad Company*, setting forth the rule of statutory construction that was named for him when the U.S. Supreme Court cited his 1872 treatise, *Municipal Corporations*, and fully adopted his reasoning in deciding *Merrill v. Monticello*.[23] He had merely said that municipal corporations—like the private ones ruled on in the *Charles River Bridge* case—possess only those powers expressly granted by the state. *Clark* involved the issuance of bonds by the City of Des Moines to raise money for a private railroad company proposing to offer service locally. The Iowa state legislature had not specifically authorized municipalities to do so. After the bonds were sold, Des Moines refused to pay. Judge Dillon agreed because, he said, the city lacked express authority to issue such bonds in the first place.

"Dillon's Rule" was nothing new. Its specific ruling can be traced to an earlier case, *Stetson v. Kemp*, in which the Massachusetts Supreme Court said that towns are solely creatures of the state and may exercise only the powers expressly granted to them.[24] If this rule of law is familiar, it is because the common law rules for construing grants of sovereign power question the plain meaning and original intent of the U.S. Constitution and state constitutions with the same respect demanded by the monarchy of England of those exercising power it had granted. Justice Roger Taney, for example, said the plain text of the corporate charter granted to the Proprietors of the Charles River Bridge did not expressly provide exclusive rights and there was no other evidence that when doing so the Massachusetts legislature intended to deprive itself of building or allowing others to build new bridges. Dillon pumped up his rule for usurping municipal government in his *Commentaries on the Law of Municipal Government* published in 1911.

> It must now be conceded that the great weight of authority denies in *toto* the existence, in the absence of special constitutional provisions, of *any inherent right of local self-government which is beyond legislative control.*[25]

"Cooley's Doctrine" arose in a quo warranto case, *People ex. rel. Leroy v. Hurlbut*,[26] challenging the right of Chauncey Hurlbut to hold office in the City of Detroit as sewer and water commissioner under so-called "ripper legislation" re-creating the commission with new state-appointed members.[27] Judge Cooley ruled against Detroit, and Hurlbut was ordered removed. Cooley, however, said it was implicit in the state constitution of 1850 that officers of a municipal board of public works should be locally elected or appointed rather than filled by the state legislature. He reasoned that state law could make only provisional appointments, leaving Detroit free to make them permanently. In justifying his remarkably two-faced decision, Justice Cooley relied on not only case law but also a whole range of literature asserting self-government to be an essential element of the English and, especially, American legal tradition. He explained his reasoning in words of exceptional passion:

> If this charter of state government we call a constitution were all there was of constitutional commands; if the usages, the customs, the maxims, that have sprung up from the habits of life, modes of thought, methods of trying facts by the neighborhood, the mutual responsibility in neighborhood interests, the precepts which have come from the revolutions which overturned tyrannies, the sentiments of manly independence and self which impelled our ancestors to summon the local community to redress local evils, instead of relying upon the King or legislature at a distance to do so, if a recognition of all these were to be stricken from the body of our constitutional law, a lifeless skeleton might remain, but the living spirit, that which gives force and attraction, which makes it valuable and draws it to the affection of the people, that which distinguishes it from numerous constitutions, so called, which in Europe have been set up and thrown down the last one hundred years, many of which in their expressions have seemed equally fair and to possess equal promise with ours, and have only been wanting in support and vitality which these alone can give, this living and breathing spirit, which supplies the interpretation of the words of the written charter, would be utterly lost and gone.[28]

Nobody has ever said it better in one magnificent sentence. Cooley's writing and faith in self-government from the ground up was embraced by the municipal home-rule movement taking root and bearing fruit by the early 1900s with the adoption by fifteen states of constitutional home-rule protections for local government, including Michigan in 1908. Meanwhile, however, widespread urban financial problems in the early 1870s had led to the first national urban crisis producing not only financial limitations on municipal borrowing but also attempts to restructure urban government. Many towns in Iowa and Michigan, and, indeed, thousands of others in the United States, made pledges of debt support under duress that failing to do so would result in a denial to them of railroad service and certain ruin for the local economy as in Iowa ruled against by Judge Dillon. Railroad lawyers and lobbyists roamed the halls of Republican state legislatures even as they sought out and corrupted the bosses and political machines in the Democratic cities with offers of big money and business ties.

Consequently, "Dillon's Rule" of statutory construction propelled the expansion of Republican Party state control over Democratic Party–ruled cities.[29] A year before Judge Dillon wrote his opinion regarding bonds issued by the City of Des Moines, Cooley, too, had decided a railroad case on different grounds involving Salem Township, which had pledged to levy taxes supporting construction of the Detroit and Howell Railroad upon its promise of local railroad service. Salem had done so as specifically authorized by the Michigan Legislature so the case involved no issue of statutory construction. Instead, Cooley said the 1864 legislation was unconstitutional because it allowed the use of public revenue for a private purpose, which was expressly prohibited by the state constitution.[30] Nonetheless, "Dillon's Rule" of conservative Republican state control won the national spotlight over "Cooley's Doctrine" of Democratic liberal home rule. The legal issue dividing them is highlighted today by the unwillingness of the U.S. Supreme Court to enforce the Constitution's protection against the impairment of contract in disputes between states and municipalities.[31]

The Street Railway Strike of 1891

As the newly formed Detroit Street Railway Company prepared to ask the Common Council for a new thirty-year franchise, unexpected unrest exploded among Hendrie's six hundred employees. On April 18, 1891, he fired three conductors working the Michigan Avenue line of the Detroit City Railway Company. Earlier in the week, he had dismissed eight others and two more from the Grand River Railway Company. All were leaders of a revived local union of street railway workers.

One of the nation's largest and most important early labor organizations, the Noble and Holy Order of the Knights of Labor, had made inroads among Detroit's street railway workers since its success against Pingree & Smith in 1885 and its defeat by William Muir's Wyandotte Iron Works and James McMillan's Michigan Car Works in 1886. At first a workingmen's fraternal organization, the Knights of Labor had been secretly formed in December 1869 by tailors in Philadelphia. As membership grew, the Knights began to function more as a labor union. Local assemblies began to initiate strikes to win concessions from employers. Its president, Terence V. Powderly, initially opposed strikes as a "relic of barbarism," but he led its membership gradually into strikes and boycotts. His greatest victories were against the Union Pacific Railroad in 1884 and the Wabash Railroad in 1885, which brought momentum and a surge to more than seven hundred thousand members.

One of Detroit's pioneer organizers with the Knights of Labor, Robert Y. Ogg, was leading this latest effort along with socialist firebrand Samuel Goldwater. Ogg had worked for Detroit's newspapers in the typographical union and had been elected to the state house of representatives.

Pingree would later reward Ogg by securing his appointment as secretary of the Board of Public Works, a position Ogg parlayed into a successful career as a manufacturer's agent representing four large companies, handling the sale of paving brick, creosoted wood blocks, Medina curbing, and granite blocks while also serving in the state senate.

Goldwater's labor-organizing career began with the largely German cigarmakers union, one of Detroit's biggest industries in the late 1800s. He remained an active Jewish leader in the labor movement as head of the Detroit Federation of Labor under its national president, Samuel Gompers. A fierce and long-winded speaker, Goldwater was a Socialist Labor Party activist, but he would win election to the Common Council as a Democrat, serving from 1891 to 1898, when he died. In 1895, he won the Democratic Party nomination for mayor, losing, however, by 10,952 votes to Pingree.

A bill introduced in the state legislature to reduce their maximum workday to ten hours accompanied the new union membership recruitment among streetcar workers. Streetcar drivers and conductors routinely worked up to seventeen-hour days on Detroit's busy streets. For a decade, the ten-hour workday had been a sentinel issue arousing low-wage workers, labor organizers, industrial tycoons, Wall Street bankers, legislators, and courtrooms in Michigan and across the country.[32] Hendrie posted petitions in the car barns opposing the ten-hour-day legislation, suggesting that wages would naturally have to be reduced if it passed.

"The company has taken no stand in reference to the ten-hour bill and does not propose to," Cameron Currie dutifully told the *Free Press*. "We shall doubtless get along as well under it, if passed, as we do now. Our system of paying by the hour was not adopted because of the bill. In fact, it was decided on months before the bill was thought of and was ready to be put in operation a year ago if we had desired. We have no fear of a strike and we cannot understand what the trouble is all about."[33]

The previous evening, April 19, the bill's legislative sponsor, Democratic Party senator Peter E. Park of Detroit, had addressed a large crowd in Brandt's Hall, 163 Michigan Avenue. Almost 75 percent of Hendrie's employees enrolled in the new union. So much for company threats of offsetting wage cuts. A union delegation meeting with company treasurer Strathearn Hendrie, general manager John F. Frye, and Currie on Monday, April 20, opened with the well-worn management question at such meetings: "Who are you representing?" Veteran conductor Robert Law responded with the well-coached union answer that he had been sent by two hundred street railway company employees to demand reinstatement of their fifteen brothers.

Strathearn Hendrie was the twenty-five-year-old son of the company owner. After attending public schools in Detroit, he had been sent East to the highly exclusive Episcopalian Trinity College in Hartford, Connecticut, where he quarterbacked the football team and graduated with a bachelor of arts degree in 1887. Well scrubbed and freshly educated, he came back to take a management position in his father's street railway companies. He would marry Katherine Moran, granddaughter of Judge Charles Moran. By sending his tall, athletic young son to the meeting with instructions to stiff-arm his workers, George Hendrie was sending exactly the wrong person with the precisely the wrong message. Strathearn Hendrie not only refused to talk about reinstatement of the fired workers but also responded in a high moral tone that he had absolutely as much right to discharge the men who were fired as they had to quit. The workers, he naively explained, were discharged because they were agitators. He insisted that it would be improper for him to keep anyone on

Strathearn Hendrie. From *A Gallery of Pen Sketches in Black and White of Our Michigan Friends "As We See 'Em,"* ed. C. O. Youngstrand (Detroit: Wm. Graham Printing Company, 1905).

the payroll who associated with professional union organizers antagonistic not only to his street railway companies but to corporations in general.

"The men discharged were persons of that kind, and they were attempting to coerce other employees into joining the movement against their will," he told the *Detroit Evening News* following the meeting. "Some of the men objected to this coercion and threatened to leave if they were not protected against these agitators. The way we treat our force is a private matter between the men and ourselves. We have received no complaint from any man in our employ, although we are always ready to hear them on any subject. These men were not satisfied to work for us, and we don't want any dissatisfied men in our employ. If any more of them wish to stir up trouble, they will be discharged."[34]

That was all that was needed by Ogg and Goldwater to ignite the fires of resentment among members of the new local union of Detroit street railway workers. On Monday evening, another meeting of Local No. 5391 of the Street Car Employees' Association was held at Brandt's Hall.

By two o'clock in the early morning, the meeting room was overflowing with workers, stirred by long and passionate speeches and barrels of beer. A vote was taken by secret ballot to suspend streetcar service on the Michigan, Trumbull, Grand River, Myrtle, Crawford, Third, Gratiot, and Chene Streets lines beginning at dawn, and the foamy meeting adjourned. Strike leaders already had eager support from the Detroit Trades and Labor Council. The *Evening News* summed up the developing situation:

> The fight presents the features of a war between a well-equipped army and an unarmed mob; the men have nothing to sustain the fight save their enthusiasm and the consciousness of what they regard as oppressive. Whether the 10-hour day law passes or not it will not make a particle of difference for the fighters as the company will see to it that their present opponents among the employees are out in the cold. It would have been much better for the employees had they kept still until this slow legislature of ours had come to some conclusions in their affairs. But they got on their ears as soon as they thought they had the state of Michigan at their back and showed their hands in advance of the game. On the other hand, the company appears to be too quick in firing men and booming an agitation that may end in adverse legislation. They had better have had the caution to bide a wee.[35]

The strike began about four o'clock in the morning, Tuesday, April 21. By a quarter to six, fifty men had gathered at the Michigan Avenue barns. Similar crowds waited at the Grand River and the Gratiot Avenue barns. Police began arriving at the Grand River and Gratiot barns, and one rowdy picketer, driver Thomas Conway, was arrested, but none of the other assigned drivers at the Grand River barns agreed to take their streetcars that morning. None of the drivers on the Gratiot lines who showed up was willing to test their picketing friends. The nasty truth of labor picketing well learned early in Detroit is that doing so is ineffective without at least the threat of violence against strikebreakers.

As the first streetcar drew out of the Michigan Avenue barn, there was a shout, and a menacing crowd rushed forward. Two men roughly pulled the driver from the front platform. Others unhitched the horses and returned them to the stable. Still others surrounded and picked up the streetcar, moving it sideways across the track. When police arrived about eight o'clock, Lewis Bates, a former driver, persisted in unhitching horses from the next streetcar started. He was arrested and sent in a patrol wagon to the Twentieth Street station. The strike was off to a rousing start because not until two o'clock in the afternoon were all thirteen assigned streetcars operating on Michigan Avenue. Sporadic acts of rock tossing had broken windows on some streetcars, rails had been torn up, and debris piled across railway tracks.

"We have plenty of men and hope to get everything running all right by tomorrow night," John Frye told the *Free Press*. "It had been a very busy day and tomorrow will probably give us plenty of work. If we can get our lines running as well as we did today in a few hours I guess we will be able to get everything straightened out in rather short order."

For the same newspaper article, the *Free Press* gathered a statement from a spokesman for the striking workers at Brandt's Hall. "The City Railway officials think the strike is broken," he said. "They claim that they have plenty of men to operate all the roads and will have them running tomorrow. We will fool them. They do not know how strong we are. They will find that they are worse off tomorrow than they were today. Wait till after the meeting tonight and we can tell what we will do."[36]

At the Common Council meeting that Tuesday evening, representatives of the Fort Wayne and Elmwood Railway Company appeared asking for a new thirty-year ordinance under which it would replace horse-drawn streetcars with electricity, cable, or compressed air. The *Free Press* hailed it as "the first step toward securing rapid transit on any of the established city railways lines . . . which has for years been a necessity in the city."[37]

Before adjourning, Republican Alderman Ernest L. Reschke offered a resolution extending "sympathy of the city council to the employees of The Detroit City Railway Company in their endeavors to reduce their hours of labor from seventeen and fifteen hours per day to ten hours and that the action of the Metropolitan Police Department, in stationing members of the force on streetcars to intimidate employees, be condemned."

Debate over the resolution was brief but remarkable. Republican Alderman Walter H. Coots protested, "Every corporation had a right to call on the police department for protection in case of necessity."

"I offered this resolution in good faith," Reschke replied. "Every car had a policeman on it to protect the same. I did not see any violence on the part of either conductors or drivers."

Democratic Alderman Michael W. McGuire complained that there were no policemen on regular duty during the day across neighborhoods of the ninth, eleventh, thirteenth, and fifteenth wards. "There was no necessity for taking them off their beats and placing them in the cars," he said. "This excited the people to trouble more than anything else. The action was an outrage and should be censured by this body." The Common Council adopted the resolution by voice vote, some members grumbling disagreement.

Inside Brandt's Hall, more workers came and those assembled agreed to increase picketing on more lines. Seventy-five new members were initiated, bringing union membership to 463. Representatives with resolutions of sympathy and aid sent into the gathering by the molders (brick makers), cigarmakers, and several other labor unions were received with great cheers. Following adjournment of the Common Council, Democratic Alderman William B. Thompson rushed over to deliver a few encouraging remarks and read the Common Council resolution.

"You'll see trouble tomorrow if the railways attempt to start a car," said the doorkeeper of the hall to a reporter for the *Free Press*. "We'll turn them bottom side up."[38]

"Detroit presented a novel appearance after seven o'clock last evening, not a streetcar being in sight at the Campus Martius," the *Free Press* reported.[39]

Hendrie had ordered a complete shutdown overnight. He worried that operating after dark would encourage strikers to acts of violence. To protect his streetcars from damage and the drivers and conductors from injury, he issued a general order to his superintendents to call in every car.

"BLOODSHED," was the *Free Press* headline describing what happened across Detroit the next day, Wednesday, April 22. "Street Car Strikers Riotous and Belligerent. Cars Thrown from the Tracks and Rails Torn Up. A Number of Men Injured and Six Strikers Arrested."

The streetcar workers started the morning refusing to work and picketing the major lines serving Woodward and East Jefferson Avenues. Many railway tracks had been torn up overnight, and obstructions had spread and grown larger with rusty roofing, lampposts, wooden blocks, and

Joseph L. Hudson.

tree stumps used to build barricades. All of Hendrie's streetcar lines were paralyzed that morning, and many thousands of Detroit's idled workers joined striking street railway employees on the streets. Strikers and bystanders threw eggs and rocks at moving streetcars, unhitched horses, and turned them back to the car barns. All day, they tore up rails and scuffled with any policemen who dared appear.

A future mayor and U. S. senator, James J. Couzens, then a burly eighteen-year-old freight car checker for the Michigan Central Railroad, was among those who joined in stoning streetcars. "During a streetcar strike in 1891 . . . he sympathized impulsively with a group of strikers he saw tossing bricks at a streetcar," wrote Harry Barnard in a 1958 biography, *Independent Man: The Life of Senator James Couzens*. "Young Couzens hurled a few bricks himself."[40]

Some downtown businesses sponsored free omnibuses and carriages on Detroit streets. A popular downtown retail merchant, Joseph L. Hudson, took a strong and public stance, putting his sales clerks out front collecting nearly $500 in contributions for striking workers and their families. He exchanged testy correspondence with George Hendrie, which they shared with Detroit's newspapers. A Michigan Avenue baker gave baskets of lunches at noon. R. H. Fyfe, who had given Mayor Pingree his first job in Detroit and who would be quoted frequently over the years during the Thirty-Year War by the *Evening News*, joined other prominent businessmen in condemning Hendrie's actions.

Sidney Davy Miller formally called on Mayor Pingree to bring in the state militia from Fort Wayne to suppress the strike. Pingree declined. Instead, he issued a statement publicly urging nonviolence by the strikers and replied in writing to George Hendrie personally asking him to suspend service and join the union in arbitrating their disagreement as Pingree himself had done with his striking shoemakers. When asked why he did not put more policemen on the streets, Mayor Pingree explained that the police department was controlled by the Board of Metropolitan Police Commissioners, whose members were appointed by the governor, one of whom, incidentally, was Sidney Davy Miller.

The *Free Press* questioned Cameron Currie following a noon meeting with George Hendrie and his son Strathearn Hendrie at the Detroit City Railway Company offices at 12 Woodward Avenue. "The elder Mr. Hendrie said he was not at all alarmed at the situation, and expressed confidence that the strike would be short-lived and that the company would be victorious," the newspaper said.[41]

"We have no difficulty in filling the places of strikers," Currie explained. "There are more applicants waiting now than we can take care of. We are going to employ every man who applies and answers our questions satisfactorily, no matter if there are 500 of them. . . . The trouble today has been principally on Jefferson avenue. The men have been drinking heavily and it is hard to do anything with them. . . . I have heard it stated that we are employing Canadians to fill the places vacated by the strikers. This is not true. Every man we employ who is not America born is required to show his citizen's papers."[42]

At Woodward and Jefferson Avenues, a mob of as many as five thousand people gathered, shouting encouragement to some strikers who derailed a streetcar. About five o'clock, serious trouble erupted at the Michigan Stove Works plant at Jefferson Avenue and Walker Street. Vandals tore down lampposts to block the track, and some attacked a streetcar driver and conductor. Police officers restored order only following a severe fight and arrest of several strikers. About nine o'clock, six men burst out the doors of a Gratiot Avenue saloon, mounted the front and rear platforms of a passing streetcar, and attacked the conductor and driver. Both resisted. The driver yanked the brake handle and struck out at his assailant. The two men clinched and fell heavily to the ground. An ambulance was called for them both.

One driver told of his experiences that day.

> My clothes were soon covered with the stains of eggs. When we got away from the barn a gang came on board and tried to capsize the car. In this, they were baffled. One man hit me with a brick, but fortunately, the wound does not amount to much. I wish the boys would leave me alone. I want to earn an honest living. I have been getting $11.35 a week all my life, and it is getting too late now to expect more. I can't last much longer anyway. I was attacked three times between Warren Avenue and the barn. Each time I thought my hour had come.[43]

A large number of women joined men hooting at, jeering at, and pelting with stones conductors and drivers on streetcars passing by the corner of East Jefferson and Belle Isle Avenues. The *Evening News* reported someone shouting, "Break out the windows. Give them a volley of anything you can lay your hands on. And if you happen to hit the cops and the scabs it'll be all right!"[44]

In a heated encounter there, rock throwers taunted Strathearn Hendrie, who was riding with armed guards. He heard a loud rehearsed personal insult: "Kill the Canuck!" He responded badly, with unrehearsed rage, shaking his fists amid the shattering and splintering of streetcar windows. The crowd joined and shouted louder: "Kill the Canuck!" Echoes followed him down East Jefferson Avenue: "Kill the Canuck!"[45]

Men, women, and children assembled on street corners along the street railway lines all over Detroit all day in crowds of twenty-five to five hundred. "The citizens of the city are in full sympathy with the strikers if their sentiments overheard on the street count for anything," the *Free Press* said.[46]

The next day, Thursday, April 23, beginning at around three o'clock in the afternoon under heavy police guard, the Detroit City Railway Company moved six streetcars onto the Woodward Avenue line, where 350 of Pingree's shoemakers were staging a sympathy march led by the Pingree & Smith's Brass Band.

Other marchers carried banners encouraging the strikers and denouncing the street railway company. Nearly four hundred police officers had stationed themselves along Woodward Avenue. Others boarded or patrolled alongside streetcars. As word spread of a possible clash, a crowd reaching twenty thousand began to congregate all along the line from Grand Circus Park to the Detroit River. Onlookers packed the sidewalks, filled the windows, climbed the trees, telegraph poles, and electric lamp masts, and rode the streets on horseback and in every other sort of vehicle.

"Never before in its history has Detroit seen stormy scenes as were enacted on Woodward Avenue," said a breathless report by the *Free Press*. "Blood flowed freely and arrests were made about every five minutes, but the strongest efforts of the police proved powerless on one occasion at least."[47]

Hendrie's son Strathearn went out on the Woodward Avenue line riding alongside his driver and conductor. His passengers included eleven police officers. Several different stories of what happened have been told. The *Evening News* and the *Free Press* published detailed eyewitness accounts of surrounding events relied upon by Graeme O'Geran in his *History of the Detroit Street Railways*.[48] Some colorful details came from one of Detroit's legendary newspapermen, Malcolm W. Bingay, who drew his 1946 story from a newspaper morgue full of clipping files and a vivid imagination.[49]

Following the prior two days' events, Strathearn Hendrie had purchased revolvers and cartridges at Field's store, which he distributed among some of his remaining loyal drivers, conductors, and hired strikebreakers. Hundreds of men and boys yelled as his streetcar came southbound across Jefferson Avenue and stopped. Several chunks of mud splattered against the streetcar. Holes could be seen in the windows on both sides. A horse and buggy stood directly across the tracks. "A policeman grabbed the animal by the bit and attempted to lead him away," the *Free Press* said. "The driver, a big, burly man, evidently drunk and with his face streaked with grime, pulled back with all his force on the reins. But the policeman finally pulled the horse and vehicle out of the way."[50]

Hendrie's streetcar proceeded toward Woodbridge Street, where the buggy driver again turned across the track. The streetcar braked but crashed into the buggy, tossing it over and throwing out the driver, who was roughly grabbed by three policemen and escorted to the Woodbridge Street police station. The streetcar continued to the foot of Woodward Avenue at the Detroit River. It was greeted with hoots and cheers. Hendrie's crew unhitched the horses and took them around for the return trip. The driver and Hendrie remounted the north end platform. Police officers guarded both platforms, and others surrounded the streetcar on foot. A police patrol wagon, which had been standing nearby, suddenly drove out onto the tracks ahead of the streetcar with a clanging gong.

"Shoot them! Lynch them! Hang the suckers!" yelled someone in the mob. Hendrie's driver urged the horses ahead and together the patrol wagon and streetcar sped back toward Jefferson Avenue past the excited mob where a large dray stood across the track. "As soon as the car came to a stop one of the strikers jumped to the horses' heads to unhook the traces," the *Free Press* said. "Strathearn Hendrie slipped out a revolver and pointing it at the man, ordered him back. He almost fell over in his haste to get out of range of the weapon."[51]

Some time later, none other than Mayor Pingree came upon the mob scene at Jefferson and Woodward Avenues as policemen were arresting two men accused of throwing bricks that had crashed through the streetcar's windows, smashing the driver on his forehead. Pingree was driving what was described as a stylish two-wheeled dogcart with Wayne County sheriff James Hanley. A police captain on the scene pleaded with Pingree to calm the excited crowd.

"Why, they are not misbehaving, are they?" Pingree responded.

"Yes sir, they are molesting the street car company's property and assaulting their employees," was the captain's response.

"Is this so?" Mayor Pingree replied and urged his horse into a slow trot, stopping a little farther on where he rose and warned those gathered round "to refrain from committing any acts that might incite others to commit acts of violence that would reflect upon the innocent and thus cause undue suffering."[52]

Woodward Avenue was filled with vehicles of all descriptions, and Pingree could proceed no further. According to the *Free Press*, Pingree "commanded the scores of vehicles in the jam there to move on. Two or three of the drivers took the hint and whipped up, their horses drove away, but the rest only grinned and held their places, at the same time advising Detroit's executive to 'get a move on' himself. After a few minutes parley with the men his honor drove Jefferson disgusted."[53]

Pingree's calm actions betrayed the experience of a self-made man whose own success "gave him confidence in the ultimate fairness of the system, but his background . . . also made him sympathetic to workers' arguments," said Richard Jules Oestreicher in 1989. "By the end of the decade Pingree had been convinced that orderly negotiations between businessmen and responsible labor leaders were both necessary and justified," Oestreicher said, quoting from an undated Pingree speech among his papers in the Burton Historical Collection. "Property rights could be secured if justice was also secure and ultimately the unity of labor is the safety valve of the civilized globe and the only prevention of the dreadful remedy of revolution. Pingree was by no means anti-business or anti-corporate but his programs anticipated Progressive notions of using state action to regulate the business system in the interests of order and efficiency and to force overly narrow-minded businessmen to behave more responsibly."[54]

Bingay was confident that Strathearn Hendrie started his own trouble by standing at the front of the streetcar urging his driver, a hired strikebreaker, up the hill from the foot of Woodward Avenue to Jefferson Avenue into a crowd of citizens peacefully watching a handful of protesting strikers. When Strathearn pulled out his revolver and waved it over his head, Bingay said, a few in the outraged crowd swarmed around his streetcar. Hendrie fled away on foot as "the mob, led by

Don Dickinson. Frances Benjamin Johnston Collection, Prints and Photographs Division, Library of Congress, LC-USZ62-2835.

former U.S. Postmaster General Don M. Dickinson, a prominent Democratic attorney, pushed the streetcar back to the foot of Woodward and dumped it into the river, whereupon Dickinson made an impassioned oration on human liberty and other matters pertaining to horse-drawn streetcars."[55]

Professor Holli added a colorful and humorous surprise ending to Strathearn Hendrie's confrontation with the rioting mob at Woodward and Jefferson Avenues ridiculing the naïve young son of wealth and privilege. Strathearn Hendrie pulled out his revolver and pointed it at the unarmed striker trying to loosen the traces; a dozen men in the crowd responded immediately by derisively brandishing their own pistols back at him.[56] Whatever the true story may be of the Woodward and Jefferson Avenues incident, after the strike ended, Strathearn Hendrie never again thrust himself out as the public face of Detroit street railway companies.[57]

The strike brought Detroit's factories and downtown businesses, theaters, and restaurants to a standstill by Thursday evening. Everyone without a horse and vehicle was walking except the very few men who owned bicycles. "The man who owns a bicycle is right in line now. He cares not if the cars are tied up and smiles in a manner which is very aggravating to the foot-sore pedestrian and noiselessly spins by the walker," quipped the *Free Press* about the bike riders without fully recognizing its implications.[58] The harsh reality of the situation created by the street railway strike came as no surprise to the union organizers, Goldwater and Ogg of the American Federation of

Labor, but it settled hard on Detroit's working-class neighborhoods, which had since 1862 spread out almost four miles down Fort Street and Michigan, Grand River, Gratiot, Woodward, and Jefferson Avenues. The livelihood of the working men and women making their homes far away from downtown Detroit depended upon the streetcar they rode every day. More important to Mayor Pingree, perhaps, by Friday morning, April 24, the strike was hitting hard against the emerging upper-class owners of Detroit's industrial plants and factories, all of which were shut down all day, including his shoe factory.

"Jefferson Avenue was so quiet that it looked like old time," the *Free Press* said of Friday morning. "A few boys sat on the Belt Line Bridge, while round about was the usual accompaniment of idle strikers. Business in all the shops about was suspended. The men sat with dinner pails in their hands, evidently ready for a holiday. When the whistles blew at seven o'clock no one was ready to obey the usual summons."[59]

"This morning the Detroit City Railway company decided upon a course of inactivity until such time as the City of Detroit can afford the needed protection for running their cars and prevent the demolition of their property," said the *Evening News*.[60]

"We will not start a car for 10 years unless the mayor notifies us that he can afford us protection," announced Strathearn Hendrie,[61] whose father, nonetheless, promptly accepted Pingree's suggestion for arbitration, and a meeting of management and labor was arranged that same evening. Pingree welcomed representatives of the Detroit Trades and Labor Council, employees, and company.[62] Jacob, too, opened his offices for streetcar and labor leader meetings, but the promanagement stance he paraded in opening remarks spoiled his opportunity to play any other role in settling differences. By one o'clock in the morning, under pressure from Mayor Pingree, Hendrie retracted his claim to summary discharge of the fired employees, and both sides agreed to wage and hour arbitration.

Meanwhile, at eight o'clock on Friday evening, the Common Council went ahead anyway with a well-attended special meeting called by its Democrats for the shameless purpose of addressing the already ended street railway strike. Republican Alderman Reschke tried to preempt the grandstanding charade by announcing that the Detroit City Railway Company already had accepted Mayor Pingree's arbitration proposal.

"I will ask the city clerk if he has received any such communication from the mayor," said Democratic Alderman McGuire.

"I have not," responded Clerk Augustus G. Kronberg, a Democrat.

"Then I withdraw my resolution," said Alderman Reschke.

Democratic Alderman William Uthes offered an empty resolution urging the Detroit City Railway and its employees to seek arbitration and directing the Common Council president to appoint a committee of five aldermen with himself as chairman for the purpose of doing so. Having already heard Reschke's announcement, those spectators gathered twittered. Alderman Anthony H. Reynolds said he thought the best way to settle the whole matter is for the Common Council to take hold of it, make up its mind what is to be done and then do it.

"It is high time that something be done by somebody," Alderman Uthes said. "And if the railway company don't want to run its cars, the streets should be given to some company that is able to give the public proper service."

Applause followed this remark and Alderman Coots said:

"The Detroit City Railway Company is not a private corporation but a creature of this council and if it is not running its cars inside of twenty-four hours, I, as a member of this council, will vote for the city to take hold of this road and run it until they can come to terms with their employees."

Uproarious cheering followed this speech and Alderman William O'Regan said:

"I fully concur in what Alderman Coots has said, and it was a great surprise to me that the mayor did not take this course himself. The Detroit City Railway gets all its privileges from the City, and gives very little in return. It's a duty we owe the citizens to furnish them transportation on their streets, and I am in favor of giving them what belongs to them, even if we have to do it ourselves."

"Let us go ahead by ourselves and put an end to this trouble," said Alderman Stephen A. Griggs.

The resolution of Alderman Uthes was then adopted unanimously, the city counselor and city attorney being added to the committee. Alderman William Richert moved that the council not adjourn, but take a recess until noon today. A member moved to amend by making the hour 10 A.M.

"No," said Coots. "There will be too much for the committee to do. We may have to get an order of court and have a trustee appointed if we find we must operate the road ourselves and 12 is none too soon."[63]

Streetcar service had already resumed Saturday morning led by what a state Bureau of Labor and Industrial Statistics report on the strike later called a "monster street parade" before the Common Council meeting at noon. Restoring streetcar service had disappeared as an issue before the Saturday meeting even began. Another arose.

Historian George Catlin politely mentioned the Saturday incident in his 1926 history of Detroit for the *Evening News* without naming Sidney Davy Miller or telling what happened next.[64] "By a curious coincidence," Catlin said, "one of the foremost street railway officials was also a police commissioner and failing to quell the strikers through his department, that official called upon the Mayor, insisting that he should ask the Governor to send the state troops to Detroit. Mr. Pingree refused, holding that the situation was not beyond local control."[65]

Sidney Davy Miller had concluded by Wednesday that Detroit's police officers could not control the strikers. Pingree maneuvered Miller into political disgrace. Pingree said:

> The company howled to me to turn out the troops, after tying my hands by bribing the Council. Of course, on the face of things, they were entitled to a show, but I didn't see why the militia should be turned out. I had a meeting with Sheriff Hanley and Judge [George] Gartner, and Hanley didn't appear to think there was any call for an extraordinary show of force. Judge [John J.] Speed, city counselor, furnished an opinion that I had no authority whatever to afford such protection as asked by Hendrie, except to request the Board of Metropolitan Police to quell the riots and preserve the public tranquility. That was written on the twenty-second day of April. The same day I sent a communication to the police board, calling the attention of the board to the matter.[66]

On Saturday at noon the Common Council's committee made a verbal report, meekly seeking more time, and the meeting was adjourned until Tuesday evening, but not before Democratic Alderman Ferdinand Amos offered a stunning resolution calling for Miller's resignation from the Board of Metropolitan Police Commissioners on which he had served since 1869, more than twenty-two years.

"Whereas, It is the clearly expressed sentiment of the majority of the people of the City of Detroit that the connection of Mr. Sidney Davy Miller with the police department of the City while he remains a director and large stockholder in the Detroit City Railway company is inimical to the public interests," the resolution began before dropping blame for the four days of rioting on Miller. "Whereas, the recent unfortunate disturbances have been largely attributable to such connection."

Thursday's editorial page of the *Evening News* had bluntly but quietly without a headline called upon Miller to resign.

> If Mr. Sidney Miller, who owns the whole of the police department of the city and considerable of the Detroit City Railway, cannot use the one to protect the other, why should he not let someone—not of the railway or of the police department. He is one of those who seldom dies and never resign, but it would be highly beneficial for the interests of the City of Detroit and of the City Railway Company that he should resign now. The double connection is getting too obvious, and both the railway and Mr. Miller will find that it is one of the main obstacles which [stands] between the company and the public sympathy.[67]

A tabling motion by Alderman Thompson saved Miller from an immediate and embarrassing public rebuke, and Tuesday's meeting of the Common Council was later quietly cancelled. Nonetheless, in 1892, Michigan's Republican legislature gave the power of appointment to Mayor Pingree, who replaced Sidney Davy Miller on the Board of Metropolitan Police Commissioners. The episode might have been the only big mistake Sidney Davy Miller ever made during his otherwise distinguished years as a professional and civic leader in Detroit.

On May 11, the street railway company and union agreed to a full settlement. Streetcar employees won a ten-hour day, wage hike from ten to eighteen cents per hour (seventeen cents for drivers), and at least one day off every two weeks. The riotous four-day strike and final agreement was a rude defeat for George Hendrie's street railway companies, a sweeping victory for Mayor Pingree's progressive Republican administration, and a lesson for everyone from the general public about their attitude toward street railway service in Detroit.

CHAPTER 5

From the Streets to the Hallways

Eighty Percent Vulnerable

Against such a highly charged political background, in May 1891, George Hendrie nonetheless launched an all-fronts campaign aimed at getting new citywide thirty-year franchises for the Detroit Street Railway Company and another for the Detroit Suburban Railway Company, which proposed electric streetcar service on the city's southwest side into Wyandotte. Cameron Currie and ex-alderman DeWitt C. Kellogg, who Holli said, "had a record as crooked as a dog's hind leg," went to work applying pressure on the Common Council's Democrats, who had been faithful company supporters.[1]

John Christian Jacob had been reelected president by an evenly divided Common Council that took 118 ballots spread over four days doing so. The first three ballots beginning at 7:30 P.M. on January 13, 1891, evenly split the Common Council, 16-16, between Democrat William O'Regan and Republican Frank N. Reves. On the fourth ballot, all of the Democrats switched their support to Jacob, resulting in a 16-16 tie with Reves. On the fifth ballot, Republican Alderman Walter Coots voted for James Brennan, giving Jacob a 16-15-1 edge, and Clerk Augustus G. Kronberg declared him the winner. Republican Alderman Stephen Griggs appealed, but Jacob avoided a vote on the parliamentary question—did the rules require that he have a majority of the full Common Council—by instead declining to take the chair. Punctuated by four recesses of five, ten, fifteen, and thirty minutes, voting continued all night, 112 ballots, each resulting in a 16-16 tie between Jacob and Reves before the Republicans walked out at 6:50 A.M. When the Common Council reconvened at 7:30 that evening, none of the Republicans appeared. Again, the following evening only sixteen Democrats answered the roll call, and the meeting adjourned. On Friday, by prearrangement, Republican Alderman Brennan broke ranks, voting for James Lennane, again giving Jacob a 16-15-1 margin. This time Republicans protested, but none appealed Kronberg's announcement that Jacob had been reelected. The lesson of his reelection as council president would not weigh heavily enough on Jacob in what was coming.

"It was notorious that the Common Council, with a few notable exceptions, were bribed in the interests of the company after they became aldermen," Mayor Pingree said. "But the company did not depend wholly upon bribing an alderman after he was elected. They resorted to another scheme, and that was to enter actively into practical politics and aid aldermen to procure nominations after exacting a promise of support."[2]

"It was common talk that the men constituting the old Council were eighty percent vulnerable," acknowledged a Detroit street railway company leader only many years later. Jere C. Hutchins came to work for Detroit's street railway companies in 1894. His privately printed autobiography, *A Personal Story*, was not otherwise especially candid.[3]

"The company had plenty of money and was no piker," he wrote. "If it was disposed to do business in that way, why did it not buy what it wanted just as it would buy a railroad, a power house unit, or a motor car? The answer is that the company wanted only a square deal. The company was often told that the only way to beat it, if the Common Council was as bad as it was alleged to be, was to buy up that group of men."[4]

Hutchins had more to say.

> It was the habit of politicians and publicists at such times to picture the company as being itself up to its neck in the playing of some deep and subtle political game which they alone could frustrate. And involved in politics the company was but it was involved in the same sense that fish are in a net, or as are sailors in a storm at sea. . . . Of course, in those days, as from the beginning of things and as probably will be the case to the end of things, it was customary to pass the hat for campaign funds for parties and for candidates. Some money is needed to maintain a party and to run for office. It is not passing strange—nor is it any secret now nor was it then—that some of the company's money, in addition to expenditures to resist attack, fell into that hat, generally in moderate but sometimes in rather sizable amount. There was no expectation that such contributions would affect any specific favors, but it was thought the recipients in return might find fewer reasons and excuses for coercing the company. The latter result did not, as a rule, materialize. Oftener than otherwise these recipients after election shouted loudest in opposition just to show their constituents they had not been influenced.[5]

Hutchins had retired to his Grosse Pointe home, fifty acres he originally purchased in 1911 directly across from the Detroit Country Club, before he wrote his book in 1938. He continued his modest confession that the street railway company was "just-playing-the-game," adding a humorless joke he should regret having made given the high sensibility and pretense of the tony neighborhood in which he lived. "There were a good many eminently practical men and some women in the community who thought not only that such a course would be entirely justifiable but, in addition, that the *atmosphere should be cleared by a few examples of well-directed homicide*" (emphasis added).[6]

Hendrie representatives spread out in a well-orchestrated campaign to arouse support from Detroit's newspapers and business community with promises of a new rapid transit system using electrically powered streetcars. Hendrie offered to sweeten his deal with Detroit by making an immediate increase in the annual franchise fee paid on the company's gross receipts from 1.5 to 2 percent, something he trumpeted as a 33 percent bonanza for the city treasury. His push for action was joined by requests from the Hendrie-owned Grand River Street Railway Company and the

Charles M. Swift. From *A Gallery of Pen Sketches in Black and White of Our Michigan Friends "As We See 'Em,"* ed. C. O. Youngstrand (Detroit: Wm. Graham Printing Company, 1905).

independent Fort Wayne and Elmwood Railway Company, with franchises expiring in 1916 and 1899, respectively, a clue that he was orchestrating all four requests.

No doubt, both the public and Hendrie's company would be better served by an electric system in place of the horsecar system and that there should be an extension of the franchise sufficient to justify spending the large amount of capital that would be needed. What happened, however, exposed Hendrie's shocking level of dishonesty and greed.

Specifically named as requesting a franchise on March 18, 1891, for the new Detroit Suburban Railway Company were Charles M. Swift, John C. Cahalan, and William P. Lane.[7] Swift was an attorney and street railway investor who worked privately with the Hendrie family on street railway matters.[8] Cahalan was a respected political leader in Wyandotte. Section 6 of the ordinance sought by the Detroit Suburban Railway Company for street railway service from downtown to Wyandotte, taken up for routine first and second reading by the Common Council on May 21, 1891, was a political blunder. It was a public reminder of what Mayor Pingree, the street railway company, and the newspapers called the "workingmen's fare."[9] Section 6 said:

> The rate of fare for a single trip shall not exceed five cents for any distance on the route and the payment of such fare shall entitle the passenger to a continuous ride between either the terminus of said

> route, or any portion of the same. They shall issue and sell tickets at the rate of *eight for twenty-five cents,* each ticket to be good as fare for transportation over any portion of or the entire length of said line for a continuous ride either way between either terminus *between the hours of 5:30–7 a.m., and 4–6:30 p.m.* (emphasis added)[10]

Introducing this language was a mistake because the working-class men and women of Detroit counted their pennies every day, and a streetcar ticket had cost five cents for many years. If they bought one, the "workingmen's fare" ticket would be a twice or more daily reminder that a streetcar ride ought to cost just three cents. Mathematical precision aside, for them, "workingmen's fare" equaled three cents. Few riders, however, could afford to buy "workingmen's fare" tickets because most of them did not have a quarter to spend all at once.

The "workingmen's fare" ticket dated back to January 3, 1889, when the Detroit City Railway Company and the Fort Wayne and Elmwood Railway Company wanted to extend service and lay double tracks on certain streets. Common Council added a provision to ordinances agreeing to the requests that required the sale of eight for twenty-five cent tickets applicable during the hours of 5:30–7:00 A.M. and 5:15–6:15 P.M. They were adopted without any particular company objection or public fanfare. Most riders, however, could not get "workingmen's fare" tickets because the street railway companies refused to distribute them to conductors to sell on streetcars. The companies also did not sell them at stations.

"The Company succeeded in very greatly curtailing the sale of these tickets by *limiting the places* where could be obtained," Pingree explained. "A workingman, or anybody else, in order to get hold of a quarter's worth of these tickets, had to go to the general office of the Company, or to the branch offices at the barns, or to some out-of-the-way saloon or grocery."[11]

Hendrie had swallowed the "workingmen's fare" language not only because he never intended to make them readily available for sale. The Detroit Suburban Railway Company would operate only on lines serving riders from whom he would demand a second ticket because they were commuting from suburbs sprouting outside of Detroit: Wyandotte, Highland Park, and the Grosse Pointes. The Detroit Suburban Railway Company ordinance generated no debate among aldermen over its "workingmen's fare" requirement even though the loophole complained against by Mayor Pingree remained. The "workingmen's fare," however, would become a colorful rallying cry among working families for three-cent tickets and universal transfers.

A full month later, on June 23, before giving a third reading to adopt the Detroit Suburban Railway Company ordinance, the Common Council took up two amendments to the existing Detroit City Railway Company ordinance, and three new ordinances agreeing to thirty-year ordinances for the Detroit Street Railway Company, the Grand River Street Railway Company, and the Fort Wayne and Elmwood Railway Company. Hendrie's full package of legislation then was being put on a fast track to adoption.

The first introduced ordinance awarded a thirty-year franchise to Hendrie's new Detroit Street Railway Company. It came cloaked in a promise of rapid transit service beginning on Jefferson Avenue within six months. It allowed him the widest possible management flexibility because the ordinance allowed either "cable, electric or other mechanical power, including steam, on all of the lines of street railway owned or operated by it, or which may hereafter be owned or operated by it" within one year except on Woodward Avenue, where the new company would be required to use cable traction unless otherwise ordered by the Common Council for which there was no deadline to begin or to finish construction.[12]

The ordinance, however, would be rendered meaningless by the second ordinance introduced that evening. It specifically extended the Detroit City Railway Company's expiration date to November 14, 1921, without requiring anything else, emptying the bottom out of any promise of immediate citywide rapid transit service. Closely reviewed today, the charade being played by Hendrie and his cronies on the Common Council was laughable. Also introduced and approved on first and second reading that evening were ordinances extending for thirty years the rights held by his Grand River Street Railway Company and the Fort Wayne and Elmwood Railway Company.

A week later, on June 30, 1891, the Common Council took up the third reading required by its parliamentary rules for adopting ordinances. "Mayor Pingree came into the chamber after the city fathers had been in session for a short time and took a seat beside the clerk's table," said the *Free Press*. "Cameron Currie, secretary of the Detroit Railway Company, was on hand early, carrying his usual smile, and freely mingling with the aldermen, who were unusually prompt in putting in an appearance."[13]

President Jacob put first up for consideration the Grand River Street Railway Company franchise. The Common Council approved some miscellaneous amendments, one of which required city residency of employees and, for them, a ten-hour workday, much to Currie's angry surprise. The ordinance then passed, 23-6. "We will not accept the franchises with that clause included," Currie declared afterward in a confrontation outside council chambers with representatives of the Street Car Employees' Association.[14]

A showboating and ambitious Democratic Party alderman, meat market owner William B. Thompson (no relation to former mayor William G. Thompson but who benefited greatly by his similar name), offered a losing three-cent fare amendment expressing a popular sentiment that Mayor Pingree did not yet fully grasp. Thompson's simple amendment said, "That in lieu of the above valuable privilege and extensions, the Grand River Railway Company charge the people no more than 3 cents for a single fare, or 10 cents for 25 tickets." Detroit newspapers embraced Thompson's three-cent fare, and he would never forget it.

"Amendments which, if adopted, would give the people some return for their valuable grant to the company were steadily voted down," said an editorial in the next day's issue of the *Free Press*.

> The council is compelling the City to pay very dearly for improving transit facilities. The mayor may, and should, interpose his veto for the protection of the interests, which the council is disposed so readily to part with, but the strong vote by which the Grand River ordinance passed indicates it is well nigh hopeless to expect that reconsideration, at the Mayor's suggestion, will change the result. At the same time, it is worth the effort. A clear and strong statement from the Mayor setting forth the great pecuniary value to the companies of the extension of the several franchises, the revenue which the City could acquire in the twelve years after 1909 from the franchises, provided there were no extension, and the fact that the substantial concessions are all on one side, may cause the council to hesitate.[15]

Last to be taken up that evening was final reading of the Detroit Street Railway Company franchise. Aldermen removed language in the ordinances unilaterally amending the existing franchises held by Detroit City Railway and Grand River Street Railway Company, which were legally unenforceable without express company agreement. Final adoption, however, was stymied by the consideration and surprise majority support for amendments that horrified onlooking Hendrie operatives. The first, offered by Alderman Michael McGuire, closed the loophole Pingree described by specifically requiring the company to supply conductors with "workingmen's tickets." The amendment's explicit use of the catch phrase was evidence of the growing sophistication of Detroit's politicians. The second amendment would require the Detroit City Railway Company to share its downtown terminal facilities with other streetcar companies. Republican Alderman Reves frantically moved to lay all street railway matters on the table and adjourn to noon, July 1. Jacob, embarrassed and furious at losing his grip on the majority, turned the gavel over to Alderman O'Regan and rushed out. "It being very seldom that he makes a request of this kind, his colleagues were disposed to grant his request and he silently stole away but returned later in the session," the *Free Press* said.[16]

Carried

On July 1, meeting again, Alderman Murray Watson presented a petition from residents asking the Common Council to pass an ordinance regulating the sale of streetcar tickets, which the majority buried by sending it to a committee. The Common Council gutted the residency clause of the Grand River Street Railway Company franchise before approving its adoption, 22-6. Jacob then took up the Detroit Street Railway Company ordinance. Alderman McGuire's amendment requiring conductors to sell "workingmen's fare" tickets for three hours each morning and two and a half hours each evening was voted down, and an amendment requiring conductors to accept them between the hours of 5 A.M. to 7 A.M. and 5 P.M. to 7 P.M. excluding Sundays, leaving the big loophole regarding their place of sale, was adopted.

"When the famous ordinances of 1891 were passed, efforts were made by several aldermen, who had the good of the people at heart, to procure the insertion of a provision requiring the company to place these tickets on sale in the hands of conductors, so that they would be easily accessible to patrons of the lines," Pingree said later. "But at the dictation of a gentleman, who sat in the lobby, and controlled by a movement of a hand, the adoption or rejection of any amendments offered, these were invariably voted down by the Gang."[17] The power of lobbyists over President Jacob and the Common Council was so firmly entrenched that on April 22, 1891, the *Free Press* joked about plans to redesign council chambers. "The proposal to remove the lobby of the Board of Aldermen to the portion of the room most remote from the president's chair must cause Mr. Jacob to feel a little insecure in his position," its editorial said. "He has depended upon the lobby for his applause and upon those whom the lobby represents for his votes." After striking otherwise legally unenforceable changes attempted to earlier-granted franchises, the Detroit Street Railway Company ordinance was adopted, 22-6.

What came along next was an ingenious and devious legal twist that could only have been stage-managed by Hendrie's legal counsel, Sidney Davy Miller. The Common Council made what appeared to be a straightforward one-word correction of an embarrassing error by the drafter and proofreaders in the separate ordinance specifically extending the Detroit City Railway Company franchise to November 14, 1921. The amendment offered by Alderman Reves corrected the original draft, which added a new section 8 to the old Detroit City Railway Company ordinance. The original amendment said:

> The powers and privileges conferred and the obligations imposed on the Detroit *City* Railway by the provisions of an ordinance entitled "An ordinance to permit certain persons to establish and to locate street railways in the City of Detroit," approved November 24, 1862, and all amendments and supplements thereto, and by the provisions of the several ordinances contained in chapter one hundred and nine of the Revised Ordinance of the City of Detroit for the year 1890, and by the terms and provisions of this Ordinance, are hereby conferred and imposed on the Detroit *City* Railway Company. (emphasis added)

Otherwise, the amendment had explicitly extended the franchise term "twelve years from and after the fourteenth day of November 1909" and further specifically provided that "the Detroit *City* Railway Company, its successors and assigns are hereby authorized and empowered to own, construct, use and operate its and their lines of street railway from the date of the passage of this ordinance to November fourteenth, 1921" (emphasis added). Hendrie and Miller apparently insisted on twice stating the franchise extension language in legally unassailable, easy to understand, plain English words. Having gotten everything they wanted in that language, however, they wanted more.

The Reves amendment was to strike the word "*City*" and insert the word "*Street*" in section 8, which would fully incorporate by reference all of the powers and privileges conferred on the Detroit City Railway Company for a term expiring November 14, 1921, directly on the new Detroit Street Railway Company. The change moved all powers and privileges granted by Detroit since 1862 from Hendrie's old Detroit City Railway Company to his new Detroit Street Railway Company. The reworded amendment created a gigantic legal loophole under which Hendrie could disregard his promise of rapid transit made in the Detroit Street Railway Company ordinance and continue using horse-drawn streetcars as the Detroit Street Railway Company until he or his purchasers decided otherwise anytime before 1921 when he would be eighty-seven years old. If Sidney Davy Miller had been involved in its original drafting, he never would have made such a typo requiring correction. He would have since concluded, however, from the votes actually cast in Hendrie's favor, and firmly brought in line since June 28, that Hendrie had the two-thirds majority needed to overturn any veto forthcoming from Mayor Pingree. Therefore, the final audacious step was taken. The official *Journal of the Common Council* reads:

> Ald. Reves moved to strike out the word City, and insert the word Street, in last line sec. 8 and second line of sec. 3.
>
> Carried.[18]

The Detroit City Railway Company ordinance amendment then passed, 22-4. Last, the Common Council took up and adopted, 22-4, the ordinance extending the Fort Wayne and Elmwood Railway Company franchise for thirty years.

"The City Railway Company had a field day yesterday at the adjourned meeting of the Common Council," said the *Free Press*. "To an observer it was manifest at the opening of the session that all matters had been prearranged. The amendments which the company desired to have were all typewritten and in charge of Ald. Reves, who led the force in behalf of the company."[19]

Few people fully understood all of what had happened that evening. The Common Council had blown up a thick smokescreen of carefully worded new ordinances and amendments before adopting Miller's last-minute obscure language change. Hendrie may have quit worrying because he had gained unchecked control over choosing among cable, electric, steam, or other mechanical power together with a thirty-year franchise.

Hendrie's five-cent horse-drawn streetcars were not only inadequately slow but also increasingly expensive for him to operate in the fast-growing city because the outer boundaries of Detroit were growing to encompass the area up to and around the vicinity of the then rapidly developing Grand Boulevard. Hendrie's street railway company needed to keep extending its lines against possible competition. Longer street railway lines were much more costly to operate because horses could pull a streetcar for no more than two four-hour daily shifts, requiring the barns and blacksmiths to make ready twelve horses every day for every streetcar on every line, increasing the cost of housing, feeding, shoeing, and day-to-day animal care while adding passengers who paid no more than five cents while taking those longer rides.

Hendrie knew that he needed a cheaper and faster means of propelling streetcars. His resistance to replacing his horse-drawn streetcars even under pressure from both his friends and enemies is not so much the story of a man blind to advancing technology as the story of a man struggling to keep what had made him one of the wealthiest men in Detroit over the last twenty-five years. Hendrie's horse-drawn streetcars poorly served the needs of Detroit's growing commercial and working-class population, which during his tenure had built homes on the now subdivided and developed old park lots and ribbon farms along Cass and Brush Avenues from Grand Circus Park north to Grand Boulevard, increasing the city's population from 20,000 to 205,000 people since his first streetcar ride almost thirty years before.

What Hendrie did not fully appreciate was that while everything had gotten faster traveling by horse-drawn streetcar in Detroit on the spokes drawn by Judge Woodward in 1805, those roads spread the city's population farther apart each year. Many more of his passengers wanted not just higher speed and greater convenience but, above all, cheaper fares and, especially, free transfers. As many more riders had settled far away from the intersection of Woodward and Jefferson Avenues, filling jobs in the industrial shops and factories across Detroit, first paying five cents riding just one line twice each day, many now traveled two, three, or more lines or lived outside city limits. Paying for transfers and second fares made daily commuting much more costly for riders, and Mayor Pingree was only beginning to see that their anger demonstrated during the four-day strike was ready to blow up again in the latest battle in the Thirty-Year War over Detroit's streetcars. Meanwhile, Hendrie could only see that the last valuable asset he held was his franchise allowing five-cent fares without transfers. Denied its extension, however, he would own nothing anybody would buy. He knew that his horse-drawn streetcars were worthless even though the nickel fare paid by riders was earning him a fortune every day. It would take a huge investment and a leap of faith for a horseman to adopt an entirely new technology bringing rapid transit to Detroit.

George Hendrie. From *A Gallery of Pen Sketches in Black and White of Our Michigan Friends "As We See 'Em,"* ed. C. O. Youngstrand (Detroit: Wm. Graham Printing Company, 1905).

"Mr. Hendrie's interests were always with horse transportation, and he felt that new methods demanded new men," said a biographical essay written in 1909. "Mr. Hendrie has always been a great lover of horses. In his younger days, he was an enthusiastic rider and driver, and later he has interested himself in the breeding of blooded stock from the large draft horse to the fleet-footed trotter and thoroughbred. His extensive breeding farm, at Royal Oak, has afforded one of his favorite recreations as has his stable of thoroughbred, which has been quite successful on the turf."[20]

Pingree understood.

> This pow wow of rapid transit talk was made a cover for getting a new franchise and for covering up their past poor service. When the dust was supposed to be well thrown into the people's eyes by the papers having a corporation alliance, a franchise giving the company a further lease of life of thirty years was sprung. The discontent of the people with the service made them seemingly ready to accept any sort of promise on the part of the company, and the company overestimated the readiness in its eagerness to make another grab. They asked extraordinary concessions in the extension of the franchise of their various lines, and the council, under the cloud raised by the cry of rapid transit, and all sorts of great improvements by the company, voted down all amendments that were not clearly in the interests of the company.[21]

The new franchise was rammed through the Common Council under the well-disciplined leadership of President Jacob, now a grisly veteran of Common Council politics, whose tenure dated back to just before adoption of the 1879 ordinance extending expiration of Hendrie's consent to use city streets personally coached by Cameron Currie. "You and your majority of the aldermen rushed in Wednesday at the special session to give the companies these privileges," he challenged Jacob personally. "Rushed as if you would break your necks."[22]

Mayor Pingree realized that vetoing the street railway ordinances would give him a potent political issue arousing the workingmen of Detroit a few months ahead of his fall reelection campaign. He saw an opportunity to launch his 1891 reelection campaign by making an enemy of George Hendrie and his street railway companies while accusing Jacob and his Common Council cronies of acting on company bribes. Pingree knew nothing of what was really going on.

Corporate Life and Death

The expiring corporate life of the Detroit City Railway Company that stirred all this activity by Hendrie and the Common Council dated back to 1863 when the Detroit City Railway Company originally was organized as a street railway corporation after obtaining consent to use Detroit roads for thirty years. Section 10 of article 15 of the state constitution of 1850 said no corporation could be authorized to do business for longer than thirty years.

In 1879, when Detroit's Common Council extended consent to 1909 in exchange for semiannual payments of 1 percent of the street railway company's gross receipts, Hendrie's legal counsel, Sidney Davy Miller, understood that the Detroit City Railway Company's corporate existence under state law would, nonetheless, expire in 1893. The thirty-year expiration set by the state constitution began running no later than May 12, 1863, when the Willcox investors filed articles of association with the secretary of state. Michigan's constitutional limitation on corporate life authorized the state legislature to make extensions for up to thirty years but only by adopting a general law, which would apply to all street railway companies. Getting such a general law passed would arouse not only the stockholders of all other Michigan street railway companies but the ever-watchful capitalist vultures with offices on Wall Street in New York City and untold others in Cleveland, Chicago, Montreal, and elsewhere. The resulting legislative hullaballoo would be, at least, entirely unpredictable.

Sidney Davy Miller knew that forming a new corporation with a thirty-year life to which he transferred all of Hendrie's street railway assets not only violated the underlying public policy of the state constitution's demand for limited corporate life but that doing so resolved only part of the problem if Detroit's 1879 extension ordinance itself violated the thirty-year constitutional limitation. If so, Hendrie could no longer operate on any of the streetcar lines constructed under the Detroit City Railway Company ordinance after midnight on November 23, 1892. Such a legal attack now would run into Miller's carefully meshed ordinances and ordinance amendments. Veto-proof majorities surely relieved Hendrie that the Common Council had defeated amendments requiring conductors to sell "workingmen's fare" tickets and passed Miller's exceptional legal handiwork.

Corporations were still relatively recent legal creations of the state legislatures. The Proprietors of the Charles River Bridge was only the third corporation in the United States when it was created by the State of Massachusetts in 1784. By 1800, there were, perhaps, fifty turnpike and bridge companies in Massachusetts and at least as many insurance, banking, and a very few manufacturing companies in the entire country. Corporations were not involved in any court cases until 1800.[23]

The state constitutional limitation on corporate life adopted by Michigan in 1850 arose from deep social and political fears. The many special privileges enjoyed by corporations denied to individuals—limited liability, liquidity of stock ownership, and existence continuing beyond the lifetimes of their shareholders, bondholders, lenders, officers, and employees—gave rise to widespread general public suspicion not only about the range of business activities in which corporations were engaged but their growing wealth and gathering of social and political power.

Chief Justice Marshall had explained:

> A corporation is an artificial being, invisible, intangible, and existing only in contemplation of law. Being the mere creature of law, it possesses only those properties which the charter of its creation confers upon it, either expressly or as incidental to its very existence. These are such as are supposed best calculated to effect the object for which it was created. Among the most important are immortality, and, if the expression may be allowed, individuality; properties by which a perpetual succession of many persons are considered as the same, and may act as a single individual. They enable a corporation to manage its own affairs, and to hold property without the perplexing intricacies, the hazardous and endless necessity of perpetual conveyances for the purpose of transmitting it from hand to hand. It is chiefly for the purpose of clothing bodies of men, in succession, with qualities and capacities, that corporations were invented, and are in use. By these means, a perpetual succession of individuals is capable of acting for the promotion of the particular object, like one immortal being.[24]

In 1819, the U.S. Supreme Court upheld against revocation by the State of New Hampshire a corporate charter granted to Dartmouth College by King George III many years before the Revolutionary War based upon a corporate charter's protection against government impairment of contracts in violation of the U.S. Constitution.[25] The ruling drew a public outcry, and many states passed constitutional amendments giving themselves more control over corporations by expressly limiting corporate life.

The First Bank of the United States was chartered in 1791. It was given a twenty-year charter. When the charter expired in 1811, Congress voted not to renew and created the Second Bank of the United States in 1816. That charter lasted for twenty years, expiring in 1836. A dispute over whether this second charter should be renewed became known as the Bank War between President Andrew Jackson and Nicholas Biddle, the bank's president. Congress passed an act to recharter the bank in 1832. Jackson vetoed it, with a message of striking intellectual clarity and rhetorical vigor, which stands as a timeless critique of corporate power still today. Jackson said that the powers, privileges, and favors bestowed in the original charter operated as a gratuity to its stockholders. If the federal government sells such monopolies and exclusive privileges, then it should at least exact from them as much as they are worth in the open market. Even though the bank ought to be perpetual, President Jackson said, its stockholders were a privileged class clothed with political power too great. They already enjoyed immense financial advantages from their connection with the government. Jackson's veto stood.

If Detroit had refused to grant a thirty-year franchise to Hendrie's new street railway company, the city could force him to idle his horse-drawn streetcars as his old company franchises expired even though nobody would argue that valuable streetcar lines should simply be destroyed. Corporate death, however, was the inevitable consequence of the state constitution. Moreover, Hendrie still lacked the municipal consent needed to install new overhead wires and to operate electric-powered streetcars because the original 1862 ordinance as amended in 1879 only allowed him to use horses. He was in a terrible position that Mayor Pingree could make worse by a successful veto.

Pingree's Veto

On July 1, Detroit's Common Council had adopted ordinances allowing Hendrie to continue operating streetcars for thirty more years without getting anything in return: no cash for the city treasury to relieve taxes on the commercial class or reduced fares for the working class, both of which had dramatically demonstrated angry discontent during the four-day streetcar strike. Five days later, at eight o'clock in the evening on July 6, four thousand of them jammed into a well-organized mass meeting at the city auditorium on Larned Street.[26]

"No one advanced any specific charges of bribery, but had the city been a jury, the Council could scarcely escape a verdict of guilty," Pingree said. "The audience was composed of no particular class or classes of citizens. Wealthy merchant princes sat side by side with the mechanic. Old and middle aged men, who saw the birth of the street railway company, jostled and were jostled by youngsters. But old and young, rich and poor, were there with one common object in view." Pingree proudly listed the vice presidents of the meeting as including Thomas Palmer, Dexter Ferry, R. H. Fyfe, Joseph Hudson, and Charles A. Kent, former dean of the University of Michigan Law School, among many other prominent men including, most notably, Captain William H. Stevens, who had earned a fortune mining silver in Colorado following the Civil War.[27]

"It included responsible citizens from the most prominent to the most obscure and was, in the sense of this inclusiveness, the best 'people's meeting' that has been held in this City, since the days of the war," said the *Free Press*. "Its officers were the representative men of the city, and the vast hall was filled with those who pay taxes and cast votes."[28]

The meeting adopted a protest resolution and appointed a citizen committee to present it to the Common Council. The next day, Tuesday, July 7, twenty-eight aldermen answered the roll call and routinely approved the *Journal* of the July 1 session. President Jacob recognized Alderman Reves, who moved to suspend the rules to hear a ten-minute presentation from the citizen committee relative to streetcar franchises. Mayor Pingree stood by anxiously with a veto message he was prepared to read into the record. Alderman Amos immediately moved to recess for ten minutes so council members, he said, could vacate their seats, and move into the audience.

"Mr. President, there is no necessity for taking a recess," one of the aldermen complained. "This committee can be heard and the aldermen who are present can retain their seats until the committee gets through. There is no need to take a recess."

"All in favor of taking a recess signify by saying, 'Aye.' Gentlemen, I want you to vote, every one of you!" President Jacob demanded. He wanted to test his majority and to consult with Hendrie's lobbyists.

"Give us a rising vote, Mr. President, please," said Alderman Charles A. Buhrer.

"All in favor of taking a recess of ten minutes will signify by rising."

Only four stood. The motion's failure was "greeted by derisive laughter and cheers from the lobby," according to the *Evening News*.[29] A vote on the motion to suspend the rules was unanimous over Jacob's objection that doing so was out of order. The citizen committee resolution was then read word for word without comment from any of the aldermen. The resolution objected to the granting of valuable thirty-year street railway franchises without cash payment. Indeed, the Common Council had three times during its consideration of the ordinances defeated amendments proposed by Republican Alderman Buhrer, which would have immediately hiked the franchise fee to 2.5 percent of gross receipts, and the aldermen had refused others which would have required payment to the city treasurer of $100,000 within one year. Since then, apparently, Mayor Pingree had been doing some figuring, because the citizen committee came armed with a much higher cash demand likely relying on information he had passed along to them.

"The fact that sagacious business men stand ready to pay millions of dollars for such franchises show what they are worth to the City," Mayor Pingree said in his veto message delivered later in the meeting. He explained why he had rejected the Detroit Street Railway Company ordinance. "If The Detroit City Railway Company, or the Detroit Street Railway Company, does not choose to give us rapid transit, the right to furnish the new and improved facilities for travel over lines operated by that, or those companies, could be sold for from three to four millions of dollars."

The protest resolution, however, demanded payment of only $1 million, which would today equate to nearly $25 million. "It is believed that the rights, privileges and franchises conferred upon such corporations, without adequate compensation, could be made to realize a million dollars or more to the City treasury, if proper competition were invited, and at the same time better service to the public be secured by suitable safeguards," the resolution said.

Unmentioned was reducing the five-cent fare collected twice or more each day from the growing number of workers also wanting universal transfers between lines and companies, an issue of no particular concern to business leaders gathered together by Mayor Pingree. During debate by the Common Council, amendments reducing fares and requiring transfers among competing companies had come up several times in addition to those requiring the sale of "workingmen's fare" tickets. The Common Council had approved a meaningless line transfer motion but defeated amendments demanding universal transfers among companies in extending the Grand River Street Railway Company's franchise. Stunned by what he saw as Democratic Party betrayal of working men who rode the streetcars every day, Louis E. Tossy, president of the Trades and Labor Council, joined the angry grumbling. His realization of what was happening strongly influenced Mayor Pingree's political calculations. "It's hard for working people to know who their friends are," Tossy said. "Now the silk stockings are opposed to the franchise, and most of those who are supposed to be the friends of the laboring people have voted against us. It is infamous and outrageous."[30]

After dutifully listening to the protest resolution, Jacob yielded the chair so he could offer a motion. Anticipating trouble and breaking ranks, Democrat Alderman Thompson moved to adjourn. It was defeated, 4-24, Thompson joining the majority, exercising a political adroitness that would serve him well in the years ahead. Before Pingree's supporters could do anything else, with the experience and skill that had earned him his role as president of the Common Council, Jacob offered a smoothly conceived motion to reconsider not the new Detroit Street Railway Company ordinance already vetoed by Mayor Pingree but rather the Grand River Street Railway Company ordinance upon which Pingree had not yet formally acted. Following Common Council parliamentary rules, Jacob claimed to have delivered to the city clerk written notice of his intent to do so within seventy-two hours of its original passage. Jacob's claim was accompanied by controversy missing from the official minutes but noted by the *Free Press* on its editorial page the next day.

"It ought to be remembered to the credit of City Clerk Augustus Kronberg that he refused to allow his office to be used to defeat the will of the people with reference to the street railway franchises. He had never heard of Jacob's motion to reconsider and he said so. This is one more man to be recorded on the right side," said the *Free Press* editorial page. "Ald. Jacob made a characteristic exhibition of himself at last night's council meeting in declining to recognize a demand for the yeas and nays upon a motion to adjourn. His action was an insult to every self-respecting alderman. The council should put a pin on the nose of the bully in the chair."[31]

Jacob lost his motion to reconsider, 13-15. He had been outflanked by Mayor Pingree. Jacob surely realized that offering motions to reconsider the other pending streetcar ordinances risked exposing himself and Hendrie to even deeper embarrassment. What he had done with his stalking-horse motion was a political mistake followed by another at the end of the meeting aimed at distracting everyone's attention.

The tense meeting continued. Kronberg delivered and the Common Council received some routine miscellaneous correspondence, including a letter from Hendrie asking the Common Council to arrange a conference with leaders of the citizen committee that was duly accepted and placed on file without comment. Finally, Pingree's veto message was formally received. Oddly, it is not clear from either the *Journal* or newspaper accounts if he was otherwise permitted to speak. Jacob then recognized Alderman Griggs, who offered a motion referring Pingree's veto to a five-member committee of aldermen "to investigate to the fullest extent their time and opportunities will permit of the entire street railway question, both as to existing and proposed corporations, and to act in conjunction with his Honor the Mayor and the Citizen Committee." It was approved, 16-12. The intent was to put Mayor Pingree's veto into parliamentary limbo while Jacob and Hendrie worked to regain their two-thirds majority. It was extraordinary that while they had already publicly lost a majority on the motion to reconsider the Grand River Street Railway Company ordinance, Hendrie and Jacob thought a conciliatory action would succeed in dissuading Mayor Pingree's new majority on the Common Council.

Jacob then abruptly adjourned the meeting, drawing catcalls and insults from the packed chamber heard up to four blocks away. A mob rushed over the room, overturning furniture and splattering ink onto the carpeting. Half a dozen chairs were demolished. The *Evening News* breathlessly reported that police officers were summoned to protect Jacob from the mob consisting not of scruffy workmen but of an audience of furious silk-stocking types, including brewer Edward W. Voigt, dry good merchant Cyrenius A. Newcomb, attorneys Levi L. Barbour, William A. Moore, and John Atkinson, physician Henry R. Carstens, and retired general contractor Homer W. Candler.

"Tar and feather Jacob!" some chatted. "Don't let Jacob get away!"[32]

Jacob fled into the clerk's office and remained there until a bodyguard escorted him away. City hall was surrounded by assembled crowds, according to the *Evening News*, who were "discussing plans for bringing to account the 22 aldermen who voted the railway franchise for no other consideration except the price of rapid transit."[33]

The *Free Press* applauded loudly. "Mayor Pingree, in his veto of the ordinance granting a franchise to the Detroit Street Railway Company temperately, yet strongly, presented the reasons for withholding his approval," the newspaper said. "Those reasons are so good that, if all of the aldermen had been in the frame of mind to listen and be convinced by argument, the veto would have been sustained by a practically unanimous vote. While this was more than could be expected, enough was developed at the session of the council to indicate that the veto will be ultimately sustained and the ordinances meet the fate they merit."[34]

The next day, Pingree decisively vetoed the remaining three ordinances and called for a special meeting of the Common Council at eight o'clock in the evening of Thursday, July 9, to take up all four. As the time approached, city hall filled with anxious men awaiting the opening of doors to the council chamber, which filled quickly and murmured with sweaty anticipation. Jacob and thirteen other aldermen never arrived. Pingree's first veto message had been the most dramatic. He opened simply.

> Private ownership of natural monopolies in cities is necessarily the cause of an immense financial loss to the citizens. It is a bad financial arrangement. It is generally believed that this is the chief source of corruption in city governments. I do not assert this could be proved in respect to our City. It is only urged as the result of general experience but that it is a foolish financial arrangement can be proved beyond question by European and American experience on a large scale. Denunciation of particular persons should be tempered by the consideration that the system is largely to blame. Still, the people cannot see why valuable public property should be given away unless through private instead of public motives.

Pingree reviewed how the ordinance granting consent to operate to the Detroit Street Railway Company neatly dovetailed with the ordinance extending the term of the Detroit City Railway Company and conferring all of its rights on the Detroit Street Railway Company.

> It is thus evident that the effect of the ordinance is: First. To enable the old City Railway Company to assign all of its franchises and property to the new corporation; and Second. To confer upon the new corporation, a franchise embracing the right to operate a street railway upon all the thoroughfares of the City for the period of 30 years, without compensation to the City. The City's valuable franchises are property, as much so as the money of the city raised by taxation in the city treasury, and, in my opinion, no property of the City should be given away, either as a reward of merit or as a subsidy. The pretense for this donation urged by the Detroit City Railway Company, otherwise known and now appearing as the Detroit Street Railway Company is that it will give Detroit rapid transit, but we cannot afford to buy rapid transit at the immense cost of these franchises. To grant what is now asked by the City Railway Company is to bind this City hand and foot for 30 years—that is to say for an entire generation.

Pingree argued that Hendrie's companies could choose not to make the investment needed to provide rapid transit as promised but instead sell the right to furnish the new and improved facilities for travel over its lines on city streets for three or four million dollars.

"In the first place, it is extremely doubtful, as I am advised, whether the franchise of the City Railway Company can last longer than thirty years from November, 1862," Pingree said, giving public notice to Hendrie's greatest fear—that the 1879 extension won with Jacob's political help had violated the state constitution's thirty-year cap on corporate life.

"But if it be true that the old company is vested with an unexpired term, and refuses to give us what the people want during that unexpired term, except upon unreasonable, not to say outrageous conditions, then the right of the City Railway Company for its unexpired term, which is undoubtedly the City Railway's property, should be taken and condemned under power of eminent domain."

Pingree explained that condemnation would require an appraisal by twelve property owners in which gross receipts reported by Hendrie for the purposes of taxation would be evidence of the franchise's value not subject to successful rebuttal. The city could then sell the monopoly right to operate on city streets for its higher actual fair market value, reaping for itself the windfall being sought instead by Hendrie.

"There is no good reason why Detroit should not follow the example of other cities and relieve the burdens of the people incurred by constantly increasing rates of taxation by selling such franchises for the benefit of the City Treasury," he continued before briefly addressing the working-class streetcar riders of Detroit. "Either that or leave the money of the people in their own pockets by reducing the fare to the minimum amount."

"Gentleman of the Council," he concluded, "I cannot believe that when these ordinances were passed that you knew that you were granting a new franchise for thirty years to a new corporation created but six months ago and you were consenting to a transfer to such new corporation, in addition to all of the new rights granted to it, all the exceptional and remarkably valuable franchises already voted to the old City Railway."

Pingree's veto message regarding the ordinance extending the Detroit City Railway Company ordinance by twelve years and conferring its rights on the new Detroit Street Railway Company was particularly harsh. His sarcastic generosity to the Common Council must have grated hard because he knew all eighteen of its thirty-two members who showed up were poised to sustain all of his vetoes.

"This ordinance, if it became a law, would be much more vicious in its tendency than the one granting a franchise for thirty years to the Detroit Street Railway Company for the reason that the latter imposes as a condition for the granting of the franchise, the obligation to equip its lines with rapid transit, which is some slight compensation to the people. The apparently innocent ordinance, however, extends the franchise of the old company twelve years from the eighteen which it now has, and then transfers the whole thirty to the new company, for absolutely no consideration whatsoever, either in rapid transit or in any other way."

The eighteen aldermen present serially moved to reconsider all of the previously adopted street railway motions regarding the new Detroit Street Railway Company, Detroit City Railway, Grand River Street Railway Company, and Fort Wayne and Elmwood Railway Company, and Pingree's veto of each was unanimously sustained. The Common Council's eager embrace of Pingree's vetoes created a political sensation in Detroit, said an editorial in the *Free Press* on July 9, 1891.

> It is usually some specific matter that calls the attention of the public to the fact it is being robbed, betrayed and insulted. So in the case of the City of Detroit, the outrageous breach of trust on the part of the members of the Board of Aldermen, in connection with the railway franchises, is the acute manifestation of a chronic disease. The people are now thoroughly aroused, and they should not stop at spiking the guns of the corruptionists who have been engaged in the disgraceful street railway deal. There is an immensity of other housecleaning to be done, and it would be a good plan to begin now and do it. . . . It has been a matter of patronage and the frying of fat long enough. Ignorant and corrupt men are swaggering about with full purses. . . . The City Hall is a stench in the nostrils of those who pay to maintain it and the time has come when all this should end.

The argument for compensation from Hendrie's street railway company to the city treasury being tossed around by Mayor Pingree and the new commercial-class men of Detroit, however, was not enough to unite the city in fighting the Thirty-Year War.

The Octopus Sold

Just two weeks after Pingree's vetoes, ex-governor Thomas M. Waller of Connecticut came out of his room at the Hotel Cadillac on July 23 to conduct a press conference. Waller announced that he and other financiers from Connecticut, New York, and Boston had agreed on terms to buy the Detroit Street Railway Company and the Grand River Railway Company, which together controlled eighty miles of railway tracks in Detroit, three hundred streetcars, and two thousand horses. His partner, William W. Cook, a Michigan native and University of Michigan Law School graduate, would be president of the new company. Waller said they would be investing $2 million in new overhead electric lines and buying electric streetcars. He refused to name any other purchasers or the price they were paying Hendrie but emphasized his desire for widespread public ownership of the street railway stock. Waller added that he wanted five hundred to a thousand new investors from all across Detroit.

Waller was a Democrat who had been defeated for reelection in 1884 after two frustrating years advocating in favor of raising school taxes and boosting internal improvements against a contrary Republican-controlled state legislature. He served as ambassador in London, England, from 1885 to 1889. The *Free Press* summed up its impression of Waller. "He is a careful and most plausible talker, conveying in all he says an impression of his personal sincerity and truthfulness. He can get over, around, above or under an embarrassing question with a deftness that scarcely leaves an impression that he is dodging, while in making a direct and positive statement he can score a bull's eye every time."[35]

"THE OCTOPUS SOLD," said the *Free Press* front-page all-capital headline the next day, July 24, 1891. "The Hendries Sell All Their Interests and Will Retire."

"It is the biggest deal that has been made in Detroit for many years," the newspaper said. "Citizens seemed to breathe freer, as if released from some sort of thralldom, and visions of electric wires and motors and other forms of rapid transit flitted before their minds, with horses and horsecars fading away in the dim and uncertain distance."

Sidney Davy Miller admitted that he and the Hendries had been negotiating with Governor Waller since before Memorial Day, explaining with a lawyerly straight face that fifty-seven-year-old Hendrie's health had been deteriorating and he wanted to relieve himself of day-to-day street railway management.[36] Rumors circulated that the price was as much as $5 million and that the Hendrie and McMillan families had retained a 45 percent stake and $750,000 in outstanding bonds.

Not until September 2 did Waller and Cook make the legal filing creating a new corporation they called the Detroit Citizens Street Railway Company.[37] Its $4 million capital stock was divided between twenty thousand preferred and twenty thousand common shares, a sophisticated financial arrangement.[38] The incorporators having eighty shares each were Waller, Cook, and Miles W. Barse, a Buffalo banker. Buying ten shares each were Dwight W. Townsend of New York, a wealthy sugar dealer and former Democratic congressman; William R. Ferguson of Newburyport, Massachusetts, electrical appliance manufacturer; Hoyt Post, a Grosse Pointe lawyer and investor; and John R. Mulliken, Pingree-appointed public works commissioner, who was, they said, to be the company's general manager.[39] Waller explained that Post was merely a representative for other investors he refused to disclose.[40] Ferguson told the Detroit newspapers that he had overseen replacing seven horse-drawn systems with electric power in the last two years. Detroit, he said, with its wide straight avenues was well suited to electricity. He insisted that electric streetcars could travel twice as fast and cause no more accidents than horse-drawn streetcars. Edward P. Shaw of Boston, an experienced street railway promoter, said he had toured all of Detroit's street railway lines and found them to be in good condition although the roadbeds needed some reconstruction.

That same day, the Detroit Citizens Street Railway Company conveyed all of its franchises and real and personal property to the Washington Trust Company of New York, to secure $3 million in new borrowing at 5 percent interest. A few days later, on September 13, Waller stepped up his posturing for a new thirty-year franchise, emphasizing an end to the Hendrie streetcar era in Detroit. He announced the purchase of an 80 percent majority interest in the new corporation by a laundry list of prominent local investors, including Dexter Ferry; M. S. Smith, president of the American Exchange National Bank; George H. Russel, president of the State Savings Bank; and Simon J. Murphy, a well-known lumberman.

"Here were men of unquestioned integrity who could appeal to the citizens of Detroit without arousing the slightest suspicion," Catlin said. "It looked for a moment as if a franchise would be immediately forthcoming. . . . They had virtually surrounded Mayor Pingree by bringing his closest friends and nearest neighbors into the deal."[41] Waller rounded up these local investors with Miller and Hendrie's guidance as a crucial part of their strategy to make it not just politically but personally difficult for Pingree to again veto a thirty-year franchise.

Miller publicly insisted that he had completely divested himself even while privately securing purchase options from at least two of the local investors, a scheme possibly followed by Hendrie, McMillan, and Muir, too. "All of the stock I owned, I have sold," Miller said. "My banking and legal affairs will occupy my time fully hereafter and I don't imagine I shall find time hanging heavily on my hands either."[42]

George H. Russel. From *A Gallery of Pen Sketches in Black and White of Our Michigan Friends "As We See 'Em,"* ed. C. O. Youngstrand (Detroit: Wm. Graham Printing Company, 1905).

Miller's papers donated to the Burton Historical Collection include next to nothing from his many years with the street railway companies. Remarkably, however, buried among the sixteen boxes spreading across twenty feet, there are two option agreements Miller made with two Detroit investors dated September 26, 1891, and October 5, 1891, which question Miller's public statements because a few months later, on November 19, 1891, he exercised those options, buying 750 shares from one and 250 shares from the other.

Waller laughed off Pingree's constitutional legal argument that the consent to use city streets held by the Detroit City Railway Company would expire in 1892, citing a legal opinion by Cook he said was further endorsed by local attorneys. Waller said smoothly:

> Oh yes, I know about the claim, but my associates have no fear of it, legally or otherwise. They are confident the people of Detroit will reciprocate good treatment and the courts of Michigan, if they

> are appealed to, will not confiscate a great property upon a mere technicality. The leading lawyers of the City, I know, do not all think alike upon this question. The new management will be perfectly willing to enter upon a contract with the City containing, if necessary, a condition that the technical question shall be left open, and if the decision is against them, the contract shall fail. You see, I do not want to go back on my profession. I want the lawyers of Detroit to have the $10,000 for which a public subscription is being raised whatever may happen to the street railroads.[43]

Following its votes sustaining Pingree's vetoes of the thirty-year franchises, the Common Council had appointed a Committee of Fifty prominent citizens to study street railway issues and to petition the mayor to take whatever action they decided was needed. Some were actively gathering donations to pay legal expenses to test the expiration date issue. Waller's conciliatory posture was right on, but his timing was badly off because Mayor Pingree was preoccupied with his first reelection campaign against a splintering Democratic Party and he was lining up strong Republican candidates to run for the Common Council where sixteen seats were on the November ballot.

A month before the election, on October 2, Cook told Detroit newspapers that they had completed buying the franchises, railways, streetcars, and horses of the Grand River Railway Company for $1 million. Cook brought no experience in the rough-and-tumble of Detroit politics to the purchase. His father, John P. Cook, had been a wealthy businessman, farmer, logger, and founder of Hillsdale, Michigan, who died leaving a large estate in 1884. The younger Cook attended Hillsdale College and graduated from the University of Michigan Law School in 1882, working for lawyers in Nebraska and Toledo during summer breaks. One of his professors was Thomas Cooley. Following graduation, he moved to Manhattan where he established himself as a corporate lawyer specializing in complex stock transactions.

Nobody except Mayor Pingree took special note of the fact that Waller and Cook had also purchased Hendrie's Grand River Railway Company, which owned the Grand River Street Railway Company. The purpose of the ordinance Pingree vetoed a few months before on July 9 was to formally extend for thirty years the franchise held by the old Grand River Street Railway Company in exchange for reducing Woodward Avenue's four tracks to three with joint use shared with Hendrie's Detroit Street Railway Company.

In compiling ordinances in 1895, city lawyers said a *full* transfer of rights was made between the old and new companies in December 1890. That seems unlikely, however, because the 1883 amendment adopted by the Common Council granting consent to operate double tracks on Woodward Avenue by the Grand River Street Railway Company provided that it "may be revoked and withdrawn by the Common Council of said City should any transfer, assignment or consolidation of said *railway company* be made or affected with any other *railway company or corporation*" (emphasis added). This loosely worded clause was included because Detroit's Board of Public Works objected to having four tracks on busy Woodward Avenue especially if one street railway company owned them all. Although such language would not bar stockholders from selling majority control, Miller would have advised against making any formal transfer of franchise rights because Hendrie wanted authority to keep four tracks on downtown Woodward Avenue at least as leverage in dealing with the city.[44]

Detroit never invoked the revocation clause. Nor did the city ever inquire into the details as evidenced by John J. Speed's vague report in 1904 of a transfer of rights he could only explain was made on "December ——, 1890." A few days after Cook's announcement, Pingree persuaded Alderman James Vernor to introduce a resolution that "it is claimed and commonly reported that a transfer to another corporation has been made by the Grand River Street Railway Company." The resolution would have revoked consent for the double track on Woodward Avenue, but it was referred to the Common Council's Committee on Streets and Ordinances, and the issue was settled behind the scenes a year later.[45]

Many leaders of the citizen committee had bought stock in the Detroit Citizens Street Railway Company, and progress at reaching a recommendation was bogged down by the November election. "Daily in the newspaper appeared the customary routine mention of what the Committee was going to do but nothing was done," Mayor Pingree said. "Meantime the company shifted names, issued new stock, and a general distribution of this stock was made among the more prominent people who were present at the Rink. Whether this was cause or not, it was plain to be seen that these prominent men had gradually grown cool, that the enthusiasm which bubbled over furiously in fiery ardor at the Rink died at committee meetings. True, they had done a great deal of interviewing with the newspapers but the fire ran low little by little until the kettle got cold and there was no more steam singing."[46]

On December 22, 1891, Mayor Pingree vetoed a resolution adopted by the Common Council allowing Caleb E. Healy to continue testing his steam-operated streetcar in Detroit. Pingree said,

> While I do not desire to do anything to discourage any effort in the direction of an improved motor for purposes of rapid transit, I feel that the City should be extremely guarded instead of, as it has formerly been, profuse and liberal in the granting of special rights and privileges in the use of its streets. It has been claimed that the intention of the resolution was simply to permit the inventor of the motor to exhibit its operation to our citizens and representatives of other cities or street railway companies from other cities who desire to investigate its merits. If this is the case, no such resolution as the one in question is necessary, inasmuch as Mr. Healy had now had, for something like a year, the tacit permission of the City authorities, no one objecting, to use the streets for that purpose.

Pingree's veto was sustained, 27-0. A defiant Hendrie inaugurated Healy steam-motor streetcar service just outside Detroit on the East Jefferson Avenue line owned by his family, running from the Water Works Park to the Grosse Pointe Club House at Fisher Road a brisk walk away from where he lived.

CHAPTER 6

The Lawyers Battle

A Disarming Strategy

Mayor Hazen Pingree's first-term accomplishments, highlighted by his streetcar vetoes following the four-day street railway strike, so divided the Democratic Party's base that its late summer nominating convention split into warring factions. Pingree was easily reelected on November 3, 1891, receiving more votes than his two Democratic opponents combined, and crucial to his wielding of political power, his Republican candidates gained majority control of the Common Council.[1] In the New Year, Democratic Party boss John Christian Jacob would be forced to again give up his control of the gavel.[2]

On December 15, 1891, Pingree pressed his advantage, urging the Common Council to initiate a legal challenge against the validity of the Detroit City Railway Company thirty-year franchise extension made in 1879. His brief correspondence was directed to a lame duck Common Council. Eight aldermen, including Jacob, were absent that night. Jacob had appointed a special committee consisting of Democratic Alderman Michael W. McGuire, Republican Aldermen Stephen A. Griggs and Joseph T. Lowry, City Counselor John J. Speed, and City Attorney Charles Casgrain to consider a petition from attorney C. J. O'Flynn, who had been elected chairman of the Committee of Fifty. Flynn's petition demanded litigation testing the expiration of the Detroit City Railway Company franchise.[3]

"I understand that your committee will tonight report recommending that the important question of the ownership of these franchises be determined by the only way of determining a legal question, *viz*: in the courts of law," Pingree wrote. "It is only recently that our citizens have come to realize the immense value of the right to operate street railways in and through our principal streets. But since they have learned that this right is of enormous value in dollars and cents, and that it is their property to be used or disposed of to the best possible advantage for them, they have shown a decided disposition on several occasions to assert and protect those rights to the uttermost."

Pingree pegged the value of the franchise owned by the Detroit City Railway Company at $4 million, the uppermost of the range he claimed it had in his veto message the previous July. "It is maintained by good legal authority that most of the street railway franchises expire within a year or so," he continued, "and on the other hand it is claimed by the companies operating under them that they do not expire for a period of seventeen or eighteen years. Indeed, it has been intimated by some of the so-called new stockholders of the Citizens Street Railway Company that the franchises will be like those procured by the notorious 'Jake Sharp' in Broadway, New York—perpetual."[4]

Therefore, Pingree asked the Common Council, "in view of the great importance of this question and of the distinguished counsel who will be employed on the other side . . . to make necessary provision to employ able legal counsel to assist the regular legal officers of the City." The Committee of Fifty, he said, was expected to hire an attorney who would join the city in challenging the thirty-year extension awarded to the Detroit City Railway Company in 1879. The Committee of Fifty, however, had not itself recommended hiring outside counsel. It asked only that the city's existing legal officers, Speed and Casgrain, be directed to commence necessary proceedings, and the Common Council agreed, 24-0.

A week later, under renewed pressure from Mayor Pingree, on December 22, the Common Council adopted a resolution, proposed by Democratic Alderman William B. Thompson, who raised his political profile still more by doing so, that authorized Pingree to engage special counsel but directed him "to submit to the Common Council all proceedings before entering into a contract for any legal assistance." Obvious friction between Pingree, Speed, and Casgrain, encouraged by Hendrie's lingering Democratic and Republican supporters on the Common Council, threatened to delay and confuse who would be in charge of any lawsuit against the 1879 franchise extension.

"The fact remains that, before investing in the stock of this company, the present owners of the stock obtained the legal opinions of some of the ablest counsel in this state concerning this question and were advised that the contention of the City has not the shadow of a basis in the law," said Dexter Ferry in a letter to the Common Council on January 1, 1892.

> The cases upholding our rights are numerous, clear, and decisive: while not a single case has been found to the contrary or even raising any doubt on the subject.
>
> Nevertheless, the attack has been continuing. And it is preventing the company from putting in a rapid transit plant. Rapid transit is not possible until the question of the right to use the streets is settled: and only two ways of settling it seem to be open. These are either litigation or recognition of the rights of the company.
>
> Litigation involves expense and delay. If there is a way in which adjudication suitable to such vast interests can be intelligently and satisfactorily obtained in a brief time, it is unknown to us. Certainly, we, who have made so large an investment in a property worth several millions, must exhaust every possible defense known to the law to defend our rights and interest.
>
> It is safe to say that, unless terminated sooner by a decision favorable to the company, no conclusion in the litigation can be reached in less than six or seven years from the commencement, this consuming over one-third of the time which is in controversy.

Ferry's letter ended with a polite request that they oppose Pingree's hiring of legal counsel: "We take opportunity to send this communication and proposition now while your honorable body is still considering the propriety and methods of starting litigation."

"Three-Cent Fares!"

Mayor Pingree's annual address to the Common Council delivered on January 12, 1892, schooled the new Republican majority on his developing progressive vision for the future of Detroit. He began:

> In assuming the duties which many of you are called upon to exercise for the first time, it will be wise for you to bear in mind the importance of the functions of the body of which you are members. The Board of Aldermen, with the Mayor, representing the inhabitants of the City of Detroit, composes the body politic and corporate known as the City of Detroit and, to all legal intents and purposes are the City of Detroit. It is therefore incumbent upon us to adopt and carry out, after wise deliberation, such measures as shall in our judgment contribute most to the health and prosperity, and therefore to the happiness, of the inhabitants of the beautiful City we represent.

The mundane, gritty work of street paving and sewer construction continued to top his agenda, hardly the stuff of populism, but he reminded the thirty-two aldermen, elected from sixteen wards, exactly who they represented. "Though you are chosen from various districts of the City, yet you represent the whole City. While guarding the special interests of localities, should not forget the necessities of the whole, bearing in mind that one member of the body politic cannot suffer except at the expense of all members."

Pingree briefly spoke with a profound understanding of what was happening in Detroit and across the United States as the twentieth century approached. "We should remember, too, that Detroit is no longer a village; that this is an age of progress and competition; that what seemed to be the wants and needs of the City twenty years ago are drawbacks to its prosperity today and stumbling blocks in its onward path to a place in the front rank of American cities; that as we are compelled to a great deal of public work for future generations, provisions should be made so that those future generations should bear a proportionate share of the burden of payment."

His remarks about the street railway situation started with gripes about the practical day-to-day roadway issues overlooked or ignored in the past by Detroit's government and by George Hendrie.

> As we advance in the era of good pavement, we should adopt and enforce more stringent rules for its preservation. The severe lessons which the street railway companies received during the past six months have not been sufficient to convince them that they are the servants and not the masters of the people, and they still refuse to comply with the just requirements of the Board of Public Works to put in satisfactory foundations under their tracks. It is a fact noticeable on every paved street in the City wherein there is a railroad track, that the part of the pavement next to the track is constantly getting out of repair, to the great injury of the remainder of the pavement, and entailing an enormous expense, which comes out of the general treasury, to keep it in even passable condition. I again recommend the speedy passage of an ordinance to compel street railway companies, in re-laying their tracks, to make foundations under them conform to that under the remainder of the street.

Mayor Pingree moved on, heaping scorn on the type of railway track used by the city's streetcar companies. "Heretofore, they have used whatever kind they pleased, which was the cheapest to them and the least satisfactory to the public," he railed. "The inconvenience to drivers of vehicles everywhere in the City resulting from the flat rail now used has always been great, and the actual damage through breakage directly attributable to this cause has been enormous."

In a city where few people enjoyed their own means of transportation, Mayor Pingree's words reached only the day-to-day lives of its many new manufacturers, merchants, and those whose growing businesses depended upon the safe and secure delivery of goods across the City. "In other cities all over the country, street railway companies, of their own accord, are reconstructing their tracks with an improved groove or slot rail, which makes a perfectly level surface over which vehicles may pass without harm or inconvenience, the same as over the remaining portion of the street."[5]

Letting his frustration and anger mount, Pingree lashed out. "It would be too much, however, in the light of their past history, to expect that the street railway companies of this city would take any steps toward the convenience of the public unless they were compelled to," he said. "It is, therefore, incumbent upon us to compel them. I call your attention to a clause which appears in all the street railway franchises."

Pingree then read what he said was boilerplate language included in all of the ordinances granting franchises. It specifically reserved to the Common Council authority to exercise the city's broad, general police power over the streetcar company by adopting new regulations to protect the public health, safety, and welfare that would not otherwise impair the obligation of contract: "It is reserved to the Common Council of the city of Detroit the right to make such further rules, orders or regulations as may, from time to time, be deemed *by the Common Council* necessary to protect the interest, safety, welfare or accommodation of the *City and public* in relation to said railways" (emphasis added).[6]

In doing so, Pingree was making more than a nasty crack about the streetcar company and a threat of more and costly litigation. First, he was raising regulatory uncertainty for the railway company's new local investors. Pingree was increasing the financial risk they would have to accept by installing any new rails, for example, not of the particular design he was demanding. Second, because the old 1862 franchise held by the Detroit City Railway Company specifically allowed only "rail of the Philadelphia or other suitable pattern," an ill-defined, thirty-year-old standard, predicting the outcome of a court fight with Pingree over the matter was impossible.

The populist Pingree then rose up, pitching his speech to arouse not his downtown commercial-class supporters but rather the many more working-class voters in the streetcar neighborhoods of Detroit, knowing that what he had said so far about street paving and rail design was not going to do so. The inexperienced Republicans filling seats on the Common Council certainly were looking to him in eager anticipation of leadership. In the hurly-burly of the election campaign, the most diligent candidates for political office talk to hundreds of people on the streets, at their front doors, and in the assembly halls. What they learn by doing so may sharpen their thinking about the issues that drive voters to the polls on Election Day, but making public policy that responds to those issues is an entirely different matter. Gifted political leaders such as Hazen S. Pingree never confuse getting elected with governing. He returned to the immediate task.

> You, as well as our citizens generally, are familiar with the street railway franchise question as it has developed during the past year. You have become aware of the rapidly increasing and now enormous

> value of the right to operate railway lines in the streets of this, and of every other large city in the country and I am pleased to note that the City, through its representatives, has joined hands with the citizens, through their committee, in determining to contest in the courts the rights to the enjoyment of these immense values, and to ascertain definitely whether they belong to the public or to private corporations.

Stinging from the rebuke of friends, Pingree spoke directly to them using a few straightforward words. "I do not think that the City owes any special consideration to the street railway companies," he continued. "Nor to the individuals who are the directors or stockholders, in this matter."

Pingree then surprised both his friends and his critics by announcing that the outcome of any streetcar litigation mattered little him as he politically reframed the issue as a battle between the rich capitalists and the average laborer in Detroit, who earned as little as $1.50 a day with monthly rent of $8.91 and a monthly food budget of $16.00, according to Detroit factory workers surveyed in 1892 by the State Bureau of Labor Statistics.

> For many years, when the rights of the street railway companies were not in dispute, they have been importuned repeatedly and continuously by our citizens to furnish them with some means of rapid transit; and though they have promised it time and again, they have never made their word good. The result is that Detroit is now practically the only city in the United States of upwards of 10,000 inhabitants, which is still dependent upon horses as a means of streetcar transit. These street car companies now assure us that if we will leave them in peaceable possession of their claim for seventeen years exclusive rights in the streets, they will furnish rapid transit at an early date. But this is the same assurance which they have been giving the public for many years, and we have no more reason to believe them now than we had years ago.

Pingree had drawn heavily on activists from Detroit's typographical union and its newspapers for key positions on his staff. Judson Grenell, printer, was a member of his personal staff. Another printer, Joseph Labadie, became a water inspector. Pingree hired Jennie Smith, an *Evening News* reporter said to have an unfathomable instinct in the art of Detroit politics. Together, they tapped Alex L. McLeod, *Evening News* city editor, as his secretary, and J. W. Walsh, an *Evening News* poet and satirist, as his speechwriter.

Their influence cannot be underestimated in the rise of the first Detroit politician pandering to the social class lines that had begun dividing the city from its surrounding suburbs in southeastern Michigan during the latter half of the nineteenth century. Pingree's next remark about Detroit's suburbs has infected Detroit's leaders ever since. They have uniformly suffered from an incurable disregard for the regional impact of their local decisions and a perverse enjoyment at exploiting to advantage their neighboring communities along the roads drawn by Judge Woodward—Fort Street and Michigan, Grand River, Gratiot, Woodward, and Jefferson Avenues.

"I feel assured that even our enterprising citizens who own large amounts of real estate in the suburbs will be as willing as those who live in the more densely populated portions of the City, to forego for a short time the advantages of rapid transit," Pingree declared, his voice rising dramatically, "if by that means they can turn into the public treasury several millions of dollars in money properly belonging to the public and secure a three-cent fare, all day, on every route in the City." Nobody could successfully run for political office in Detroit again during the Thirty-Year War without demanding three-cent fares.

"While the standard fare for streetcar rides in American cities has generally been five cents, with or without transfers, as the case may be, there have been many variations from this standard," wrote street railway expert Delos F. Wilcox. "Indeed, lower streetcar fares have been one of the most potent political issues in a number of important American cities. . . . Mayor Hazen S. Pingree of Detroit was a pioneer in the low-fare movement."[7]

"Believing, as he doubtless did—New England born as he was—that three cents was as much as should be paid for a streetcar ride, he adopted 'Three-Cent Fares' as his main political slogan," Jere Hutchins said.[8]

By taking up three-cent fares, Pingree was demanding a 40 percent reduction in daily passenger receipts paid by Detroit's working class, all of which would come directly out of the pockets of the street railway stockholders he had counted among his personal friends. They were coming to understand that the stock they bought from Hendrie, Thomas M. Waller, and William W. Cook was worthless unless they won the battle over expiration of the Detroit City Railway Company franchise. Over the next three years, they would end up giving away their 326 streetcars and selling their 1,949 horses for five dollars each. They had to scrap their old rails and tear down their livestock barns. All they had paid for was some real estate and those franchises.

The Hendrie Toll Gate Company

In his annual address to the Common Council on January 12, 1892, Pingree also spoke about Detroit's many despised old plank roads. He called them "relics of barbarism," applying to them an even then hoary old Republican epithet for slavery coined during the Civil War. Pingree eased into the subject.

> Through the indiscretion, generosity, or short-sightedness of some of those who have gone before us, Detroit seems to be tied up more than any other city in the country, with special privileges granted to corporations. The person who drives three miles out East Jefferson Avenue, two and one-half miles out Gratiot Avenue, or two or three miles out Woodward, Grand River or Michigan Avenues, over a pavement built originally by the abutting owners, pays tolls, or tribute, or blackmail, for it is little better than blackmail, to various companies organized under the laws of the State, and given the right to levy blackmail on our citizens by the legislators at Lansing. The City has from time to time paid lump sums of four and five thousand dollars to these various tollgate companies, to move their gates beyond the City limits as they have been extended. But these specially privileged companies have never relinquished their claims to collect toll from City Hall and they tell us now that they have some thirty years more in which to levy this tribute to our citizens.

Pingree had decided to engage George Hendrie on another front, this time over his tollgate on the East Jefferson Avenue plank road three miles away from city hall that was daily charging tolls to city workers dispatched from Water Works Park. George Hendrie's family owned the Hendrie Toll Gate Company, which operated the East Jefferson Avenue plank road ending in today's Grosse

Pointe Farms south of Gaukler Pointe where Henry and Josephine Ford would later build a three-hundred-acre estate. In 1891, Hendrie had extended street railways from Detroit's Water Works Park to Fisher Road. When Lakeshore Drive residents objected, Hendrie and his partner John B. Dyar graciously relocated their Lake St. Clair Railway to Grosse Pointe Boulevard, protecting the scenic beauty of the lakefront in Grosse Pointe Farms.

Originally called the Detroit and Grosse Pointe Plank Road Company when it was formed in 1851, Hendrie's tollgates were located at today's Dequindre Road and Van Dyke Avenue in Detroit and Beaconsfield Road in Grosse Pointe Park. Before it was completed, driving a horse and buggy to and from Detroit in muddy weather could take up to five hours.

Plank roads were an advance on corduroy roads, which were also popular in Michigan during the early nineteenth century. Corduroy roads were made by placing logs, often of different sizes, over a low or swampy area. Although depressions were filled with gravel or with smaller logs, they were rough and often dangerous. Logs floated and rolled in the slippery mud into which horses, frightened by the unstable footing, sometimes plunged and floundered and at times fully sank one or more legs. Plank roads, on the other hand, originally were made of fitted boards and, with necessary maintenance, provided a smooth surface. They were constructed by laying planks of pine or, preferably, oak, eight to sixteen feet long and three to four inches thick, across stringers placed parallel to the direction of the road. Workers dug ditches on either side of the road for drainage.

Some highway historians claim that plank road companies were first introduced by the State of New York in 1846.[9] Seven years earlier, however, Michigan granted a corporate charter to the Detroit, Plymouth, and Ann Arbor Turnpike Company for a "turnpike or timbered road. . . . constructing the same of good hewn timber where the alluvial nature of the soil renders it impracticable to construct a good earth road."[10] The state legislature created many other plank road companies. So great was the demand that the state legislature passed a general Plank Road Act, Act No. 62 of the Public Acts of 1848. It required plank road companies to follow certain minimum construction standards. Namely, that the road be two to four rods wide, sixteen feet of which was to be "a good, smooth, permanent road, well drained by ditches on either side." At least eight feet of the road surface was to be covered with wood planks at least three inches thick. Builders used no nails or otherwise fastened the planks together because nails worked loose and caused injuries to the hooves of horses. The Plank Road Act said no grade could be greater than one in ten and that the company life would be sixty years, and thirty years before the state legislature could make any regulatory changes. Despite the tremendous influx of settlers to Michigan after 1830 as the state population rose from 31,640 to 212,267 in 1840, and to 341,591 in 1850, Michigan did practically nothing to provide roads.[11] Local units of government made feeble attempts to build them. The results were hopelessly inadequate. Even the federal government failed to meet the needs of Michigan settlers. Prior to 1837, Congress had authorized the construction of a number of territorial roads for use by the military, but little work was even started on them. Thus, the task of road construction fell by default to plank road companies.

Financial support for the plank road companies came mainly from local users: well-to-do farmers, manufacturers, merchants, and real estate developers. Prominent backers of the Detroit and Howell Plank Road Company, and most of the other roads serving Detroit, included Lewis Cass and Charles C. Trowbridge. The cost of building plank roads reached $3,000 per mile, depending upon the condition of the roadbed and the accessibility of timber and gravel. The many needed bridges, too, put a heavy financial burden on plank road companies. Some companies, like the Detroit and Mt. Clemens Plank Road Company, purchased large stands of timber and a lumber mill to guarantee an adequate supply of planks.

The state legislature not only set up specifications for the construction of the plank roads, but it regulated tolls, which limited the investors to a return of 3 percent or less annually. A toll of no more than one cent per mile could be charged for one horse and rider or any vehicle drawn by one horse. A charge of two cents a mile could be made for a vehicle drawn by two horses. If more than two horses were used, there could be an additional charge of three-quarters of a cent per mile for each additional animal. Tolls of one-half cent a mile could be levied for every score of sheep or swine but two cents a mile for cattle. The state legislature never allowed any increase in tolls.

At first, plank roads were highly popular, delivering much improved transportation, increased commerce, and heightened real estate values to the communities they served. Great fanfare often accompanied their opening. In Lansing, citizens gathered to celebrate the Lansing to Howell plank road. Spectators heard the stagecoach carrying the speaker for the ceremony approaching from a full mile away. As long as they were properly maintained, the plank roads were a great improvement over dirt roads that were impassable many weeks of the year. Plank roads were as popular in rural areas as in towns and cities. Farmers could carry greater loads to market, and many of them preferred to use the cheaper, more convenient plank roads rather than the railroads. In fact, in rural communities, the plank roads were commonly called the farmer's railroad. More than two hundred plank road companies operated across Michigan. Not surprisingly, eight plank roads served Detroit, which spread out like spokes in a wheel along Fort Street and Mount Elliott, Woodward, Michigan, Grand River, Gratiot, and Jefferson Avenues, costing their investors an estimated $300,000. "They have never been profitable and could probably be bought at one quarter of their cost," Farmer said. "Some of them pay small dividends, others none at all, and all of them, at times, have suspended dividends, but the original proprietors of the principal roads have retained their shares, and managed the roads as carefully as if they had been profitable."[12]

Farmer's congratulatory opinion was not shared by anyone who had ever used them. Despite their initial success, the craze did not last long because plank roads remained in good condition only for three or four years. Then the planks loosened, warped, decayed, and had to be replaced. Annual maintenance and repair costs were 20 to 30 percent of the original cost, and there were other fixed costs that had to be paid. Tollbooths had to be maintained, and a full-time superintendent employed throughout the year. Because of the heavy expense of lumber, some companies began substituting gravel as planks decayed, giving rise to complaints over dust clouds arising from dirt and sand. Some companies used unscreened gravel, which was dangerous to heavily loaded teams. Erin Township successfully sued the Detroit and Erin Plank Road Company in 1898 against using unscreened gravel on Gratiot Avenue in today's city of Roseville.[13]

By 1900, only twenty-three plank roads continued in operation, and of these, only a short stretch of the road from Detroit to Howell was actually made of planks. All of the others had long since replaced wood with gravel, although they were still popularly called plank roads. In the first

Plank Road Companies Serving Detroit

NAME OF COMPANY	STREET	MILES	DATE	GATES
Detroit & Pontiac	Woodward	18	1849	3
Detroit & Saline	Michigan	40	1850	8
Detroit & Erin	Gratiot	30	1852	6
Detroit & Howell	Grand River	49	1851	10
Detroit & Grosse Pte.	Jefferson	9	1851	3

Source: Farmer, *History of Detroit*, 926.

decade of the twentieth century, the remaining private roads, coming increasingly under public scorn, were turned over to the state or purchased by street railway companies.

Mark Twain left the classic description of Michigan's plank roads. Asked how he liked his trip from Kalamazoo to Grand Rapids, he replied, "It would have been good if some unconscionable scoundrel had not now and then dropped a plank across it."[14]

By inaugurating his campaign to eliminate all of the toll booths standing across Detroit's main thoroughfares, collecting tolls from two-thirds of the traffic coming and going each day, against the Hendrie Toll Gate Company, Pingree was taking on an obviously formidable now favorite opponent, who rarely before, if ever, had not gotten exactly what he wanted from city hall. Hendrie's plank road was in particularly wretched condition because he owned the street railway line and recognized no reason to pay for plank road repair and maintenance. Hendrie's plank road on East Jefferson Avenue occupied a sixteen-foot swatch directly down the middle of the sixty-six-foot-wide right of way. Often, in the late winter and spring, the mud on either side was hub deep. Various legal remedies against the plank road companies had been tried and failed. Over the years, the Michigan Supreme Court was called upon to decide more than 230 plank road cases. Years before, in 1879, Detroit lobbied the state legislature to prohibit tollgates within its corporate limits by adopting a general amendment against them that applied within all cities and villages. The legislation targeted a tollgate maintained by the Detroit and Howell Plank Road Company along two and a half miles of Grand River Avenue. Justice Cooley wrote a Michigan Supreme Court opinion describing the legislation as violating the constitutional prohibition against impairing obligation of contract.

> And it cannot be necessary at this day to enter upon a discussion in denial of the right of the government to take from either individuals or corporations any property which they may rightfully have acquired. In the most arbitrary times such an act was recognized as pure tyranny, and it has been forbidden in England ever since Magna Carta and in this country always. . . . It may be that what the legislature of 1879 proposed to accomplish would, in itself, work no hardship to [the plank road company] and would be highly desirable to the city; but the principle violated is the fundamental principle that underlies all property, and the first successful inroad upon it that obtains judicial sanction may be a precedent that shall let in innumerable evils.[15]

In closing his opinion for the unanimous three-member supreme court, Justice Cooley generously pointed out that the city could exercise its power of condemnation to rid itself of the tollgate by fairly buying the plank road company's right to collect fares from users along the contested section of Grand River Avenue. "Courts must look beyond the particular case to the governing principle, and be governed by that, regardless of the temporary and special inconveniences," he said. "But even such inconveniences must be trivial, since the power to appropriate private property to public uses is always ample and always at command."[16]

Mayor Pingree made buy-out offers but was often rebuffed. Opposing him in general were members of the Common Council loyal to their tollbooth supporters, and they made difficult getting the votes needed to pass road appropriations. Condemnation, never locally popular and also expensive and time-consuming, was a choice of last resort for politicians, especially for impatient men such as Mayor Pingree who, instead, advised citizens to refuse to pay tolls on grounds that Hendrie had forfeited his right to operate his plank road company because of gross negligence. "If they won't get out, the people should organize and drive out these leeches on the municipality," he announced. "The fact these relics of pioneer days should be able to prevent public improvements on a street within the limits of the City, and to collect tolls for travel over our City pavement is repugnant to all ideas of justice."

When Strathearn Hendrie obtained a court injunction stopping the city from paving at his East Jefferson Avenue tollgate, Pingree sent his road-building crew right up to and around it with a sixty-foot-wide crushed-rock roadway, leaving the tollbooth stranded in the middle. Strathearn Hendrie defiantly applied for another injunction, which was still pending at the time of Pingree's annual address to the Common Council on January 9, 1894. The circuit court eventually ruled that since Hendrie's company owned rights only to the sixteen-foot strip in the center of East Jefferson Avenue, tolls were uncollectable from drivers going around on the forty-four feet of outside paving. Thus, by the middle of 1896, every toll road company had been effectively ousted from the city. "Now we can drive over our streets feeling that we are free men," declared Mayor Pingree.[17]

In the meantime, the deals Detroit successfully negotiated with other plank road companies pushed surrounding areas into litigation. In 1893, for example, the Village of Highland Park, where Hendrie owned the Detroit and Birmingham Plank Road Company, sued to prevent the building of a new tollgate there. Detroit had paid Hendrie's plank road company $5,000 for an agreement against tollgates within five miles of city hall and "to collect no tolls from persons traveling over the portion of the road south of the gate to be established beyond said five-mile limit, except as they should pass though said gate." The village's lawsuit failed, of course, on the same ground that Detroit lost its Grand River Avenue case.

"We see no difference in principle between the cases," said Chief Justice Frank A. Hooker. "The plank road act gave to the defendant a right to build and maintain its gates where it might deem necessary, which is as much one of the contract rights to maintain an existing gate would be, while to compel it to surrender half a mile of its road in Highland Park is, in principle, exactly the same as to take two or more miles from the Detroit and Howell Company in the City of Detroit."[18]

A routine bill introduced in the state legislature on February 5, 1893, regarding the sale and condemnation of plank roads, was the subject of some legislative mischief on behalf of Detroit. Article 4, section 28 of the state constitution required that no bill may be introduced after the first fifty days of each legislative session. Timely introduced, House Bill No. 247 served as a vehicle for substitute language adopted by the state house of representatives on May 24 that, instead, completely dissolved the Detroit and Saline Plank Road Company. A few months later, when the state attorney general sued to wind up the company, Justice John McGrath's opinion for the supreme court said the bill violated the fifty-day requirement, "otherwise, by the use of scissors and mucilage the constitutional provision may be easily evaded."[19]

Litigation Hardball

By early February 1892, Mayor Pingree persuaded two of Detroit's leading lawyers, Don Dickinson and Alfred Russell, former U.S. attorney in Detroit, to take the case, but more than two months passed before they did anything. Instead of litigating, the political trouble surrounding their hiring erupted into a legal scandal. While Dickinson and Russell were supposedly studying the Michigan Constitution and the Street-Railway Act, reading three hundred court cases, and working out a legal strategy for getting a judge to decide that the 1879 ordinance was illegal, the street railway company succeeded in turning both men against Detroit.

Dickinson was in Washington, D.C., to testify before a U.S. Senate committee about his former service as postmaster general on March 10, 1892, when he insisted, in response to a question from a reporter for the *Evening News*, that he had, in fact, never accepted the case.

> All I know about it is this: February second the council passed a resolution authorizing the mayor to retain Hon. Alfred Russell and myself at a retainer of $1,000. On February three, on seeing this action in the morning papers, I sent a note to the mayor that I did not see my way clear to accept money from the City in a matter which was the result of a quasi-political agitation in which I had been more or less prominent. I had been called upon to preside at the citizens' meeting. I said to the mayor that it might be thought right by nine men in ten but whether right or wrong, I could not feel comfortable about it. The mayor broke his arm and we have not met to speak about it since.[20]

Dickinson continued, muddling his explanation with a suggestion that he was concerned about being paid enough. "That is all there is about it, except that I said to the City counselor at Lansing the other day that if I did not act as paid counsel I did not see my way to volunteering professional services against private interests. To do that would be an undoubtedly unprofessional act. I would like to be in the fight if it comes, but I hope it will be adjusted without a fight."[21]

When agreeing to their hiring, 26-2, on February 2, 1892, aldermen had tossed around paying Dickinson and Russell $500 each as a retainer and $200 per day, but they made no appropriation.[22] Citizen committee members said by Waller to be gathering legal subscriptions failed to raise the $10,000 Dickinson may have wanted to take the case. In fact, the Committee of Fifty appointed by the Common Council just faded away. It was never heard from again as Mayor Pingree began his second term of office.

Four days after Dickinson quit came another devastating bombshell in the Thirty-Year War. Russell, too, abruptly and publicly resigned, explaining that he had accepted what he described as a "splendid offer" from the Detroit Citizens Street Railway Company. Russell was sixty-two years old and had enjoyed a distinguished career since graduating from the Harvard Law School in 1852 and moving to Detroit. By quitting, his reputation was destroyed. He ended up working as a general attorney for the Wabash Railroad Company. A front-page story in the *Evening News* of March 16, 1892, dramatically reported Russell's noon meeting with Mayor Pingree. "Now the council haggled about a paltry $500 as a retainer for me. The City won't pay me a day's wages for doing this work in their behalf. I'm a poor man," Russell said. "I can't afford to work for glory, when men like James McMillan and D. M. Ferry offer me a very large amount of money to work for their side of the case. I am actually compelled by my necessities to accept. I regret that I have to do this, but it's simply a matter of business to me."[23]

Mayor Pingree publicly fumed, calling Russell's hiring away subordination of treason by the street railway company. Today, Russell's betrayal would have gotten him brought up on charges by the Attorney Grievance Commission. Dickinson's political career may have been threatened, and he, too, may have been offered other opportunities because a few weeks later he was selected to head Michigan's delegation to the Democratic National Convention. Dickinson and Waller were well acquainted. They had been instrumental in securing the first presidential nomination of Grover Cleveland, who went on to win the 1884 election.

Senator McMillan denied any personal involvement, and Cameron Currie insisted that bondholders he represented were blameless. Russell, however, acknowledged that Waller and Cook were in charge from New York City, an admission that another attorney for the bondholders called "the most stupid blunder I ever heard."[24] The episode debunked the myth of local ownership, exposing a split between the company's local stockholders, on the one hand, and Hendrie, Waller, and Cook on the other, who had unwittingly demonstrated that they remained firmly in control.

George H. Russel, company treasurer, apologized, saying, ridiculously, "Do you think the directors are such a parcel of fools as to hire Russell away from the City? Why, if we did so there would be another riot and $100,000 would be raised by subscription in Detroit to employ counsel to fight the company."[25]

R. H. Fyfe was outraged. "As I came down in the streetcar this morning, citizens were mad," he told the *Evening News*. "They wanted to get out and tear up some streetcar rails. I tell you, there will be a riot again if the streetcar company doesn't look out."[26]

Pingree turned to two able lawyers lacking Detroit roots. "On looking around for the essential legal talent to replace these gentlemen, I found that the company had retained for its services almost everything with even the color of the required talent," Mayor Pingree said. Eventually he recruited Charles Kent and Benton Hanchett to take the case. "These gentlemen took up the legal weapons at the point where the others had dropped them."[27]

Kent had been dean of the University of Michigan Law School. A Saginaw lawyer with a sterling legal reputation, Hanchett's selection was a highly political choice by Pingree. A former Saginaw mayor, Hanchett was an active Republican and a friend of Senator McMillan. President Harrison had nominated him to a vacancy on the U.S. Sixth Circuit Court of Appeals on February 22, 1892. It came so late in Harrison's term that the nomination died without getting a Senate confirmation vote, a clear signal that a cynical McMillan had been trying to buy him away from Detroit.[28]

On March 15, 1892, the *Street Railway Review*, a national industry newsletter published in Chicago,

Charles A. Kent. Courtesy of the University of Michigan faculty and staff portrait collection, Bentley Historical Library, University of Michigan.

Benton Hanchett. From *A Gallery of Pen Sketches in Black and White of Our Michigan Friends "As We See 'Em,"* ed. C. O. Youngstrand (Detroit: Wm. Graham Printing Company, 1905).

headlined a full-page editorial "Blocking the Wheels of Commerce." It quoted from a letter sent to the Common Council by the Detroit Citizens Street Railway Company.

> You ask the question, "Why should the company be much less able to provide rapid transit when, according to your own figures, it is the cheaper of the two?" We would have commenced putting in a rapid transit plant before this time, had it not been for the question that has been raised as to our rights under the present ordinances, but we would not be able to provide such facilities under more onerous provisions. . . . We cannot raise the $2,000,000 unless the investor is certain that the principal and interest will be paid within the next seventeen years, the time when our main franchises expire.

Speed drafted two new ordinances for the Common Council. The first specifically set the expiration date of the original street railway ordinance as May 9, 1893, for the apparent purpose of avoiding later arguments over the exact date. The second ordinance repealed that part of the 1879 ordinance that extended its expiration date to 1909. The Common Council passed both, and Mayor Pingree signed them on March 29, 1892. No judge would pay any attention to either one because the original ordinances comprised a bilateral contract agreed upon by the city and the Detroit City Railway Company in 1862 and 1879. Giving them unilateral effect would violate, at least, the state and federal constitutional impairment of contracts clauses. The street railway company could never agree to them without breaching its duty of prudent care to stockholders. Such a futile legal volley may be perceived as putting the city on the offensive, but it would neither persuade the company to surrender nor win the case in court.

Having done what little they could to clean up the ordinance, without awaiting final Common Council action on Mayor Pingree's hiring of new outside counsel, on March 15, 1892, Speed filed a one-hundred-page typewritten lawsuit in the Wayne County Circuit Court. It asked for a declaration that the Detroit City Railway Company's franchise would expire on May 9, 1893, and an injunction ordering the company to vacate the streets of Detroit by then. Speed committed a first-class legal blunder by naming as one of the defendants the New York City–based Washington Trust Company, a mistake made without any personal involvement by Kent or Hanchett.[29] By doing so, Speed guaranteed at least a four-month delay in getting any court rulings in the case and, as would be seen, other legal maneuvering.

State legislatures and the federal courts had jockeyed for years over the scope of protection afforded by the due process clause of the U.S. Constitution to out-of-state defendants sued in state courts. Michigan had tried to preserve the exercise of state court jurisdiction by giving them 120 days to respond to lawsuits.[30] On March 22, 1892, Speed obtained a routine order for service by publication against the out-of-state defendant. All of the other defendants were personally served in Detroit and timely filed separate answers. Nevertheless, the Washington Trust did nothing while the clock ticked by more than 120 days.

Meanwhile, on April 5, 1892, the company announced that it was replacing horse-drawn service on the East Jefferson Avenue line with overheard electric streetcars even though the original ordinance specifically authorized only horse-drawn service. Work was not begun until June, however, delayed by inaction on construction permits needed from the city's Board of Public Works, over which Mayor Pingree exercised considerable influence.

Not until August 13, 1892, did Detroit file its proof of publication in the Wayne County Circuit Court along with a pro confesso order against the Washington Trust Company of New York for failing to timely answer or otherwise take action to defend against the lawsuit by July 20, 1892, when the 120-day deadline expired. With most of Detroit's closely knit legal community having offices in the Hammond Building and frequently seeing each other in and around the court buildings, professional courtesy would ordinarily make them reluctant to take advantage of procedural rules against one another. Furthermore, no doubt, Sidney Davy Miller's role as trustee for at least some streetcar company bondholders renders suspect any suggestion that the Washington Trust Company of New York did not timely receive actual notice from him sufficient to obtain local counsel. Either its lawyers neglected the case or they had some reasonable explanation for failing to sooner take appropriate action. The delayed taking of a pro confesso order—Latin meaning the allegations made by the city would be indisputable in court—was an indication that the attorneys for both sides were in no hurry to resolve the case. Mayor Pingree had unsuccessfully sought nomination for Michigan governor at the Republican Party's summer convention in Saginaw on July 20 and lost to John T. Rich, which may have contributed to the delay.[31] Something broke down between the attorneys, and Detroit's lawyers decided to embarrass their colleagues representing the Washington Trust Company of New York because, unless set aside, the pro confesso order would bar their client from actively defending the high-stakes case.[32]

Service by publication, the subsequent four-month delay in answering, and the filing of a pro confesso order under such circumstances are indicative of hardball tactics being employed by both sides in this litigation.[33] Six days later, however, one of Detroit's lawyers nonetheless agreed to set aside the default and, on the same day, the Washington Trust Company of New York filed its answer. The Detroit Citizens Street Railway Company had already filed a highly aggressive defense to the lawsuit, itself asking injunctive relief against the city's recent repeal of key language in the 1879 ordinance as violating the impairment of contract clause of the U.S. Constitution, which, of course, it did.

On August 23, 1892, the city served routine paperwork on all the attorneys in the case giving formal notice that the case was ready for hearing just as Detroit's newspapers reported the successful early morning test ride of a new overhead electric streetcar. Driver John Cochrane gingerly maneuvered the trolley arm to the overhead wire and, with a whir and a crunch, the forty-horsepower electric streetcar built by the Brownell Car Company of St. Louis at a cost of $10,000 emerged from its barn at St. Antoine and Woodbridge Streets at 7:42 A.M., reaching Jefferson Avenue having once fallen off the tracks. The car, a single truck-type with hand brakes and heated by a coal stove, continued to Baldwin Avenue in about eighteen minutes. On the return trip, the cowcatcher struck a paving stone at the Detroit, Grand Haven, and Milwaukee Railroad viaduct and splintered. It was removed, and the new electric streetcar returned without other trouble.

The *Detroit Tribune*'s enthusiastic coverage said, "The unfamiliar sound of the new vehicle brought people from their breakfast tables to gaze with delight at the car while they shouted praises and waved their napkins as it sped by."[34] A horse-drawn streetcar would have required an hour to make the trip. The new electric streetcar covered the same ground in thirty minutes. By November, twelve electric cars were running on Jefferson Avenue from Woodward Avenue to the Water Works Park.

On October 18, 1892, before anything was done by Judge George Gartner, the Wayne County Circuit Court judge assigned to handle the case, the Washington Trust Company of New York filed an ex parte motion and obtained an order from U.S. District Judge Henry H. Swan removing the case to the U.S. Circuit Court for the Eastern District of Michigan on grounds of local prejudice.[35] Lawyers filing an ex parte motion typically give no advance warning to the other side even though they are supposed to try. They may have tried but without exerting any diligence, failing at what they perceived as just response to the city's earlier taking of an embarrassing default against them.

In 1892, federal district courts had jurisdiction only to hear cases involving violation of a federal statute, a treaty, or the U.S. Constitution. Some cases filed in the state courts not involving federal law, however, could be transferred to a three-judge panel of what were called the federal circuit courts if any of the defendants were residents of a different state and they presented facts showing local prejudice that would prevent them from getting a fair hearing in the state court.[36] The U.S. Congress had adopted the Jurisdiction and Removal Act of 1875, dramatically enlarging the role that federal courts could play in protecting railroads and other corporations doing interstate business by allowing them to move their cases out of state courts.[37] The panel would consist of a circuit judge from the newly organized Sixth Circuit Court of Appeals serving Michigan, Ohio, Kentucky, and Tennessee and two district judges serving Michigan. U.S. Circuit Judge William Howard Taft and District Judges Swan and Henry F. Severens were assigned to the case,[38] and together they would read the legal briefs, attend the hearings, and listen to courtroom arguments from a roomful of lawyers representing the city, the Detroit Citizens Street Railway Company, and the Washington Trust Company of New York.[39]

By making the Washington Trust Company of New York one of the parties to the case, following the violent four-day streetcar strike and mass rally protesting the new thirty-year ordinances, Speed had opened the door for the case to be heard in the federal court.[40] Furious at the preemptory and unexpected turn of events, Mayor Pingree directed Kent and Hanchett to seek reversal of Judge Swan's decision. "A stock broker working for the trust company conveniently appeared, attached his name, and swore to a statement prepared by a local attorney, which was a mass of fabrications and exaggerations, as to the truth or falsity of which the broker made claim to no personal knowledge whatever," Mayor Pingree explained in his annual address to the Common Council on January 10, 1893.

> This ghost story was quietly presented one day to a judge of the United States Court, who was assisted to his life appointment on the Federal Bench by a large stockholder in the Detroit Citizens Street Railway Company.[41] This judge listened to the reading of what was an insult to the citizens of Detroit, and then directed the clerk to enter an order of court removing the case from the state courts to the United States Courts on the ground of local prejudice. The lawyers who were retained to defend the interests of the City in this suit were not notified that such a request was to be made of the Federal Judge; were not given an opportunity to show that justice could be done in the Michigan courts as well as in the United States courts; and, in fact, were not permitted to read the fairy tale of the New York stock broker, until the Federal Judge had done his work. At the urgent solicitation, or, perhaps, more properly speaking, the imperative demand of Professor Kent, one of the City's counsels, he and his colleague, Hon. Benton Hanchett, of Saginaw, were finally given an opportunity to ask the Federal Court to remand this case to the Wayne Circuit Court, and to state their reasons therefore. The argument on the motion to remand was made two months ago, and the Federal Court still has the matter under advisement. It is to be hoped that the Federal judges will make up their minds before they die, or become incapacitated through old age.

The motion to send the case back to the Wayne County Circuit Court, however, had already been decided against Detroit on January 5, 1893.[42] Either Mayor Pingree had not yet received a copy as of Tuesday, January 10, 1893, or he had already written his speech and decided to deliver these intemperate remarks anyway as a rebuke to the slowness and procedural tangles of the state and federal judicial system he had suffered over the last year. Nothing had been accomplished to decide the merits of the city's expensive streetcar lawsuit or toward persuading Waller, Cook, Hendrie, and its local owners to make an offer of settlement to his liking. Circuit Judge Taft's seventeen-page opinion denying the motion to remand displayed an intimate knowledge of earlier events in Detroit. "If the facts stated do not show prejudice and local influence in the community of the City of Detroit against the defendants in this case, then it is difficult to imagine facts that would," Taft said. "It is very clear that the citizens of Detroit generally are impressed with a feeling that the street railway company has abused its privileges, that the continued enjoyment by it of the franchises will be an injustice to the City."[43]

Detroit's lawyers argued in vain that even if the community was angry at the street railway company there was no evidence the defendants could not obtain justice from the judge assigned in the Wayne County Circuit Court. Judge Taft brushed that aside in keeping the case in federal court. "A decision in this case adverse to the City of Detroit would probably cause many electors of the City in the approaching judicial election, convinced of the righteousness of the City's cause, to vote against the judge rendering the decision, and no judge could be unconscious of that fact in passing upon the case," he said.[44]

This is a sensitive issue for judges in the state and federal courts of a particular community who went to law school, practiced law, and socialized with one another. The lifetime appointment of federal judges protects them from worry about the impact of their rulings on the next election. That is not so with state court judges in Michigan, who also rely on the lawyers appearing before them to help pay campaign expenses but necessarily make decisions unpopular with more or less half of them appearing in court every day. In those few cases garnering any general public attention, the law and justice sometimes demand from them rulings protecting otherwise detestable persons and causes. Judge Taft explained his reasoning for the wider audience of Detroit residents his opinion would reach.

> We entertain the highest respect for our brother judges of the state court, as we ought, for those exercising concurrent jurisdiction with us. Nor, in reaching this conclusion, do we attack the whole system of an elective judiciary. . . . We simply hold that, under extraordinary circumstances, judges elected by a community must be presumed to be affected by a prejudice shown to pervade the entire community, so as to make it unjust to compel a nonresident to try his controversy with the community before its own judges. If this holding is an attack on the system of an elective judiciary, it is the constitution and laws of the United States which are responsible for the attack, and not the courts which administer them.[45]

In response, a few weeks later, Detroit's lawyers tried to dismiss the entire case so they could start over again in state court. "The motion is accompanied with the frank statement that the complainant prefers another tribunal than this in which to litigate its rights," wrote Judge Taft in a March 16, 1893, opinion refusing to do so even though the Washington Trust Company of New York, which had obtained removal from the state to the federal court, itself sought no affirmative relief and, therefore, could be dismissed without prejudice. "While it may not be usual to have so candid an avowal of the facts made, the federal courts are frequently compelled to administer justice in cases where one of the parties would prefer another forum."[46]

Judge Taft pointed out that the Detroit Citizens Street Railway Company had filed an answer seeking affirmative relief and objected to dismissal as against the Washington Trust Company of New York. "The complainant cannot dismiss its bill against the trust company without also dismissing it against all the other defendants, and so long as they object to the dismissal and prevent it, the Washington Trust Company must remain, because it is a necessary party to the litigation [under a cross-bill filed by the street railway company],"[47] Judge Taft concluded in an opinion he delivered from the bench. The case proceeded immediately to a hearing on Detroit's legal claim that the 1879 ordinance extending the expiration date of its consent was void under the state constitution.

Judge Taft's Ruling

On Saturday, January 21, 1893, Pingree told a reporter for the *Evening News* that he had been offered $100,000 and the governorship if he would abandon the street railway fight. "He made the further statement that he has documentary proof that during the past 25 years aldermen have been in the habit of receiving monthly stipends from the predecessors of the Citizens Street Railway," the newspaper said, prompting preemptory denials from Jacob and formal action by the Common Council to appoint a committee to investigate.[48] Nobody ever pursued prosecution, but the taint of Pingree's allegations stuck.

The Detroit Citizens Street Railway Company's lawyers had mounted a highly aggressive defense. In response to the city's pleadings, it had not only filed paperwork routinely denying that the 1879 ordinance was illegal but went on the offensive, seeking an injunction permanently restraining enforcement of the thirty-year expiration clause in the Street-Railway Act on grounds that it violated the impairment of contracts provision of the U.S. Constitution. On May 31, 1893, Judge Taft sided with Detroit based upon Michigan's thirty-year cap on the corporate life of a street railway company over the dissenting opinion of Judge Swan. The 1879 ordinance giving the Detroit City Railway Company rights in the street after May 9, 1893 was void, Taft said, because the extension exceeded the limited measure of state sovereign power delegated to the city by the Street-Railway Act.[49]

Before entering a final order, Judge Taft explicitly gave the street railway company an opportunity to settle its differences with the City, even though the original ordinance had already expired. In the meantime, Judge Taft asked for new written legal briefs and oral arguments specifically regarding franchises granted to the Congress and Baker Street Railway Company and Cass Avenue Railway Company. In an opinion dated January 31, 1984, he decided that they survived their assignment to the Detroit City Railway Company and, therefore, would not expire until 1907 and 1909, respectively.[50]

Judge Swan had written an elegant but angry opinion dissenting from the earlier Detroit City Railway decision,[51] prompting a belated but candid response from Judge Taft illustrating both his professional generosity and their differing judicial philosophy. "It is quite likely that he is right, and I am wrong, but meeting the responsibility which the law imposes on me, I must hold that the complainant in the bill is entitled to relief prayed for," Taft wrote in an opinion giving the streetcar company three full months to remove all of its railway tracks from city streets. "In view of the division of the court, and the magnitude of the interests involved, the case will, of course, be taken, as it ought to be, to a reviewing court. It can be heard in the court of appeals in May next, and an early decision had. Upon the company's giving a bond in the sum of $10,000, conditioned in the usual form, the decree may be superceded, and the operation of the injunction will be stayed pending the appeal."[52]

Taft's original thirty-eight-page opinion had explained why the law required him to issue a mandatory injunction ordering the Detroit City Railway Company to cease operating its horse-drawn streetcars and remove its railway tracks despite the obvious and enormous inconvenience suffered by the public and financial loss incurred by the company, its stockholders and bondholders, and other creditors. Historian Doris Kearns Goodwin said no one on the circuit court was more widely respected or better loved than Judge Taft. "The work itself was intellectually challenging, requiring him to reach decisions and write opinions on far-reaching issues regarding labor strikes, injunctions, workplace injuries, street railways, and monopolies," she wrote. "He was allowed the time necessary to study cases thoroughly, reviewing precedents and refining his position. Most important, he was able to draft, revise, and edit his decisions 'over again and again' until he had honed the language to his satisfaction. His opinions earned the admiration of lawyers across the nation, building a reputation that bolstered his dream of one day sitting on the Supreme Court."[53]

A large body of street railway law had developed across the country since 1862 when the Detroit City Railway Company obtained its thirty-year franchise. The 749-page first edition of Henry R. Booth's *Treatise on the Law of Street Railways,* published in 1892, reported on more than 2,600 cases from across the United States and Canada. Many of those mostly state court decisions looked back to how they had decided cases involving grants to ferry and bridge companies. Under the English common law tradition, judges decide cases by applying the law arising from earlier court rulings to the present set of circumstances while trying to respond wisely to society's economic, social, and other needs and technological advancements as the U.S. Supreme Court had done in deciding the *Charles River Bridge* case in 1837. The abiding rule intended to make courts reliable is what judges call stare decisis—"to stand by what is decided"—under which an issue of law and facts once decided persuasively should not be revisited and rarely reversed. Judges do not make rulings otherwise than by a plaintiff complaining against a defendant. The impact of judicial decisions is slowed dramatically by the appellate process, the carefully deliberative review of a single case in which one or the other of the parties was willing to invest more of their time and money in legal wrangling. The choosing of what to decide by the appellate process is strictly reserved to judges without any possibility of review by the other branches of government.

Judge Taft began by framing the question simply: Did the Common Council have the power in 1879 to extend its consent originally granted in 1862 for sixteen years beyond the corporate life of the Detroit City Railway Company? The defendants, he said, asserted that the power of extension existed under both the street railway acts and the city charter. Judge Taft observed that in construing them he would be guided by the general rule applied by Michigan courts in cases involving grants by the state legislature to other corporations.

"Any ambiguity or doubt arising out of the terms used by the legislature must be resolved in favor of the public," he said, quoting from a U.S. Supreme Court case. "This principle has been so often followed in the construction of corporate powers that we need not stop to refer to authorities." Judge Taft continued.

> There is no reason, therefore, why the strict rule of construing the powers of municipal corporations should be departed from in Michigan. We have the highest authority for this conclusion. In the case of *Taylor v. Bay City Street Railway Company,* 80 Mich. 77 (1890) where the effect of a legislative grant of power to a city in reference to street railways was under consideration, Justice Grant, speaking for the supreme court of Michigan, said: "Municipal corporations derive their sole source of power from legislative enactments. The rule has long been unquestionably established that municipal corporations are limited to those powers which are granted—First, in express words; second necessarily incident to the powers expressly granted, and, third, those which are essential and indispensable to the declared objects and purposes of the corporation."[54]

Michigan Supreme Court Judge Cladius B. Grant, a Republican from the Upper Peninsula, was quoting directly from Dillon's *Treatise on the Law of Municipal Corporations*. Had Judge Grant instead applied Cooley's Doctrine to the case, Judge Taft may have reached a different conclusion in this early part of the Progressive Era. It is ironic that while Judge Cooley may have disagreed with Judge Taft that Detroit lacked authority to extend its consent, the result of his doing so would have been a victory for the street railway company while Dillon's Rule required its defeat. Judge Taft cited Dillon's treatise directly in explaining why he rejected arguments by the street railway company that Detroit could extend its consent under its state-granted charter authority to regulate the use of streets. "It is hardly probable that Judge Dillon's language is to be given the meaning claimed by defendants because . . . he emphatically approves the language of Judge Comstock in the case of *Davis v. City of New York*, 14 N.Y. 506 (1856) expressly negativing the power of a city council having control and regulation of the use of the streets to make an irrevocable grant of an easement therein to construct and operate a street railway."[55]

Judge Taft carefully dissected the state constitution, Tram-Railway Act, and several street railway acts adopted over the years. He narrowed his attention to section 34 of the Street-Railway Act of 1867, which, he said, limited the state-granted franchise to construct and operate a street railway by making it operative only on municipal consent subject to whatever limitations the local government imposed on granting its consent.

> An inevitable limitation thus arising is that the easement shall not endure beyond the life of the franchise for which the easement is given. I cannot escape the conclusion . . . that the power of consent is limited in time to the life of the franchise to be consented to. . . . If such a delegation may be authorized by an act of the legislature, certainly the power to make it cannot be inferred from a mere power to consent. . . . It necessarily follows that the power of the city to consent to the exercise of the franchise conferred upon the railway company was also limited in its duration to the life of the corporation. Either the limitation stated exists, or the power of the city is unlimited, and it may create in the streets, by virtue of the power to grant an easement . . . an estate in perpetuity. . . . The 30 years mentioned in the statute can have no effect to limit the duration of the consent or easement which the city confers, except by reason of the fact that this is the time beyond which the life of the franchise and corporation cannot extend.[56]

Judge Taft concluded by referring back to the thirty-year limitation on corporate life set forth in the state constitution and a recently decided case by the Michigan Supreme Court, *Kent County Agricultural Society v. Houseman*,

> "The evident intent of this section was to prevent the perpetuation of corporate power and corporate life, so as to place it practically beyond the reach of the people or the legislature. It was intended to apply to corporations of a private character, organized for profit and the accumulation of wealth, and not to those, which are public in their character, and designed solely for the purposes of education and improvement."[57] . . . [I]t would hardly be proper for a court to be swayed from a conclusion as to the meaning of a statute by the claim that it involves an anomaly, when the anomaly has no existence, except

> in the view that a corporation may in fact perpetuate its wealth and franchises, and remain identically the same entity, no matter how many different names it bears, or how many formal conveyances of property and franchises are necessary to continue its existence.[58]

In his dissenting opinion, Judge Swan more or less conceded that Detroit lacked authority to extend its consent beyond thirty years. He objected, however, to the inequitable result because the street railway company had been operating under the 1879 ordinance for so many years. "If acted upon for 14 years, and regarded by both parties as superseding a prior contract and defining their relations, and affirmed by one party as the basis of recovery against the other, by successful litigation, there is no principle, consistent with sound morality, that will permit its reasonableness, over even its constitutionality, to be questioned now, at the suit of the grantor, who seeks, in bad faith, to impugn its own grant," he concluded.[59]

Taft explained why he differed from Judge Swan. "The case of the city is different from that of a private corporation," he said. "The city council, for the time being, is the trustee, in control of the streets for the benefit of the public; and, although former trustees may have attempted to do that which they had no power to do, the public cannot be prevented from having asserted in its favor the ordinary equitable remedies to maintain its rights in the streets."[60]

The Street Railway Review, an industry newsletter, was horrified by the outcome and re-cast the factual setting to sensationalize its account of the case. "Detroit plodded along for years with the street railway service of an overgrown country town," the *Review* said on June 15, 1893.

> At last eastern capital was interested in its behalf and the old Detroit City and several smaller lines were sold to the new syndicate—the Citizens. The chief factor in the sale was an extension of thirty years, which the old road secured about two years before its corporate existence expired. Acting in perfect good faith the new company was allowed to enter into possession and to invest a large amount of money. Then began a systematic warfare on their new benefactors, and every possible effort, in which Mayor Pingree specifically distinguished himself, was made to hamper and cripple the new enterprise. A crisis was finally reached May 31 last, when the United States Court handed down a most remarkable decision, Judge Swan dissenting, in which it was declared the new company ceased to hold operative title to all but two minor lines, on May 9, 1893, which was the date of expiration of the state charter of the old Detroit City Railway. The mayor and city authorities indulged in a ghost dance of ghoulish glee over the victory.[61]

The Detroit Citizens Street Railway Company put electric streetcars on Jefferson, Woodward, and Mack Avenues by the end of 1892 when all construction stopped. It otherwise schemed to evade the five-cent limit on fares and continued to resist accepting transfers even while passenger service and capital maintenance suffered under a national economic depression that had begun in 1893. Some of Detroit's biggest industries were forced to shut down. The railroad car shops and the stove factories were among them. An estimated twenty-five thousand workers were unemployed.

Let's Make a Deal

In the wake of Judge's Taft's opinion, the Detroit Citizens Street Railway Company began scrambling for a deal. Oddly, thrust into the delicate role was its new general manager, James D. Hawks. On July 29, 1893, Hawks delivered the first of many settlement offers exchanged during the Thirty-Year War. He promised electric streetcars operating on all roads within two years. He offered to require conductors to sell a "workingmen's fare" of six tickets for twenty-five cents during certain hours each day but otherwise keeping five-cent fares. The compromise he proposed guaranteed stockholder dividends up to 8 percent per year before the city could enlarge the hours during which the "workingmen's fare" would apply. Hawks also offered to sell the streetcar company for $4 million—par value of its authorized stock—upon receiving six months' notice.[62]

"It takes $3 million to equip all our lines," he said. "That means $150,000 interest every year or an increase of $500,000 in our gross earnings each year to pay the interest, while our receipts don't come in til the line is equipped."[63]

Mayor Pingree balked at continuing the five-cent fare and vetoed a deal based on Hawks's proposal championed by Alderman Vernor. Pingree's veto was upheld, 17-13, and he refused to make any counteroffer until after easily winning reelection in November 1893 by a 5,800-vote margin over his Democratic Party opponent, Marshall H. Godfrey. In his annual address to the Common Council on January 9, 1894, Pingree confidently asserted, "the courts have decided the franchises on all the main lines have terminated or will terminate within the next four years. The Citizens Street Railway Company as a corporation is practically bankrupt and at the mercy of the holders of its bonds. Outside capitalists stand ready to take the property of the Citizens Company, and of its bondholders, off their hands at more than its actual value and to give the people of Detroit first-class service for a three-cent fare, if the city does the paving. I have given the subject much careful thought and painstaking investigation."

Even while hinting that he had buyers in his pocket, Pingree said he would agree to extend the existing franchises by fifteen years but only if the company would install citywide overhead electric street railways within three years using grooved rail tracks and agree to transfer complete ownership on demand by the city at a price determined by arbitration. He would then lease everything back at annual rental starting at $1,500 for a single track and $3,500 for a double track, increasing to $2,500 for a single and $6,000 for a double during the last five years of the fifteen-year term. Tickets could still be sold for five cents but with universal transfers and workingmen's fares of eight for twenty-five cents from 5:30 A.M. to half past midnight.

A Nasty Personal Backlash

The mayor was driving a hard bargain because he had in hand Judge Taft's favorable ruling and he did not know with whom he was negotiating. He certainly believed that Waller, Cook, Hendrie, and the local investors were struggling among themselves over the company's future. Maybe, in addition, he was trying to drive a wedge between them, protecting the many local investors he had counted among his friends. They were not persuaded, and they were very angry.

Pingree's reelection in 1891 and again in 1893 over the confused opposition of the Republican

James D. Hawks. From *A Gallery of Pen Sketches in Black and White of Our Michigan Friends "As We See 'Em,"* ed. C. O. Youngstrand (Detroit: Wm. Graham Printing Company, 1905).

and the Democratic Party bosses of Detroit and his successful litigation against George Hendrie's street railway company propelled a nasty personal and financial backlash against him and his family. The old, established, reactionary wealthy families and power brokers moved against him, his key appointees, and political supporters in all of the ways they knew had been persuasive of lesser men, and the newspapers unmercifully lampooned, caricatured, and misrepresented him, and refused him space to respond.

He and his wife Fanny, son Hazen Jr., and daughters Gertrude and Hazel lost their family pew at the socially fashionable Woodward Avenue Baptist Church. All the other pews, church leaders told Pingree, were reserved. They generously offered free seating in the pews at the back of the church. Pingree only mentioned the incident briefly in an otherwise polemical book he published in 1895 called *Facts and Opinions; or, Dangers that Beset Us*. "I was even pursued into the sanctuary and pushed out as though I have been a mere money changer," Pingree wrote.[64]

The Woodward Avenue Baptist Church six blocks north of Grand Circus Park had Detroit's largest congregation when it was dedicated on January 19, 1887. The church stood along a stretch of Woodward Avenue once known as Piety Hill because of its twenty-two architecturally magnificent churches and eighty-five breathtakingly beautiful mansions lining its cedar block pavement.[65] Among those filling the front pews of this gray limestone late Victorian Gothic church were the families of Walter W. Smith, Schuyler S. Olds, Thomas W. Palmer, John D. Standish, and Stephen V. R. Trowbridge, whom George Hendrie's wife counted among her influential relatives.

Pingree's opponents in Detroit also worked through the banks, orchestrating his ouster as director of the Preston National Bank of which he was a founder and owner of $27,000 stock. They organized Detroit's other banks against his shoe manufacturing plant, refusing their banking business and strangling then cutting off financial lines of credit. "The local banks caught the itch of petty persecution, and ordinary accommodations were refused," Pingree said. "My intimate friends and supporters were served in the same way. As a manufacturer of undisputed responsibility, whose business required the customary accommodations, I was still pursued to the East, where the trade of the firm is large, but the pursuit in that direction was profitless to the pursuers."[66]

In resigning his seat on the Common Council from the fourth ward on February 7, 1893, a plumbing contractor, Edwin F. Webster, announced that he had succumbed to the pressure. "I believe Mayor Pingree to be right and therefore have supported him but it is only too plain that if I want to keep up my business I cannot continue in the council and support him. I will not remain and antagonize him, so there is nothing left for me to do but resign. I am not like some other aldermen who can draw their business support from the voters, who are with Mr. Pingree as a rule. My business depends upon the wealthy class whose interests the mayor is fighting."[67]

City Controller Clarence Black, highest paid of Pingree's appointees, resisted. "At my club and at my bank pressure is brought to bear to induce me to leave Pingree, and little insinuations that hurt my business and social standing are thrown out."[68]

The old money movers and shakers pressured Detroit's retail merchants and sent word across the country warning others against stocking Pingree's boots and shoes. "Personal attacks of all descriptions, of the meanest and even of the vilest kind may be anticipated, as the corporation sleuth hounds stop at nothing," Pingree said. "The least hole in the private character of a man who goes up against corporations will be noted and enlarged upon. It they are not there, all sorts of attempts will be made to make holes to order."[69]

In these remarks, he may have been speaking about an incident related to his oldest daughter, Gertrude Elizabeth Pingree, who died of severe tuberculosis complications at one o'clock in the morning on March 26, 1894. She was nineteen years old.[70] His young daughter's death by tuberculosis may have been complicated by Down syndrome, a child who suffered mental retardation. Gertrude never attended Detroit's public schools. Instead, she was enrolled at the Detroit Seminary, which occupied two buildings overlooking Grand Circus Park on Adams Avenue, maintained by Misses Harriet B. Pope and Anna M. Cutcheon. Ads described it as a home school for girls. Gertrude wears the typical facial features of Down syndrome in the only known photograph of her, taken about 1885 when she was eleven years old. In her obituary, the *Free Press* described Gertrude on March 27, 1894, as "a gentle, home-loving girl, kindly, of sweet disposition and of marked musical tastes." Her original death certificate is missing from Detroit's records today. The Michigan Department of Community Health record of her death was not routinely filed in Lansing as required by law until more than a year later on June 1, 1895.

Pingree had sent Gertrude away with his trusted friend, Clarence Black, to California's warm climate during the summer of 1893, and the family took her to San Antonio the following winter, where her health deteriorated during an unexpected Texas cold snap. The *Free Press* published a florid but empty account of her funeral service, attended only by friends and family of Mayor Pingree and his wife, Frances.

Gertrude Elizabeth Pingree. Courtesy of the Walter P. Reuther Library, Archives of Labor and Urban Affairs, Wayne State University.

"Death put forth his most tender touch, when his arms reached out for all that was earthly of Miss Gertrude Pingree, and the form of the grim reaper wore nature's fairest colors in wafting that gentle spirit to her heavenly home," the newspaper report began. "As her sweet face lay before the mourning gaze of her host of friends in the parlor of her home yesterday afternoon, it looked like the spirituelle lines of some wanderer of another sphere, so calmly sweet did her features rest in the bed of flowers that encompassed her."[71]

Pingree's emotions would have split between grief and relief over the loss of a daughter whose loving character masked the severe mental and physical handicaps she suffered. English physician John Langdon Down first characterized the syndrome as a distinct form of mental disability in 1862 whose victims share facial similarities Dr. Down described as mongoloid. Most children with Down syndrome were institutionalized, few of their associated medical problems were treated, and most died in infancy or early adult life. The personal shame and intense guilt endured by some parents of Down syndrome children may have filled Pingree with anger over a courtroom episode he later said he had endured. "They have been prowling around my skirts for years, and have finally concluded I must be insane," Pingree wrote a year after her death in *Facts and Opinion*. "Whether they reached that conclusion by finding that I was strangely different from the men with whom they usually came in contact and who were more compliant or not, I do not know."

Pingree then singled out for vulgar insult a particular but unnamed person who would have been readily identifiable by the judge, clerks, and other lawyers who were present or by long, perhaps futile, searching of courtroom transcripts, if they could be found today. "I was seriously asked by a corporation attorney, while I was testifying as a witness, if some of my progenitors had not been insane." Lingering rage at the intensely personal question put to him around the time of Gertrude's death may have prompted his inflammatory public accusation. "So accustomed had this corporation lawyer become to male prostitutes that a man in normal condition of mental health appeared to him as abnormal."[72]

A mixed quartet opened Gertrude's service singing the exquisitely lovely John Henry Newman lyrics written in 1833, "Lead, Kindly Light." Presiding at the funeral service was the aged Rev. A. E. Mather of Fenton, who had ministered to the family of Pingree's wife since her childhood in Mount Clemens, and Dr. Donald D. MacLaurin of the Woodward Avenue Baptist Church. MacLaurin had filled the vacancy created by Rev. Henderson's departure in October 1892. MacLaurin led Detroit's Civic Federation for five years before he moved to Rochester, New York. The National Civic Federation, an organization of corporate businessmen, trade union leaders, and social reformers, played an important role in the progressive reform movement, highlighted by its strong and successful agitation for state regulation of privately owned and operated public utilities such as natural gas and electricity and its widely circulated and influential report on municipal ownership in the early years of the twentieth century. Under MacLaurin's leadership, the Detroit branch avoided such matters but rather heavily campaigned for the closing of saloons during his tenure.[73]

Following the funeral service, Pingree's family conducted a private burial at the Elmwood Cemetery. Detroit's newspapers were told her burial would be at the Woodmere Cemetery, where he had buried his father and mother. Instead, her body was placed in a cemetery vault at Elmwood.[74]

The eventual personal toll on his family of his battles in the Thirty-Year War was heavy. His son, Hazen S. Pingree Jr., born May 22, 1877, had been a star halfback on the University of Michigan football team and joined his father's shoe manufacturing business. The son's marriage fell apart. His divorce judgment entered in 1906 required that he pay permanent alimony of $250 a month. Hazen Jr. remarried and was living at 409 Cadillac Avenue where he died at age thirty-three on May 7, 1910, of a massive infection, including pluero-pneumonia, enteritis, and embolism of the brain.[75] His ex-wife sued the estate for half of his factory stock on behalf of herself and their son, Gilbert Bissell Pingree, winning little because the boot factory closed just a few years later.[76]

An Unappealing Compromise

While offers and counteroffers continued, the Detroit City Railway Company, Miller, and Charles Swift, new cotrustee for the Washington Trust Company named following the death of William K.

Muir, bypassed the U.S. Circuit Court of Appeals and appealed Judge Taft's rulings directly to the U.S. Supreme Court, which on May 14, 1894, refused to take the case. The court issued a one-line order dismissing for lack of jurisdiction.[77] The Detroit City Railway Company had also appealed to the U.S. Sixth Circuit Court of Appeals and posted a $10,000 bond to stay enforcement pending a decision. The November 14, 1892, expiration date of the original ordinance granting consent had already come and gone. Detroit's daily commuting workers continued to ride horse-drawn streetcars paying five cents.

While the seesaw legal battle dragged on, two weeks before the death of his daughter, Mayor Pingree prepared a fully drafted ordinance he asked the Common Council to adopt as a settlement offer on March 13, 1894. "It is also proper to say that the plan for municipal ownership of tracks, provided in the draft of an ordinance submitted with my annual message was abandoned," he explained. "Principally because as the charter of the City now stands, of the lack of authority to carry it out."

Mayor Pingree's generous new proposal was to grant a twenty-seven-year extension to June 24, 1921, requiring around-the-clock sale of eight tickets for twenty-five cents good for a single ride. A transfer ticket would still cost five cents. The company would be required to construct and operate an overhead electric street railway system within three years.

On April 2, the Common Council's Committee on Streets and Ordinances recommended approval but demanded transfers within fifteen minutes on major routes for all tickets. At Pingree's urging, they also demanded full municipal ownership upon expiration in twenty-seven years, a flip-flopping offer he told the committee he was inspired to ask for by proposals he had received from a syndicate of Denver capitalists who were interested in buying. The *Free Press* reported on March 28, 1894, that the so-called "Rocky Mountain syndicate" had already decided against stepping in unless there was a deal among Waller, Cook, Hendrie, McMillan, and the many local shareholders.[78] On April 30, 1894, after battling back and forth over details of a workingmen's fare requirement, recovery of attorney fees owed to Kent and Hanchett, and ward politics-driven tinkering with service routes, the Common Council adopted, 31-0, Pingree's plan with full municipal ownership upon expiration and, the next evening, defeated a motion to reconsider, 10-20. The board of directors of the Detroit Citizens Street Railway Company rejected it on May 7.[79] President Dexter Ferry sent a letter to the Common Council pointing the way to reaching a deal.

> This is the first proposal which has been made by the city government for a settlement of the controversy between it and the street railway company and it seems to have been made in good faith, seeking a final settlement. Rather than continue the present controversy the company is willing to accept the ordinance proposed by the Mayor March 13, 1894. Our opinion is that, even under that ordinance it will be impossible to furnish such accommodations as the public should have but we are willing to make the experiment and do the best we can, rather than continue the controversy and litigation which have been so injurious, not only to our own, but to the public interests.

The obvious and only obstacle to a settlement was full municipal ownership upon expiration in 1921. Mayor Pingree's March 13 proposal had explicitly conceded municipal ownership as illegal under the city charter, which was, nonetheless, revived by the Common Council with his active encouragement. If Mayor Pingree really wanted a settlement as strongly encouraged by Judge Taft,[80] citywide three-cent fares could have been achieved by persuading the Common Council to strip away the illegal full municipal ownership clause.

"Oh, they want to run the whole thing, do they?" Mayor Pingree instead perversely told the *Free Press* in response to Ferry. "Want to lay down their own terms? They'll tell the City how this thing shall be done? What's the use of offering a franchise to people on a basis fair to the city—people that won't put enough money into it to buy a load of hay for their horses? They want to raise all the money on watered stock."[81]

Even while politically posturing for his next gubernatorial campaign, Mayor Pingree was making a narrowly targeted point for the company's local investors. Nothing more than the street railway company's worthless horse-drawn streetcars supported the stock they had purchased from Hendrie, Waller, and Cook. Pingree must have thought that yielding municipal ownership in twenty-seven years would be a modest concession on their part because whatever their investment would eventually return to them ultimately depended on securing an extension from the city even if the circuit court of appeals reversed Judge Taft, which nobody reasonably expected.

Then Major John Byrne, a New Jersey railroad president who was a director of the Detroit City Gas Company, obtained an option to buy from local stockholders. Mayor Pingree believed that Byrne was secretly representing Collis Potter Huntington, transcontinental railroad magnate who built the Central Pacific Railroad. Byrne aroused support from Joseph L. Hudson. On June 26, responding to a petition from three hundred other prominent Detroit businessmen supporting Byrne, Alderman Lowry introduced another settlement that required the sale on streetcars of eight tickets for twenty-five cents and universal transfers during workingmen's fare hours but not until January 1, 1897. The ordinance included full municipal ownership of the streetcars, rails, ties, wires, poles, and power station upon expiration with the price determined by arbitration. Mayor Pingree stubbornly objected to delaying three-cent fares but conceded his support if it went into effect by October 1, 1895, a few weeks before the November election at which he would be on the ballot for either mayor or governor.

What he did next was reckless if not intentionally damaging to reaching agreement with those friends of his who owned a controlling majority of the Detroit Citizens Street Railway Company. He tossed a monkey wrench into the Common Council's deliberations, claiming that while aldermen were considering his March 13 proposal, local stockholders raised $75,000 among themselves and others "to be used in procuring the passage and approval of the proposed ordinance."[82]

"While this ordinance was pending one of the board of directors of the Detroit Citizens Street Railway Company sent word that he desired to see me," Pingree told the Common Council in a letter dated June 26, 1894.

> He said . . . that it having been ascertained that he and one other of the stockholders and directors were opposed to the raising of money for such purposes, that he and the other gentleman had been requested to remain away from the next meeting. This is one of the reasons, gentlemen, why I opposed the passage of the ordinance and announced that if it was passed, I would not approve it. I say this in order that you and the public may know the character of the men in high circles who are seeking to make millions in the sale of watered street railway stock and bonds at the expense of the people of Detroit.

At a special meeting the next evening, June 27, Alderman Lowry, nonetheless, secured Common Council adoption, 22-8, amended to delay three-cent fares until January 1, 1896. Byrne responded on July 3.

> In pursuance of the instructions of my principals, I have heretofore done my utmost to meet all reasonable demands of the executive and legislative branches of the city government consistently with the safety of the capital invested in this property and, indeed, accepted terms agreeable to both in every respect, except the single and trifling condition of a brief postponement of the new rates until the company should have completed the equipment of the lines.
>
> At this point his honor the Mayor in an official letter to the Council and in repeated public interviews in the press, denounces the proceedings heretofore had in the matter as tainted by corruption. The owners of the property who I represent are not compelled to accept any ordinance regardless of its terms, and are not desirous of accepting any, which is not absolutely free from even the suspicion of impropriety. They regret the action the Mayor's course has compelled them to take but must leave the initiative to the further discussion of this subject to the city authorities. When the latter shall, without further suggestion from the owners of the property, offer an ordinance worthy of consideration, the company will cordially, and in good faith, consider it; but the company must decline all negotiations so long as they can be entered into only at the cost of vituperation from his honor the Mayor, and his allies.

Lowry's motion to reconsider and indefinitely table the ordinance was unanimously adopted. An unlikely pair pounced on the indecision. Cameron Currie and Thomas Nevins, a New Jersey street railway and natural gas utility financier,[83] had acquired a new option from local stockholders to buy their controlling interest, subject to the city granting a new and favorable thirty-year franchise by July 9. They had no success in getting any attention from the mayor or Common Council before their option expired.

Listless negotiations continued back and forth all summer focusing on paving delays and three-cent fares while Pingree campaigned for nomination as governor by the Republican Party and lost again to John T. Rich. On July 3, 1894, in the midst of his campaign, an impatient Mayor Pingree complained that Judge Taft's decision had rendered unenforceable the city's street paving and cleaning requirements. The street railway companies refused cooperation with the Board of Public Works. Consequently, "paving operations that have been held in abeyance because of the hope of settling the street railway problem should now be pushed for their fullest extent."

On August 2, 1894, the Common Council adopted, 19-9, a thirty-year ordinance championed by Alderman Vernor with three-cent fares requiring payment to the city of 4 percent of gross revenues and full municipal ownership upon expiration by arbitration that would require payment to take "into consideration as an element of value, the earning capacity of said property and business." It was vetoed by Mayor Pingree, who complained, "It is rapidly becoming a settled conviction in the minds of thinking citizens that the City should not release the control of its streets, even temporarily, to any private individual or corporation."

On the one hand, Pingree's veto message warned that "the growth of great corporations and the concentration of capital and power thereby in the hands of comparatively few persons, to the injury of the public in general, and individuals in particular, has become one of the great dangers of civilization." Then, on the other hand, he ticked off a long list of street improvement projects that were being delayed or costing more to complete without the street railway company's cooperation because of the pending litigation. On August 7, 1894, the Common Council failed to override Pingree's veto, 13-17, and Alderman Lowry introduced a new ordinance that eventually was adopted, vetoed, reconsidered, tabled, and finally, tied up by another vote against, 13-17, on August 21.

Nevins and Currie secured a second option from the local stockholders expiring September 1 for which they paid $32,000 cash. Closing a deal with Waller and Cook was delayed by more infighting. Different persons offered different explanations. One said that Nevins wanted to finance the purchase price in bonds issued by a new company, which the local stockholders refused. Another said details of the deal required notice and approval by a stockholder's meeting. Still another said New York capitalist Harry B. Hollins had offered the Hendrie and McMillan families a better price. Nevins and Currie, however, had found a buyer who could afford to pay a lot of money and risk losing everything.

The Confederate Carpetbagger

Nevins and Currie completed their small part of the deal on September 1, 1894, assigning their option to R. T. Wilson & Company, a Wall Street banking firm owned by Richard T. Wilson, a former major in the Confederate army's commissary department. Wilson had sent one of his New York City lawyers, Frank Sullivan Smith, to close the deal and talk to the Detroit newspapers, which never reported anything about Wilson's Civil War record. Instead, they were captivated by Smith's revelation that Wilson's son had recently married one of the Astor family daughters.

Born in 1831 to a Scottish tanner near Gainesville, Hall County, in northern Georgia, after the death of his father in 1849, Wilson became a commission merchant in Loudon, Tennessee.[84] At the outbreak of the Civil War, he went into the business of supplying Confederate troops with salt pork and bacon, drawing the attention of President Jefferson Davis, who invited him to join the staff of the commissary general. Wilson oversaw the highly risky but enormously profitable business of running Southern cotton through federal blockades, while engaging in cotton, gold, currency, and real estate speculations for himself and the South's military and political leaders. Some said he profiteered by selling cotton blankets to Confederate troops when he was supposed to be supplying wool blankets. As the war raged, Wilson and his family fled Tennessee to Atlanta by railroad ahead of Union troops, then again to North Carolina, and finally by steamship to Bermuda, Nova Scotia, and Liverpool, England. Wilson was in London handling the entire Confederate cotton trade when the Civil War ended, leaving him as a foreign agent controlling an estimated $500,000 without a nation to which it belonged. With a pledge of allegiance to the Union, and a letter of support from Tennessee's governor, he gained a presidential pardon.[85]

Wilson brought his fortune to New York City, where he did legitimately what he had done illegitimately: engaging in cotton trading as English agent for the entire Southern cotton crop, buying and rebuilding Southern railroads, salt and gypsum mining, and chemical, natural gas, and street railway investments.[86] He also brought to Wall Street a wide circle of political and financial contacts from across the Confederacy, England, and the postwar United States.[87] The colorful and handsome Confederate carpetbagger could have been Margaret Mitchell's model for Rhett Butler

Richard T. Wilson. Courtesy of Tommy Stokes Design and the City of Loudon, Tennessee.

in *Gone with the Wind*. If so, his charming and attractive wife, Melissa Clementine Johnston, who rose to the top of New York City society despite her Dixie roots, was his Scarlett O'Hara.

Their son Marshall had, indeed, married into the Astor family. Another, Richard T. Wilson Jr., entered the investment banking business with his father and was a celebrated thoroughbred racehorse breeder. A daughter, Grace, married Cornelius Vanderbilt III, whose sister was married to prominent horseman Harry P. Whitney. In 1896, Wilson Jr. and Whitney bought the Saratoga Race Course. Together their horses won many important races, including the Toronto Cup Handicap, Belmont, and Preakness Stakes. Two other daughters married suitors of wealthy New York and Newport, Rhode Island, high-society families. When he died on November 26, 1910, Wilson was surrounded by family in his New York Fifth Avenue mansion, formerly owned by Boss Tweed, with a personal fortune of an estimated $40 million.[88]

A report on Wilson's purchase of Detroit's street railway companies in the *New York Times* on September 2, 1894, said Nevins made a "fine profit." Currie went unmentioned.[89] Wilson promptly exercised the Nevins option, assuming company debts totaling $3,250,000, while gaining control of 6,025 of the street railway company's 10,000 outstanding shares, paying $620,000 cash, leaving Hendrie with a stake perhaps as large as one-third. Waller, Cook, and all of the Detroit investors had bailed out, selling their stock to Wilson at losses of twenty-five cents on the dollar.[90]

Wilson went about quietly recruiting a new local leadership team, who could get a thirty-year renewal keeping five-cent fares over Mayor Pingree's objection. Wilson chose well. He tapped Democratic Congressman Tom Loftin Johnson of Cleveland with whom he made a speculative

Tom Loftin Johnson. Prints and Photographs Division, Library of Congress, LC-USZ62-41906.

Jere C. Hutchins. The photograph originally appeared in Robert B. Ross and George B. Catlin, *Landmarks of Detroit: A History of the City*, rev. Clarence M. Burton (Detroit: Evening News Association, 1898), 556.

one-fifth profit-sharing deal. An energetic and agreeable young man from the Illinois Central Railroad Company named Jere C. Hutchins was brought in to serve as vice president and general manager.

Some years later, Hutchins was sitting with Wilson, when a young man stuck his head through a crack in the door and said, "Good morning, Mr. Wilson. Do you wish to participate in the Morgan railway underwriting?"

"Yes," answered Wilson.

"How much, sir?"

"Half a million."

"All right, sir. Thank you, sir."

Hutchins, whose curiosity was excited by the methods of Wall Street in transactions of such magnitude, asked Wilson what the next step would be and how soon this half a million dollar matter would be concluded.

"I'll next hear from it in about a month when I am called upon to pay the sum I mentioned."

"Suppose, at the end of the month, you should not find it convenient to meet so large a payment?"

"Ah! In that case," said Wilson, "I could no longer live on Wall Street."[91]

Judge Taft Reversed

Just a few weeks later, on October 2, 1894, a three-judge panel of the U.S. Sixth Circuit Court of Appeals unanimously reversed Judge Taft.[92] The stunning nineteen-page opinion written by Circuit Judge Horace H. Lurton neatly sidestepped Detroit's corporate life argument entirely, ending any talk of settling the Thirty-Year War.

"These street railway acts directly confer upon the municipalities [the sovereign] power to grant such an easement of way in the streets as is requisite for the purposes to be accomplished. . . . without any expressed words of limitation," Lurton explained. Judge Lurton said the 1879 ordinance extending the consent for thirty years, therefore, was fully within Detroit's authority even though the street railway's corporate life ended in 1893 because the ordinance he loosely described as an easement could be assigned to another street railway company that had continuing life.[93]

"While, therefore, neither party supposed that it was in the power of the city council to extend the corporate life or corporate franchises of the Detroit City Railway Company beyond the term prescribed in the law which gave it birth, yet it was supposed and believed by each that the value of the extended term would consist of its assignability to a grantee endowed with the franchises essential to the enjoyment of the City's consent to the use of its streets for street railway purposes,"[94] Judge Lurton explained. He concluded:

> The evils to be apprehended from long grants of easements to such companies seem not to us to be such as to justify a constructive limitation on that account. The power to make an irrevocable contract giving an easement of some considerable duration is an inseparable incident in any scheme for furnishing such public facilities as a street railroad. The duration of such grants must be a question of discretion to be exercised by some public authority. That the exercise of that discretion should be left to the local government as a question of purely local interest seems most consistent with the proprieties of the case, and most in accord with the decentralizing policy so peculiar to the state of Michigan.[95]

The Street-Railway Act requirement for obtaining municipal consent did not itself expressly require Detroit to do so by entering into a franchise agreement—a bilateral contract—setting forth detailed terms and conditions and, more importantly, an expiration date. If a municipality consented by entering into a bilateral contract adopted as an ordinance setting its own expiration date beyond corporate life, Judge Lurton said, courts could not interfere because doing so would violate the protection against impairment of contracts. In sum, Judge Lurton's opinion told Mayor Pingree that the limit on corporate life set forth in the state constitution did not limit Detroit's authority to extend the duration of its consent by amending its bilateral contract with the Detroit City Railway Company.

At the time, nobody investigated whether there were any ties between Wilson and Judge Lurton, who had also been a Confederate army first lieutenant. They were from opposite sides of Tennessee, and their different roles in the Civil War would not have necessarily brought them together.[96] Judge Lurton was at least acquainted with Wilson, having decided a Tennessee Supreme Court case in 1889 in which R. T. Wilson & Company was a defendant.[97] Furthermore, Lurton practiced law and served as the leading banker in Clarksville, Tennessee, from 1878 to 1886, when Wilson was

Judge Horace H. Lurton. Harris and Ewing Collection, Prints and Photographs Division, Library of Congress, LC-DIG-hec-16450.

rebuilding Clarksville's railroad, the Louisville and Nashville.[98] Pingree was resourceful enough to have learned of their connections and to be suspicious.

"What reason these capitalists had for thinking the stock of a company whose franchises had already been declared void by one tribunal, and were not yet passed upon by the Appellate Court, a safe investment, will possibly never be publicly known," he said in his annual message delivered to the Common Council on January 8, 1895, before dropping the matter.

Pingree's next hopeless legal maneuver was political genius. He asked Democratic State Attorney General Adolphus A. Ellis to commence litigation seeking immediate relief ordering the railways removed anyway. To the great surprise of the people and Pingree's feigned anger, on October 23, 1894, Ellis, who had an otherwise rocky relationship with Mayor Pingree,[99] pointedly declined, saying he agreed with Judge Lurton that the easement of way to use Detroit streets for street railways extended by thirty years in 1879 was a protected constitutional property right owned by the Detroit Citizens Street Railway Company or its assignees until it expired in 1909. Ellis argued that he was, therefore, barred from filing new litigation because no good public purpose would be served by doing so. Consequently, Ellis was defeated for reelection a few weeks later by Kent County Republican Fred A. Maynard. Mayor Pingree piled on the lame duck Ellis, filing suit against him directly in the Michigan Supreme Court, which heard oral arguments on December 2, 1894. Pingree's lawsuit for an order of mandamus argued that Ellis had a clear legal duty to act on behalf of the city.

"If by any chance the Michigan Supreme Court should agree with the U.S. Court of Appeals, then

I shall advise an amendment of the street railroad act and submit a draft of a bill," Pingree told the Common Council in his annual message delivered just a few days before January 22, 1895, when the Michigan Supreme Court agreed with the U.S. Sixth Circuit Court of Appeals in a unanimous opinion refusing to compel the attorney general to take any action.[100]

Consequently, fully ousting the Detroit Citizens Street Railway Company from the streets would have to wait many years because the Grand River Street Railway Company's valuable franchise, which Wilson controlled, too, had been extended to December 31, 1915.

The Missouri Compromiser

When he arrived in Detroit, late in the afternoon of Election Day, November 6, 1894, Jere C. Hutchins read in the evening newspaper that an indignant mob had that morning stopped his new company's streetcars from operating in Highland Park by tearing up some railways.[101] The next morning, he would confront and resolve the Highland Park problem even while a much larger issue arose. Among other election results, a referendum on municipal ownership of street railway tracks was decided by Detroit's voters, winning by an overwhelming, 12,619-3,044.[102]

"Though named in honor of his maternal grandfather, the last two syllables of the first name were omitted, and all of his life his name was written and pronounced 'Jere,'" he explained, without expressly denying that his full legal name was Jeremiah.[103] His grandfather Dr. Jeremiah Chamberlain had been a Presbyterian minister of Scotch-Irish descent stationed in Bedford Springs, Pennsylvania. His great-grandfather Colonel James Chamberlain emigrated from Londonderry, Ireland, and served as an officer under President Washington in the Revolutionary War. In the early 1820s, Dr. Chamberlain went south and at Rodney, Mississippi, established Oakland College, for white men only. In 1851, a deranged student stabbed him to death and ended his own life by taking poison.[104] The college closed during the Civil War and reopened as a black-only, land-grant college named after Governor James L. Alcorn, who was a high-ranking Confederate general during the Civil War but who became a leading Republican scalawag favoring the end of slavery.

Fair-haired and clean-shaven, always pictured with his head held high and wearing a high-button wool jacket and trousers, starched collar, and subdued silk tie, Hutchins carried a calm, confident Southern gentleman's courtesy about him although he had twice won hair-raising gunfights. Hutchins was raised by an aristocratic family of the old South on a hemp plantation called Prairie Lea, about ten miles from Lexington on the Missouri River. His father was a native of Natchez, Mississippi. His grandfather Anthony Hutchins was a captain in the British army during the French and Indian War of the 1760s. He fought with Bouquet's Brigade against various Indian tribes led by Chief Pontiac at Detroit. At the conclusion of the war, Anthony Hutchins went back south, settling in Natchez, Missouri, building the family plantation.

Hutchins's father fought in the Confederate army in a state that was divided against itself. The great Missouri Compromise of 1820 had allowed the free state of Maine and the slave state of Missouri into the Union while otherwise forbidding slavery elsewhere in the former Louisiana Territory. Neighbors lined up against neighbors. Half of them volunteered to fight under Confederate General Sterling Price, and the other half joined the army of Union General Nathaniel Lyon, giving rise to severe bitterness that was not healed for many years.

A Federal cavalry captain captured Hutchins's father as he ate family breakfast at home on furlough. He was taken prisoner to Lexington. Some brief months later, Anthony Hutchins was paroled. Following President Lincoln's Emancipation Proclamation, all of their slaves disappeared, Hutchins said, leaving Prairie Lea to grow over in weeds. The family left the farm, reunited, and took a home in Lexington.

Hutchins joined a railroad construction company as a timekeeper and payroll clerk at age nineteen and, later, supervised field workers laying track and building bridges. He moved around from job to job during those railroad construction boom years in Missouri, Oklahoma, and Kansas, taking him finally at age twenty-three to Texas for five years where he went to work as a newspaper reporter and later editor of the *Waco Examiner*. He married in 1880 and rejoined the railroad construction business, again moving from project to project, eventually taking charge of building a railroad line between Vicksburg and Memphis financed by R. T. Wilson & Company. Hutchins rose to serve as general superintendent of railway for the Illinois Central Railroad Company from which Wilson tapped him for the Detroit job.

Hutchins needed all of his skills as Southern gentleman and railway manager to deal with the problems in Highland Park that immediately confronted him on his arrival in Detroit. Nothing much happened in Highland Park without at least Captain William H. Stevens's knowledge. He had bought at least 450 acres of virgin land in Greenfield Township, six miles north of Detroit along Woodward Avenue, the settlement once called Woodwardville but popularly renamed Whitewood for the spruce trees growing tall and thick north of a vast swamp separating it from Detroit. Stevens organized a village government, incorporated by the state legislature in 1889, that formally changed its name to Highland Park with a population of 450.

Stevens owned the two-story McAlpine Shoe Factory building at the corner of Woodward Avenue and Colorado Street where the village council held its meetings. Stevens and Frank Snow had gotten a street railway franchise from Greenfield Township to operate on Woodward Avenue, which was binding still within the village. Snow also was general manager of the East Detroit and Grosse Pointe Railway. Stevens put in three and a half miles of three-rail line north from the Detroit and Milwaukee Railroad crossing, where the Detroit City Railway Company had a transfer station. They started converting to overhead electric streetcars in 1889, losing money by the bucket every day because their overhead line ended two miles short of the village. The Detroit and Birmingham Plank Road Company, owned by the Hendrie family, had leveraged its rights along the center of Woodward Avenue by refusing to give Stevens the permission he needed to rebuild double tracks. They succeeded and their Detroit Suburban Railway Company bought him out in 1893. All hell broke loose because Detroit was paving Woodward Avenue from Pallister Avenue to the village of Highland Park and the railway tracks were on the west side of the road. Mayor Pingree wanted them moved to the center. Hendrie's plank road company refused to cooperate, so public works crews removed the rails and repaved, leaving a long unpaved strip down the middle of Woodward Avenue the newspapers called "Pig Lane."[105]

All service on the line was suspended. Detroit Suburban sold its powerhouse to the Detroit Electric Works with payments to be made from power usage. Detroit Suburban finished the overhead lines a month before Hutchins arrived and had the line operating again with new electric streetcars bearing the Detroit City Railway Company name. That started more trouble because the

Pingree rouses the armory mass meeting described by Jere C. Hutchins. The drawing originally illustrated "Twas Plain: The Feeling Against Dr. Duncan McLeod Shown Last Night at the Mass Meeting," *Detroit Free Press*, January 27, 1895, 1.

company no longer needed to transfer riders at the Grand Trunk station. Detroit Suburban posted new fare at ten cents from Highland Park, it being six miles distant from the Detroit City Railway line's five-cent fare. Before the suspension, Highland Park riders had been paying eight cents for a transfer ticket, and the agitation was immediate.[106]

Captain Stevens and his family had a large mansion on Woodward Avenue.[107] When calling at the Stevens house the next day, Hutchins would have been greeted at the doorway by a young maid speaking with a German accent. Mr. Stevens denied any personal knowledge of any recent troubling disturbances in the village but said he was well acquainted with two brothers, village council members, who could be of some assistance. He summoned them by telephone.

They arrived within ten minutes and told a story of street railway abuses; chief among the grievances was the recent fare increase to ten cents now charged to passengers boarding in Highland Park. The ordinance granting a franchise to the Highland Park Railway Company on July 13, 1886, to construct railways on Woodward Avenue stipulated a five-cent fare within Greenfield Township, but transfers into Detroit were a matter over which the township, therefore the village, had no power under the franchise or otherwise.[108]

Hutchins told them he had been there less than twenty-four hours, and he offered to meet with the Village Council in a spirit of fair adjustment. In the meantime, he said, repairs would be promptly made and service resumed and continued as though nothing had happened.

"Sounds reasonable," remarked Stevens.

"So it does," replied a brother.

"And there will be no further interference," added the other who took up the telephone. Following a few quick words, the conversation ended.[109]

Jere Hutchins described Mayor Pingree as a "man in the prime of a vigorous life, amiable, honest, and well-liked. . . . Pingree had first been elected as a conservative, but ambitious for further political honors and a born fighter, he had come to be a Tartar," Hutchins said. "The things said . . . about him from day-to-day were enough to fill the newspapers and to afford cartoonists the opportunities of a lifetime."[110]

Hutchins said he prepared himself for dealing with the mayor by attending what he called a protest rally at the armory, the city's largest hall, shortly after his arrival. "Just as one speaker was condemning him heatedly as a foe of the people and a demagogue of beastly proportions, Pingree forced his way through the crowd to the platform and to a position at the speakers side," Hutchins wrote.[111]

Both men tried to talk at the same time. The noise was simply terrific. Shouts or derision, catcalls, and the stamping of feet drowned all other sounds. After a time, the first speaker retired in disgust to the rear. The mayor stood facing the crowd alone. There was no cessation. The uproar became even louder. Above the din, Hutchins heard only shouts from the mayor.

> "I'm Pingree.
> "I'm a shoemaker.
> "I'm your mayor."

The exhausted crowd quieted and listened as Mayor Pingree, perspiration streaming down his cheeks, mouth flying open and shut, launched into a condemnation of George Hendrie, his son Strathearn Hendrie, and their alleged successors. "Pigs and Niggers," he called them for not giving the people three-cent fares.[112]

"Pingree believed the Hendries to be still in control behind the scenes. As a matter of fact, the Hendries had nothing to do with the new management, although they had not yet sold their stock. They eventually sold their stock through the offices of Cameron Currie, their young associate, to Wilson and Company."[113] All of the prominent local investors who had acquired majority control had already sold. "It was believed in the beginning that these men would escape criticism. But this proved a painful mistake. . . . It deeply pained most of them to see in the newspaper columns the stories he told of their delinquencies. Nor were they or their families flattered by the cartoons that also appeared in the public press. Not hard-boiled enough placidly to absorb this kind of punishment, they had been glad at the end of about three years of it and before Hutchins' arrival in Detroit to sell their stock for less than it cost them."[114]

Pingree rallied the crowd that evening against "Wall Street Sharks" and "Foreigners" taking over the city's street railways. "Pingree had listened in silence when told by Mr. Wilson that, conditioned upon the pledge that a first-class electric system should be immediately installed, the City in return should at once grant a new thirty-year franchise, with five cents as the minimum rate of fare. This suggestion and the fact that it came from Wall Street supplied further ammunition," Hutchins said.

> "Three-Cent Fares."
> "Wall Street Sharks!"
> "Foreigners!"

"They became joint catch phrases that were to go clanking down the pathway of time," Hutchins said. "The local malefactors had been bad enough, but the incoming sharpsters, pretending to have succeeded them, were even worse."[115]

The Three-Cent Lines

Just two weeks after Hutchins arrived, attorney Charles Flowers, a close friend of Mayor Pingree, appeared before the Common Council on November 20, 1894, with a petition from Albert and Greene Pack, Alpena lumbermen, and from Henry A. Everett and Edward W. Moore, Cleveland capitalists who already owned street railways in London, Toronto, Montreal, and Winnipeg. They would, Flowers said, build a competitive street railway company offering three-cent fares in Detroit.[116]

Mayor Pingree had easily persuaded them.[117] Confirmation of passenger-volume estimates Mayor Pingree obtained from the Detroit City Railway Company's former purchasing agent were crucial to convincing what became known as the Pack-Everett syndicate to accept the challenge of building an entirely new electric streetcar railway system in Detroit with three-cent fares despite lacking rights to operate on the five main roads designed by Judge Woodward. Instead, they would operate on sixty miles of secondary and, especially, crosstown streets of Warren, Forest, Fourteenth, Hastings, Sherman, Harper, Catherine (Madison), and others but free from any requirement for paving between the tracks. The former company insider, Andrew S. Gray, said he thought Hendrie had sold his stake in the company to Wilson and, therefore, saw no harm to his former boss in cooperating with Mayor Pingree.

Pingree made the most of the deal by leaking news of what was happening to the newspapers. "There is a big sensation on . . . for the council meeting to-night. . . . It is nothing more nor less than that a new street car company will to-night offer to the council an entirely new plan of street railway service for this city," the *Free Press* said. "His Honor, it appears, has given up the idea of fighting it out with the old company and their latest successors and gone out of town for a new company."[118]

The Common Council duly referred an ordinance granting consent proposed by Flowers to its Committee on Streets and Ordinances, which held a public hearing attended by more than two hundred people that began early in the afternoon and stretched late into the evening of November 26. Residents living along the proposed lines presented thirteen petitions urging approval. The newspapers and some aldermen expressed suspicions arising from the appearance at the hearing of Albert Johnson on behalf of the Detroit Citizens Street Railway Company, arguing against allowing competition. He was known to be an owner of a Cleveland street railway company along with Everett, so confusion reigned because the role of his brother, Congressman Tom Johnson, remained under wraps.

Moving quickly under pressure from Mayor Pingree, the Common Council met again on November 28. Its committee favorably reported the ordinance. The Detroit Citizens Street Railway Company again formally protested, reminding the Common Council that the 1862 ordinance gave it exclusive rights to the use of all city streets. "The Company, therefore, respectfully but earnestly protests against the adoption or the taking of any action by your Honorable Body granting any other person or corporation the right to construct street railway lines or routes on any of the routes of this city, without first giving the Company the opportunity to construct the same," Sidney Davy Miller wrote.

At a special meeting the next evening, the Common Council took up the ordinance for adoption, and the chief opponent was Alderman Vernor, who objected that it relieved the Pack-Everett syndicate of paving between the tracks. He failed to convince anyone else and it passed, 29-1. Vernor might have protested that the costly paving concession did not actually get three-cent fares but rather an agreement for eight tickets for twenty-five cents from 5:45 A.M. to 8 P.M., and six tickets for twenty-five cents the balance of the day. Single fares would remain five cents but with universal transfers. Nonetheless, on December 4, the Common Council rejected Republican Alderman John A. Fisher's motion to reconsider by simple voice vote—Fisher, Vernor, and Jacob were heard objecting—and Mayor Pingree signed the ordinance in his office within minutes. "I cannot refrain from tendering my hearty congratulations to the Common Council and to the people of Detroit on the passage of a street car franchise on terms for which we have been fighting for the last four years," he declared.[119] The Pack-Everett syndicate incorporated as the Detroit Railway and started construction on December 13, 1894.[120]

Johnson later insisted that he had not tried to block the thirty-year franchise obtained by his three-cent fare competitor, despite the appearance of his brother against it. "My brother Albert and R. T. Wilson of New York, a man high up in the business and financial world, had purchased the street railways of Detroit, an old broken down horse car system with a few worn-out electrically equipped cars," Johnson wrote in an autobiography, *My Story*, published in 1911. "When I was defeated for Congress they knew I would soon be free for business again and came to me with a proposal that I undertake the management of this road on a profit-sharing basis. I didn't want to do it and I told them I was thinking of quitting business, but they insisted. What finally induced me to accept was not so much the pecuniary reward, which the undertaking promised, as the chance to build unhampered by lack of funds a modern street railroad in a growing city. This looked like something worth doing."[121]

Johnson's explanation failed to mention that since 1884 he had owned the nation's largest manufacturer of streetcar rails, the Johnson Company of Johnstown, Pennsylvania, and that in 1894 he was building one of the country's largest steel mills at Lorraine, Ohio. He invented and patented the Johnson girder rail from which he would profit handsomely by competition in Detroit. "I stipulated to Mr. Wilson and my brother that I was not to be expected to try to defeat the mayor's three-cent fare project except by improved facilities on our lines. I was to so remodel our railroad that it should have the advantage on its merits, rather than to go before the Common Council and engage in a scramble and put a lot of obstacles in the way of the Everett grant. Neither the Mayor nor Mr. Everett knew anything of this agreement of course."[122]

With Johnson's brazen two-faced strategy playing out, Hutchins, the practical day-to-day manager, saw trouble coming. "The rates were low enough to satisfy Pingree and to cause a sneeze of disgust throughout the streetcar world," Hutchins said. "Even the projectors knew the rates were too low but they hoped to gain control of all lines in Detroit and later effect a satisfactory compromise. Anyhow, there was the devil to pay."[123]

"He had kept the New York office fully informed," an overwhelmed Hutchins said while he awaited Johnson's arrival from Washington, D.C. "He now urged that the company's Grand River line should be immediately electrified—wintertime though it was—as an earnest of the company's good intentions and that franchise extension and rates should be left to the future. This policy was adopted."[124]

Hutchins undertook the project despite severe weather conditions in Detroit during the winter of 1894 when extremely low temperatures and heavy snow made construction unusually difficult. "Nevertheless, supports for a transmission line were dug into five or six feet of frozen earth; the rails, which happened to be heavy enough to support the weight of electric cars were properly bonded, some additional power was hired, a full equipment of nobby electric cars that had been built for spring delivery to a company in another city was secured, and, on a zero day in February, horses were withdrawn, and the new service started on Grand River amid the tinkling of sleigh bells and shouting of a multitude of delighted citizens," Hutchins said. "Press and public expressed gratification."[125]

Tom Johnson

After final adjournment of the U.S. Congress on March 4, 1895, Tom Johnson came to Detroit accompanied by Antoine B. DuPont Jr. One branch of the famous DuPont family that built a financial empire on gunpowder, chemicals, and rubber had settled in Louisville, Kentucky, where Johnson managed its electric railway designed by Thomas Edison for a national exposition from 1883 to 1887. The railway took visitors around the grounds through tunnels of incandescent lights. The sprawling site of the exposition, today's Louisville Central Park, was donated by the DuPont family to the city in 1904.

DuPont's task in Detroit was the engineering and building of the citywide $6 million, ninety-seven-mile electrical system for which he earned the praise of everyone involved. Street railway companies throughout the United States adopted his many innovations and inventions, including a new electric heating and ventilating system for large streetcars. He enjoyed such good employee relations that the one-thousand-member Amalgamated Association of Street and Railway Employees of America held a farewell banquet in his honor when he moved from Detroit to St. Louis in 1900.[126] "When he came to Detroit, DuPont was thirty years old, tall, and athletic," Hutchins said. "Careless of dress and amiable, though a bit lacking in diplomacy, DuPont possessed an inventive mind and was a skillful mechanical and electrical engineer."[127]

Johnson was the son of an impoverished Confederate army colonel who lost his one-hundred-slave plantation in Beaver Bayou, Arkansas, and moved to Louisville following the Civil War. Tom

Johnson was barely fifteen years old when he went to work in 1869 for a Louisville street railway company owned by two members of the wealthy DuPont family of which he was a distant relative by marriage. In 1873, Johnson invented a glass-and-metal streetcar fare receptacle. In earlier years, conductors would walk around the streetcar, collecting fares by hand, ringing them up on an overhead fare register mounted on one of the bulkheads near the ceiling. This system worked fine but did lead to a problem the industry called "knocking down"—conductors who pocketed instead of ringing up fares as collected. Many street railway companies resorted to hiring spotters. Johnson's glass fare box, hand-cranked by drivers as each passenger boarded, eliminated the need for conductors and spotters. With his fare box earning, Johnson bought street railway companies, first in Indianapolis, then in Cleveland, and later in Brooklyn, St. Louis, and Johnstown. In 1883, he opened steel mills to manufacture street railways in Pennsylvania. Johnson served two lackluster terms in the U.S. House of Representatives before losing reelection in 1894. "Past his middle forties, short of stature, rotund, weighing more than 250 pounds, quick on his feet and energetic, Tom Johnson was intelligent, resourceful, instant in decisions, a good speaker, well up in street railway manipulation, and a keen politician,"[128] Hutchins said, the description of someone who never did get to know him personally.

Johnson told the press that he came to Detroit prepared for the next battle in the Thirty-Year War. "It's for blood," he announced. "Somebody is going to get skinned and skinned thoroughly. This is a fight for gore, and it will be carried right along to the finish."[129] Johnson was much less combative and much more generous to Mayor Pingree in his autobiography.

> His attitude at our first meeting was very hostile. When he had stated two or three ultimatums of street railway policy to which I agreed he was greatly surprised but still skeptical. There were plenty of influences at work to prejudice Mayor Pingree against me. The newspapers added to this prejudice by saying that I was coming to Detroit to hypnotize him and nothing made him so mad as that. As we proceeded to tear up old tracks and rebuild the road complying with the mayor's suggestions as to construction, doing the very things the City had been unable to compel the former owners to do and asking no favors in return, the mayor commenced to melt a little. We spent $6 million in cash on that railroad and the result was the best electrically equipped street railroad in existence anywhere.
>
> When some of the councilmen who were known to be friends of the old system told the mayor I had advised them to vote with him for the three-cent grant and had advised against imposing any hardship on Everett and his friends, he was thoroughly mystified. When we met, he asked me in his frank manly way to explain my attitude. I told him the City needed additional street railway facilities. It was evident our company couldn't get any concessions and that the new company ought to have them. My reason for wanting the grants made to the new company on as fair a basis as possible was purely selfish, for it would be only a question of time until the old company would acquire them. To impose unfair conditions in the new grants would be simply putting burdens on our own backs when these lines came to be absorbed by ours. This amused the mayor and he called my attention to a provision in the grant, which said that if the new company should consolidate with or sell out to the old the grant became void. I replied that notwithstanding that provision or any other they could frame into words nothing could prevent us from acquiring the other railroad. This rather staggered Mr. Pingree and in his childlike way he asked, "Mr. Johnson, explain that to me, won't you?"

> I will not consolidate with the new company or make any attempt to buy. But some day I will have a friend of mine down in New York or West Virginia or somewhere else, whom I shall call Smith for convenience, acquire the stock of the railroad by purchase. Mr. Mayor, if you attempt to put in a provision to prevent Smith from doing this, you will simply defeat your own ends, for railroad stocks to be useful must be saleable.[130]

It was evident to Johnson, if not Mayor Pingree, that the manner in which Judge Woodward had laid out Detroit in 1805 would naturally compel the merging of the new three-cent lines with a franchise not expiring until 1924 into the old five-cent system with its franchise on Woodward's roads expiring in 1909.

"In laying out the plan of the city, much was due to splendid judgment of Judge Woodward," wrote Paul Leake, a former financial editor of the *Free Press* in 1912.

> The Judge, in laying out the plan, gave rise to the "Hub" idea. . . . Taking the City Hall as a pivotal spot, Judge Woodward laid out the city in an elliptical form, the center being the City Hall. The streets reaching into what was then the country, but which is now well within the city limits, radiating from the common center of the City Hall and the Campus Martius. This design simplified matters for the street railway builders and promoters. The main arteries of travel from this common center were East Jefferson, Grand River, Woodward, Gratiot, Michigan, and Fort. In the development of the streetcar service, naturally these main thoroughfares were utilized. This was done because they were the shortest distances between the terminal points and the center of the city. . . . In considering the present street car situation in Detroit, the fact must be taken into consideration that none of the so-called three-cent lines under the Pingree franchise hit any of these main radial streets, save in their entrance to the center of the city.[131]

CHAPTER 7

Competitive Fight Really Begins

Representative Fisk's Preemptive Legislation

Albert Pack was a former Republican member of the state legislature widely known throughout the state. He went back to Lansing for the beginning of the Michigan Legislature's 1895 session seeking passage of preemptive legislation that would permit his new company to use any of the railway tracks of Tom Johnson's company within one mile of Grand Circus Park, breaking Johnson's monopoly on service to Woodward and Jefferson Avenues through the heart of downtown Detroit. In a competitive fight at the scale underway between Johnson and the Pack-Everett syndicate, each side calls on all the help they can get against each other not only from judges but also from legislators because reducing prices and increasing service is financially ruinous. While Johnson filed suit in the Wayne County Circuit Court claiming exclusive rights, Pack went lobbying the state legislature against them.

On February 19, 1895, at Pack's request, Representative Charles H. Fisk of Detroit introduced House Bill No. 815, and Senator F. Markham Briggs of Plymouth introduced identical legislation, Senate Bill No. 319. In the days to come, Johnson hired Schuyler S. Olds, a legendary Republican railroad lawyer and lobbyist, who put Senator James McMillan's Republican machine to work on state legislators. "Although Hazen Pingree had come to expect just about anything from Senator McMillan, he was surprised this maneuver because McMillan, as chairman of the Senate Committee for the District of Columbia, had permitted the multiple use of street railway lines on Pennsylvania Avenue. Pingree snorted: 'Vote for papa! What the people of Detroit want cuts no figure if it happens to conflict in some way with papa's financial interests,'" Melvin G. Holli wrote.[1]

McMillan's political influence had been demonstrated on January 15, 1895, when the only Democratic Party member of the state house of representatives, Representative John Donovan of Bay City, crossed over and voted for McMillan, making him the first and only person from Michigan ever unanimously elected to a full six-year term in the U.S. Senate. Donovan explained that the Democratic Party candidate, Edwin F. Uhl, had prevailed upon him to vote instead for McMillan. The house of representatives responded warmly, adopting a resolution extending "the thanks of the Republican members of this House to Hon. John Donovan for his courtesy in voting for Hon. James McMillan."

"The ensuing fight conducted in the lobbies and committee rooms at Lansing, and lasting several weeks, was led by Pack on the one side and by Tom Johnson on the other side," Hutchins said. "Pingree backed Pack dutifully but not enthusiastically. Many of Michigan's most prominent men took some part for or against."[2]

"'I don't know what to do,' a desperate Michigan legislator muttered. 'If I vote against the bill, the friends of the Packs say they will scalp me. If I vote for it, I shall be accused of ingratitude to McMillan. I'll get the worst of it either way. It was wrong to bring politics into this matter, and the Republican Party will suffer, no matter which way it goes.' Representative William E. Rice protested, 'I want to ask if Senator McMillan owns this legislature. We paid our debt to him by re-electing him Senator. . . . He ought not to try and coerce us into opposing this bill because he may be interested in it,'" Holli wrote.[3]

On April 4, Representative Fisk read at length and placed in the *House Journal* a petition from "R. H. Traver, Hunter, Glenn & Hunter, R. H. Fyfe . . . and several thousand citizens and business houses in the City of Detroit" asking for passage of his bill. The petition began:

> The undersigned citizens of Detroit respectfully petition your honorable body that favorable consideration may be given to a certain bill, introduced by Representative Fisk of Wayne county, in the House of Representatives, and by Senator Briggs, also of Wayne county, in Senate, which bill, by its terms, enables one street railway company to condemn a right of way over portions of the tracks of another company, where the public necessity demands, and to make use of the said tracks upon the payment of such damages as may be awarded by the jury in condemnation proceedings.

The petition explained that "a new street railway company has been granted franchises in over forty miles of streets; but it is unable to brings passengers into the business part of said City owing to the fact that the Detroit Citizens Street Railway Company is already in possession of all the main thoroughfares with its tracks, and the construction of new tracks for the new company, in said streets, would leave no room between the curbs for driving purposes."

The bill had been referred to the House Committee on City Corporations of which Fisk was chairman, a signal to opponents that the bill was on a fast track for passage. Committee debate opened early in the evening on April 16, a meeting the *Free Press* described as "Hotter than Ever."[4] On April 17, Fisk won a 5-2 committee vote to report to the floor with a substitute bill that also required the Detroit Citizens Street Railway Company to share use of its key terminal at Woodward and Jefferson Avenues with Pack's Detroit Railway Company.[5] Supporters defeated a motion to postpone action for one week sought by the opposition leader, Representative Henry H. Alpin of West Bay City. Pack and Fisk were moving quickly, and they secured a vote on adopting the bill by special order at ten o'clock the next morning, April 18. Overnight, telegrams went out to members from McMillan's son, William, saying: 'Knowing you are a friend of father's, you will vote against the bill.'"[6]

Promptly at ten o'clock in the morning, on Fisk's motion, the house went into Committee of the Whole, under which the entire legislative body operates informally to consider bills. Speaker William D. Gordon of Midland turned the gavel over to Representative John W. Norman of Lexington. The bill emerged from the Committee of the Whole without further amendment and with a favorable recommendation, indicating a high likelihood of final passage. Fierce debate against the Pack bill consumed two hours, during which opponents twisted the arms of wavering members before the house recessed for lunch.

Speaker Gordon opened the session at two o'clock sharp, and the argument continued into the early evening, interrupted twice by previously scheduled special order votes, which were promptly postponed on motions by Representative Fisk.

Finally, the house voted against the Pack bill, 40-52, a remarkable turn of events.[7] Fisk, having joined the majority, moved for immediate reconsideration. Representative George G. Covell of Traverse City moved to table. During a calling of the roll, Covell withdrew his motion, confident Fisk would lose. The house then divided equally over reconsideration, 47-47, a breathtaking defeat by the closest possible margin. The key votes cast came from Representatives Eugene Hicks of Brighton and Edmund S. Amidon of Sturgis, who reversed their earlier favorable votes. Two other representatives, George B. Davis of Utica and John Baird of Zilwaukee, absent from the first roll call, also voted against reconsideration.

"Finally, when floor tactics and speech making, in which nearly every legislator had his say, were over, and a vote was taken," Hutchins said, "Tom Johnson's consummate skill had won the battle. Pack lost by eight votes. Thus ended that chapter."[8] Johnson, however, had not himself won the battle. "One could almost hear the crack of the party whip as the bill was defeated," a newspaper reporter remarked.[9]

"We would have easily won our fight for terminal facilities on Woodward Avenue," declared Albert Pack, "had not the great influence of Senator McMillan and control of public offices and the active work of his lieutenants, been exerted to defeat us. Of course his wishes had great weight with a legislature, many members of which had been personally assisted by him in their election last fall. I cannot recall another instance in the history of the state where a United States senator's name and influence have been so extensively used to defeat a measure, even though the senator had some small personal interest in the matter."[10]

"The Citizens Co. won't get very much from me," Pingree told the *Free Press*. "I have said all along that Senator McMillan owns the legislature of Michigan, and would do what he pleased about the bill."[11]

When Does Exclusive Really Mean Exclusive?

The Detroit Citizens Street Railway Company suit against the city defending its monopoly on Detroit streets argued directly from the language of the original street railway ordinance approved on November 24, 1862. The Detroit City Railway Company was "*exclusively* authorized to construct and operate railways . . . as may from time to time be fixed and determined by vote of the common council of said city of Detroit" (emphasis added). The ordinance also granted a separate more specific privilege to construct and operate on all other streets "provided, the corporation does not assent in writing, within thirty days after the passage of said resolution of the Council, ordering the formation of new routes, then the Common Council may give the privilege to any other company to build such route."

In addition, section 34 of the Street-Railway Act provided that "all corporations formed for such purposes shall have the *exclusive right to use and operate any street railways constructed, owned, or held by them*." The Street-Railway Act further provided that "no such corporation shall be authorized to construct a railway under this act through the streets of any town or city without the consent of the municipal authorities of such town or city and under such regulations and *upon such terms and conditions as said authorities may from time to time prescribe*" (emphasis added).[12]

Anyone reading all of those words would pause only briefly before concluding that they granted an exclusive right to install and operate horse-drawn streetcars not only on the specifically designated Detroit streets specifically confirmed by the ordinance granting its consent in 1862 but a first option to do so on all other streets, too. The legislators who adopted the Street-Railway Act, the original railway company incorporators who sought Detroit's consent, and the mayor and aldermen who granted it, all reasonably understood that the Detroit City Railway Company should face no competition for passengers if it agreed to provide service on streets demanded by notice from the city.

Remarkably, the Wayne County Circuit Court refused to grant a preliminary injunction, and construction by the Detroit Railway Company continued while the lawsuit was being argued. On March 2, 1896, the circuit court ruled against Johnson, who sought review by the Michigan Supreme Court, which, on July 28, 1896, fully agreed in a unanimous opinion written by Judge Robert M. Montgomery.[13] Somehow, neither the plain language of the Street-Railway Act nor the ordinance and the persuasive legal arguments made against competition persuaded even one judge of the supreme court, over which Senator McMillan exercised considerable reelection influence.

"As a judge, Montgomery was exceedingly painstaking," said supreme court historian George I. Reed. "On any doubtful question, he invariably supplemented the briefs and arguments of counsel by the most rigid examination of the law of the case before him, by a thorough search of the authorities and in the light of his own reason."[14] Montgomery's opinion in *Detroit Citizens Street Railway Company v. City of Detroit*, however, is not an example of such painstaking research and writing. His legal analysis of the Street-Railway Act was singularly unpersuasive. "We think the act in question cannot be construed as conferring the power upon the common council to grant such a privilege," he wrote. "Certainly, there is no express grant of the right to confer exclusive privileges, nor do we think that there is any clear implication of any such power arising out of the *terms* of the act" (emphasis added).[15]

Montgomery comfortably failed to explain his reasoning but rather stated nothing more than a bald conclusion. He never addressed what exclusive right the street railway company obtained by the specific language of section 34 or by Detroit's contractual agreement to a first option if not a privilege against competitors such as the so-called three-cent company building forty miles of new railway tracks across Detroit never first offered to the Detroit Citizens Street Railway Company.[16]

Montgomery conceded that "under our constitution the sovereign power over all public streets and highways . . . is taken from the state legislature, and distributed among the townships, cities, and villages of the state."[17] However, he insisted, following the *Charles River Bridge* case,

> As the power to grant an exclusive privilege was not expressly conferred, it was not to be implied. Indeed, the argument in favor of the necessity that the power to grant exclusive privileges be lodged

> somewhere would apply with substantially the same force in case of a delegation of power, which the legislature may exercise directly, as in a case where the power is conferred upon local authorities as the only means of granting an easement. . . . One very solid ground upon which the cases which hold that authority of a municipality to grant an exclusive privilege is not to be inferred in the absence of an express grant is that a franchise of that nature is in restraint of free competition.[18]

The Street-Railway Act, however, expressly conferred on the Detroit City Railway Company at least an "*exclusive right* to use and operate any street railways constructed, owned, or held by them . . . under such regulations and *upon such terms and conditions as said authorities may from time to time prescribe*" (emphasis added). Judge Montgomery never addressed this broad legislative grant in construing the Street-Railway Act. To the contrary, he concluded that the city nonetheless lacked express authority from the state legislature to agree that its consent would exclude competitors. The ruling demonstrated to the city and its street railway companies that any exclusive franchise would never find support in the supreme court without changes to the state constitution explicitly allowing exclusive franchises to be granted by municipalities. It was wrongly decided despite the U.S. Supreme Court's agreement on subsequent appeal by Johnson.[19]

Cooperating Competitors

On July 7, 1895, the Detroit Railway Company inaugurated its so-called three-cent fares on Warren and Forest Avenues. Mayor Pingree himself took charge of its new overhead electric streetcar wearing a motorman's cap to the delight of hundreds gathered along the route. Invited aldermen followed in a ceremonial second car. Some spectators threw bouquets of flowers into the mayor's passing streetcar, and he was so busy waving to the crowd that he almost ran down a herd of cows at Riopelle Street.[20] Pingree had become a pioneer in the low-fare movement. Street railway expert Delos Wilcox said, "This franchise was the earliest important low-fare ordinance granted by any American city."[21]

By the end of the year, the Detroit Railway Company was offering three-cent fares on all the crosstown and Belle Isle lines, including Catherine, Sherman, Fourteenth, Oakland, Porter, and Mount Elliott Streets, and Jere Hutchins had made a good friend in Albert Pack. They often met to talk, at first banteringly and later seriously, about the street railway business, Hutchins said. On several occasions, they went off to New York together. Hutchins said it was plain to both of them that the logic of the Detroit situation demanded cooperation.

So, for example, on April 9, 1895, the Common Council adopted and Mayor Pingree signed an amendment to the Detroit Railway Company franchise, which, buried among a host of route changes, subject to agreement from the Detroit Citizens Street Railway Company, authorized "joint use of the tracks extending southerly from State Street on Woodward Avenue to the Detroit River with convenient loop lines enabling it to reach the foot of Woodward by its entire system of tracks and cars." This simple clause, facilitating cooperation between competitive rivals on the most crucial stretch of downtown Woodward Avenue, would have unanticipated consequence upon expiration of the old Detroit City Railway Company franchise in 1909. A few weeks later, on June 4, 1895, the Detroit Railway Company obtained the city's consent to construct double tracks

Mayor Pingree takes the motorman position for an inaugural ride on the new three-cent streetcar. Courtesy of the Research Library of Kenneth E. Schramm.

along Abbott Street from Eighth to Second Streets for the joint construction and use of the two companies at the option of the Detroit Citizens Street Railway Company. The joint arrangement was amended by the city at the request of both companies on August 13, 1895, to apply to Abbott and Porter Streets between Trumbull and Michigan Avenues.

"Before I got through with the Detroit enterprise, Pingree and I became warm friends," Johnson said. "One night after a supper together in my room we talked for a long time over our cigars."

> An ordinance was pending granting our lines a double track privilege [on Trumbull Avenue] where there was now a single track. "Of course, Johnson, I'm going to veto that ordinance if it passes; but I don't know why. The people out that way all want it; it seems like a necessary improvement, but I'm against it. I wish you'd tell me what's wrong with it."
>
> I said there wasn't much wrong with it but that if I were a member of the Common Council, I'd see Tom Johnson in the hot place before I'd vote for it. The next day at a committee meeting Pingree made a speech against the ordinance and when he said, "If I tell you what a man said to me last night, not one of you will dare to vote for this measure," I suspected what was coming. He repeated my exact words and appealed to me to verify them, which, of course, I did. The ordinance didn't get a vote, not one.
>
> If anybody but Pingree had done that, I should have resented it. He hadn't promised not to use my word against me but I never dreamed that he would hold me up to public ridicule in that fashion.

> Yet I couldn't resent it in him. He said afterwards that he was in a mighty tight place and that he had to do it because he didn't know what else to do.[22]

Johnson said he came to admire the man he was up against in the Thirty-Year War because they were so much alike. "Pingree was charged with being a political boss, but he wasn't one, for a political boss is a man whose word is his capital and it must be absolutely good," Johnson said. "Pingree was a political idol. He was always in a fight and always on the popular side. Thoroughly honest and trustworthy except when he was in a political contest, then, as he said of himself, he never hesitated to promise the same place to more than one man. Once before a whole roomful of people he stated that he was out of ammunition, for he had promised every job at least twice."[23]

Johnson, nonetheless, signed an agreement with the Detroit Railway Company allowing it to operate streetcars on the north track along a section of Michigan Avenue from Griswold to Porter across to Second, and on the south track from Griswold to Abbott across to Fourth. The companies went to the Common Council to confirm the deal on October 4, 1895.[24] Anticipating further trouble from Johnson, before Pingree left Detroit to attend a national convention of the Grand Army of the Republic, he had sought pledges from aldermen to resist Johnson's continuing pleas. In Pingree's absence, nonetheless, Johnson moved quickly. He promised the Common Council:

> In view of some criticism in regard to the ordinance recently adopted by a unanimous vote of your honorable body, and afterwards vetoed by his honor, the Mayor, permit us to say by the authority of our board of directors that we hereby agree if the ordinance should be passed over the Mayor's veto, and in consideration thereof, we will accept the same within ten days, and we agree that while operating under our present grants and any amendments thereto, to sell tickets entitling passengers to six rides for twenty-five cents, and good on all lines owned by this company within the city limits, full privilege of transfers.[25]

When he returned, Pingree learned that Johnson had, thus, won adoption of the Trumbull Avenue ordinance over acting mayor William Richert's veto and secured a new Baker Street ordinance, too, which remained subject to veto. Discouraged by the Common Council's backsliding, Pingree signed the Baker Street ordinance. Pingree said he was particularly upset that a majority of the aldermen had accepted Johnson's workingmen's fare promise rather than writing it into the ordinance. Pingree warned them again that Johnson's promises were worthless. Mayor Pingree grew more suspicious and then angry as rumors grew in the days ahead of the November election in 1895 of a citywide takeover by the Detroit Citizens Street Railway Company. Hutchins explained what happened. He boarded a night train and went up to Alpena to visit Albert Pack and his wife on a long weekend.

"As out of the clear sky, in the late afternoon," Hutchins recalled that Pack asked him a startling question.

"Would you take charge of our lines as a director and as vice-president and general manager?"

After only a moment's consideration, Hutchins eagerly replied. "I'll confer by wire with New York and let you know tomorrow."

Hutchins only said that Richard T. Wilson encouraged him to use own judgment. Pack wired his directors to call a meeting. The next day they went back to Detroit together, and Pack's board elected Hutchins.[26]

Detroit's Last Horse-Driven Streetcar

Just after three o'clock on a rainy Saturday afternoon, November 9, 1895, a few days after Pingree's reelection trouncing of Democratic Party nominee Samuel H. Godfrey, a crowd gathered at Monroe and Chene Streets. Detroit's last horse-drawn streetcar, No. 10, pulled forward. The two-horse team turned onto Monroe and stopped. Signs covered each side of the old streetcar: "The Last Horse Car." The horsecar pulled onto Woodward Avenue where it stopped in front of city hall surrounded by a vast array of umbrellas. The well-coached Pingree & Smith Company band played "Johnny, Get Your Gun" to the crowd's special amusement.[27] After a brief speech, Hutchins conducted a mock auction of the two horses, which were unhitched and led away. Hutchins announced a $100 donation to a relief fund established by Mayor Pingree, who failed to attend. Ceremonies continued under a steady rain. The last horse-drawn streetcar was attached to an electric car for a ceremonial last ride on Woodward Avenue up to Mayor Pingree's home less than two miles away. Someone stole the bell rope and then the bell disappeared. One of the passengers removed one of the many ceiling advertisements of Detroit's leading merchants. Other riders joined, ripping from their fastenings other ads from pill manufacturers throughout the country. Spectators started pulling off the outside ads and then punched in the sides. By the time it reached Pingree's residence and turned around, all of the windows had been smashed, the platform roofs were broken, the seats were removed, and the doors were missing. Nothing but the frame remained when the streetcar returned to the carbarn. "Even if its passing was marked with destruction it also recalled the fact that Detroit is becoming a great and more magnificent city and that the day for slow travel has passed from the City of the Straits," said the *Evening News*.[28]

Pingree's Bold Stunt

Johnson decided to demonstrate to Mayor Pingree what he was capable of doing if a thirty-year franchise was not forthcoming from his administration. On November 19, 1895, he announced that six tickets for twenty-five cents with universal transfers during all hours as he had promised to the Common Council would no longer be available. Outside workingmen's fare hours, all riders, instead, he decided, would be charged five cents as permitted by the terms of the original ordinances. Johnson initiated his new policy five days later, after recalling all six for twenty-five-cent tickets from conductors and sending them new strips of five for twenty-five tickets that had to be separated during workingmen's fare hours, beginning on Sunday, November 24, eliminating twenty thousand free transfers daily.[29] Pingree called for a public boycott of the Detroit Citizens Street Railway Company. He argued that the company should be driven from the streets as another "relic of barbarism."

One thousand employees at Parke, Davis & Company, joined by men at the Ideal Manufacturing Company, initiated petitions condemning Johnson and pledging not to use the Detroit Citizens Street Railway Company lines.[30] Conductors reported that riders had refused to pay the extra fares

Detroit's last horse-driven streetcar. The drawing originally illustrated "Last Horse Car," *Detroit Free Press*, November 10, 1895, 23.

and vowed to walk.[31] One of Detroit's newspapers called Johnson a cunning, unscrupulous schemer. Holli wrote, "His business methods are treacherous and political methods are shady. . . . He has recently attempted to hold up our citizens in broad daylight in order to get revenge on Pingree, the one man who stood like a rock of adamant between Johnson's greed and the People's Rights."[32] The *Free Press* warned Johnson that if he was using the fare increase to drive Pingree into granting him a new thirty-year franchise, "he may as well abandon the hope of doing anything of the kind. It was upon a franchise extension that the original warfare began. . . . If that is really what he means—as is pretty plainly intimated—he is playing directly into Mayor Pingree's hands."[33]

Mayor Pingree's next move was political street theater. Even though Johnson's streetcars passed his Woodward Avenue home, he walked through rain and slush several blocks to ride the three-cent Detroit Railway line. "Going to come down that way every morning," he told a gathering of newspaper reporters on November 24. "Not quite so near, but it's all right. Good service. Got a seat. Warm cars. No smell of gas from the stoves. No old rattletrap cars such as Tom Johnson runs."[34] That same morning, L. S. Paige, a manager for the *Evening News* described how he had boarded a streetcar on Johnson's line and received a single ticket and twenty cents change when he tried to buy six tickets for a quarter.

"What does this mean?" he asked.

"Straight five cent fare this morning," replied the conductor.

"Give me back that five cents and stop at the next corner," demanded Page.

The conductor obeyed.[35]

The Detroit Railway's three-cent lines reported passenger traffic up 35 percent by November 26 and 50 percent the next day, when it was carrying an additional 11,800 fares daily. "The company gained no advantage," confessed Hutchins. "On the contrary, so many deserted the lines that revenues fell off materially and the rival company benefited."[36]

A few weeks later, on December 13, Mayor Pingree himself rounded up a squad of newspaper reporters and went out with a quarter to buy six workingmen's fare tickets. This was high political street theater. That morning, instead, the conductor, H. H. Ballard, had let him ride free. The conductor was suspended by the company pending investigation. "Ballard is not in such a terrible hole as it seemed," said the *Free Press*. "Mayor Pingree will get him a job on the Detroit Railway if he loses the one he now has. In case he does not get that job, the mayor is able to get a City Hall position, as has been done for other men that suffered in the Pingree cause."[37]

That evening, a *Free Press* reporter said a colored conductor, J. P. Anderson, greeted Pingree at the Detroit Opera House crossing of the Woodward Avenue line.

"Good Lawd! There comes Mayor Pingree!"

"Got any six-for-a-quarter tickets?"

"Good evening, Mayor Pingree," Anderson said. "Fare, please."

"Here I have twenty-five cents: give me six tickets."

Anderson laughed and reached for the quarter. Mayor Pingree would not let go.

"Oh, come now, Mr. Pingree, I cannot sell you any tickets. Please don't make me any trouble," Anderson begged.

"I don't want to make you any trouble, but I do want to see if Tom Johnson is bluffing," Mayor Pingree replied and turned to others on the rear platform. "Any of you people want to ride with me on six-tickets-for-a-quarter?"

"Now, Mr. Pingree, you either have to pay your fare or get off. The man you rode down with this morning was laid off because he did not collect your fare. I do not want to put you off but I must if you insist."

Ed E. Kane, a lawyer who had a flare for getting publicity and an office in the Moffat Building, 723 Jefferson Avenue, generously offered to pay the mayor's fare. Pingree refused. Anderson went forward and returned with the motorman who carried a menacing detachable motor lever in his hand.

"You refuse to sell me six tickets for twenty-five cents and order me off the car if I will not pay five cents; do you?"

"Yes!"

"All right, I will get off."

Pingree turned and stepped off the platform, the crowd applauded, and Anderson chuckled to himself.[38]

The newspaper stories the next day were a sensation across Detroit. Overnight, ridership on Johnson's streetcars dropped precipitously. The episode pushed Mayor Pingree into issuing an angry proclamation on December 14, 1895, which gave voice to growing sentiment among riders of Detroit's streetcars that would set the course for coming events in the Thirty-Year War. "For no accountable reasons the rates had been raised in the face of a plainly implied contract to the contrary," he said. "The fares were raised against the will of the public. The people have the right

. . . to tender twenty-five cents for six tickets, and if that fare, which has prevailed for thirty years, is refused, then to claim the right to ride until such tender is accepted."

Mayor Pingree added to his proclamation in plain and simple words a profound conclusion arising from his four years of personal and political experience with Detroit's street railway companies that marked a striking evolution in his populist thinking. Another generation of Detroit political leaders and streetcar riders would continue to rally around his "three-cent fare" political slogan without understanding the obvious implication of what Mayor Pingree had come to differently realize about private, corporate ownership of Detroit's street railways. "A street railway is primarily for the convenience of the public and not for private profit making," he said.

Plummeting fare box collections persuaded Johnson to abandon his fare hike on December 31. Not only had he been forced to rescind his five-cent fare but he had lost what little public goodwill he had gained since coming to Detroit with new electric streetcars. As he put six-for-a-quarter tickets back into effect, Johnson offered Common Council a new thirty-year ordinance that it eagerly adopted on December 31. Rumors of graft ran rampant. Alderman Frank J. Licht said Johnson offered him a $6,000 bribe to gather support for the ordinance. Johnson admitted only that he had applied "pressure" upon Licht. Real estate developer Homer Warren admitted that he had advanced $1,000 to facilitate passage in the hope of getting Johnson to extend a new street line to 140 acres that Warren was trying to develop. Pingree, bristling with anger, asked who owned the City, and denounced the "fire-in-the-rear fellows over at the Chamber of Commerce," which supported the ordinance. "They're dangerous men," he said, "and the sooner they get out of town the better it'll be for Detroit."[39]

In a heavy-handed veto message on January 7, 1896, Mayor Pingree criticized the Common Council for passing an ordinance that not only gave Johnson a special tax exemption but lacked provisions for transfers with three-cent fares, no children's fare, no limit on employee hours, and no clause for continued joint use of downtown tracks or for future municipal ownership. His veto was upheld, 25-6.

"The history of what has been called the streetcar war has demonstrated the fact that competition in the streetcar business is healthful and necessary," Mayor Pingree said in his annual address to Common Council on January 14, 1896. "It produces good service and fair treatment. It prevents stagnation. Whatever favors are granted to the people will be returned by them four-fold. . . . The people of the whole country have been attracted by our labors in streetcar matters. They are looking to Detroit for good examples. A settlement, which would lead to a consolidation of the three roads, in my opinion, would be a public calamity, unless coupled with the principle of municipal control. The moment the spirit of competition is destroyed, the public service will be weakened."[40]

Johnson continued offering three-cent fares while he worried what he could do next in the Thirty-Year War.

The Horseless Carriage

At eleven o'clock on a cold, foggy evening, March 6, 1896, twenty-eight-year-old Charles Brady King drove his four-cylinder, gasoline-powered automobile away from John Lauer's machine shop at St. Antoine and Congress Streets at six miles an hour. King drove south to Jefferson Avenue, turned right, and proceeded to Woodward Avenue. He continued two miles north to Mayor Pingree's home at Warren Avenue, where he turned around and headed back. Interviewed by a reporter for the *Detroit Journal*, he said, "I am convinced they will in time supersede the horse."[41]

A Friend of Mine Named Smith

Three-cent fares continued across Detroit into the summer of 1896. Mayor Pingree believed that he had succeeded in getting citywide three-cent fares. Pingree solicited and got Pack's vigorous outstate support for his gubernatorial campaign. As the Republican convention neared, the Detroit Railway Company was sold to The Detroit Electric Railway Company.[42] The new company's articles of association had been filed with the secretary of state on July 10, 1896, with but $5,000 capital stock. The listed shareholders were Pack, Henry A. Everett, Edward W. Moore, Amos B. McNairy, and John B. Corliss.[43] A few days later, however, they increased the capital stock to $1 million and made an exchange of its stock for $1 million in 5 percent bonds issued by the new company with which it refinanced outstanding debt with an additional bond issue of $1.8 million. A two-paragraph article in the *New York Times* on July 14, 1896, reported that Wilson bought four-fifths of the new stock.[44] He had done what Johnson predicted, but none of Detroit's newspapers said anything about what had happened until several months later. Even then, nobody in Detroit found any evidence of Wilson's ownership or that his having acquired majority control violated a provision in the state constitution that prohibited the merger of competing railroad lines.[45]

"I announced it to the mayor one day by inviting him to take a ride in a private trolley car and telling him, at the moment we stepped onto the Everett line," Johnson said, "that this property had just passed into the hands of a friend of mine named Smith."[46]

Then, a few days after Pingree won the Republican nomination for governor on August 6,[47] Johnson announced that he was abandoning three-cent fares. Over the next few months, the three-cent lines now owned by The Detroit Electric Railway Company merged its physical plant with that of the Detroit Citizens Street Railway Company, beginning with the closing of its powerhouse on September 16, 1896.

"The effect of this consolidation has been to cripple the service upon the Detroit Railway, where the lower fare is charged," Pingree exclaimed. "Its powerhouse has been closed and many men have been thrown out of employment; cars are crowded and the general public is compelled to suffer great inconvenience and discomfort."

Albert Pack's support of his gubernatorial nomination and Johnson's three-cent fares had been intended to move Pingree out of Detroit into Lansing. Engaged in the most heated political campaigns of his career, Pingree stormed furiously but helplessly. "Pingree, a master craftsman of municipal politics, countered Johnson's tactic in the fashion that he knew best," wrote Holli. "Pingree announced that he would wage relentless 'guerrilla warfare' against the street railways, which would require many additional privileges and favors from the aldermen in the years ahead. "I am going to see that sixteen aldermen, favorable to three-cent fares on all roads are elected this fall," Holli quoted Pingree. "Three-cent fares will be the campaign cry in the local election."[48]

What he could not do in the courts, he would do with the political power of a governor. Pingree announced that he would require that any ordinance granting a franchise be confirmed by citywide voter referendum, which he hoped would prevent unscrupulous railway operators from bribing Detroit's Common Council. Pingree made a final promise, too: "I'll resign my place as governor of Michigan and go back to Detroit next fall and run for mayor again," Pingree said. "If none of the men who want to be mayor have the courage to stand out against Tom Johnson and his crowd, I will continue to be mayor until their present franchises run out."[49]

So, even though he won the governorship election, 304,431-221,022, on November 3, 1896, Pingree refused to give up his position as mayor of Detroit. "Pingree is quoted as declaring his intention to be mayor and governor at the same time," the *Evening News* said.[50]

A few weeks later, having already taken the constitutional oath of office as governor, Mayor Pingree delivered his annual message to the Common Council. His remarks that evening, January 12, 1897, had special significance:

> If the concentration and consolidation . . . had stopped . . . it would not have been so bad because there still existed a company which has heretofore been supposed to be free from entangling alliances and this company was in a position to receive valuable concessions had it desired to accept them.
>
> But within the past few weeks it too has entered into the combination and become a party to the illegal contract. When those who combine for their own selfish ends against the people who furnish them the means of support are active and aggressive, and with secret schemes even go so far as to violate constitutions, the people's representatives should be equally active and aggressive and should not only demand but enforce strict obedience to existing contracts.
>
> The question of whether an illegal consolidation has been made is a question which should be fully investigated. How far the violators of constitutions and laws can go and be supported by the courts should be tested and I know of no better time than the present and no better place than the state of Michigan to make such a contest.

Attorneys for Detroit and the Detroit Electric Railway Company disagreed that the constitutional prohibition even applied to street railways and, if so, whether it prevented stockholders of one street railway company from buying a controlling interest in a competing street railway company. Moreover, they pointed out, section 15 of the Street-Railway Act adopted in 1867 specifically provided:

> Any street railway company may also purchase, acquire, either at public or private sale, whether judicial or otherwise, or may hire any street railway in any city, village or township, owned by any other corporation or company, together with all the real and personal estate belonging thereto, and the rights, privileges and franchises thereof, and may use, maintain and complete such road, and may use and enjoy the rights, privileges and franchises of such company, the same, and upon the same terms as the company whose road and franchises were so acquired might have done.

A confident and defiant Johnson had announced on January 4, 1897, that he had secured a complete streetcar monopoly in Detroit by acquiring the Fort Wayne and Belle Isle Railway Company.[51] The Common Council tabled Alderman William B. Thompson's resolution to challenge the consolidation of Detroit's street railway companies on January 26, February 2, and February 9, and defeated it, 12-18, on February 16, sending it to back to committee on February 28 over fears fruitless litigation would cost upwards of $75,000. Finally, on March 9, the Common Council narrowly, 15-14, agreed to support litigation that was overtaken by events of the next few weeks.

Still on the job in Detroit, a dutiful Mayor Pingree went personally inspecting concrete paving laid under the supervision of a very politically powerful public works commissioner, Dewitt H. Moreland. Pingree found that a contractor had shorted the job, and a Common Council investigation quickly urged Moreland's removal. Moreland retaliated by filing suit demanding Pingree's removal as mayor. The Wayne County Circuit Court decided on March 1 that Moreland lacked standing. The attorney general himself eagerly took up the case. Acting quickly, on March 19, 1897, the Michigan Supreme Court ruled against Pingree holding both offices.[52]

In the absence of Mayor Pingree from city hall and the election of Democrat William C. Maybury to replace him on April 7, 1897,[53] no lawsuit testing legality of R. T. Wilson's ownership of the competing street railway companies was filed until many months later, on October 11, 1897. The case sat inactive in the Wayne County Circuit Court through at least 1903. *City of Detroit v. Detroit Railway*, Wayne County Circuit Court in Chancery, No. 18404, apparently never was decided.[54]

The Funeral Car

Weekend ridership reports to the city's three main cemeteries, Mount Elliott, Elmwood, and Woodmere, in the early months of 1897, may have surprised Hutchins. He was the kind of man who spent Sunday at his desk with the newspapers, streetcar journals, and company reports, making notes. He would have noticed that families taking picnics, especially, jammed the East Jefferson line on weekends with Catholic families visiting Mount Elliott and Protestants visiting Elmwood. Riders paid only one cent each. Just as many rode the Fort Street line to Woodmere Cemetery, the working-class burial ground of Detroit's west side despite its full five-cent fare. The streetcar companies had built sidings at all three cemeteries to serve riders attending funerals. They were followed many minutes later by a horse-drawn hearse, bringing the coffin. Hutchins had ordered Car No. 1 of the Detroit Citizens Street Railway Company that had been retired in storage for a few years to be refitted as a funeral car and put back into service. The funeral car was painted black, with no name or number. "SPECIAL" was stenciled in gold on the right front. A large opening on the side was added to receive the casket into the center of the streetcar. Twenty-eight mourners could ride in seating around the outside right along with the coffin. Fine black velvet drapes with golden-yellow tassels graced the windows, and a delicate glass electric-lighted chandelier hung close to the roof.

When he read of a young motorman's death of appendicitis on June 15, 1897, Hutchins would have put himself and, for the first time, the refitted streetcar, at his family's disposal for the burial ceremony two days later.[55] Hutchins would have boarded the funeral car at the downtown yard. Thirty maintenance crew workers stood in two neat rows with heads solemnly bowed as the car slowly exited the shed followed by four others. The streetcar moved onto East Jefferson Avenue and proceeded west toward the Hamel Funeral Home, where the motorman slowed and stopped the streetcar. The funeral party milled about outside. In a few moments, six pallbearers all wearing company uniforms emerged into the late morning sunlight. They approached the streetcar and, guided by Mr. Hutchins, positioned the coffin on the polished center flooring while

Funeral car. Courtesy of the Research Library of Kenneth E. Schramm.

the family of George Sheldon filed into the streetcar, where Hutchins could take each by the hand and exchange a few sympathetic words. The streetcar moved away with twenty-eight passengers toward the Woodmere Cemetery with a hiss of static and a crackle of sparks from overhead. Following were four regular cars draped in black. The nearly thirty-year-old, two-hundred-acre cemetery was several miles away. It's stately, rough-hewn stone gatehouse with a slate roof was a Fort Street landmark.

The cemetery came into view, and the motorman signaled his arrival with two clangs of the bell. A driver with two horses pulling a wagon waited at the gate for the coffin. As soon as the pallbearers unloaded the coffin, the funeral car clanged and sped away to duty elsewhere. The road ahead to the gravesite wound gently around to the left through a broad area over which tall oak trees provided pleasant shade. A few minutes later, the funeral party paused as they reached a brightly sunlit area on the right well cleared of trees. Three unattended, ragged, single horse-drawn wagons, a well-dressed driver, and carriage parked by the roadside. The air was moist and still that day. Back a few steps from a narrow rising slope stood the undertaker wearing a black top hat and shiny leather boots covering his calves. A handful of mourners milled around.

"Please proceed carefully," the undertaker likely announced.

Sheldon's family moved up the slope and gathered at the far side of the grave. Hutchins would have followed to the rear, awaiting with the others the six pallbearers bringing up the coffin. When the ceremony ended, Hutchins probably joined the others in passing by the coffin, which he touched with delicate fingertips. He would have walked quickly to catch the next regular streetcar back to his Woodward Avenue office.

The funeral car was always heavily booked. Eventually, the company promoted four motormen to special car operators who, following personal interviews, Mr. Hutchins agreed, had the right combination of driving experience, grooming, and demeanor. Use of the funeral car was available to the Woodmere, Elmwood, Mount Elliott, German Lutheran, Crematorium, Beth Olem, Woodlawn, Evergreen, Forest Lawn, Mt. Olivet, Gethsemane, Beth David, Roseland, Grand Lawn, Grotto, Grosse Pointe, Royal Oak, Oak View, and Machpalah cemeteries.

The service almost ended six months later, when the Rapid's Bridge over the Clinton River collapsed under the funeral car returning from duty in Marine City. The accident was blamed on winter pack ice, an overloaded car, and torque created by the speeding car coming out of a poorly designed "S" curve just ahead of the crossing. The funeral car suffered remarkably little damage, was repaired, and was put back into service. In 1902, it was replaced with a much larger thirty-eight-passenger interurban car. Two more were added in 1911. They provided funeral service until 1919, when demand for their use dwindled because funeral directors were purchasing automotive hearses, originally too expensive at $6,000. They were by then much cheaper and much speedier—reaching thirty miles per hour—meaning more funerals per day.

CHAPTER 8

Three-Cent Fares or Municipal Ownership

Hutchins Makes His Last Settlement Offer

On December 12, 1898, at the invitation of the Common Council's Committee on Streets and Ordinances, Jere Hutchins agreed to personally present a settlement proposal by which, he said, "we burn all bridges behind us. I confess I am sorry that matter is up at this time. If you think best, drop it and let us wait."[1] He came to the committee's meeting that evening with a fully drafted ordinance that would award a new franchise covering all streetcar lines for thirty years, with eight-for-a-quarter tickets between the hours of 5:30 and 7:30 A.M. and 5:00 and 6:30 P.M., and six-for-a-quarter tickets during all other hours with universal transfers for continuous rides. The company, he said, would agree to pave between the tracks and pay 2 percent of its gross earning to the city. He insisted:

> The rates of fare are twenty-five percent or thirty percent below those in effect in any other American city. No other railway management in the world would probably consider such a proposition. We may be able to live under it. . . . Three or four years ago, it was largely on my advice that my associates in and out of Detroit were induced to stake their fortunes on Detroit. That advice was predicated on my unswerving belief that in this American city we could count on ultimate fair play. If this ordinance is adopted, it will be on my advice that it may be accepted. Four years ago, the bicycle cloud was no larger than a man's hand. Today there is a cloud of more than 50,000 bicycles in this city. No man may foretell what the evolution of city transportation may be. The risk is ours.

Hutchins continued, asserting plainly that he was finished trying to make a deal while making an extraordinarily candid accusation and promise to the thirty-four members of the Common Council.

> There is a phase of this matter to which I wish specially to allude. Their records show that no measure introduced in the Common Council antagonistic to the interests I represent has ever failed of passage by a practically unanimous vote, and none of any other tenor has ever been introduced. The people

> are doubtless willing that right shall prevail, but have been led to believe that their interests may suffer through the dishonesty of their own servants. It is said that some of these very servants are dishonest in a mercenary sense, and that others are dishonest in the sense that they would annoy us for political advantage. I attack no man's integrity but trust that all may now be honest. We shall do nothing that is not open and above board. Not one dollar shall be paid to any man, directly or indirectly, in any way to influence his action in this connection.

His ordinance was taken up two days later and rejected, 3-30. "This proposition of the street railway company I consider an insult to the intelligence of the people of Detroit," declared Alderman William H. Beamer. "Four years ago, the people of the city of Detroit declared for municipal ownership of street car tracks, and this idea is gaining ground daily. . . . A bill will be introduced in this legislature authorizing the City to build and own its own tracks. True the gentlemen asked the company to bring in a petition, but I don't think the gentlemen supposed that they would bring in an ordinance of this kind."[2]

Hutchins never again offered a settlement to Detroit's Common Council. A few days later, on December 20, 1898, the Common Council took up a motion to rescind a resolution it had adopted on February 8, 1898, that no franchise be granted without first securing a favorable popular vote. It was referred to the Committee on Streets and Ordinances, 20-12, where it died.

The McLeod Act

Tom Johnson had moved to New York City following Pingree's 1896 election as governor, doubling Hutchins's and Antoine B. DuPont's salaries and leaving them in full charge of Detroit's street railways until early 1899. That fall, Maybury, demanding three-cent fares and voter approval for any franchise, defeated Republican Captain Albert E. Stewart, from whom Pingree withheld active support because Stewart opposed municipal ownership of street railways.

"One day, Tom suddenly appeared in Detroit to launch a scheme he and Governor Pingree had agreed upon in a private conference at Buffalo a day or two previously," Hutchins said in his autobiography.[3] Otherwise, he said nothing about what Johnson and Pingree had agreed upon, but Hutchins would play a surprising and intimate role in events as they unfolded over the next three months.

Taking four sumptuous rooms at the Russell House in Detroit for himself and his valet, in early April, Johnson announced that he and Governor Pingree had agreed on terms of sale under new state legislation allowing an independent street railway commission to buy and operate street railways without using any Detroit taxpayer money. "S. B. Clark, a keen lawyer from New York, is with him," an industry journal reported. "Mr. Clark is said to know more about the legal phases of street railway franchises than any other man in this country. He was a former partner of Elihu Root. It is supposed that he will draft the papers when the street railway commission takes charge for the people."[4]

Under Pingree's plan, the commission would acquire the entire street railway system subject to a long-term bond issue secured by an equally long-term security franchise. The mayor and Common Council would gain immediate control over fares, transfers, pavement maintenance, schedules, track locations, inspection of the books, and the hours of employee labor under a working franchise with the commission. Pingree insisted that three-cent fares would be enough for the commission to operate the streetcars and pay off the bonds in a city of 290,000 residents. For Johnson, the long-term security franchise would boost the value of outstanding company bonds, which had been in a depressed state on the market because, if the commission defaulted on its bond payments, the company could foreclose, taking back ownership of the street railway system subject to more favorable terms of the security franchise.

Representative Malcolm J. McLeod, a thirty-one-year-old first-term Republican from Detroit, had introduced legislation creating the street railway commission in the state house on February 21, 1899.[5] Detroit's newspapers never even mentioned the bill's introduction.[6] Born on January 22, 1868, McLeod's Canadian parents sent him to the public schools in Sarnia before moving to Lapeer County's Attica Township. He clerked in a grocery store there from 1888 until 1891 when he went to work on the St. Clair railroad tunnel. McLeod came to work in Detroit as a streetcar conductor and, within four years, was named business agent for the street railway union.

His bill was referred by house leadership to the Committee on City Corporations, which reported with a substitute that passed without floor debate, 79-0, on March 22. The Senate concurred, 26-2, the next day, and Governor Pingree signed the McLeod Act on March 24.[7] Mayor Maybury protested that the legislation did not require confirmation by Detroit voters.[8]

The McLeod Act, Local Act No. 338 of the Public Acts of 1899, authorized Detroit's Common Council to appoint a three-member street railway commission to acquire any "street railway or railways existing at the time of the passage of this act lying wholly within or partly within and *partly without said City*" (emphasis added). In doing so, the commission could incur no obligation on behalf of the city or state and would be entirely independent, a bold move creating an ingenious legal defense upon which, if challenged, to argue that it did not come within Michigan's constitutional prohibition against the making of internal improvements. Otherwise, the McLeod Act vested the commission with the same powers and duties as any other private street railway corporation.[9]

A week later, on April 1, Republican leaders of Detroit's thirty-four-member Common Council took up the politically sensitive matter of appointing its initial members because the McLeod Act gave no legal role in doing so to Mayor Maybury.[10] Most of Detroit's newspapers joined him in vehemently demanding a public vote on municipal ownership.

"In the matter of public franchises, which contemplate the private use of our highways, I see no reason to depart from the recommendation of my former message that . . . it should be done only after mature deliberation for a just equivalent and when the people themselves by direct vote have been permitted to confirm or reject the action proposed," Maybury had reminded the Common Council on January 10, 1899. "The franchises now existing on most of the important avenues of the City will expire in a very few years. As we approach that date from day-to-day the opportunity for a favorable bargain on the part of the city increases. All advantages of delay will accrue to the City and none to the other side. This is a very important step. Let us make haste slowly."

Before making the appointments, Republican Alderman George Dingwall proposed that the commission not "close any bargain for the acquisition of any street railway properties until it shall have first made a report to the Common Council and take no final action until the Common Council has acted on such report." It was unanimously adopted, 32-0.

Council President William Beamer, a Republican who would never again vote with those favoring the McLeod Act, then recognized Democratic Alderman Walter H. Coots, who attempted to stall further action. He moved to require a two-thirds vote of the Common Council to make any appointments and to postpone doing so until April 11. Alderman Oscar B. Marx, a Republican, jumped in offering a resolution that named to the commission Hazen S. Pingree, Elliott G. Stevenson, and Carl E. Schmidt, a close friend and Republican political advisor relied upon by Governor Pingree. Stevenson was a respected corporate lawyer in partnership with Don Dickinson. Stevenson was a Democratic Party activist and former mayor of Port Huron.[11] Schmidt owned a successful Detroit tannery. Neither had any experience with street railways so they would bring little more than the appearance of political balance to the commission, which Pingree, doubtless, would dominate.

Marx then read into the record correspondence he had requested from Governor Pingree:

> My Dear Sir—In answer to your inquiry, I would say that my opinion is that whoever are appointed members of the Street Railway Commission ought not enter into a binding agreement without first submitting the matter to the Common Council for its favorable action.
>
> Yours respectfully,
>
> H.S. Pingree.

Two more parliamentary delaying motions by Alderman Homer McGraw failed. The Common Council voted, 15-16, defeating his motion referring appointments to a five-member committee for a report no sooner than April 11. His next motion to adjourn lost, 9-21. Over objection by Marx, Beamer put the Coots two-thirds requirement and postponement on the floor. It failed, 5-24. The Common Council then voted, 21-11, to appoint Governor Pingree, Stevenson, and Schmidt. Within three days, negotiations would begin between the Pingree commission and the Detroit Citizens Street Railway Company.

The Republican-leaning *Detroit Tribune* summed up the situation:

> It is seldom that a municipality is called upon to entrust so much to three men but so far as ordinary human wisdom may judge, the council has acted wisely. . . . The people have merely delegated to a commission of three representative citizens, men of unusual foresight and business ability, men of unquestioned probity, a business proposition concerning which not one resident in one hundred is able to form an acceptable judgment. . . . Under such conditions, it is absolutely certain that the commission will be governed by conservatism; that the three men will exercise the same caution when acting in the interest of the city as they would when staking their own fortunes in a business venture.[12]

The level of trust needed from the people of Detroit by Governor Pingree's plan with Tom Johnson would rise even higher as events unfolded. On April 4, Mayor Maybury personally came before the Common Council to announce that he had formally vetoed the appointments. In an act of unabashed political posturing, Maybury read into the record a well-researched and written argument against the McLeod Act.

Elliott G. Stevenson. From *A Gallery of Pen Sketches in Black and White of Our Michigan Friends "As We See 'Em,"* ed. C. O. Youngstrand (Detroit: Wm. Graham Printing Company, 1905).

> In the interests of the people of Detroit, as they appear to me, and in compliance with my official duty, I interpose my veto upon the proceedings of your honorable body as aforesaid. This intervention on my part is not controlled by any hostility to the purposes of your honorable body in any lawful effort that may be made to bring about municipal ownership of street railways in the city.
>
> The question will doubtless be raised as to my right to interpose a veto on your proceedings. Under the provisions of the charter of the City, the Mayor has no authority to veto appointments made by your honorable body. Nor is such authority conferred under the provisions of the McLeod Act.

In his empty veto message, Maybury never mentioned the state constitution's prohibition against government involvement in the making of internal improvements. It was a purely political message reminding everyone that he could veto the two franchise ordinances needed to close a municipal ownership deal between Pingree and Johnson, who would need twenty-three votes from the thirty-four-member Common Council to override by a two-thirds majority.

Maybury closed his veto message by promising that he would not cooperate unless the McLeod Act was amended to require approval not only from the Common Council but also from the voters for any purchase of the street railway company. Following Maybury's appearance, Council President Beamer brushed aside Alderman Frank J. Licht's motion to reconsider appointment of the governor's slate, saying, "The mayor has no vetoing power in the matter."

A few minutes later, during the same Common Council meeting of April 4, the Pingree commission submitted an exchange of correspondence by which it had already formally initiated completing the deal struck by Pingree and Johnson, the general terms of which were believed by some to be set forth in a written option agreement that never was made public. When asked for its details, Pingree only hinted that speedy action was required. The *Free Press* said that Johnson held an option from Richard T. Wilson of "extremely short duration."[13]

The reply to Pingree's correspondence came signed not by Tom Johnson but rather by Bernard Clark, who was majority owner of 246 shares of an entirely new street railway company named the Metropolitan Railway Company, organized in Lansing on April 3.[14] Clark was an unlikely person to take the public lead in such a high-stakes deal because he was no more than a junior accountant with the Rapid Railroad Company, which provided streetcar service from downtown Detroit to Mount Clemens along Gratiot Avenue. Frank W. Brooks, Hutchins's brother-in-law, headed the Rapid Railroad Company.[15] The Metropolitan Railway's other shareholders were Clark M. Bates of New York and Stephen Baldwin, Frederick A. Baker III, and his son, George J. Baker, all of Detroit, each of whom held just one share.[16] Bates was a business crony of Johnson and Johnson's son, Loftin, who worked on their street railway companies in New Jersey, Pennsylvania, and Cleveland.[17] Stephen Baldwin was a wealthy, semiretired lumber investor living in Oakland County. Baker was an attorney with ties to both Governor Pingree and Detroit's street railway companies. This new cast of characters surprised everyone and, perhaps, Governor Pingree, too. Getting a formal reply from Clark instead of Johnson should have suggested to Pingree that mistrust and tension existed between Johnson and Wilson.

Clark wrote that his company was prepared to acquire the Detroit Citizens Street Railway Company, Detroit Suburban Railway Company, Fort Wayne and Belle Isle Railway Company, and Detroit Electric Railway Company. Pingree's reply was pointed and, perhaps, angry. "We do not regard this as the proper time to discuss the question of the method by which we can acquire such properties, except that we proceed upon the understanding as outlined in ours of yesterday, that it must be some method which will not in any way involve the credit of the City," he said. "We therefore must indicate at this time that except in the event of the negotiations terminating in the purchase of the property by the commission for the city, that we do not in any way consent to a consolidation of the property of the different railway companies."

Tom Johnson's arrival in Detroit had enflamed an already skeptical city. He was portrayed in the newspapers as a tough and unscrupulous bargainer, whose actions throughout the next few months instead betrayed self-serving financial motives, arising from the murky financial agreement he had with Wilson that nobody in Detroit, including Pingree, fully understood.

"If Tom L. Johnson has not always been an enemy of the people, then in the name of common sense who has?" asked William B. Thompson, Democratic Party city treasurer since 1896. "Since when did he become a friend of the people?"

"The Tom Johnson of five years ago is the Tom Johnson of today, a smart, shrewd, jollying promoter," Council President Beamer warned.

"Have the horns and cloven feet been so suddenly transformed into wings of white?" asked Alderman Licht, who reminded Detroiters that Johnson had attempted to bribe him in 1896.

"Much opposition developed among property owners, including a good many men who did not like Pingree," said Hutchins. "In fact, bedlam turned loose."[18]

"The simple fact that [Tom Johnson] wants to sell should put the City on its guard," Joseph Hudson exclaimed.[19] Hudson formed yet another group of downtown merchants and businessmen he called the Citizens Committee of 62 to oppose the purchase, citing as their major reasons the loss of the $23,000 property taxes paid each year by the street railway companies, the sizable amount of paving being done by them, and the city's liability for streetcar accidents. Hudson's committee led a hostile crusade against Tom Johnson in particular, proclaiming him a liar and a thief, claiming that any proposal of his had to be dishonest. They retained the legal services of Professor Charles A. Kent to seek an injunction in the Michigan Supreme Court on grounds that the sale was illegal under the state constitution's internal improvements clause. Kent harbored deeper political and social objections. Kent said:

> This is the first tangible movement in the direction of socialism. It is the first evidence of a concerted action and is the first indication of the crystallization of a communistic sentiment, which has been preached and initiated with much vigor for the last decade. We do not know what the limitations of such a movement will be when once it is started. We cannot conceive whether they will result in confiscation and the curtailing of private rights. If the city goes into the street railway business, there is nothing to prevent it from organizing itself into a socialist commonwealth.
>
> This is a case where the Detroit Street Railway Commission and the street railway company of this city are alone interested. There is not a great public utility operated by a corporation in the country that is not more or less affected by this experiment, and there is not one of them that will not feel the danger of socialist tendencies if they ever get a start. The decision, which will be given by the Supreme Court, will spread its influence all over the whole world, into the homes of all classes of people. It is not a decree of the law so much as it is a decree of sociological importance, and places or fails to place the limitation upon socialistic enterprises.[20]

Professor Kent's public rant expressed the unspoken fears of Detroit's ruling class that underlaid Pingree's struggle for three-cent fares. Kent may have been one of the first in Detroit to give voice to this incendiary political rhetoric against municipal ownership, and he would not be the last. Pingree would later respond:

> This is one of the principal objections urged against municipal ownership of street railways. It has its origin, of course, in the offices of private railway corporations and other natural monopoly corporations. It is repeated by their attorneys. It finds an echoing response among other people of high financial and social standing, whose fortunes have been made by means of special privileges and favors, granted, and bought from legislative bodies.
>
> The streets . . . belong to the people. There is no reason why a favored few should make money out of them at the expense of the real owners. Private companies have no right to that kind of business. They are the usurpers, although they would have us believe that municipal ownership is an effort to

> rob them of vested and natural rights—a claim that is preposterous when we know to whom the streets belong. It is absurd, therefore, to say that municipal ownership of street railways leads naturally to municipal ownership of drug stores, dry good stores, grocery stores, etc. Yet that claim is frequently made, and advocates of municipal ownership are consequently called Socialists.[21]

Kent's legal brief against the McLeod Act, however, would focus squarely on the internal improvements clause and section 5 of the McLeod Act, which authorized Pingree's street railway commission to purchase any "street railway or railways existing at the time of the passage of this act and lying wholly within or partly within and *partly without said City*" (emphasis added). Pingree's attorneys would struggle to argue that the street railway commission was constitutional because it would buy only those street railway lines lying solely within the city. On April 24, 1899, Pingree, Stevenson, and Schmidt agreed to join with Hudson's committee in asking Attorney General Horace M. Oren to file original proceedings in the Michigan Supreme Court testing whether the McLeod Act violated the state constitution's internal improvement clause. Oren did so on April 25, filing an action in quo warranto seeking ouster from office of the street railway commissioners.

Meanwhile, continuing with exceptional speed, the Pingree commission hired seven valuation experts led by Professor Mortimer E. Cooley of the University of Michigan School of Engineering. They were put to work appraising the real estate, power plants, barns, street railways, streetcars, equipment, and supplies of the Detroit Citizens Street Railway Company. Edward W. Bemis of the Kansas State Agricultural College, a pioneer in the field of public utility valuation, tackled the tricky job of putting a dollar value on the existing municipal franchises.[22] Theirs was a hurried job and they finished in a hurry. They were appointed on April 11, and they submitted their final report on April 30. It set the total value of the street railway property and franchise rights at $16,478,653.86.[23]

Bemis computed the present value of the net earnings of each streetcar line for each year remaining in the term of the various franchises with a 6 percent annual increase in traffic. The $8,478,000 valuation he assigned to franchise rights created a lot of buzz in Detroit because they had cost nothing. In 1891, Pingree had seized upon the financial bonanza having a municipal franchise was for company stockholders in arousing the city against George Hendrie's extension request. Now, Mayor Pingree's arguments echoed against him. Already past the May 14 option agreement deadline apparently set by Wilson, the Pingree commission presented the Common Council on May 23 with an outline of purchase terms reached with Johnson.

> After Prof. Bemis had given us the result of his investigations and calculations, the railway companies' representatives submitted their first definite offer as to price, fixing their price for the all the railway properties and rights at $17,500,000, the proposition being that a new security franchise covering all the lines be granted to a new company, which new company would execute bonds secured by mortgage on all the property of the companies and the security franchise for $17,500,000, and then the city would acquire such property subject to the payment of such mortgage indebtedness. We have strenuously endeavored to obtain concessions in the matter of price and have succeeded to this extent only: The company offers to turn over to the commission, to be used for the purpose of making extensions, payment of interest, or carrying out the sinking fund provisions of the mortgage referred to, $400,000 of bonds, and one of the parties interested has offered to turn over, for the same purpose, an

additional $300,000 of bonds, which would provide $700,000 as a safety fund and practically reduce the purchase price to $16,800,000.

The Pingree commission and company representatives had agreed to ask the Common Council to award a forty-eight-year security franchise, persuaded that anything shorter would require interest and sinking fund payments so large it would jeopardize sale of the bonds and Pingree's promise of three-cent fares. In the event of default, the security franchise would preserve three-cent fares currently required on the Detroit Citizens Street Railway streetcar lines until they expired in twenty-six years while requiring citywide workingmen's and school children fares and universal transfers. One of Johnson's primary demands had been ending three-cent fares from the security franchise. On this point, Pingree absolutely refused to compromise.

The final disagreement between Johnson and Pingree had involved the question of who would sell the bonds: the street railway commission or the street railway companies. Johnson insisted that if he personally handled the sale, the company would accept $15,325,000 of the cash generated. Critics quickly pointed out that the difference between the $17.5 million bond issue and the cash price would be a tidy windfall for Johnson if the bonds sold at face value. It was also convincingly argued that the depressed condition of existing company bonds was due to its expiring franchises and the company's long adversarial relationship with Governor Pingree and Detroit. Bond market dealers said no discount would be needed to sell bonds with a forty-eight-year security franchise behind them, and they argued that since Detroit school bonds had recently sold above face value, it was very likely that the street railway commission's bonds would sell at least at face value. The Pingree commission pressed its advantage and took the bond sale away from Johnson. As salesman, Johnson later said he had been willing to deduct his commission from the sale price and claimed in his autobiography that he was sincerely interested in assisting Detroit to obtain municipal ownership.[24] With the fat extracted from the deal, Johnson appeared to lose interest, close observers said.[25]

"This we report as the best price, terms, etc., we have been able to secure, the best we believe that can be secured," the commission report concluded before making a surprising admission and an even more surprising recommendation. "The question as to whether they are such as to warrant their acceptance is one which we feel ought to be settled by the electors of this municipality. *It is a responsibility that the undersigned are not willing to assume* without the sanction of the electors of the municipality, and we therefore report the situation to you with the recommendation that, at the proper time, the question be submitted to the people for their decision" (emphasis added).

Pingree's Desperate Idea

Anticipating defeat in the supreme court any day, Pingree, Stevenson, and Schmidt said they "have worked out a plan, which if acceptable to the owners of the railways, and should be approved by your honorable body and the electors of the city, would enable the people of Detroit . . . to avail themselves of such advantages, under *private ownership* surrounded by such safeguards as will protect the people in their enjoyment, until the power shall be secured to enter upon municipal ownership and operation, if such power does not now exist" (emphasis added).

Having heard their personal doubts about the sale, the already skeptical Common Council took no action before moving on to the day's routine business. Not until two weeks later, on June 6, would the Common Council take any further action, and then, without debate, the aldermen simply sent the deal to its Committee on Streets and Ordinances, which reported nothing back at the June 13 or June 20 meetings. Obviously, Common Council leadership was stalling.

Nineteen aldermen demanded a special session of the Common Council on June 22 to vote on putting Pingree's municipal ownership plan to a public vote at a special election on July 10. Surprising everyone in Detroit, the special meeting request said the street railway commissioners now wanted the deal handed over to an entirely private street railway company the Pingree commission would organize to complete the negotiated purchase and give the people three-cent fares with universal transfers regardless of what the Michigan Supreme Court decided in the pending litigation. Evidently, unlike the mayor and the Common Council, Governor Pingree was racing ahead of whatever the supreme court might decide.

When President Beamer called the meeting to order at two o'clock in the afternoon, only sixteen members were present, less than a quorum. Alderman Anthony Weiler moved to recess for ten minutes to gather those missing. When the Common Council reconvened, all thirty-four aldermen answered the roll call. Alderman Max C. Koch's motion to hold a July 10 special election was met by a motion to adjourn, which was defeated, 16-18. Beamer then ruled the special election resolution out of order, and Alderman McGraw moved to appoint a special committee of three members with power to seek legal advice. The Common Council unanimously amended the motion, sending the special election request again to its Committee on Streets and Ordinances with permission to seek legal counsel. On June 27, the committee recommended rejecting Pingree's referendum request. "Your Committee has sought and received advice from the corporation counsel and other legal authority, which satisfies your committee that the Common Council is without warrant of law to order such an election at the expense of the city, nor is it deemed expedient or advisable that such election be undertaken by the city authorities, even though funds for the necessary expense be contributed," they said.

The Common Council adopted the recommendation without a roll call vote. Instead of adjourning, however, the meeting was recessed for two days, until ten o'clock in the morning of June 29, when President Beamer was forced to recess twice more for lack of a quorum. Twenty-three members finally took their seats, and they unanimously tabled an ordinance that would have allowed Pingree, Stevenson, and Schmidt to move ahead with their private ownership plan. Once again, action on Pingree's plan was delayed awaiting a ruling from the Michigan Supreme Court.

Finally, on July 5, the Michigan Supreme Court declared that the McLeod Act was unconstitutional because allowing the street railway commission to operate outside the city of Detroit violated the internal improvements clause of the state constitution of 1850. Justice Joseph B. Moore wrote the unanimous opinion.

> To say the system of railroads as it existed in 1850 constituted internal improvements, within the meaning of the constitution, and the system of roads existing in Detroit, which are to be taken over by this commission, and the lines leading thereto, with which said commission is allowed to make agreements for deeds, leases, and in relation to the exchange of tickets and transfers, is not a system

of internal improvements, within the meaning of the constitution is to deny to words in common use their ordinary and accepted meaning . . . The law under consideration involves much more than the simple question of municipal ownership of the tracks within the corporate limits.[26]

Judge Moore said the McLeod Act was unconstitutional because it allowed the Detroit Street Railway Commission to engage in making internal improvements outside city limits in violation of the state constitution, regardless of what Governor Pingree said he was actually going to do. Even if the McLeod Act had been more narrowly drawn, critics pointed out, the growing progressive movement for municipal ownership of street railways was ripe for outright judicial rejection. Indeed, several years later, the Michigan Supreme Court decided, 4-3, that the internal improvements clause rendered unconstitutional municipal construction of street railways, even completely within city limits.[27]

Undeterred, on July 11, Governor Pingree pushed the Common Council ahead with his bold private ownership plan sidestepping the supreme court's ruling against the McLeod Act. That same day, representatives of Hazen S. Pingree, Elliott G. Stevenson, and Jere C. Hutchins had filed articles of association with the secretary of state in Lansing, creating a new street railway company they called the Detroit Municipal Railway, with 250 shares at par value of $100 each. The filing said that Governor Pingree bought one hundred shares while Stevenson and Hutchins bought seventy-five shares each. Altogether, the filing said, they had paid $6,250 of the $25,000 owed.[28] Schmidt delivered a letter to the Common Council explaining to its already skeptical aldermen why he had resigned in favor of Hutchins.

> Objections to the proposed plan have been urged by people (whose good faith cannot be questioned) that the proposed incorporators of the Municipal Railway did not include one person of practical experience in street railway operations; also that the proposed organization would likely degenerate into a political machine in the interest of Gov. Pingree, whose warm and personal friend I have been for many years. These considerations, in connection with increasing demands upon my time, have constrained me to suggest that Mr. J. C. Hutchins, a gentleman who enjoys the confidence of the people of Detroit, and who has demonstrated that he is a most successful manager of street railway operations, be substituted in my place in the proposed corporation.

Hutchins owed nothing to Johnson, but he would not have agreed to join Governor Pingree without the direct blessing of Wilson. The special meeting of the Common Council beginning at three o'clock on July 11 suddenly lurched ahead. Pingree explained that he had organized the private street railway company to complete the purchase and operate the street railways only until the state constitution could be amended to allow direct municipal ownership. The aldermen voted, 23-8, to take up the report of June 27 and raced through first and second reading of an ordinance awarding Pingree's new company a forty-eight-year security franchise to secure the issuance of 4 percent gold bonds totaling $17.5 million for the purchase of the four street railway companies in the city of Detroit. After adopting a series of relatively minor changes and defeating a motion requiring submission to the voters, 14-18, the Common Council received for the record a brief note from Pingree and Stevenson revealing how close they were to completing the sale.

"The plan submitted contemplates the granting of the so-called security franchise, and as soon as it is mortgaged—as is outlined—to have the working 3-cent fare ordinance adopted," they said. "The latter ordinance will be accepted by the Municipal Railway as soon as adopted, *tomorrow*, if the mortgage can be executed, and the council will adjourn until *tomorrow* for the purpose of adopting the working 3-cent franchise. As soon as the ordinance referred to shall be passed, it will be accepted, and the people at once enter upon the enjoyment of 3-cent fares, as proposed" (emphasis added).

Debate continued furiously over the fare provisions of the security franchise until 7:30 in the evening when the Common Council recessed for thirty minutes. Upon reconvening, Alderman Marx moved to recess for ten more minutes to await latecomers. Republican Peter Knauss, who had replaced Democrat John Christian Jacob, was the only alderman missing. A motion to send the ordinance back to the Committee on Streets and Ordinances lost, 15-18, and the Common Council voted its adoption, 19-14, not the two-thirds majority needed to overcome a mayoral veto.

Following the security franchise vote, Marx put adoption of the working franchise before the Common Council. However, his motion was tabled, 21-12. Conspicuously missing from Governor Pingree's note to the Common Council was any acknowledgement of the need for Mayor Maybury's signature on both ordinances before the street railway companies could accept an exchange of bonds for ownership of their valuable assets. The aldermen who refused to take up the working franchise knew that Pingree would never get the votes he needed if Maybury stuck to his promised veto. The Pingree plan was dying.

A few weeks later, Bemis wrote an article for the September 1899 issue of *Municipal Affairs*. "The great stumbling block, however, was the claim of Mayor Maybury and his friends that the decision of the Michigan Supreme Court practically rendered illegal the working franchise," Bemis said. "There was enough plausibility at least in his contention to have weight with many when joined with the natural feeling of dislike to buying back, for over $8,000,000, franchises which had cost the companies nothing. The desire to prevent political capital accruing to the Republican Governor of the state doubtless influenced the Democratic Mayor of Detroit and some of his friends."[29]

Under the City Charter, Maybury had seven days until the next regular meeting to exercise his veto against the security franchise. He just waited. Pingree managed to persuade twelve aldermen to call another special meeting on July 14 to adopt the working franchise.

That morning, at the urging of Governor Pingree, Johnson ordered three-cent fares and universal transfers citywide. Streetcars were plastered with big notices, "Three-cent Fares" printed in flashing red letters. Pingree produced and arranged for the delivery of a flier to all streetcar passengers and others along their routes. It was headlined "3C FARE." He wrote:

> We have put the plan of 3-cent fares into operation. You are in the presence of the real thing, and it is no longer necessary to talk about ghosts. This plan will be continued until your enemies put a stop to it. It is for you to say whether they can do it.[30]

Just moments after gathering for the three o'clock special meeting, on motion by Alderman Coots, the working franchise was again referred to the Committee on Streets and Ordinances, and the Common Council adjourned without a dissenting voice. The jammed council chambers could not contain the crowd that had pressed for admittance, but the entire session lasted little more than fifteen minutes.[31] It was now obvious to everyone except Governor Pingree that his municipal ownership plan was dead. Pingree delivered another flier to streetcar riders the next morning. It said:

> You are now able to ride to any part of the city upon the streetcars for a straight three-cent fare, and you can get a transfer from any line to any other line. The present street railway companies have established three-cent fares at the request of my associates and myself. You will always be entitled to ride for three cents unless the ordinances which we have asked the Council to pass are defeated by the Mayor, a sufficient number of the aldermen, and the *Free Press, Journal, Evening News*, and *Tribune*, all of whom are either intimidated or cajoled by the threats and pleading and flattery of their wealthy friends and advertisers, who wouldn't object even to a ten-cent fare.[32]

Pingree's fliers touting three-cent fares continued several times daily ahead of the Common Council regular meeting on Tuesday, July 18. One said:

> I say to you that I will risk my whole reputation on the statement that three-cent fares are here to stay unless the Mayor and a few aldermen defeat them by their veto and votes on Tuesday night.[33]

Instead, on Tuesday night, July 18, the Common Council abruptly adopted motions to reconsider and indefinitely postpone any further action on the security franchise, 29-0, burying Governor Pingree's municipal ownership plan without subjecting themselves to the veto that Maybury was eager to deliver. Later that evening, heaping scorn on the already defeated Pingree and Johnson deal, the Common Council formally received a joint resolution adopted on July 14 by the Merchants and Manufacturers Exchange, Board of Trade, Chamber of Commerce, and Citizen's Committee of 62 protesting Pingree's scheme:

> We denounce and condemn the action of the Pingree-Municipal Railway-Tom Johnson combination, in an attempt to prostitute the public conscience, and blind the issue before the public, by temporarily offering and establishing a three-cent fare, with universal transfers, on all lines, when the real purpose is to blind the public as to the character of the franchise sought by such combination and to secure a public franchise for nearly half a century upon conditions which may ultimately develop or ripen into a right to use such franchises for such long period, upon a five-cent basis.

Governor Pingree continued producing his fliers a few more days, desperately trying to salvage his municipal takeover of the street railway system. Wilson was furious with Johnson's agreement to institute citywide three-cent fares. On July 16, formal announcement that Wilson was finished dealing with Detroit came not from Pingree or Johnson but from Bernard Clark acting on orders evidently received directly from Wilson.

"We are satisfied that it is not feasible to consummate, under existing conditions, the plan of transferring the street railway property to your company," Clark said in a letter formally addressed to H. S. Pingree of the Detroit Municipal Railway, Detroit, Michigan.

> We must face squarely the proposition which the opponents of the plan put forward, that our franchises are running out and that when they do expire we shall have an expensive plan on our hands which the opponents of the plan say they can compel us to sell at a ruinous sacrifice unless we are willing to accept a new franchise on their terms. We must so manage the railways in the meantime as, if possible, to prevent the loss so threatened. Low fares and short franchises are incompatible if railways are to be run for profit as a private enterprise. In bringing our negotiations to an end we thank you heartily for the courtesy and fairness which you have shown us throughout.[34]

Newspapers across the country published a syndicated article about the Detroit streetcar situation. It said Johnson, Stevenson, and Hutchins had all traveled to New York City. Wilson had been skeptical of Johnson's plan all along. "Never for a moment, however, did he contemplate the 3-cent fare object lesson and he sent a telegram which caused Mr. Johnson's sudden journey eastward. . . . Mr. Wilson is not at all sorry that the deal fell through. It will eliminate Tom L. Johnson from the Detroit field."

Governor Pingree sent Stevenson and Hutchins

> to see R. T. Wilson, who owns the majority of stock in the Detroit lines . . . with a view to getting Mr. Wilson's consent to allow the 3-cent fare to continue.
>
> Governor Pingree said:
>
> "We have got the 3-cent fares now and I would like to see the man who will stop it. No, sir. It will continue."

The newspaper report continued: "Further than this, he would not talk but this is taken as an indication that 3-cent fares will continue by some sort of deal until November and that Governor Pingree will run for mayor with that as a slogan. How he expects to accomplish it is not known but the confident manner in which he made the assertion gives every reason to believe that he had found a way out of the dilemma."[35]

Wilson abruptly revoked the citywide three-cent fares on July 21. He let universal transfers continue, a small concession recognizing the increased ridership they had generated. Mayor Maybury leaped into the political wreckage, calling a special meeting of the Common Council for ten o'clock on Saturday morning, July 22, for "considering the order of the Citizens Street Railway Company returning to a straight five-cent fare with universal transfers after giving the city three cents for the past six days."

At the meeting, the Common Council responded by adopting a resolution, 26-4, that "such action in increasing the fares to a straight five-cent basis is an unwarranted act of bad faith on the part of the railroads and is in violation of law." Four days later, Mayor Maybury proposed amending all of the city's ordinances granting street railway franchises to impose three-cent fares, which the Common Council referred to its Committee on Judiciary and to the corporation counsel.

"I believe I am right in assuming that honorable body has obtained sufficient information very recently regarding the income of the railway companies, certainly sufficient to enable you to act with intelligence in this matter," said Mayor Maybury at a Common Council meeting on July 25. "I believe it was demonstrated to you that a three-cent fare was entirely adequate for the support of all the reasonable interests involved in operating railroads in this city, and this was confirmed by a voluntary reduction of the fare to this rate for a period of six days by the railway companies on their own motion." Maybury's straight-faced conclusion was not without irony for Governor Pingree. He lost his municipal ownership campaign in great part because of public fears stoked by Mayor Maybury and others that Governor Pingree could not earn enough income with three-cent fares to pay off the bonds and that Johnson would take back the street railway companies with a five-cent franchise renewal extending even more than thirty years.

Johnson would regret sharing the income and financial inner-workings of his street railway companies because what emerged from the Common Council on August 16 by votes of 17-1 were five ordinance amendments ordering a citywide reduction in fares to eight tickets for twenty-five cents. The Detroit Citizens Street Railway Company scrambled to get a preliminary injunction from the friendly U.S. District Court blocking enforcement. On March 19, 1900, Judge Swan handed down a final decision in favor of the street railway company.[36]

And the fallout continued. On April 18, 1900, the Common Council rejected the street railway company's appeal from a decision of the city's Board of Assessors that having valued the company for property tax purposes of $2,600,000 in 1899, revised it upwards to $10,247,000 for 1900, based on the valuation put upon the street railway franchise by Bemis for Pingree's Street Railway Commission. The Michigan Supreme Court affirmed the city's decision on February 12, 1901.[37]

Detroit had handed Governor Pingree and Johnson a humiliating defeat. Johnson failed to obtain a franchise renewal for his company. Pingree failed to get citywide three-cent fares. A further indignity was heaped upon them both when Detroit rejected their ingenious municipal ownership plan. It must have struck Pingree and Johnson hard that they could not win when they were either for or against each other. The Thirty-Year War would continue.

Johnson's One-Fifth Deal

With the three-cent fare ordinances blocked by Judge Swan, Wilson proceeded to cut a deal on November 24, 1900, to sell all of his Detroit street railway companies to Albert Pack and Henry A. Everett for $12.5 million.[38] When he learned, Johnson filed a partnership dissolution lawsuit in the New York Supreme Court to block the closing. Some details of their one-fifth agreement exposed by this litigation may explain Johnson's actions and inactions in Detroit during Governor Pingree's failed municipal ownership campaign.

Johnson's lawsuit alleged that his 1895 agreement with Wilson entitled him to participate as a one-fifth partner in all stocks purchased by Wilson in connection with consolidating all of the street railways in Detroit. Johnson was to have charge of the working of the different streetcar lines acquired and was to act as president of the company at a salary of $10,000 per year. Wilson was to have management of the financial affairs of the corporation and could form syndicates and outside arrangements with regard to all stocks as he saw fit. Their original agreement expired in 1898, but it was extended from time to time while Johnson tried to secure control of the Pack-Everett three-cent lines in Detroit. Pack-Everett had finally agreed to sell 70 percent control to Wilson. Unknown to Johnson, however, they continued private negotiations on purchasing back from him the entire Detroit street railway system.[39]

Wilson responded to Johnson's lawsuit simply. He had paid $5 million for the streetcar lines, and Johnson had never paid his $1 million. Therefore, Johnson had no one-fifth ownership claim to make.

This explains Johnson's desire to personally handle the sale of bonds, the mysterious $300,000 sweeter, and his subsequent failure to win the Common Council votes needed to approve the municipal ownership plan.[40] If Johnson lacked the cash needed to secure his one-fifth partnership share from Wilson, he may have preferred to fail. Johnson's autobiography tells a story about a midnight meeting with Wilson that has been retold differently by earlier historians. Johnson wrote,

> While I was interested with a lot of people who were accustomed to deal in rather big transactions, and during a time of great business depression, I received a call from Mr. Wilson one night long after midnight. He came to my room at the Waldorf in New York and asked me to forgive him for waking me, but said he was in a state of terrible depression and felt that he must have me talk to him and cheer him up. We chatted for some time on various topics and when I had finally succeeded in getting him into a more tranquil frame of mind, I asked him why he didn't give up business since it worried him so excessively. He was worth many millions and with his simple tastes couldn't spend his income.
>
> "Yes, yes," he said, "I ought to stop business. I know it and I've tried it. My family seems to get some enjoyment out of life and I ought to. But I can't—not away from the office. I have stayed away for weeks at a time as a trial, and then I get so blue that I have to rush back. Then after I've been at the grind awhile I am overwhelmed with the awfulness of it all, as I was tonight when I had to come down here to see you."
>
> "Well," I answered, "if you will play the game, you've got to take the thumps."
>
> He answered that he saw no relief in any course he could now take.[41]

Eugene C. Murdock's biography, *Tom Johnson of Cleveland*, tells the same tale setting the scene specifically in 1898 when there was a national business depression and when Wilson and Johnson were contending with each other over the sale of their stock in the Nassau Electric Railroad Company of Brooklyn and its consolidation with the Brooklyn Rapid Transit Company.[42]

Schramm and Henning, however, embellished their version of the story with some colorful details of Wilson's career as an overseas cotton dealer for the Confederate army and wrongly set the incident two years later. They concluded by saying, "R. T. Wilson up to his old tricks of fast dealing was trying to short change Tom Johnson. Therefore in late December, 1900, Johnson took Wilson to court to get his fair share of the new organization."[43]

Actually, Wilson was a step ahead of Johnson, who wrongly believed that Wilson was buying the Pack-Everett three-cent lines in Detroit. It is a tribute to Wilson's deal-making skills that he fooled not only Johnson but also some earlier historians. Johnson settled his lawsuit on December 28, 1900, accepting an undisclosed sum.[44] Johnson returned to Cleveland, where he would adopt Pingree's mayoral platform and successfully run for mayor the following year.[45] DuPont left to take general management of a St. Louis street railway company. The decisive meeting between Wilson, Pack, and Everett was held two days later on December 30, 1900, in Wilson's private office in New York.

"This meeting, attended by the interested parties and their several attorneys, some twelve or fifteen men in all, did not open promisingly," Hutchins said. "Stern determination seemed written on every face, and talk was limited to monosyllables. Each interest wanted something more than the others, in previous smaller meetings, had been willing to concede."

Hutchins recalled that the door to Wilson's office opened partially and through a crack appeared hesitatingly the head and shoulders of a good-looking man.

"Come in," said Wilson. In walked Victor Cline, a prominent Cleveland lawyer whose clients included John D. Rockefeller. Before being seated Cline assumed a look of relieved embarrassment.

"I feared I might not be welcome at this meeting," he said. "In fact, I thought I might share the fate of the man who, being bounced out of a saloon, gathered himself up and said, 'I knowed I wasn't wanted in there the minute I struck the sidewalk.'"[46]

Within an hour, it was unanimously agreed that all of the stock in the five companies—Detroit Railway; Detroit Electric Railway; Detroit, Fort Wayne and Belle Isle Railway; Detroit Citizens Street Railway; and Detroit Suburban Railway—would be exchanged for stock in a new company on the basis outlined on a slip of paper Wilson passed around. The Detroit Citizens Railway Company received 81,043 shares, giving it 65 percent of the 125,000 shares of the new company. This was not classic corporate merger but rather a simple exchange of stock. Detroit's litigation against consolidation was still pending but could not overturn what was done.

"And by what name shall the new babe be called?" somebody asked.

"How would Detroit United Railway do?" Hutchins suggested.[47]

Articles of association for the new company, capitalized at $12.5 million, were filed with the Michigan secretary of state on December 31, 1900, listing as the incorporators Wilson and his son, Marshall; Major J. M. Edwards; Everett; Hutchins; Albert E. Peters of Detroit; and Ralph A. Harmon of Cleveland. Everett formed a syndicate in Cleveland to purchase Wilson's holdings. It priced the stock at $70 per share. Wilson may have made a profit of more than $3 million.[48] Everett said he and his partner, Edward W. Moore, and their Cleveland friends ended up with all but thirty-one thousand Detroit United Railway (DUR) shares.[49] New York financier Robert B. Van Cortlandt bought five thousand shares.[50] One thousand were sold to DUR employees, and the controlling majority was sold to investors in Montreal.

Pingree's African Safari

Pingree's political career ended December 31, 1900, entangled in a sensational $40,000 embezzlement scandal involving his most trusted aide, Eli Ransom Sutton, a young lawyer from Detroit's corporation counsel office, that featured a series of sensational Ingham County grand jury hearings, indictments, trials, appeals, pardons, and a contempt of court warrant for Governor Pingree's arrest that followed him until his death.

Sutton was born in Greeley, Kansas, on August 25, 1868. After graduating from the Kansas State Normal School in 1888, he attended the University of Michigan, earning a master of laws in 1892. He was working for the city's legal offices when Pingree appointed him to a senior military post on the governor's staff in 1897 and arranged for his nomination by the Republican Party and election to the Board of Regents of the University of Michigan in April 1899. Sutton was widely and jealously recognized in Lansing as Governor's Pingree's closest friend and political advisor.

LIST OF CONSTITUENT COMPANIES FORMING THE DETROIT UNITED RAILWAY SYSTEM IN THE CITY OF DETROIT AND CONTIGUOUS TERRITORY

- **Detroit United Railway.** Incorporated Dec. 31, 1900.
  - Detroit Citizens St. Ry. Co. Incorporated Aug. 31, 1891. Acquired by Detroit United Ry., Dec. 31, 1900.
    - Detroit City Ry. Co. Incorporated Dec. 1, 1890. Acquired by Detroit Citizens St. Ry. Co., Sept. 16, 1891.
      - Detroit City Ry. Co. Incorporated May 12, 1863. Acquired by Detroit St. Ry. Co., Dec. 1, 1890.
    - Grand River Ry. Co. Incorporated Dec. 1, 1890. Acquired by Detroit Citizens St. Ry. Co. Oct. 1, 1891.
      - Grand River St. Ry. Incorporated Feb. 27, 1869. Acquired by Grand River Ry. Co., Dec. —. 1890.
    - Oakland Railway Co. Incorporated Jan 24, 1895.
      - Highland Park Railway. Incorporated May 12, 1886.
  - Detroit, Fort Wayne & Belle Isle Ry. Co. Incorporated March 1, 1898. Acquired by Detroit United Railway, Dec. 31, 1900.
    - Fort Wayne & Belle Isle Ry. Co. Incorporated May 23, 1892. Acquired by Detroit, Fort Wayne & Belle Isle Ry. Co. April 1, 1898.
      - Fort St. & Elmwood Ave. Ry. Incorporated Feb. 9, 1865. Special Act of Legislature changed name to Fort Wayne & Elmwood Ry. Co. (Act of 1871). Acquired by Fort Wayne & Belle Isle Ry. Co., July 1, 1892.
  - Detroit Suburban Ry. Co. Incorporated Nov. 1, 1892. Acquired by Detroit United Railway, Dec. 31, 1900.
    - Highland Park Railway. Incorporated May 12, 1886. Acquired by Detroit Suburban Ry. Co., Feb. 1, 1893.
      - F. E. Snow, *et al.* Grant, 10-17-1885, from twp. of Greenfield. Acquired by Highland Park Railway. Grant 7-13-1886. Grant 4-18-1891, from twp. of Hamtramck.
    - Detroit Electric Ry. Co. Incorporated May 19, 1896. Acquired by Detroit Suburban Ry. Co., Nov. 1, 1892.
      - Dix Ave. Railway. Incorporated.
      - Geo. Dorr, *et al.* Acquired by Detroit Electric Ry.
    - Jefferson Ave. Railway. Incorporated. Acquired by Detroit Suburban Railway Co.
      - Geo. Hendrie, *et al.*—Grant, 4-14-1891, from twp. of Hamtramck—Perpetual. Acquired by Jefferson Ave. Railway.
    - Gratiot Ave. Railway Co. Incorporated Dec. 9, 1891. Acquired by Detroit Suburban Ry. Co., Nov. 1, 1892.
      - Henry Plass, *et al.*—Grant, 5-7-1891, from twp. of Hamtramck—Perpetual. Acquired by Gratiot Ave. Ry. Co., Dec. 10, 1891.
  - Detroit Electric Railway. Incorporated May 19, 1896. Acquired by Detroit United Railway, Dec. 31, 1900.
    - Detroit Railway. Incorporated Dec. 10, 1894. Acquired by Detroit Electric Railway, July 29, 1896.
      - H. A. Everett, *et al.*—Grant, 12-4-1894—30 years. Acquired by Detroit Railway, Dec., 1894. Grant, 3-9-1895, from twp. of Springwells.

- C. S. Bushnell, *et al.*—
  Grant, 11-24-1862.
  Acquired by Detroit City Ry. Co.
- Congress & Baker St. Ry. Co.
  Incorporated Sept. 17, 1875.
  Acquired by Detroit City Ry.
  Co. June 22, 1882.
  - Detroit & Grand Trunk Junction Ry. Co.
    Incorporated.
    Grant repealed and subjected to Detroit City Ry. Co.—
    Ordinance on. 11-14-1879.
    Acquired by Congress & Baker St. Ry. Co.
    - Grant,
      6-13-1873.
- Cass Ave. Ry. Co.
  Incorporated Aug. 23, 1877.
  Acquired by Detroit City Ry.
  Co., June 22, 1882.
  - Central Market, Cass Ave. & Third St. Ry. Co.
    Incorporated 5-31-1873.
    Acquired by Cass Ave. Ry. Co.
    - Grant, 6-13-1873.
      Grant repealed and subjectedto Detroit City Ry. Co.
      Ordinance on, 11-14-1879.
- Congress & Baker St. Ry. Co.
  Incorporated Sept. 17, 1875.
  Acquired by Detroit City Ry.
  Co. June 22, 1882.
  - Grand Trunk Junction Ry.
    Acquired by Fred. Cariale and then
    by Congress & Baker St. Ry.
    - Grant, 4-11-1873, from
      twp. of Springwells.
- Hamtramck St. Ry.
  Incorporated May 1, 1869.
  Acquired by Detroit City Ry. Co.
  - Original Grant, 8-12-1873, to Moses W. Field, *et al.*
    Confirmed, 11-1-1881.
    From twp. of Hamtramck.
    Perpetual.

- N. Prouty, *et al.*—
  Grant, 1-31-1865.
  Acquired by Grand River St. Ry.

- Grant, 10-27-1890.
  From village of Highland Park.

- F. Buhl, *et al.*—Grant of 1-31-1865.
  Acquired by Fort St. & Elmwood Ave. Ry.
  Grant of June 17, 1880, from twp. of Springwells.
  Grant of July 26, 1886, from twp. of Springwells. Extended, March 9, 1895, for 30 years.
  Grant of March 31, 1888, from twp. of Springwells.
- Detroit River Rouge &
  Dearborn St. Ry. Co.
  Incorporated.
  Acquired by Fort Wayne &
  Elmwood Ry. Co.
  - Detroit, Springwells & Dearborn
    Ry. Co.
    Incorporated.
    Acquired by Detroit River,
    Rouge & Dearborn St. Ry. Co.
    - Grant of 6-24-1889 from
      twp. of Springwells to
      Albert E. Pepper *et al.*

- Geo. Dorr, *et al.*—Grant, 4-17-1886, 25 years.
  Acquired by Dix Ave. Railway.

- Grant, 5-10-1886.
  From twp. of Springwells—30 years.

Company history of the Detroit United Railway compiled by Robert B. Rifenberick, DUR valuation engineer, in the early 1900s.

In September 1899, another ambitious young Republican, Arthur J. Tuttle, prosecuting attorney of Ingham County, eager for publicity and currying favor with Senator James H. McMillan's political machine, pounced upon Sutton in a series of grand jury hearings investigating graft in the sale of surplus Spanish-American War military supplies by the State Military Board. Tuttle and Circuit Judge Rollin H. Person of Ingham County targeted senior military officials surrounding Governor Pingree. Highly prejudicial daily leaks to the press in Lansing and Detroit from the secret grand jury hearings shocked and enraged Governor Pingree.

In December 1899, Tuttle obtained indictments against Sutton, two brigadier generals, Quartermaster General William L. White of Grand Rapids and Inspector General Arthur F. Marsh of Allegan, and others, including Assistant Quartermaster General Lieutenant Colonel Harold A. Smith of Grand Rapids, for conspiring with Samuel N. Bickerstaff, superintendent of the Henderson-Ames Company of Kalamazoo, one of the largest suppliers of uniforms and regalia in the country. They were accused of selling the state's surplus military supplies at salvage prices, buying them back at full price, and splitting the profits.

Pingree immediately demanded resignations from White and Marsh and the prosecution of everyone else involved at the Henderson-Ames Company. Bickerstaff and the Henderson-Ames Company, however, made full restitution and were never prosecuted. Sutton was acquitted. Smith pled guilty and paid a fine of $1,200. White pled guilty and was sentenced to ten years in prison. Marsh was convicted, and he was awaiting sentence when, on December 4, 1900, Governor Pingree pardoned them both. Then, on Christmas Eve, Ingham County Circuit Judge Howard Wiest, who had presided over the trials of White and Marsh, ordered Governor Pingree to show cause why he should not be punished for contempt of court arising from an interview published in the *Detroit Tribune* on December 7, in which Pingree bitterly attacked Judge Wiest and Tuttle. Pingree's friend, attorney Elliott Stevenson, applied to the Michigan Supreme Court for a writ of prohibition to restrain Judge Wiest's contempt proceeding. The appeal was argued in February and still awaiting a decision when Pingree died on June 18, 1901.

In an astounding, endless speech filling twenty-three columns of the *Evening News*,[51] delivered to a joint session of the state legislature on January 3, 1901, three days after his last day in office,[52] Pingree prefaced his message with some extemporaneous remarks in which he attacked the courts, the legislature, and the press. Pingree said:

> In regard to my being locked up for contempt to Ingham County's boy judge, I want to say that I think that this judge and his associate certainly owe an apology to the people of the State of Michigan for insulting their Governors.
>
> I want to say that if this young man thinks he has a monopoly on my contempt and that I have contempt for just his court alone, he is mistaken, for I have contempt for dozens of courts in this State.

He ended his speech on an especially bitter personal note.

> The office which I have held for the last four years should have commanded the respect of every loyal citizen in the State, whatever the opinion of myself may have been. That it did not command the respect of the people in Lansing is proved by the fact that during the whole four years of my term as

Arthur J. Tuttle. From *A Gallery of Pen Sketches in Black and White of Our Michigan Friends "As We See 'Em,"* ed. C. O. Youngstrand (Detroit: Wm. Graham Printing Company, 1905).

> Governor, I have only once been invited to the home of a single resident of the capital city of Michigan. My experience during my political life, extending over a period of twelve years, has convinced me that in order to secure the full commendation of those who consider themselves the "better classes," the Governor and the other high officials must do nothing to antagonize the great corporations and the wealthy people. I am satisfied that I could have had the praise and support of our "better citizens" and our "best society" and of the press of the State generally, if I had upheld those who have for years attempted to control legislation in their own interests, to the end that they might be relieved from sharing equally with the poor and the lowly the burden of taxation. I would have been pronounced a good fellow and a great statesman.[53]

On February 10, 1901, Pingree left the country on a trip to South Africa and Germany, traveling with Sutton and with his son Hazen Jr. Over the next few months, the *Evening News* published several of his dispatches about the Boer War. While visiting Germany's Black Forest, according to one account, he drank brackish water that brought on a violent attack of a chronic ailment contracted while he was a prisoner in Andersonville. On June 15, his son sent a cable home announcing that Pingree was stricken with peritonitis and too ill to leave the Grand Hotel in London. The next day, Mrs. Pingree and their daughter, Hazel, boarded a train to New York City to catch a transatlantic liner. Before they sailed word came that Pingree had died.[54]

His body was returned on the Red Star line steamer *Zeeland* for one of the largest funerals in Michigan history, observed over two days. On July 5, his body lay in state in city hall. An estimated seventy-five thousand people came to pay their last respects. School and fire station bells rang across Detroit as his funeral procession began a five-mile march from Pingree's home to the Elmwood Cemetery along Woodward and Jefferson Avenues, closely lined by thousands of spectators. Among those ordered by Governor Aaron T. Bliss to participate in the cortege following Pingree's flag-draped caisson was the Michigan Naval Brigade under the command of Strathearn Hendrie.

Sutton had quietly returned to Detroit ahead of Governor Pingree's body. He resigned from the University of Michigan Board of Regents in June 1902, when Brigadier General White publicly confessed that he, Marsh, and Sutton had, indeed, profited $10,000 each in the military scandal. Tuttle again indicted Sutton, this time for perjury. Sutton fled to Mexico City. His wife, Grace Louise Williams, and her child, Dorothy Hathaway, followed a few days later. Sutton returned to upstate New York in September 1903, where he reached an agreement with Tuttle to plead guilty to a charge of conspiracy. He was fined $2,000 and disbarred from the practice of law. Sutton moved to California, where he was science editor of the *Los Angeles Times* when he died of a heart attack on October 16, 1934.[55] Tuttle's eventual reward was appointment by Republican President Taft as U.S. attorney for the Eastern District of Michigan in 1911 and to the U.S. District Court for the Eastern District of Michigan in 1912. He died on December 3, 1944, having enjoyed a celebrated career on the federal bench in Detroit.

Keep Your Bazoo Shut!

When the Detroit City Railway Company lost its bid for an extension in 1891, it is not surprising that Cameron Currie lost his job, too. His firing by the new owners was indicative of what he was being paid to do but failed to do for the old owners. What is surprising is that more than a decade later he was heading his own stock brokerage firm, investing heavily in Upper Peninsula copper mines and enjoying prominence in Grosse Pointe social circles. When he died on September 16, 1942, a brief, four-paragraph obituary in the *New York Times* said:

> Cameron Currie, Detroit banker and broker, and leader in civic affairs, died at his home today after a short illness. He was 82 years old.
>
> The firm of Cameron Currie & Company of which he was senior partner, failed in July 1908, with liabilities of $3,600,000.
>
> Mr. Currie served overseas with the Red Cross during the First World War and organized relief work among refugees when the Germans made their big drive of 1918. He was a member of leading clubs.
>
> He leaves a widow, Harriette Lewis Currie, a daughter, Countess Cyril Tolster [*sic*], and a son, John D. Currie.

The story of Currie's career after Thomas M. Waller and William W. Cook fired him in 1891 illustrates the shadier side of the wealth and social status enjoyed by one of the celebrated "McMillan Boys" of Grosse Pointe society as they were called.

Currie was born of old Scottish ancestry in London, Ontario, on May 4, 1860. After graduating from Hellmuth College, he went to work as a clerk for the Great Western Railway of Canada. Undoubtedly, he came to work in Detroit for George Hendrie because of connections William K. Muir, McMillan, and Hendrie had made with London's Scottish families. He arrived to work at the

Cameron Currie and his daughter, the Countess Cyril Petrovitch Tolstoy.

Detroit City Railway Company in 1879 just as Hendrie was getting its much-litigated thirty-year extension eased through the Common Council by John Christian Jacob with whom Currie would continue to work closely over the next twelve years. Theirs was reputed to be a corrupt friendship fueled by Hendrie's generous bribes. Clearly, regardless, Currie learned well the ways of making lots of money from business and political friendships.

His biggest customer at Cameron Currie & Company had been a man named Frank C. Andrews, who splashed onto the scene in Detroit in 1892 as a real estate loan manager for a big Detroit real estate developer, Homer Warren and Company. Andrews and John Winter, who had worked with Currie at the Detroit City Railway Company, were the prime movers behind the Detroit, Rochester, Romeo, and Lake Orion Railway in 1899 that was sold to the DUR. On May 4, 1901, Mayor Maybury appointed Andrews as Detroit's police commissioner. What happened while Andrews was Maybury's police commissioner, from which Cameron's social standing emerged unscathed, is simply astonishing today.

Andrews was born on his father's farm probably in today's Shelby Township near Twenty-Six Mile and Mound Roads on March 20, 1871. He went to work as a clerk for Homer Warren's real estate office in about 1890. Over the next decade, Andrews invested his real estate earnings in several banks in addition to interurban railroads likely because of his growing business with Cameron Currie. He became vice president of the City Savings Bank, a vice president and director of the Preston National Bank, and big owner of the Romeo Savings Bank.[56]

Andrews had invested particularly heavily in speculative copper mining stocks, including Amalgamated Copper Company, a Rockefeller family company. Andrews told the *Successful American*, a vanity magazine published in August 1901, "In the stock excitement of 1898–99, he had invested wisely and *quit* with a large balance in his favor" (emphasis added).[57] Andrews may have quit but he had relied upon his copper stock in making many other speculative investments. The *Evening News* traced Andrews's financial downfall to a 60 percent drop in Amalgamated Copper stock in October 1901. Andrews began furiously buying and selling stocks and bonds through Cameron Currie & Company and another brokerage firm, reaching $6 million per month. He was frantically kiting checks and looting the City Savings Bank of as much as $700,000 in one day.[58]

Andrews's method was to buy stocks or bonds on the New York City markets through a Detroit broker. When the certificates were delivered to a Detroit bank, he would pay with a certified check drawn on his personal account at the City Savings Bank. Then he would take the securities to another bank for a loan and use the money to cover his certified check at the City Savings Bank. He would be back to the second bank the next day or so with another certified check to pay off the loan, and take the securities to a third bank to borrow against them to buy more securities or to cover other certified checks. His was a classic check-kiting scheme.

On February 5, 1902, Andrews bought $90,000 Union Pacific convertible 4 percent bonds through Currie's firm. Andrews arranged for payment by certified check drawn on his account at the City Savings Bank. Currie's firm endorsed the check and deposited it at the First National Bank, which wired $50,000 to New York.[59] On February 7, the City Savings Bank was unable to pay the $50,000 to the First National Bank. Four other banks came forward with certified checks from Andrews amounting to $662,000. Over the next few days, it became clear to Detroit's banking community that not only was Andrews overdrawn but the City Savings Bank had no money left to pay any of its depositors, large or small.[60] The state banking commissioner stepped in and closed the bank's doors on February 10. An examination of the books found that the City Savings Bank had allowed Andrews to overdraw his account by $914,000. Especially hard hit was the Detroit Board of Education, which had deposited $467,000, the Library Commission, $38,000,[61] the Wayne County Board of Auditors, $150,000, and the State of Michigan, $80,000. The resulting avalanche of litigation forced Frank C. Pingree, bank president, into personal bankruptcy and the loss of his shoe factory stock.[62] Pingree and the other directors issued a brief statement when the City Savings Bank closed that might itself explain why he would take such a terrible loss: "The Banking Commissioner has deemed it the wisest policy to close the bank for the present, for the best interest of all depositors. Outside of Frank C. Andrews's indebtedness and checks, *the bank was never in a better condition*," they said (emphasis added).[63] Commenting on Pingree's condition, a Detroit newspaper said, "At the time he suffered a nervous collapse, accompanied by a slight stroke of apoplexy, from which he never really recovered."[64] He died April 2, 1910.

Despite digging over the next several years, bank receivers were unable to recover from Andrews any more than 35 percent of what its many working-class customers had deposited with the City

Cameron Currie. From *A Gallery of Pen Sketches in Black and White of Our Michigan Friends "As We See 'Em,"* ed. C. O. Youngstrand (Detroit: Wm. Graham Printing Company, 1905).

Savings Bank. Commercial customers got less than 13 percent. Andrews was prosecuted, convicted, and sentenced to fifteen years in prison, but, incredibly, Governor Bliss granted him full parole on December 22, 1903. His release was greeted by a statewide uproar of protest. Bliss explained that he paroled Andrews to assist bank receivers in recovering what he had stolen. Andrews did not, and Bliss did not seek reelection. Andrews died of bronchial pneumonia in New York on December 12, 1918.[65] "It is said that in later years Mr. Andrews had succeeded in laying the foundation for another fortune," said the *Michigan Manufacturer and Financial Record* on December 21, 1918. The *New York Times* bluntly disagreed. "When he left prison at the age of 32, he was a broken man," his obituary said. "An attempt to come back failed."[66]

In 1902, while the Andrews financial scandal swirled around him, Currie took on a partner, Louis H. Case.[67] They continued to do business through the Panic of 1907 until July 18, 1908, when Currie put the firm into receivership, owing $1,045,000, he said, due to Case taking orders for stock and bonds without being fully paid by customers.[68] Currie asked for dissolution of the partnership, which had been kiting checks for months before its collapse. Blaming Case for engaging in margin buying for several years without his active knowledge and participation is utterly unconvincing because the firm had been insolvent by at least $300,000 for a full year before it collapsed.[69]

2
CENTRAL DEPOT
WATER WORKS
2
H. & C. P. RY CO.

AVENUE 326

WOODWARD AVENUE
DETROIT CITY RAILWAY.

66 GRATIOT 66
DETROIT CITY RAILWAY.

CONGRESS & BAKER STS.
92

112

MICHIGAN AVENUE
90
DETROIT CITY RAILWAY

Detroit's many different streetcars from 1862 to 1922. Courtesy of the Detroit Historical Society.

"During the financial depression which occurred during the latter part of 1907 they were in sore straits and resorted to irregular and dishonest practices, which were followed, when emergencies arose, until their failure," said the Michigan Supreme Court in deciding the principal piece of litigation arising from the case in which there were four hundred intervening parties. "They concealed and covered up their true condition by fraudulently hypothecating securities under their control, delaying delivery by specious excuse, by a system of having commercial paper afloat, called 'kiting paper,' making overdrafts and wiring money at the last moment to cover them, and other similar expedients."[70]

The case ended in personal bankruptcy proceedings in which Currie's lawyers persisted in blaming Case. Currie never personally testified, and he was denied discharge for failing to supervise and keep proper books and records.[71] The bankruptcy court noted that many of the firm's accounts listed fictitious names. The firm was not only carrying on its books $67,138.67 owed by Frank C. Andrews, but it had opened a new account for him under the name A. C. Frank.[72]

Currie and his wife were living at 675 East Jefferson Avenue during the 1910 census with their daughter Gwendolyn, age eighteen, son John, age seventeen, and three female servants, who were from Scottish families from Canada. Gwendolyn was a five-foot-five, blue-eyed brunette, an exceptionally attractive woman, who may have preserved her father's social cachet because he was living at 5 Berkeley Place in Grosse Pointe Farms during the 1930 census. Gwendolyn married twice. It was her second marriage in New York City to a distant relative of Leo Tolstoy that captivated Grosse Pointe. Count Cyril Petrovich Tolstoy was a second cousin of the Russian novelist. Following the Bolshevik revolution, Cyril Tolstoy fled to Seattle where he married a Seattle heiress, whom he divorced in 1927. Two years later, he married Gwendolyn Currie Seyburn at New York City's Russian Orthodox Church of Christ the Savior at East 121st Street on June 15, 1929.

Cameron Currie remained at the top of Detroit's high society, of whom it goes without saying that he was a member of the Yondotega Club, one of the most exclusive men-only dining clubs in the United States with today's membership limited to one hundred or so with no new member being admitted until an old member dies. Long-time club members included all of his cronies from street railway days: George and Strathearn Hendrie, the Muirs, the McMillans, and Hutchins. Visitors have rarely been admitted—and women never—but include such notables as Admiral Richard Byrd and Theodore Roosevelt. The clubhouse moved from the path of the Chrysler Freeway to its present home at 518 East Jefferson Avenue in the 1960s. At the time, society page writer Jane Schermerhorn said the late Cameron Currie was still remembered as the club's No. 1 member. "He was a graceful speaker, a gourmet, a connoisseur whose ideas gave the club distinction," she said. "He served one of the longest terms as chairman, and during those years the club year book printed a verse advising the pattern of closed-mouthedness: 'Good friende, for friendship's sake forebeare. . . . To utter what is gossip heare . . . In social chatt, lest, it may be. . . . Thy tongue do wrong to us and thee.' A 20th century member, endeavoring to quote the gentle poetry, boiled it down to . . . 'Keep your bazoo shut.'"[73]

CHAPTER 9

Every Mayor Had a Three-Cent Fare Plan

The Codd-Hutchins Ordinance

With but two years of political experience as a member of the Common Council, Republican George P. Codd, a popular and athletic young lawyer, defeated Maybury in November 1904.[1] Codd avoided engaging with the Detroit United Railway (DUR) until the second year of his term when a short section of one of its franchises to operate on Woodward Avenue from the railway crossing to Pallister Avenue was expiring. Mayor Codd had promised voters that he would sign no franchise until the voters approved it.

In his annual message to the Common Council on January 9, 1906, Mayor Codd had emphasized Detroit's stubborn insistence on getting three-cent fares.

> It is gratifying to note the policy in regard to streetcar matters which I believe pervade your honorable body that no further rights or concessions, which, as a matter of course, strengthen the street railway company's rights, shall be given unless an adequate return is made to the City. As long as the present company has contract arrangements with the City, which do not expire for three or four years from now, the entire question can best be settled by agreement. In this matter we should stand strictly by our pledges to the people, and no agreement of any kind should be made unless based upon the great desideratum, three-cent fares, or their equivalent; and any agreement must, in any event, be submitted to a vote of the people for their approval before its final adoption.

Hutchins saw his expiring Highland Park franchise as an opportunity to renew all of his other franchises on terms outlined by Mayor Codd. "I wish you would sow into the mind of your good friend, Mayor Codd, the thought that something better than three-cent fares for those in Detroit most needing cheap fares is quite possible," Hutchins urged General Henry M. Duffield, a distinguished military general during the Civil War and Spanish-American War.[2] Duffield had been Detroit's corporation counsel for many years and first president of the Michigan State Bar Association, and he was active in Republican politics.[3]

Mayor George P. Codd. From *A Gallery of Pen Sketches in Black and White of Our Michigan Friends "As We See 'Em,"* ed. C. O. Youngstrand (Detroit: Wm. Graham Printing Company, 1905).

Duffield arranged for a meeting between Hutchins and Mayor Codd the next evening, followed by more meetings between Detroit and DUR attorneys to assist in the drafting of what came to be called the Codd-Hutchins ordinance, the central feature of which, Hutchins said, "was a provision that all riders during the several hours morning and evening when the industrial armies in factory, shop, and office were moving to and from their work, should be carried at the rate of ten tickets for twenty-five cents."[4]

When they finished, Hutchins called a special meeting of his board of directors in Cleveland to avoid premature publicity and at that meeting submitted the ordinance with his recommendation that it be accepted. "A five-cent fare was little enough anywhere," they told him. "Two rides for five cents simply out of the question. There was no use talking. The directors simply would not approve." Hutchins agreed to tell Mayor Codd but added that, after doing so, he thought it would be best for him to go abroad with his wife, Sarah, for two or three months.[5]

During his trip to the Mediterranean, his directors reversed themselves. "The Cleveland financier who had previously objected so strenuously rose to his feet and said he had decided to withdraw his objections and would say that if the president were of unchanged mind, he would gladly approve acceptance of the ordinance," Hutchins said. "The entire board concurred. When informed of these conclusions, Codd was overjoyed."[6]

Franchise Expiration Dates and Mileage

EXPIRATION DATE	ORIGINAL COMPANY	MILEAGE	EXPIRATION DATE	ORIGINAL COMPANY	MILEAGE
July 12, 1906	Highland Park Railway	0.8	December 4, 1924	Detroit Railway	59.6
November 14, 1909	Detroit City Railway	63.8	July 1, 1927	Detroit Electric Railway	1.1
July 23, 1910	Fort Wayne and Belle Isle Railway	3.8	May 14, 1928	Detroit Electric Railway	2.7
December 31, 1915	Grand River Street Railway	15.9	May 2, 1935	Detroit United Railway	0.5
December 14, 1921	Fort Wayne and Elmwood Railway	9.8	Perpetual	Hamtramck Street Railway	5.0

Prepared from a voluminous collection of street railway ordinances and resolutions gathered and summarized by attorney Clyde L. Webster for Mayor Phillip Breitmeyer's Committee of Fifty in 1909 and from mileage estimates compiled by Delos Wilcox in 1908.[7]

Codd insisted that the question must go to the people at the fall election, now only a few months away, at which he would be seeking reelection. Hutchins had unwittingly tied himself into campaigning not only for the Codd-Hutchins ordinance but also inevitably for Mayor Codd, a role for which he was particularly ill suited by his Missouri temperament.[8]

Mayor Codd submitted the ordinance to the Common Council on July 31, 1906. "I respectfully transmit herewith for the consideration of your honorable body and for the purpose of submitting the same to the people of the City of Detroit an ordinance for the operation of street cars lines within the City for a term expiring December 4, 1924, the date of expiration of the Detroit Railway franchise," he said. "This ordinance embodies an understanding arrived at with the offices of the Detroit United Railway, after numerous conferences extending over the period of the past year."

The Common Council's Committee on Franchises favorably reported back on September 11, 1906, making no changes to the all-important industrial fare provision:

> The said grantee shall also keep for sale on its cars tickets at the rate of 10 for 25 cents each of which shall be received for the carriage of any passenger in one direction on any route in said City between the hours of 5:00 and 8:00 o'clock a.m., and 4:30 and 6:30 o'clock p.m., and shall entitle said passenger between said hours to all the rights and privileges of transfer granted by this ordinance to any passenger paying a higher rate of fare.

Minor amendments were taken up and adopted on September 18 and more on October 2 when the Common Council voted, 31-4, to put the question on the November 6 ballot.

Among the brightest of Detroit's lawyers was Patrick J. M. Hally, former city attorney, born on August 22, 1867, in Wales Center. He graduated from the University of Michigan Law School in 1888. Mayor Maybury had appointed him city assessor in 1898. He became a tax expert. In 1900, he joined the corporation counsel's office. He became a street railway expert. Edward H. Doyle, a mutual friend, suggested to Hutchins that Hally, available and invaluable, should be added to the company's legal staff.[9] "That can be arranged," Hutchins replied.[10]

Hally was away from town on a three-week vacation, and before Doyle could contact him, Hally appeared in the newspapers in opposition to the Codd-Hutchins ordinance. It was only

Patrick J. M. Hally. From *A Gallery of Pen Sketches in Black and White of Our Michigan Friends "As We See 'Em,"* ed. C. O. Youngstrand (Detroit: Wm. Graham Printing Company, 1905).

the opening gun in a very nasty campaign. Hally had been called back to town by City Treasurer William B. Thompson, Democratic Party nominee for mayor, who had offered Hally appointment to his executive staff, if they could defeat Codd. Thompson's platform promised three-cent fares at all hours as opposed to Codd's two and a half cents only during certain hours.

Other opposition came from unexpected sources. Unhappy because Codd had won the Republican nomination from him two years earlier, Clarence Black wrongly believed, Hutchins said, that the DUR had helped to elect Codd. "No one connected with the company had anything whatever to do with Black's defeat," Hutchins said.[11] Black organized an opposition committee, including among its hundred members R. H. Fyfe, Frank C. Pingree, and Herman Krolik.[12] They hired Jennie Smith, Pingree's political wizard, to produce an opposition circular. In 1895, she had married George Beck, president of Michigan Beef and Provision Company. He had been a member of Pingree's first Republican majority on the Common Council in 1892. The committee distributed sixty-five thousand copies of opposition circulars written in English and Polish.[13]

"Her work during the campaign was done in a way to prejudice a good many voters," Hutchins said. "Hotter and hotter grew the campaign. The campaign must have cost Clarence Black a rather

Judge Robert E. Frazer. From *A Gallery of Pen Sketches in Black and White of Our Michigan Friends "As We See 'Em,"* ed. C. O. Youngstrand (Detroit: Wm. Graham Printing Company, 1905).

sizable sum. What satisfaction he got from it is not known, but not long after it was over, he closed out his interests in Detroit and moved away to spend the rest of his lifetime in California."[14]

The DUR bought half-page and full-page ads in nearly all the daily and the weekly newspapers promoting the Codd-Hutchins ordinance, prompting some to accuse Detroit's newspapers of abandoning themselves to bribery. "For three months, the Detroit United Railway has been giving in Detroit an exhibition of the power of a public-service corporation to persuade newspapers to swallow their principles and betray the people in a crisis," said a national public policy journal. "That the newspapers that are not fighting the franchise have been bribed by the advertising the street railway company has given them, and the street railway company intended the advertising as a bribe, is plain."[15] Hutchins saw what he did differently and with some regret. "The real question was whether Codd or Thompson should be elected," Hutchins said.[16]

Speeding about the city in an automobile, attending as many as six rallies every night, Codd argued that his industrial fare ordinance required the lowest fares ever offered anywhere in the country while Thompson promised three-cent fares for all of the people all of the time. Among those appearing frequently on the stump and in the newspapers speaking for Codd's side of the case was Judge Robert E. Frazer of the Wayne County Circuit Court. The sixty-six-year-old Judge Frazer defended Codd and Hutchins against the many accusations that opponents tossed at them with incisive wit and eloquent, forceful speeches.[17] Mayor Tom Johnson and Antoine DuPont came from Cleveland to set up a circus tent for big Thompson political rallies in wards lacking halls. "Always a good speaker, Tom had a knack of making friends by his answers to questions," Hutchins said. "It was his habit at the close of his speech to invite questions. After he had tickled the audience with several of his answers, someone said he had heard that Jere Hutchins was being paid a salary of more than $25,000 or more per annum."

"And now I ask," said the interlocutor, "if the company paid him less, couldn't it give us three-cent fares?"

"Tom's answer was, 'I don't know what salary Jere Hutchins gets but whatever it is, he earns it.'"[18]

Johnson made an easy target for Mayor Codd. "Tom Johnson doesn't want the proposed street railway ordinance adopted in Detroit for the reason that he's mayor of a neighboring city and has failed absolutely for six long years to get his people anything as good!" Codd argued. "I say that it's presumptive for a man who failed so completely to accomplish things in his own city to come here and try to settle our affairs."[19]

Hutchins put the proposed industrial fare into effect for the last two weeks of the campaign—to no avail.

Hutchins told a story of a saloonkeeper he called Pat who operated in the Fourth Ward. On Election Day, being a ward leader as well, Pat alternated, as one of the judges of the election, between his saloon and the ballot box. In the late afternoon, one of his henchmen rushed up to him and excitedly exclaimed, "God, man! Don't you see they are stuffing that box against us?"

"Sh, sh, sh!" whispered Pat. "Let the boys have their fun. We're not going to use that box."[20]

The people rejected the Codd-Hutchins ordinance, 14,411-30,978, and Thompson was narrowly elected.

The 1908 Constitution and Municipal Home Rule

On April 2, 1906, the state legislature asked Michigan voters if they wanted to rewrite the state constitution of 1850. They agreed, 196,780-127,189, ninety-six delegates were elected on September 17, 1907, and the convention convened in Lansing on October 22, 1907. A corporate railroad lawyer, John J. Carton of Flint, a notorious machine politician, who had twice served as Republican speaker of the House of Representatives, was unanimously elected to preside over its otherwise prolonged deliberations.[21] The convention was not finished until March 1908 because the progressives and the reactionaries among its delegates actually had about equal strength.[22] The draft they adopted reflected some important characteristics of the progressive reform movement begun by Mayor Pingree. It was approved by the voters in November 1908 by a statewide vote, 244,705-130,783.

The new state constitution granted powers of municipal home rule or local self-government to city and villages and expressly permitted cities, villages, and townships to operate public utilities, including street railways, gas, and electric lighting, subject to a three-fifths affirmative vote in a local election.[23] The constitution restricted the borrowing of money to acquire public utilities to mortgaging the utility itself instead of pledging municipal taxation. It also directed the state

John J. Carton. From *A Gallery of Pen Sketches in Black and White of Our Michigan Friends "As We See 'Em,"* ed. C. O. Youngstrand (Detroit: Wm. Graham Printing Company, 1905).

legislature to enact a general law providing for the incorporation of cities and villages.[24] Instead of having their municipal charters handed to them by special act of the state legislature, cities and villages would be allowed to draft their own.[25] All appeared ready for Detroit's five hundred thousand residents spread across forty-one square miles to move toward municipal ownership of its street railway.

"Between the bungling of the Legislature, the imperfect initiative of the City and the interference of the courts, five years more were consumed before the abstract question of municipal ownership of street railways as a policy could be got before the voters for decision," observed Delos Wilcox.[26]

The state legislature did move quickly, passing the Home Rule Act, Act No. 279 of the Public Acts of 1909, but an August 1910 referendum on specifically amending Detroit's charter to give the city the right to own and operate the street railways, however, was blocked by the Michigan Supreme Court on grounds that the new Home Rule Act did not allow Detroit to do so in piecemeal fashion.[27]

During its 1911 term, the state legislature fixed the problem. It adopted Act No. 203 of the Public Acts of 1911, which amended the Home Rule Act to say that cities could piecemeal amend an existing municipal charter. Detroit went ahead with a special election on a charter amendment specifically authorizing municipal ownership of streetcar lines introduced by Republican Alderman Thomas Glinnan. He was then under indictment along with seven other aldermen for accepting bribes.[28]

The municipal ownership charter amendment was caught up in a fight by Alderman James Vernor, who was championing a civil service amendment that the Common Council refused to put before the voters. Vernor sued to force his proposal onto the ballot. The Michigan Supreme Court balked, now saying that Act No. 203 unconstitutionally authorized piecemeal amending of municipal charters, consequently knocking the municipal ownership question off the ballot, too.[29]

"Necessarily, the revising of an old charter under the new general law would be in conformity with such general law and would its mandates and inhibitions to the extent as in the framing of a new charter," Judge Charles A. Blair wrote for a unanimous court on January 15, 1912. "Not so in the case of mere amendments to specific sections, which might leave the charters repugnant to the general law adopted under article 8, § 20, of the Constitution, so that cities claiming to operate under a general law intended to operate uniformly upon the local legislatures of all cities would be subject to such limitations as they should choose to accept and might adopt such provisions as they deemed beneficial."[30] Once again, the Michigan Supreme Court had blocked Detroit from moving ahead with municipal ownership of street railways that would have ended the Thirty-Year War.

"Detroit, Mich., has become distinguished among the important cities of the United States by reason of its deplorable street railway conditions and the apparent hopelessness of its situation in this respect," declared an article in the *Public Service* magazine in April 1912. "For more than 20 years Detroit has been struggling with a big street railway problem and has not been able to solve it because of politics."[31] Surely, the supreme court deserved a large measure of blame.

A special session of the state legislature in 1912 put a constitutional amendment on the ballot authorizing cities to amend existing charters. Voters approved in the statewide election on November 5, 1912. In turn, that required amending the Home Rule Act again. The state legislature adopted and gave immediate effect to the so-called Verdier Act on March 11, 1913,[32] and Detroit put another charter amendment on the ballot authorizing municipal street railway ownership. It would empower the mayor to appoint three street railway commissioners to build competing lines or to purchase the DUR. The Wayne County Circuit Court refused to enjoin the ballot question and the measure passed, 42,714-10,031, on April 7, 1913.

Opponents were not finished. They sought to restrain appointment of street commissioners on grounds that the Verdier Act violated the immediate effect clause of the state constitution, which allowed the state legislature to give any legislation immediate effect only if necessary to preserve the public peace, health, or safety. Republican Attorney General Grant Fellows had written a lengthy legal opinion for the state legislature on February 17, 1913, arguing that deciding necessity was a legal rather than a political question under section 21 of article 5 of the new state constitution. Fellows concluded that authorizing cities to amend their municipal charters piecemeal was unnecessary. On January 23, 1914, the supreme court disagreed, issuing four different opinions but upholding, 5-1, the state legislature's decision giving immediate effect to the Verdier Act.[33] Finally, Detroit could confront its street railway company with a choice between offering three-cent fares or suffering a municipal takeover. What would happen next was not any prettier, and getting from there to an end was a long, ugly chapter in the Thirty-Year War.

The Hally Ordinance

Detroit had elected the man who invented the three-cent fare political slogan. Mayor William B. Thompson was convinced of two things about the Codd-Hutchins loss and his victory. First, no settlement of the question could meet approval of the people except three-cent fares with universal transfers. Second, the DUR would never come to him with a settlement during his term of office.[34] Thompson had to take up a new line of attack if he was going to get three-cent fares. Hally had drafted an ordinance originally introduced on September 26, 1905 under Mayor Codd that Delos Wilcox, street railway expert, called "certainly novel and remarkable."[35]

> Detroit is particularly fortunate among the cities of America in having a number of great diagonal thoroughfares leading to a common center. These naturally furnish the skeleton of the transportation system. On Woodward Avenue, the most important street of the city, is found the stretch of track where the company's franchise has already expired. This stretch of track is situated about three miles from the center of the City and a mile and a half inside the City limits. Most of the franchises on the main thoroughfares of the City expire in 1909 or 1910. . . . One would naturally suppose, under such circumstances, that the City would be in a position to dictate terms to the street railway company. But all efforts to do so have hitherto been unavailing, principally because the City has no alternative under the constitution and laws of the state except to renew the company's franchises on such terms as the company was willing to give, or to grant a competing franchise to some other company on other streets.[36]

The Hally ordinance declared that no street railway company could continue to operate any streetcar on any street after its franchise expired anywhere else in the city without thereby agreeing to three-cent fares with universal transfers everywhere. It was a tour de force of creative legal imagination. Hally was careful to require notice and a hearing before the city could deem its terms accepted.

Lacking any other means of engaging the DUR, Thompson persuaded the Common Council to take up its first and second reading but was blocked at the last minute from its final adoption by a temporary restraining order obtained by the Guaranty Trust Company of New York from U.S. Circuit Court Judge Henry H. Swan on July 23, 1907.[37] The Guaranty Trust held $22 million in mortgage bonds secured by all assets of the DUR. Before giving the city a hearing at which to object, Judge Swan left the bench on a lengthy vacation away from Detroit.

"The DUR has obviously started on a campaign designed to tire and worry the City of Detroit into giving up its fight for 3-cent fares," said *The Public*, a national public affairs journal published weekly, quoting the *Detroit Evening News*. "The biggest question raised is as to the firmness and patience of the people of Detroit in meeting the vexatious and procrastinating tactics of their ancient foe."[38]

The Common Council, weary of pushing back demands for streetcar service from neighborhoods across the city and frustrated by lack of any settlement with the DUR ahead of the annual election, put two proposals on the ballot, September 17, 1907. They would allow the DUR to build eleven of the most frequently demanded railway line extensions clamored for by residents living far from streets served by the existing three- and five-cent lines. Mayor Thompson and the *Evening News* opposed their adoption without a requirement for across-the-board three-cent fares. Both were soundly defeated, 3,004-9,554 and 3,738-10,502.

In his annual message on January 14, 1908, Thompson looked to the future. Thompson said it better than Pingree ever had.

> We are now within a little more than a year of our day of reckoning, when the shackles of existing contracts shall, by limitation, be struck off, after 30 years of servitude, and we can, if we will, become again a free city. Through these years of struggle we have learned much: we have learned the binding force of franchise contracts; the galling weight of public service monopoly; the haste and solicitude of courts to protect vested rights; and the need of caution in making any new contracts. The lesson has been bitter, but out of the struggle and the sacrifice has been born the indestructible resolve to finally get back our rights and keep them. The end crowns the work.

When he returned to the bench eight months later, Judge Swan admitted that he had been at least premature and dissolved his restraining order against adoption of the Hally ordinance. At its meeting that same night, March 3, 1908, the Common Council unanimously adopted a less sweeping version of the Hally ordinance, 31-0, requiring five for fifteen-cent fares and universal transfers on about five miles of the 180-mile street railway system where the DUR's consent to operate had expired. Mayor Thompson stayed up late that night to sign it. Guaranty Trust's lawyers stayed up still later, and an agreeable Judge Swan was available to sign an order enjoining the city clerk from its publication. Until published the ordinance was ineffective under the city charter.

By making the DUR a codefendant and filing new federal litigation, lawyers for the Guaranty Trust not only succeeded in delaying any hearing on the underlying main issue, but they confounded the city's otherwise hapless defense. Judge Swan held a perfunctory hearing on April 6, 1908, at which he orally granted a preliminary injunction against the city "from publishing or enforcing said ordinance, and the defendant Detroit United Railway from doing any act or thing that would directly or indirectly constitute an acceptance."[39]

Although Detroit took an immediate appeal from the preliminary injunction, the U.S. Sixth Circuit Court of Appeals would not decide the case until nearly a year later on March 17, 1909, when it was rejected on procedural grounds that the DUR was a necessary party the city had failed to name on appeal. The opinion written by U.S. District Judge Andrew McConnell January Cochran of Kentucky was noteworthy not only for his long name celebrating both his mother and grandfather but the fact that the other two judges on the appeals court panel were Judges Horace H. Lurton and Henry F. Severens, both of whom had personal judicial experience with Detroit streetcar litigation dating back to 1893. "It may be said that the interest of the railway was not against the order granting the preliminary injunction, but in having it stand, and that, therefore, it had no right to appeal therefrom, or to unite with appellants in the appeal they took," wrote Judge Cochran in concluding his opinion for the three-judge panel.

Nonetheless, he tossed out the appeal. "We do not find it necessary to consider and determine this position. All that follows from it, if it be correct, is that the railway should have been made a respondent to the appeal. . . . Appellants have ignored the railway entirely. They have treated it as if it had no interest in the order appealed from. It has not appeared here, and it is by no act or neglect on its part that it is not here."[40]

Even while recognizing that the Guaranty Trust and DUR shared not only an identical interest but also active participation in the case before Judge Swan against Detroit, the appeals court rendered a perverse technical ruling against hearing the legal merits of the case, which went back to Detroit where it would remain ignored on Judge Swan's docket.

The Grey Nuns of Montreal

"In the fall of 1907, there came almost out of a clear sky another obstacle in the form of a widespread and very serious financial panic," Hutchins said, describing the Panic of 1907.

> With money easy to get, the company had used its full credit purchasing cars, dynamos, steel rails, rights-of-way, terminal grounds, yard sites, and many other things, besides owing large sums to both home and eastern banks, all running into millions of dollar. . . .
>
> Dividends beginning at four and later raised to six dollars per annum, had been regularly paid quarterly; but at a board meeting held in New York about the middle of September in 1907, action in that particular was deferred to the thirteenth of the following month, by which date, with time enough left for the required closing of the books, a dividend could, if warranted, be declared payable November first, as usual. But when the board reassembled October thirteenth, conditions had not improved; on the contrary, they were so much worse that some directors found it difficult to get their checks cashed for money enough to pay their fare back home. . . .
>
> Everett and Moore wondered if, by withholding all payments to creditors, the dividend might not be paid out of current receipts. This, it was admitted, could be done; but no one could tell how long the prevailing panic might endure, and Hutchins asked, "Would we not show better faith by distributing these receipts among our creditors as is now being done than by distributing these receipts among ourselves as stockholders?" . . .
>
> In the end, by unanimous action of the board, the dividend was passed; and, in less than five minutes this fact came to be known on the stock exchanges of both New York and Montreal, with the result that the stock took an immediate downward plunge of about forty dollars a share.[41]

"Panic in Montreal Stock Exchange" was the headline written by the *New York Times* on October 16, 1907. "The local stock market experienced a panic this morning as the result of the passing of the quarterly dividend on the Detroit United Railways. This stock is very largely held here. From 50 at the close of the market yesterday to 40 at the opening today was the first drop, and later it dropped to 28½. The Street is full of stories of people who have lost heavily by the slump."

"Montreal was much excited," Hutchins said. "Telegrams came pouring in." Telling only his board of directors, Hutchins caught the first train for Montreal, where he arrived by breakfast the next morning to be greeted by six stockholders waiting in the hotel lobby. "I cheerfully told them only that a room as large as the hotel could provide would be engaged and that at eleven o'clock he would tell such stockholders as should assemble there all that he knew of their company's affairs,"

Hutchins said. "By the time set the room designed for such purposes was filled to overflowing with stockholders talking excitedly among themselves in two languages."[42]

Investors in Montreal, who had acquired much of Wilson's stock in 1901, purchased significantly more in the wake of the 1902 collapse of the Everett-Moore syndicate. Angered at the personal criticism he was hearing, DUR director Herbert S. Holt of Montreal announced his intention to resign. Holt was an Irish-born Canadian civil engineer who became a businessman, banker, and corporate director with a ruthless reputation. He was president of the Royal Bank of Canada and of Montreal Light, Heat & Power, and a director of 250 companies worldwide. He was regarded as the richest man in Canada. And when his death was announced during the fifth inning of a baseball game in 1941, the Jarry Park crowd cheered.

"Lively indeed was this informal meeting," Hutchins said. "A barrage of assertions and questions assailed the visitor, seated at the head of a long table. Why had he not advised them the passing of the dividend was contemplated? Its passing was no more nor less than a stock-jobbing scheme. Doubtless, Henry Everett and Edward Moore, who had sold them their stock originally, were now conspiring to pull off bigger profits."[43] It was not true, Hutchins said, that either Everett or Moore, who was still a director, or anybody else had used the present situation to the stockholder's disadvantage.

Many in Detroit had long questioned why Montreal investors held so much DUR stock. "Isn't there a significance in the fact that the city in which the shares of this company are most generally held is a city distant by nearly 600 miles from Detroit, and located in a jurisdiction in which exact knowledge of the important conditions affecting the company's future would not, in the nature of things be as widely disseminated as in an American city?" asked the *Free Press* editorial page on October 18, 1907.

> The expiring franchises constitute the backbone of the D.U.R., the value of their goodwill is greater than that of all the other D.U.R. properties combined. They will never be renewed on terms enabling the company to make as great profits in the future as in the past, and there is always the danger that the management through mistaken policies of antagonism may not succeed in obtaining a renewal at all. In this latter event, those Montrealers who are resentful because they had to sell under 30 might have reason to congratulate themselves that they got out in as good shape as they did get out.[44]

Hutchins had gone to Montreal only to deal with the immediate crisis. "He had believed it best in the interests of the stockholders themselves to conserve the company's resources by passing the dividend and having himself urged the directors to that course, the responsibility lay entirely upon him as head of the corporation," Hutchins said he told the gathered shareholders in Montreal contrary to what he actually told the board in New York. "Hold tight, all of you, till this storm blows over, and you will come out all right."[45] Hutchins recalled that a unanimous vote of confidence followed his pep talk.

Montreal's stockholders, however, insisted on adding three directors of their choosing to the board. Hutchins agreed but urged them to keep Holt, who accepted. They nominated two others—Senator Joseph M. Wilson, a French-Canadian capitalist from Montreal, and A. J. Ferguson, of the Montreal investment banking firm of Hansons & Ferguson. Before the day was over, Hutchins said, the stock regained most of its loss on the Montreal and New York stock exchanges. The DUR's Montreal stockholders would thereafter be referred to in Detroit as the Grey Nuns of Montreal.[46]

The Barcroft Fiasco

Mayor Thompson, having been unable to make good his campaign for three-cent fares, was defeated for reelection in November 1908 by Republican Philip Breitmeyer, who eagerly promised to settle the streetcar issue in a businesslike manner by municipal purchase before the old Detroit City Railway franchise expired a year later on November 14, 1909. He did so even though it was now widely understood by Detroit voters that simply waiting until the franchise expired would immeasurably strengthen Detroit's position. Breitmeyer, who had been president of the hugely successful Florists' Telegraph Delivery, appointed another Committee of Fifty, headed by Frank W. Eddy, a wealthy Republican rubber goods and chemical manufacturer. A poll of its fifty members betrayed Breitmeyer's promise of municipal ownership. The tally of his appointees found only two who favored municipal ownership. All the others favored a settlement with the DUR under the Taylor Plan adopted in Cleveland by Mayor Tom Johnson.

U.S. District Judge Robert W. Taylor of the Northern District of Ohio gave name to the Taylor Plan. He had been jointly appointed to settle streetcars fares by Mayor Johnson and the Cleveland Electric Railway Company. Judge Taylor had determined the value of the streetcar plant and franchise, upon which it was agreed that the company should earn a 6 percent profit in pricing streetcar fares from which Judge Taylor set a three-cent fare. Before Detroit could adopt the Taylor Plan, the value of the company's physical property and its unexpired franchises had to be agreed upon by the city and the DUR.

Breitmeyer's Committee of Fifty formally organized itself into twelve subcommittees assigned to investigate various aspects of street railway service. Because their funding was coming from a closely watching Common Council, they decided to operate as if they, too, were a public body. On February 25, 1909, the key subcommittee on appraisal headed by Joseph Boyer, president of the Burroughs Adding Machine Company, was unfortunate in selecting as its chief appraiser Frederick T. Barcroft, a thirty-six-year-old civil engineer and architect.[47] He had served as an assistant engineer for several railroads before settling in Detroit and gaining the political favor of Mayor Breitmeyer, who had recently appointed him to Detroit's new Plan and Improvement Commission. The Committee of Fifty followed Breitmeyer's lead. What Barcroft lacked in street railway experience he made up for in bravado. He told the Committee of Fifty he would complete a full appraisal of the DUR in less than eight weeks at a cost of less than $4,500. It actually took him more than eight months at a cost of more than $30,000.[48]

Hutchins's appraisal of Barcroft's work was scathing. "After the man they had chosen had been fooling around several months," he said, "it was discovered that what he had done was worse than useless."[49]

Barcroft's 237-page report on Detroit's street railways was a genuinely pioneering work, however, that he based on the depreciated value of the street railway system as opposed to the cost of its reproduction. He did not include the cost of paving. Not doing so, justifiably, was his only major difference with the street railway company, a fact that got lost in the resulting controversy. "An

Mayor Philip Breitmeyer. From *A Gallery of Pen Sketches in Black and White of Our Michigan Friends "As We See 'Em,"* ed. C. O. Youngstrand (Detroit: Wm. Graham Printing Company, 1905).

appraisal of all the street railways of Detroit has recently been completed under the direction of Mr. Frederick T. Barcroft," wrote the weekly *Engineering-Contracting* magazine published in Chicago. "Mr. Barcroft's report is the *most complete* published record of its kind that we have *ever seen*" (emphasis added).[50]

On February 15, 1909, Hutchins had added to the DUR staff his own expert, Robert B. Rifenberick, a civil engineer and street railway expert with experience in New Orleans and Cleveland, whom Hutchins assigned to work with and follow fast behind Barcroft. They poured over the same comprehensive inventory—forty thousand typewritten pages compiled by two hundred clerks over three months listing every bolt, nut, screw, hammer, power generator, railway, streetcar, and everything else owned by the DUR. Rifenberick privately concluded that the entire physical plant should be valued at $24,798,275 using the reproduction cost method.

Supremely confident but politically inept, Barcroft leaked his report to the Detroit press ahead of its official delivery to the Committee of Fifty on October 1. He announced that the entire physical plant should be valued at $11,121,725 on the depreciated value basis. A few days later the DUR leaked Rifenberick's valuation. So great was the resulting misunderstanding and controversy that Rifenberick gathered together and republished his fifty-one-page critique in pamphlet form for distribution to the street railway industry in August 1910. It was titled "A Statement of 'Facts' concerning the so-called 'Barcroft appraisal' of the Detroit United Railway lines in the City of Detroit."

Initially, DUR general manager Frank Brooks had candidly admitted that

> we do not figure in this the actual condition of the lines. We have figures to show this but this particular report is based on what it would cost to reproduce the system as a going concern. Our engineers have had wide experience and daily contact with the business of building and operating street railways. They have given deep study to the whole question of values. . . . Of course, we have no knowledge of what the Committee of Fifty engineers have found, but if they resemble the published figures we assume the Fifty will permit us to know what the figures are and how they happen to be so widely at variance with what we know.[51]

But what the DUR did to destroy the work and reputation of Mayor Breitmeyer's chosen expert during the next few months was at the cutthroat highest level. The result was made worse by Barcroft's professionally naive refusal to defend his conclusion to the Committee of Fifty or anyone else until he was he paid more for doing so, doubling his exposure to ridicule from the DUR, Committee of Fifty, Common Council members, and Detroit's newspapers.

On November 4, 1909, Frank Brooks crossed paths with Barcroft in the lobby of the Ponchartrain Hotel. "You're the —— appraiser who says the DUR is worth only $12,500,000 and now it is $10,500,000," Brooks exclaimed. "You're a —— of an appraiser." Mayor Breitmeyer, who happened to be nearby, stepped between the two men. "Barcroft made a dignified retreat."[52]

Barcroft later described the scene: "On Thursday evening, November 4th, when I left the office at the Pontchartrain with a friend, I was assailed in the most intemperate manner by the General Manager of the Detroit United Railway, who loudly and boastingly stated he not only knew all the Committee's transactions but further stated, in most vicious language, what his company intended to do to the City, the Committee, my men and myself."[53]

The Committee of Fifty stumbled around for months before appointing a board of arbitration to decide the valuation consisting of Wayne Circuit Judge James O. Murfin, former Michigan Supreme Court Judge Claudius B. Grant, and Judge Taylor of Cleveland. Barcroft, however, refused to come forward to defend his report. Even Mayor Breitmeyer pressured Barcroft.

"It is incomprehensible that the Mayor cannot seem to understand my position and that financial remuneration cannot change it," Barcroft told the *Evening News*. "I will appear before any board of arbitration that is given official standing with a definite purpose fixed in advance, that has police power and power to subpoena witnesses, and that has the sanction of the city and the company to the extent that both will be bound by the result. In such a body, I must have an opportunity to aid in preparation of my own case. I must have funds for such purpose and I must have sympathetic legal assistance. These are only necessary contingencies. I must repeat that my position cannot change."[54]

Eddy was thoroughly disgusted with Barcroft.

> The public can judge for itself the motives of a man who disregards a pledge of that kind, who not only leaves in the lurch the very men who appointed him and paid him, but who goes out of his way to injure the very cause for which he was employed, on the success of which these men have set their hearts. To me it is obvious that he is opposed to a fair settlement of the streetcar question, and that he

> is in league with others to prevent it. . . . If Mr. Barcroft does not feel capable of backing up his report, all right. He has displayed so much animus and prejudice that I am inclined to believe he would not be of value as a witness in any event.[55]

Barcroft still refused to appear before the arbitration panel.

"Of course, this slip handicapped both the committee and the company," Hutchins said. "In fact, it finished the Taylor Plan. This committee of representative citizens tried hard to find a fair solution that press and public would accept, but it was not in the cards that they could do so. And this added to the conviction that the company's salvation lay in the building of a plant large and useful enough to down all opposition. Breitmeyer's efforts, strengthened by his Committee of Fifty, to bring about an adjustment on the basis of fares at cost, plus six per cent on invested capital, failed."[56]

Equity Abhors a Forfeiture

The DUR's original franchise as extended in 1879 to operate on the busier downtown streets was nearing expiration on November 14, 1909. Long stretches of Judge Woodward's radial system of roads, however, were occupied under even longer rights that had been originally granted by the neighboring townships before the expansion of Detroit's city limits. More significantly, few politicians and even fewer voters remembered that the three-cent fare company had years ago acquired rights to operate over the original Detroit City Railway lines of 1862 in downtown Detroit in a deal quietly engineered in 1895 by Tom Johnson. By their merger, the DUR would still have use of them until 1924, when the franchise granted to Pingree's three-cent lines expired.

"Beyond and connected with the tracks of the city system there fanned out, like the spokes of a wheel, hundreds of miles of tracks that served rich countryside and many growing and prosperous cities, towns, and villages. Rates of fare on these outside lines were low, being less than one-third that of the steam railways," Hutchins wrote. "Because the franchises expired at different times on various routes and in many instances at different times on the same street, it did not seem reasonable that the company could be stopped some night at midnight when one of these thirty-year franchises expired."[57]

"Questions of plain and simple equity were involved," Hutchins continued. "Some of the company's lawyers, particularly Frederick A. Baker III were of the opinion that the city, after having invited the expenditures of millions in its streets, could not arbitrarily confiscate the millions so entrapped. Baker quoted law and adage in support of his theories, dating all along the way from the present time back to the beginning of civilization, but could cite no decision by an American court for the simple reason that no case involving expired franchises had ever been tried in an American court."[58]

In 1910, Baker self-published *Duration of Municipal Street Grants*, a 237-page legal argument with a 174-page appendix consisting of lengthy street railway ordinances adopted in Chicago and Indianapolis. His legal argument tried to avoid making a naked appeal to fairness and equity as Judge Swan did in his dissent against Judge Taft years before by instead exhaustively arguing that the common law of implied contracts gave the DUR not only a right but a public duty to continue carrying passengers indefinitely at a fare to be decided by the courts, in part, because the Detroit's ordinance granting consent did not specifically require that the DUR surrender its possession of the streets upon expiration even though construing the ordinance in favor of the city made such an argument far-fetched at best. In the *Charles River Bridge* case the U.S. Supreme Court had expressly decided, "In grants by the public, *nothing passes by implication*" (emphasis added).[59] Baker all but admitted as much in making the argument central to his book. He said:

> An implied covenant on the part of the City of Detroit that it would not prevent the Detroit City Railway Company, its successors and assigns, from continuing beyond the period of thirty years the service the street railways render the public, is much more in accord with the facts of the case and the law applicable thereto, than an *implied covenant* on the part of the company that at the end of the thirty years it would cease operating its railways, and would remove the tracks and other structures from the streets.
>
> Any such surrender by the company would be a public disaster. New street railways could not be built and put in operation for many months; and when we give due consideration to the legal obligation of the company to continue to serve the public, and to the legal obligation of the city as trustee for the general public, to protect and improve its streets as to make them convenient and useful, the conclusion is inevitable that the City must have contracted with a full recognition of its own and the company's obligation, and that the company has a right to remain in the street beyond thirty years. (emphasis added)[60]

Directly refuting Baker's argument, in concluding its decision affirming the Michigan Supreme Court's 1898 ruling against exclusive rights, the U.S. Supreme Court had already specifically said, "Easements in the public streets for a limited time are different and have different consequences from those given in perpetuity. . . . *Consequently those given in perpetuity . . . must have for their authority explicit permission, or, if inferred from other powers, it is not enough that the authority is convenient to them, but it must be indispensable to them*" (emphasis added).[61]

Baker argued otherwise. "It is impossible to escape the conviction that street railways . . . are at their inception intended to be permanent public improvements and not mere temporary affairs. . . . If an express stipulation, that at the end of the term, the tracks should be taken out of the streets, and the service stopped, even for the length of time it would take to build new street railways, it would have been laughed at as absurd, and some provision would have been found to prevent any such thing."[62]

To the contrary, more specifically, the limited privilege to operate a street railway company was never a laughing matter under the state constitution and the Street-Railway Act. Upon expiration of its thirty-year corporate life, a street railway company was automatically dissolved and required to wind up its affairs by simple operation of law. Nothing else was necessary before the city could demand removal of its tracks from the streets if a buyer with municipal consent to use them had not already been found. More difficult, not only for Baker but also for everyone else, was making an implied contract argument favoring a street railway company that had entered into a contract such as the Detroit City Railway with itself a specific expiration date.

In Detroit, on October 9, 1909, the Common Council had unanimously adopted, 35-0, a resolution describing most of the streets on which the DUR operated and concluded:

> That all right and title on the part of said company, the Detroit United Railway, to such franchises and tracks maintained thereunder in the said streets above mentioned, have heretofore terminated or will have terminated on November 14, 1909; and any further use on the part of the said company of said tracks located as above set forth above, where the right to operate cars has expired, is by sufferance only and without expressed or implied waiver upon the part of the city of Detroit to enforce its rights in regard to such streets and to re-possess itself of the same; and that any further use on the part of said company of said tracks where the right to operate cars will be expired November 14, 1909, after said date, is by sufferance only and without express or implied waiver on the part of the City of Detroit to enforce its rights in regard to such streets and to re-possess itself of the same.

A few days later, on October 26, 1909, by a vote of 32-0, the Common Council adopted another resolution subject to revocation at will demanding that the DUR pay $300 per day to continue operating on streets where its franchise had expired. Hutchins agreed to pay in correspondence dated November 13, 1909.[63]

"I submit this question," Baker wrote. "Which would be more in accord with the American system of jurisprudence, and with the sentiments of a thoroughly civilized race of men, to make the truce permanent, and settle the controversy by submitting the question whether the rates of fare charged by the street railway company are excessive or not, to a court of competent jurisdiction, possessed of the necessary legal machinery, and charged with the duty, of doing equal and exact justice, or to renew a barbarous struggle, in which each of the husky warriors seek to decide the issue himself, and proposes to use whatever power he may possess to accomplish his own purpose?"[64]

The Thompson-Hally Ordinance

Thompson was reelected mayor in November 1911 on his repeated pledge to make the DUR agree to three-cent fares. "Thompson spent several months of his new term trying to induce the company to make good his promise, while at the same time Hally looked sharply for legal weapons of assault," Hutchins said. "Resourceful and desperately in earnest, Hally picked some weapons that to the company staff of lawyers looked exceedingly dangerous."[65]

Some of the best lawyers in Detroit—Baker, Elliott G. Stevenson, John C. Donnelly, William L. Carpenter, and Charles D. Joslyn—were handling DUR legal matters. "Nevertheless, thinking that some fresh legal mind outside of Detroit might see points that would be overlooked at close range, Hutchins—without consulting anybody—went to New York, with Elihu Root in mind," Hutchins said.[66]

Root is one of the most admired lawyers in American history. He was born in 1845 in Clinton, New York, son of a professor of mathematics at Hamilton College. At Hamilton College, Root graduated first in his class in 1864. He taught school for a year, graduated from the New York University Law School in 1867, founded a law firm, and by the age of thirty had established himself as a preeminent lawyer in corporate affairs. In 1899, President McKinley appointed him secretary of war. He returned to his private legal practice in 1904. A year later, President Theodore Roosevelt appointed him secretary of state. He served in the U.S. Senate from 1909 to 1915.

John C. Donnelly. From *A Gallery of Pen Sketches in Black and White of Our Michigan Friends "As We See 'Em,"* ed. C. O. Youngstrand (Detroit: Wm. Graham Printing Company, 1905).

Elihu Root. Prints and Photographs Division, Library of Congress, LC-USZ62-72828.

> Mr. Root's former partner, Mr. Bronson Winthrop, said he could see no reason why Mr. Root, then a United States Senator at Washington, should not act as counsel for the company were he disposed to do so. It was arranged that this gentleman would confer by letter with Mr. Root and would ask him—should he be interested—to name a time and place for a desired conference. Two or three days later Mr. Root wired that he would be pleased to see Hutchins at Clinton, New York, the next Monday morning. This appointment was promptly kept. Clinton is the seat of Hamilton College. The conference took place in the modest house in which Mr. Root was born and in which his father lived for forty years while serving as a professor in the college.[67]

Root listened patiently for three hours, asking many questions and showing the deepest interest, Hutchins said.

> Then, after requesting that Donnelly should write him regarding one certain fact, he promised that as soon as possible he would forward his opinion, adding that he thought a strong case had been presented.

> And, thus, the keen brain of Elihu Root was set to work in a just case. . . . About a month later the promised opinion was received, accompanied by a letter promising that the writer, if called upon to do so, would gladly defend that opinion in the United States Supreme Court.[68]

A day or two later, at a meeting in the offices of DUR attorney John Donnelly, Hutchins delivered copies of the Root opinion to Mayor Thompson and Hally. "Hally read it aloud, combed his abundant hair through his fingers, read it once again, and said his respect for Elihu Root was such that he would have to recede from his attitude that three-cent fares could be forced by litigation."[69]

"This decision brought about other tactics," Hutchins said. "Thompson urged that, if the company would accept an ordinance providing for an extension of its franchises at five-cent cash fares and eight tickets for twenty-five cents good at all hours, he would cooperate to that end and everybody would be happy. In the meantime, the company's interurban lines, with their largely increased passenger and freight earnings, were returning substantial profits, while the city lines in a fast-growing city were also prospering and all were being operated as one unit. It seemed the time had come when these rates would suffice."[70] Hutchins told Thompson and Hally to proceed. They called in Antoine DuPont from Cleveland to assist in negotiating and drafting the ordinance for which he was paid $5,000. Because the new state constitution prohibited the city from granting a franchise not revocable at will by the city without a three-fifths popular vote, it was agreed that the DUR would immediately start the construction of some much-needed railways under revocable so-called day-to-day permits—a significant and risky concession by Hutchins that he would regret making. The city's main growth had been along Judge Woodward's several great diagonal streets in territory extending far beyond its earlier limits. Upon these diagonals, tracks already existed, but there had been enormous growth between them that had long been inadequately served.

"In pursuance of the policy to expand, regardless of franchises, some millions of dollars were expended to build new lines, . . ." Hutchins said, "though it was stipulated in the permits to build that the City could at will require the immediate removal of these tracks or could take them over at cost less depreciation. And other very large sums were at the same time spent for cars and equipment to keep the service up to date."[71]

Thompson and Hally carefully drafted the new franchise. It fixed rates at eight tickets for twenty-five cents from 5 A.M. to 8 P.M., with transfers, required paving by the city, and secured line extensions, and gave Detroit the right to purchase on six months' notice, assigning no value to franchise rights while setting December 4, 1924, as the uniform expiration date of all DUR franchises.

"In so doing they were justly proud because it practically provided the rate of fare that Thompson had promised to bring about in his two elections to the mayoralty," Hutchins said. "Then the day came when their achievement was sprung on the people. At first, as in the cases of Codd and Breitmeyer, there were joyous expressions of approval. Now, thought many thousands of people, we are to get what we have long wanted, and the age-old streetcar fuss is ended."[72]

But the *Evening News* objected. "Alackaday!" said Hutchins. "Up rose the same old newspaper in full-page opposition. If the company could make money at that rate—was its plea—the city by owning the railways can make more money at a lesser rate."[73]

The *Evening News* "has made use of the street railway situation at all times as a means of making capital with the class of readers to which it caters," observed one industry journal. "The policy of this

Mayor William B. Thompson. From *The Government of the City of Detroit and Wayne County, Michigan, 1701 to 1907* (Detroit: Mannausa & Weiber, 1907), 52.

paper has been to make war on the street railway company at all times, without regard to the issue. For 17 years, Thompson has been 'fighting against the company'—as he expresses it himself—and throughout that time he had the support of the newspaper in question. But when there was hope of a settlement according to the Thompson plan the newspaper made a bitter campaign against it."[74]

The *Free Press* on December 7, 1911, argued that for twenty years the people had listened to demagogues "and for twenty years the people had not got a new mile of track out of the agitation and litigation which have thus been provoked, and have continued to pay a straight five-cent fare instead of the six for a quarter fares they enjoyed before the wind jammers began jamming the wind. . . . If the people choose to vote for this enormous improvement in the streetcar service, they can get it almost at once. If they choose to vote against it, they will go on possibly another twenty years with the same inadequate service and the same high rate of fare."[75]

Frank Brooks was resigned.

> We accepted that plan just as we have accepted every other definite proposition from the City for a settlement of the street railway question. We agreed to accept Mayor Pingree's plan for the City to buy the street railway; then, when Mayor Maybury took office and did nothing we fell in his policy and let

our affairs rest as they were. We agreed to accept Mayor Codd's plan, and when that was rejected by the people and Mayor Breitmeyer proposed the appointment of a committee of 50 citizens to devise a plan we agreed to that. Finally, we agreed to the Thompson-Hally ordinance. We have stood ready at any time to meet the City half way in any effort to arrange a settlement.[76]

On January 23, 1912, the Thompson-Hally ordinance was submitted to the voters. It lost, 22,308-30,733. Mayor Thompson said a few days later:

The people want a 3-cent fare. And that is why we have been trying all these years to get it for them. Our idea is simply this—the people of Cleveland can ride for three pennies, so why not the people of Detroit? It is true, the company tells us that the three-cent fare would be unprofitable; that it is operating its lines in the city at a loss even now, and that the losses on its Detroit business must be made up from receipts of the outside part of the system; but that is part of the company's troubles and we will let the company look after it. What we're after is a three-cent fare and we will keep after it until we get it. The adoption of the Thompson-Hally ordinance would have saved the people $1,500,000 this year in street car fares.[77]

The Battle of Fort Wayne

A few days later, on January 30, 1912, in the wake his proposal's defeat at the polls, Mayor Thompson directed Corporation Counsel Richard I. Lawson to vigorously proceed with litigation that been suspended pending outcome of the vote. Among others, he specifically mentioned a Wayne County Circuit Court case involving an arcane legal dispute over the expiration dates of the street railway company's franchises to operate its Fort Street lines that turned into the decisive legal battle of the Thirty-Year War.

Six years earlier, on May 2, 1906, the city and the DUR had agreed to a workingmen's fare ordinance specifically applying on Fort Wayne and Elmwood Railway Company lines in recently annexed parts of Springwells Township that had originally granted five-cent franchises in 1889 and 1891. They would not expire until December 13, 1921. The township franchises affected no territory east of Artillery Avenue, which was the western limit of a third township grant and two city grants that had expired in 1910. The 1906 ordinance said:

The Detroit United Railway shall *for the full term of said township grant*, issue and sell tickets at the rate of eight tickets for twenty-five cents, each of said tickets to be good for a continuous route between any two points on what is known as the routes of the Fort Wayne & Elmwood Railway lines, so called, whether constructed under grants from the township of Springwells or from the city of Detroit, between the hours from 5 a.m. to 6:30 a.m. and the hours of 4:45 and 5:45 p.m.; but the terms of said township grants in all other respects shall not be modified nor changed, nor shall this ordinance and the acceptance thereof be construed to abridge, enlarge or extend any rights acquired by said railway company, its assignors, or predecessors in title to said several grants from the township of Springwells. (emphasis added)

The highlighted phrase gave rise to Thompson's push for a ruling in this litigation between the city and the DUR because "the full term of said township grant" was December 14, 1921. Restrained against publishing the Hally ordinance by the Guaranty Trust lawsuit still awaiting trial by Judge Swan in the U.S. District Court, in defiance the Common Council adopted a resolution on July 19, 1910, requiring the DUR to pay $200 per day if it continued to operate streetcars on the Fort Wayne and Elmwood Street lines after its franchises from the city expired by July 24, 1910. Hutchins refused to pay, arguing that the 1906 ordinance had extended the franchise to December 14, 1921. "We are compelled to advise you that we deny the statement contained in the preamble . . . to the effect that the rights of the company have expired," Hutchins wrote.[78]

On September 15, 1910, the city sued in Wayne County Circuit Court to enforce its $200 per day rental resolution. A three-judge panel rejected both the DUR's argument that its franchises had not expired and the city's demand for $200 per day. The opinion written by Judge Alfred J. Murphy said the city's only remedy was ejectment—which would require the DUR to cease providing service and to remove its street railways.[79] Neither the city nor the DUR sought entry of final order doing so pending settlement negotiations of the federal court case and a vote on the Thompson-Hally ordinance.

On January 30, 1912, at Mayor Thompson's urging, the Common Council voted, 30-0, to seek entry of a formal decree so that the ruling could be appealed to the Michigan Supreme Court. Judge Aaron V. McAlvay wrote a unanimous opinion delivered on October 1, 1912, with Judge John E. Bird writing in a concurring opinion, "in doing so I do not want to be understood as holding that the city may not recover damages in an appropriate proceeding for defendant's trespass in refusing to vacate the streets after the franchises expired."[80] That was a doubly troubling warning to the DUR because Judge McAlvay had so briskly rejected the DUR's extension argument. "We think that it is not necessary to give this ordinance a construction by inference and presumption, and hold that by its plain and unambiguous terms it was restricted to a modification of the township grants as to rate of fare, and any and all other changes or modifications of the terms of said *township grants* to this railway company were expressly excluded," he said (emphasis added).[81]

Actually, the DUR was arguing that the 1906 ordinance extended until 1921 the two expired *city grants* and one *township grant*. Judge McAlvay's confusion is understandable. It was a remarkably confusing case arising from a poorly drafted ordinance. The phrase "for the full term of said township grant" added nothing but the possibility of misunderstanding to the 1906 ordinance under review by Judge McAlvay. Justice William R. Day, writing for the U.S. Supreme Court, however, explained it correctly.

> The argument is that, as this [1906] ordinance obligates the railway for the full term of the township grants, which do not expire until December 14, 1921, to sell tickets and transport passengers over its railway, including the portion covered by the now expired grants, the last-named grants of the railway were thereby extended to expire at the same time with the township grants, because only by such construction can the obligation of the railway to furnish transportation for the full term of the township grants be complied with; that this was a contractual obligation proposed by the city and accepted by the railway, and necessarily extended the grants of the railway.[82]

Having rejected the DUR's extension argument, much more important for the city and the DUR was what Judge McAlvay consequently decided about their legal relationship with each other following expiration of the last of those three franchises on July 24, 1910. "The matter of defining the relations between these parties under the circumstances of this case is not without its difficulties," he said. "We think, however, that complainant in stating its contention that the relations in all respects are analogous to the relations between landlords and tenants of real estate under similar circumstances makes an impossible comparison, for the reason that similar circumstances could not arise between an ordinary landlord and tenant. . . . The right of the defendant was an incorporeal right, created for the public use, which imposed no additional servitude upon the public streets."[83]

Judge McAlvay summarily rejected Baker's implied contract theory out of hand.[84] "We think that in advancing this argument the fact is overlooked that constitutionally enacted statutes and ordinances have provided when the terms of these franchises expire, and also determined the contractual relations, which were created by the acceptance of franchises lawfully granted. Taking, as we do, this view of the situation, we do not recognize the existence of the implied obligation claimed."[85]

More simply, Judge McAlvay said that the DUR's intangible right to operate had expired. Despite its installation of railways, poles, and wires in the streets, Judge McAlvay refused to recognize that a municipal franchise granting consent to operate conveyed any right attached to the land. The city's consent had granted no right to occupancy of the streets that was legally distinguishable from that enjoyed by the general public—pedestrians, bicyclists, horseback riders, horse-drawn wagons, motorcar drivers, and streetcars all shared the public right-of-way. Having found no existing legal or equitable remedy for the DUR's expired consent, Judge McAlvay moved to the more troublesome issue of what the city could do as a consequence. First, he ruled against Hally's $200-a-day resolution. "No authority has been cited to the effect that a municipality may arbitrarily, without consent of the grantee, impose terms upon a street railway in granting franchises. Such a holding would be repugnant to the universally accepted doctrine that such franchises are mutual contracts," he said.[86]

Judge McAlvay struggled mightily with the rule that had been cemented into the common law across the country by the *Charles River Bridge* case so many years before that legislative grants to privately owned companies using public lands such as rivers and roads must be narrowly construed in favor of state and municipal government. What he finally said doomed the DUR:

> The conclusion to be drawn from our determination of the different propositions discussed is that the contractual relations between the parties ended upon the expiration of the franchises, and all rights of the defendant company to occupy the city streets, and maintain and operate a street railway thereon, then terminated, and defendant thereafter became a trespasser; that complainant had the absolute and unquestioned right at any time to compel the defendant company to vacate the streets upon which these franchises have expired, and to require it to remove its property therefrom within a reasonable time, and, if necessary, for that purpose, to enforce its rights by a writ of assistance from this court.[87]

The Michigan Supreme Court's formal decree, delayed by jockeying among attorneys for the city

Mayor Oscar B. Marx. From Clarence M. Burton, William Stocking, and Gordon K. Miller, *The City of Detroit, Michigan, 1701–1922* (Detroit: S. J. Clarke, 1922), 3:608.

and the DUR, was not entered until February 27, 1913. It directed the Wayne County Circuit Court to enter an order saying the DUR must stop operating streetcars on its Fort Wayne and Elmwood Street lines upon ten-day notice and remove all of its property from the streets upon ninety-day notice. The DUR obtained a stay from the U.S. Supreme Court on March 14, 1913, while its hopeless appeal to the U.S. Supreme Court was pending.

Mayor Marx's Appointee from the Ford Motor Company

Well versed in municipal affairs, a thoroughly practical Republican politician bankrolled by John F. Dodge, automotive parts manufacturer, Oscar B. Marx defeated Thompson's bid for reelection in November 1912. Marx was born on July 14, 1866, the son of German immigrants. He attended the Detroit public schools and the German-American Seminary but spent much of his early life farming. As Detroit grew, the encroaching city swallowed the family farm in Hamtramck Township. Marx's father sold the farm, giving each of his sons several thousand dollars. Oscar Marx used his money in 1891 to buy into a bankrupt optical firm, the Michigan Optical Company, which he steered into becoming one of the largest in the country. Marx was vice president of the Robert Oakman Land Company. Oakman, Dodge, and Marx together controlled all of the political apparatus of the state

Henry Ford. From *A Gallery of Pen Sketches in Black and White of Our Michigan Friends "As We See 'Em,"* ed. C. O. Youngstrand (Detroit: Wm. Graham Printing Company, 1905).

Republican Party. Marx was first elected to the Common Council in 1895. He lost a race for city treasurer in 1904 to Thompson's reelection.

"He knew the ropes," said Hutchins. "Popular and of a naturally kind disposition, he privately eschewed municipal ownership and all similar plans, but publicly having fallen into the *Evening News* policies to defeat Thompson, he proved himself quite willing to drift headlong in that fateful direction."[88]

Sooner than anyone expected, on May 26, 1913, the U.S. Supreme Court affirmed the Michigan Supreme Court's decision regarding the fate of the expired Fort Wayne and Elmwood Street franchises.[89] Enforcing the decision, however, terminating service to thousands of daily streetcar riders, presented Mayor Marx with a huge political problem because he was neither confident nor strong enough to do what was needed. He stumbled into finding someone who was.

The day following the big April 7 election victory for municipal ownership authorized by the Verdier Act, Marx had announced that he intended to appoint Joseph S. Stringham, a successful construction engineer and manufacturing executive, William H. Maybury, former public works commissioner, and William T. Dust, long active in municipal affairs, all Republicans, to the newly created Detroit Board of Street Railway Commissioners.[90] None of them ended up serving. Rather, in May, Marx instead formally named Stringham, John F. Dodge, and William D. Mahon, national president of the Amalgamated Association of Street and Electric Railway Employees of America. Mahon was a former coal miner and streetcar driver who led the national streetcar union from

James J. Couzens. From *A Gallery of Pen Sketches in Black and White of Our Michigan Friends "As We See 'Em,"* ed. C. O. Youngstrand (Detroit: Wm. Graham Printing Company, 1905).

1893 until his retirement in 1946. Stringham bowed out, clearing the way for Mayor Marx, on July 23, 1913, at the suggestion of Dodge, to appoint James J. Couzens.

At the time of his appointment, Couzens was vice president and general manager of the Ford Motor Company, Henry Ford's financial wizard, and later known as one of Detroit's gasoline millionaires. James Joseph Couzens Jr. was born to English immigrants in Chatham, Ontario, on August 26, 1872. His father, who worked as a grocer's clerk, laborer, and salesman for a soap factory, took his son along while making sales calls. By age nine, Couzens held multiple jobs, too. On Sundays, he pumped the organ at St. Andrews Presbyterian Church. He was the town lamp-tender, and he sold soap for his father, who started his own soap works. At age twelve, he fled the soap factory and found work as a bookkeeper at a flourmill, even though he had no accounting experience. When his boss fired him, to avoid going back the soap factory, Couzens returned to high school, graduated, and enrolled in a two-year bookkeeping course at the Canada Business College. His first job upon graduation was as a news butcher on the Erie and Huron Railroad. When he moved to Detroit in 1890, the Michigan Central Railroad hired him as a car checker, putting him to work twelve hours a day, seven days a week. Coal dealer Alex Malcolmson recognized his intelligent, no-nonsense approach and hired him away as an assistant bookkeeper in 1895. Couzens was a well-groomed, standoffish, but blunt and tough young man at age twenty-one, and Malcolmson made him manager of one of his seven freight offices.

When he agreed to invest $3,000 in partnership with Henry Ford to build a new automobile,

Malcolmson insisted on putting Couzens in charge of Ford's business office and brought Couzens into most of his negotiations with suppliers and others for getting cars produced, including a contract with John and Horace Dodge to produce 650 chassis at $250 each over the next year. At one of their meetings, John Dodge proposed a payment schedule, to which Couzens strongly objected.

> "I won't stand for that!"
>
> Not many persons had ever dared to talk that bluntly to muscular, brusque John Dodge.
>
> "Who the hell are you?" demanded Dodge.
>
> "That's all right," Malcolmson said. "Couzens is my advisor in this."

And a deal was struck.[91]

When the Ford Motor Company was formally incorporated in 1903, Ford, Malcolmson, the Dodge brothers, and Couzens were among its twelve stockholders. Couzens invested $2,500, of which $100 came from his sister, Rosetta, a schoolteacher in Chatham, Ontario. Malcolmson's banker, John S. Gray, was president, Ford was vice president and general manager, Malcolmson was treasurer, and Couzens was secretary and business manager. When Malcolmson sold his one-fourth ownership to Ford in May 1906, for $175,000, Couzens succeeded him as treasurer, too.

Couzens and his wife, Margaret, rented a room in her widowed mother's boarding house after their marriage on August 31, 1898, the year he became a naturalized citizen. They had three sons—one died in infancy, another as a teenager—and three daughters. In the 1930s, he donated $1 million to the Children's Hospital of Michigan, in response to a birthday wish of his wife, who asked for a simple box in which to keep her pearls. Couzens included a note in the box describing his donation. "My dear, your new pearls will be all the children who are eventually treated there."[92]

By 1913, Couzens enjoyed a summer residence he called Wabeek on a farm south of Pontiac, several miles west of Woodward Avenue, distancing himself from the old money families of Grosse Pointe. The National Bank of Commerce, the Old Detroit National Bank, and the Detroit Trust Company had eagerly made him a member of their boards, and much to their annoyance, he would organize his own bank, the Highland Park State Bank, which prospered by his practice of depositing money there that was due to Ford's suppliers. His resume of directorships would include the Scotten Tobacco Company, the Kansas City Mexico and Orient Railroad, and the Detroit Salt Company. He invested in downtown real estate, building the Couzens Building on Woodward Avenue, and he entered the retail shoe business, the Rogers Shoe Company, part of the estate of his wife's brother. Couzens joined the Detroit Athletic Club, contributed to the Republican Party, and became active in the Detroit Board of Commerce, serving as its president in 1913.

Under Couzens's leadership, the Ford Motor Company would more than double daily wages earned on its Highland Park assembly line under his $5-a-day plan beginning January 12, 1914, a step he called "the greatest revolution in the matters of rewards for its workers ever known in the industrial world."[93]

He would describe the $5 workday in terms that would have completely disheartened Hutchins. "It is our belief that social justice begins at home," Couzens explained. "We want those who have helped us to produce this great institution and who are helping to maintain it to share our prosperity. We want them to have present profits and future prospects. Thrift and good service and sobriety all

John and Horace Dodge. From *A Gallery of Pen Sketches in Black and White of Our Michigan Friends "As We See 'Em,"* ed. C. O. Youngstrand (Detroit: Wm. Graham Printing Company, 1905).

will be encouraged and recognized. . . . Believing as we do, that a division of our earnings between capital and labor is unequal, we have sought a plan of relief suitable to our business."[94]

Hutchins was, nonetheless, surprised at his first tangle with Couzens. "At least 99 out of every 100 members of the Board of Commerce were naturally opposed to municipal ownership and all similar governmental experiments," he said. "It was reasonable to suppose that Couzens would be of the ninety and nine, and not the one to stray. In reality, however, when a man trained in his own line of business once gets into politics with his ear to the ground trying to hear what the people want him to do that man is likely to exhibit some very unexpected traits."[95]

When Mayor Marx appointed Couzens in 1913, the Dodge brothers had informed Henry Ford that they would no longer produce his parts. Instead, they would build their own automobiles. At about the same time, Couzens told Ford that he wanted to resign his day-to-day role in managing the Ford Motor Company. He was tired and bored. With encouragement from Ford, however, Couzens decided to stay, but he accepted Marx's appointment and thrust himself into leading the Board of Street Railway Commissioners even while giving the chairmanship to Dodge, who had just spent three months in Europe, where he claimed to have been studying public ownership of streetcars, including Glasgow, Liverpool, and Sheffield. John Dodge was a street-wise SOB and braggart. Couzens was even tougher but smarter and straightforward.

"The commission will get down to work as soon as organized and will push forward as rapidly as possible toward municipal ownership," Couzens told Detroit's newspapers. "There are undoubtedly several problems to solve and there is much work ahead of the commission. I feel and I am sure that the other members of the commission will agree that the commission should carry out the spirit of the municipal ownership election and do it as rapidly as we can."[96]

Events were unfolding rapidly. Just a few days after Couzens's appointment, the Common Council adopted an ordinance taking effect on August 7 that demanded three-cent fares with universal transfers in exchange for suspending enforcement of the *Fort Wayne and Elmwood Street* decree.

The DUR announced the following order to its crews: "If any passenger offers a three-cent fare, refuse it at once. If the passenger insists, stop the car at once." Police Commissioner John Gillespie gave this order to his officers: "Arrest all conductors who refuse three-cent fares and attempt to forcibly oust a passenger. If necessity demands it, the police will take charge of the cars and operate them."[97]

Couzens and Hutchins privately met to talk matters over. Couzens brought with him a promise from the Ford Motor Company if the DUR discontinued service on August 7. "Couzens was anxious that something should be done that would be immediately pleasing to the general public," Hutchins said. "At that time, its franchises on downtown portions of certain streets having expired, the company by temporary consent was paying a rental of $500 a day."[98]

Couzens was aggressive and direct. "If you do not take this proposition, we will stop your cars and I will supply one thousand Ford automobiles to replace the service."[99]

"An understanding was reached," Hutchins said later. "Rental was to stop. Couzens was to check hostile legislation then pending in the Common Council, and, on its part, the company was to put in effect seven tickets for twenty-five cents in place of six tickets for twenty-five cents on all city lines, without disturbing the eight tickets for a quarter that were good at certain hours. This arrangement, benefiting a great many thousands of individual citizens but costing the company in reduced revenues more than $2,000 a day, was put into effect." Couzens personally made the announcement and, of course, received all the political credit.

"Possibly it might have been wiser, even if less ethical, to use this $2,000 a day to smash the political and publicity machine that he may or may not have had in mind at the time," Hutchins said. "Instead . . . , the company, by rearranging its schedules in a way to carry about two additional passengers on each car and by deferring some reconstruction expenses, was able to recoup this loss, while at the same time it continued to enlarge its facilities inside and especially outside of the city."[100]

The tense agreement that Couzens reached with Hutchins on August 7, 1913, was a ticking time bomb because it was revocable at will by the either the DUR or the city.

Couzens's Pig in a Poke Plan

In April 1914, Mahon abruptly resigned from the Board of Street Railway Commissioners on grounds that Mayor Marx had failed to make any progress toward municipal ownership. Mahon had been an active member of the municipal ownership subcommittee of Mayor Breitmeyer's Committee of Fifty in 1909. He was the only person who favored purchase of the DUR, confident in his belief that Detroit could operate a municipally owned streetcar system at a cheaper fare. The summer after quitting the Board, Mahon joined a union colleague on a tour of Europe to investigate the condition of municipal and privately owned street railway systems. He concluded that the municipally owned lines of European cities cost passengers more, gave less adequate service, and paid less wages to employees than did the privately owned streetcar lines of American cities. His report had no influence on Couzens or anybody else in Detroit.[101] Marx appointed James Wilkie, superintendent of the mechanical department of Parke, Davis & Company, to fill his vacancy. Wilkie never did anything of note.

"In the early spring of 1914 Couzens returned refreshed and full of ginger from a visit to California," Hutchins said. "The first intimation of his return was his voice over a telephone wire saying to President Hutchins, 'We propose to buy your properties used for street railway purposes in Detroit. How much do you want for them?'"

> "The dickens you say!" was answered. "It has seemed to us the people are quite content with conditions as they are."
>
> "Not at all! What is wanted is municipal ownership. For what price will you sell?"
>
> "They are not my properties to sell, and besides I do not know what they are worth."
>
> "I could tell you in five minutes what the Ford properties are worth."
>
> "If I should hazard a figure as to what the Detroit United properties are worth, that figure might not be acceptable to the owners, and I doubt if you, in behalf of the city, would accept it as final."
>
> "Then what is to be done about it?"
>
> "That's up to you. We are not eager to sell. You say you want to buy. You make an offer and I'll submit it."
>
> "Will you attend a meeting of the commission tomorrow morning at ten?"
>
> "Yes."[102]

Many months before, in August 1913, Hutchins had agreed to supply the board with inventories and his engineer's estimates of reproduction values of the DUR's lines. The DUR filed a report on December 15, 1913, claiming a value of $31,038,982.

"We had supposed that the engineers of the City would proceed to check these inventories and investments, applying proper standards of depreciation, to determine the value at some given date of the company's properties," Hutchins dryly explained in formal correspondence prepared for the board meeting described by Hutchins that was actually held in late spring. "We have been advised that the commission, without resorting to the delays of such technical and scientific methods, would like us to name a price at which the company would sell its properties in Detroit. While anxious to meet the wishes of the commission in every way possible, we greatly fear that any figure we might find it possible to name would at once be criticized as being excessive, to the embarrassment both of ourselves and the commission."[103]

Hutchins offered a bare glimpse at a price he would sell, saying that the DUR had a value on an investment basis of $47 million consisting of its $20 million bonds, $12.5 million capital stock, $2 million notes, and $12.5 million in earnings otherwise invested in improvements since December 31, 1900.

"I have no doubt that the creation of a property in Detroit such as the company possesses would cost as much or more than the aggregate of all expenditures to which reference is made," he said.

"Just what amount these properties would be shown to be worth by the application of existing standards of depreciation and obsolescence, I am unable to say in advance of an analysis by expert engineers representing both ourselves and the city."[104]

The board responded in July 1914 by hiring Edward Bemis to conduct an in-depth appraisal of the DUR at a cost not to exceed $46,000. Bemis had done similar work for Governor Pingree in 1899. "Now, Professor Bemis . . . inclined—as a man named Barcroft, who had attempted some similar work for the city under the Breitmeyer administration—to limit values to what his employers might like, was not the type of man the company had any notion of depending upon," Hutchins wrote.[105]

The Michigan State Railway Commission, which had jurisdiction over interurban freight charges, had broached the subject of appraising the DUR. "The company had side-stepped that suggestion in the belief that such an appraisal would result in increased taxation," Hutchins readily admitted. "No advantage could result as a basis for rate fixing because rates of the company were already below those of its competitors and it did not want to raise them. Now, however, there was reason for wanting an appraisal under state auspices. An emissary sent to Lansing reported that the State Railway Commissioners would appoint a commission, made up of heads of the Engineering Department of the University of Michigan, to make the desired appraisal, provided the company would bear the expense."[106]

The State Railway Commission appointed Dean Mortimer E. Cooley, Professor Henry E. Riggs, and Professor Henry C. Anderson, heads respectively of the Departments of Civil and Mechanical Engineering. Cooley had been the lead appraiser for Governor Pingree in 1899. Riggs was an up-and-coming star of doing so. Their conclusion would be difficult for anyone to refute.

"Thoroughly scientific, used to purely logical methods, and experienced in practical engineering, these three men entered upon the work assigned to them with a purpose to ascertain and disclose the exact facts," said Hutchins. "No three men in America more honorable or better qualified could have been selected. While their work was in progress, in which more than two hundred assistants were employed, spread out in groups over the system of hundreds of miles, the books and records of the company were thrown wide open to Professor Bemis and the State Railway Commission."[107]

In the meantime, Hutchins attended weekly meetings of the board, and before the Bemis appraisal was completed, he and Couzens agreed upon general terms of purchase. Only the final price remained to be decided. On January 19, 1915, Bemis reported his physical valuation of $17,476,742. In addition, he valued the franchise at $2.5 million. Instead of offering $19,976,742, Couzens generously proposed to assume the DUR's entire bonded indebtedness of $24.9 million—payments on which Couzens believed could be made entirely from fare receipts. DUR stockholders eagerly accepted on March 31, 1915.

"Something happened!" Hutchins explained. "A young reporter, in looking through the files of his newspaper, discovered the last annual report of the company. There it was shown that of the bonds named in this agreement some to the value of $1.4 million were held in the company's treasury. And this kid played up his discovery in a sensational screed of considerable length claiming that the company had put something over on the Commission. This had a most disturbing effect."[108]

The street railway board called a special meeting.

"Why did you not tell us those were treasury bonds?" was asked.

"That fact is published to the world in the company's annual report. For months you have had unrestrained access to all company records and besides it makes no difference. Those bonds are more embarrassingly outstanding than if they were in the hands of the public because they are pledged as collateral to loans for money used to create some of the property you are buying, and those loans must be paid off in cash. Indeed, it would make no difference in the matter of our agreement with you were all of the company's bonds in its treasury."

"It makes all the difference in the world," said a commissioner. "It makes so much difference that unless you agree to strike the amount of those treasury bonds from the purchase price, we'll declare the deal off, and we'll set about doing the next best thing. . . .

A commissioner asked, "Will you take the matter up with your people and answer as soon as possible the question of deducting these bonds?"

"It is not necessary," was the reply, "to take that subject up with anybody. I'm obliged to answer now that we will do nothing of the kind."[109]

The stockholders of the company at a special meeting had accepted Couzens's original offer as set forth in a letter he had signed himself. "It would look like child's play to go back to them for a change of terms in a bargain already struck, notwithstanding the seriousness of the company's situation," Hutchins said. "In Detroit the DUR was thrust into the limelight by the politicians on every possible pretext. . . . Then, too, a streetcar rumbling through the streets was rather a big object at which to shoot. What the Commission meant by the next best thing was the building of rival lines."[110]

Hutchins recognized the possibility of even greater danger on the course Couzens was taking because of the recent Michigan Supreme Court decision in the *Fort Wayne* case that the city could at will stop operation and enforce removal of the company's tracks.

In May, Detroit's street railway commissioners announced that they would assume no more than $23,285,000 in bonded debt—deducting from its original offer $1,715,000 in treasury bonds. The DUR refused.[111] Some days later, while the city was considering its next step, Hutchins suggested to his board of directors a shrewd alternate plan. It provided that the price would be fixed instead by an arbitration panel consisting of all of the judges of the Circuit Court of Wayne County. The proposition would be submitted to a vote of the people. If approved, the property would at once be turned over to the city without waiting for the court's valuation. Detroit and the DUR would be contractually bound to accept whatever price the judges might fix.

"If the people accept this proposition you get a street railway system for nothing," Dodge confidently told the *Evening News*. "You are going to get a property that will pay for itself. Under municipal ownership, countless thousands of dollars can be saved every year by the haulage on the City's car lines of refuse, garbage, ashes, and paving materials. We can flush our streets at one-quarter the cost. In 10 years, Detroit's car-riding public has increased 180 percent. The tracks of the D.U.R. have increased less than 15 percent. For its population Detroit has the smallest area of any city in the United States. This is because the Detroit United Railway will not build extensions until a section is built up solid."[112]

Couzens jumped at the suggestion as neatly sidestepping questions over the treasury bonds. A contract was drawn up, and he opened a campaign for ratification by the people. Couzens sidestepped into muck. The newspapers went crazy, denouncing it as "a pig in a poke." Others, including the Municipal Ownership League, Federation of Labor, and streetcar employees union, called it the "blank check" plan. Worse, in a publicity coup engineered by Hutchins, seven days before the election, the State Railway Commission published its appraisal prepared by Dean Cooley, who set the physical value of the plant alone—not including the going concern franchise value—at $23,608,865.

"This appraisal report, along with a chest full of documentary detail, now rests in the archives of the state," Hutchins said. "It is as scientifically accurate and complete as any such report could possibly be. The work cost the company a large sum of money—upwards of $200,000."[113]

Couzens, nonetheless, determined to be finished with the DUR, dug into his own pocket to pay for the printing of literature in favor of purchasing the street railway system. In addition, Couzens cleverly had persuaded the Common Council to put a charter amendment on the November 2, 1915, ballot. Detroit voters had already approved a proposal authorizing municipal ownership. His new city charter amendment would make *mandatory* the municipal ownership of street railways in Detroit. It could trace its history back to the internal improvements clause included in Michigan's ill-fated first state constitution. Couzens carried the last days of the campaign on his own shoulders, telling the *Evening News* on September 15, 1915,

> There is no other issue. Fear of graft, fear of politics, fear of high taxes—all these objections have been raised to the purchase of the Detroit United Railway but each and all emanate in disbelief in municipal ownership.
>
> I don't think any one of the objections is well grounded. The people will pay such close attention to the operation of the care lines that graft will be insignificant. I do not believe politics will be tolerated in the management of the car lines. The Board of Street Railway Commissioners is convinced that the purchase of the car lines can be negotiated out of the earnings of the lines and will not affect the taxes.
>
> Well, speaking of graft, how about private business? There is more favoritism, more politics, and more graft in private business—and I should know—then in any city government in America. If you can't run your lines and keep out graft, you are a poor lot of citizens.
>
> What does the Detroit United Railway care about you? All they care about is your fares. The streetcar line is by nature a monopoly and you should own it.[114]

By refusing to set a price, Hutchins had fed the pig-in-a-poke slogan, and by arranging last-minute release of the state appraisal he heightened popular distrust. Voters would be going to the polls with doubt more than enough for its defeat. A group led by Clarence Burton, nonetheless, sought an injunction against the referendum on grounds that circuit courts lacked jurisdiction to decide the purchase price. "I want to smash municipal ownership of street railways now and forever," Burton said. "I don't care about the merits of this or any other plan. I want the courts to say that municipal ownership of street railways is illegal and can never be in this city."[115] On October 16, the Wayne County Circuit Court refused to bar the referendum.

"Then came election day—a fair autumn day," Hutchins said.[116] The municipal ownership charter amendment was narrowly approved, 32,739-32,618, but the DUR purchase, which needed a three-fifths majority under the new state constitution, lost badly, 32,514-35,676.

Jere C. Hutchins. From *A Gallery of Pen Sketches in Black and White of Our Michigan Friends "As We See 'Em,"* ed. C. O. Youngstrand (Detroit: Wm. Graham Printing Company, 1905).

Jay G. Hayden, secretary of the Board of Street Railway Commissioners, who would become a national correspondent for the *Evening News*, said the difference in the vote between the two propositions was due to the fact that under the new state constitution women taxpayers were permitted to vote on the municipal purchase but not on the charter amendment.

Hutchins Retires

Woodward Avenue had only recently been paved sixteen feet wide for one automobile lane each way as far as the City of Pontiac when at a regular meeting of the DUR board of directors on May

31, 1916, sixty-three-year-old Jere C. Hutchins surprised everyone with his resignation as company president.

"For some time past I have been coming to feel that the duties imposed by my present position are greater than I have the strength to bear," he began.

> Observing retrospectively, I would say that one may suffer being knocked down many times for the compensation to be attained in as often getting up again. And I would also observe that there are many situations and experiences in all departments of our complex civil life that are as exhilarating as the charging of a battery. Never having felt the lure of excessive pecuniary fortune, I have, nevertheless, been more than fortunate in having a goodly share of the adventure, and the sport, and the joy of service. The promotion of the company's interests, as being identical with the true interests of the great public we serve, has in truth been the chief aim of my waking hours and often the subject of my dreams at night. . . . And now, gentlemen, with a heart full of thanks for all that has been done for me, I ask your acceptance of my resignation.[117]

He nominated as replacement his brother-in-law, Frank W. Brooks. They agreed but elected Hutchins as chairman of the board at a salary higher than he had received as president and appointed a committee to secure for him a painting. "Some masterpiece that would grace his home and be pleasing there," Hutchins wrote.

"The emancipated official went home that evening relieved and satisfied."

And well he might.

"But now, his active life completed, with savings enough, thanks largely to Sarah's wise regulation of expenditures, to provide for their modest wants and some to spare for others, they could in future come and go and do as they pleased, even though his total capital was not nearly as much as his company's two principal antagonists were receiving for life in annual—if not in semiannual—dividends and in coupons from their bonds. This was a pleasing prospect."[118]

Or so he thought.

Pingree's Ploy Redux

On September 28, 1916, Couzens accepted appointment as Detroit's police commissioner, saving, the newspapers said, the reelection of Mayor Marx, who had been handicapped by lax law enforcement. Marx had again consulted John Dodge. Couzens, demanding a free hand without political interference, got such a promise.

In no hurry to confront the street railway company, Mayor Marx not did appoint replacements to the Board of Street Railway Commissioners until April 1917 when he named Francis C. McMath, president of the Canadian Bridge & Iron Works, and Julius H. Haas, president of the Wayne County and Home Savings Bank and art collector, to replace Couzens and Wilkie, who had resigned due to ill health. Hutchins said McMath and Haass favored the Taylor Plan over municipal ownership. They accomplished nothing despite downtown Detroit's worsening automobile and streetcar traffic.

Hutchins was aware of his responsibility to the country during World War I despite the ongoing

Thirty-Year War with Detroit. "More than a million Americans by this time had gone overseas to join in fighting World War I," he wrote.

> Thousands more were shipping daily. And other millions were making themselves ready to go. Detroit's streets were filled with marching soldiers. Its factories and shipyards were running day and night to provide cannon, ammunition, ships, airplanes, trucks, gun carriages, and other implements of war. There were not men and women enough in Detroit to supply the demand, though trainloads of families seeking work were coming in from other parts of the country every day.
>
> Not nearly enough men could be found to man the streetcars. Several hundred young women were employed as conductors. Looking neat in the uniform provided for them, these women not only did their work exceptionally well, but proved quite able to take care of themselves in mixed crowds on the cars. In one instance, one of them, after removing from her head her cap with its insignia of office, stepped from the car to the ground in advance of a husky young tough who had insulted her, and handed him a blow on the chin that left him lying at full length in the street. She was not disciplined. The only trouble about this class of conductors was that one by one they constantly abandoned the service to fulfill a greater destiny by getting married.[119]

On December 1, 1917, Brooks revoked the seven for twenty-five cent ticket agreement Hutchins had reached with Couzens in 1913, and the DUR began charging five-cent fares on all but the few remaining three-cent lines—Sherman, Fourteenth, Crosstown, and Harper Avenue. By this time, the DUR had built fifty-one miles of new railways subject to day-to-day agreement. "For reasons well known to the public as being entirely beyond our control, it is absolutely necessary to suspend the day-to-day agreement we are working under in relation to Detroit City rates of fare, and for the time being to resume the rates in effect prior to August 7, 1913," Brooks wrote.[120]

In response, on December 4, the Common Council adopted a resolution demanding $10,000 per day rental for streets on which the franchises had expired despite the Michigan Supreme Court's *Fort Wayne* decision that the city could not arbitrarily do so. The Common Council also rescinded permission for the company to operate skip-stops,[121] rerouted many of its downtown lines, and appropriated $35,000 for the Board of Street Railway Commissioners to investigate whether the fare increase was financially justifiable.

"We had unmistakable information that at no time did either of the political factions intend that any relief should be provided to meet the war-time conditions," said a DUR-issued statement. "On the other hand each faction planned to outdo the other to hold up the matter indefinitely for whatever advantage might come to them politically. Each wanted the slogan 'We Kept Car Fares Down' for use in the next election."[122]

Nobody expected the city to take advantage of the *Fort Wayne* case because doing so would cripple Detroit's war plants. In April, moreover, U.S. President Woodrow W. Wilson had created a National War Labor Board headed by former president William Howard Taft and labor union lawyer Frank P. Walsh. The board provided unions and employers with a federal arbitration panel intended to eliminate strikes at a time of great demand for war materials, higher wages, and better working conditions. At the same time, unrest among Detroit's motormen and conductors created dissension with local union leadership. The employees were demanding increased wages and an end to hiring women at lower rates of pay. Employees also wanted to prohibit hated "split-run" shifts that stretched a nine-hour day into fifteen to eighteen hours.[123] In a revolt, the rank-and-file members elected new officers and unanimously voted to strike beginning at five o'clock on Wednesday morning, April 24, 1918. Streetcar service across Detroit was tied up all day. Mayor Marx announced that he would call in state troops to run the streetcars.

Colonel William G. Latimer of the state militia's 550th Regiment responded aggressively. "My men are ready," he announced. "We have six machine guns. These guns can fire 1,500 shots each minute. We will place them in the square and meet the situation thus if need be. I think we can cope with any disorder."[124]

The following day, Mayor Marx, Colonel Latimer, Mahon, international union president, and Fred L. Feick, representative of the War Labor Board, appeared together at a mass meeting of striking employees. The employees agreed to return to work and to submit their demands to arbitration by the new War Labor Board, and the DUR accepted.

On June 25, 1918, Detroit voters adopted a completely new municipal charter under the Home Rule Act. The charter, among other features, more or less novel, required a nonpartisan nine-member Common Council and mayor. "But, of course, this action broke down all party responsibility and discipline," Hutchins said. "In effect, too, it made the newspapers for the time being through their columns of printed matter, or in their manipulations behind closed doors, tremendously more powerful."[125]

Couzens announced his candidacy for mayor. "They said about him exactly what had been said of Hazen S. Pingree: one so lacking in political tact and diplomacy could not be elected mayor of Detroit," Barnard wrote. "John Dodge assured him that he could not be elected 'dog catcher or coroner.'"[126]

On July 31, 1918, Taft and Walsh of the War Labor Board awarded DUR workers a raise from forty to forty-eight cents an hour, which union officials accepted. Although the Labor Board had no authority over fares, Taft and Walsh, nonetheless, made a strong appeal to Detroit's politicians and streetcar riders.

> The fares allowed to the Detroit Railway are exceptionally low, being 3 cents a passenger on some lines, 4 cents on others, and 5 cents on others. They should all be raised to meet the increased operating cost due to the high prices of needed material and equipment and the increased pay herein awarded.
>
> We have recommended to the President that special congressional legislation be enacted to enable some executive agency of the Federal Government to consider, and raise fares in each case in which the circumstances require it. We believe it to be a war necessity justifying Federal interference. Should this be deemed unwise, however, we urge upon the local authorities and the people of the locality the pressing need for such increase adequate to meet the added cost of operation.
>
> This is not a question turning on the history of the relation between the local street railways and the municipalities in which they operate. The just claim for an increase in fares does not rest upon any right to a dividend upon capital long invested in the enterprise. The increase in fares must be given because of the immediate pressure for money receipts now to keep their street railways running so that they may meet the local and national demand for their service.[127]

Taft, who was well aware of the Thirty-Year War going on between Detroit and its street railway company, said,

> Overcapitalization, corrupt methods, exorbitant dividends in the past are not relevant to the question of policy in the present exigency. In justice, the public should pay an adequate war compensation for a service which cannot be rendered for war prices.
>
> The credit of these companies in floating bonds is gone. Their ability to borrow on short notes is most limited. In the face of added expenses, which this and other awards of needed and fair compensation to their employees will involve, such credit will completely disappear. Bankruptcy, receiverships, and demoralization, with failure of service, must be the result. Hence, our urgent recommendation on this head.[128]

Brooks, too, pleaded for fare relief from Mayor Marx and the Common Council. They refused. Consequently, Brooks announced that he would abolish eight for twenty-five cent workingmen's tickets and raise fares on all expired lines to six cents. Brooks had stockpiled two million pennies so that conductors could make four-cent change for its estimated 726,000 daily riders.

Couzens, who had resigned as police commissioner, announced that he would personally institute court action to block six-cent fares.[129] Edward T. Fitzgerald, Mayor Marx's secretary and newly installed Couzens campaign manager, had an even better idea. Couzens agreed.[130]

On the morning of the fare increase, Thursday, August 8, 1918, three weeks before the primary, wearing a light-colored suit and Panama hat, his private car sitting nearby, Couzens boarded a streetcar on the expired Fort Street line, dropped a nickel in the fare box, and proceeded to a seat.

"The fare is six cents, sir," said the conductor.

"I won't pay it. The company has no right to charge six cents," Couzens replied, taking a seat.

"You'll pay six cents or you'll get off the car."

The conductor pulled the cord, signaling for a stop.

"Why don't you pay the six cents or else get off? These people want to go downtown."

Other cars piled up behind and traffic was blocked.

"I'm sorry to inconvenience them but I have paid all the fare the company has a right to collect and I will not get off."

"You don't look like a man I'd have to throw off."

"I won't get off voluntarily, though, of course, I won't forcibly resist you."

"Oh, now I know who you are. I read about what you were going to do in The Free Press this morning. Come on!"

The conductor gently urged Couzens off the rear platform while a crowd of political aides, reporters, and a moving picture cameraman stood by to record it all. Couzens climbed into his waiting auto as bystanders cheered.[131]

The next day thousands of riders mimicked Couzens's reenactment of Mayor Pingree's stunt. The DUR instructed its streetcar drivers to meet the rebellion by stopping all cars on which a rider refused to pay the extra penny. The result was rioting all over Detroit.

"During the riots the company was forced to abandon service on four or five lines to save the employees from violence and to protect property from destruction," said the *Electric Railway*

Journal. "In dozens of cases when passengers refused to pay more than five cents the car crews refused to move the cars or ran the cars onto side tracks and left them there. Saturday and Sunday riots were of frequent occurrence in the downtown streets, while in the factory districts cars were overturned and wrecked. In a statement to the public on August 13, President Brooks of the company placed the responsibility for the rioting, robbery and destruction of property on the politicians, the Common Council, and the newspapers."[132]

Some were outraged at Couzens. Among them was John Dodge, who accused Couzens of "encouraging the thousands of Bolsheviks and Anarchists in the city. . . . He ought to be put in jail!" Dodge concluded.[133] "No one in the Detroit of that period was more often called a 'Bolshevist' than Couzens himself—mainly because of his battle to establish municipal ownership of the city's streetcar lines," wrote Barnard.[134]

"Traffic on all lines of the Detroit United Railways was paralyzed nearly all day when thousands of passengers refused to pay 6-cent fares," said the *New York Times.*

> Riots in which streetcars were overturned and angry working men threatened violence to conductors and motormen, started in various sections of the city as the evening rush hour neared and the street railway company insisted in its policy of halting cars when one or more passengers refused to pay the new six-cent fare.
>
> Thousands of Ford motor employees, balked in their desire to get home by a number of men who refused to pay more than five cents or get off, rushed the cars, and after those passengers already inside had climbed out, tipped the cars on their sides. Police reserves were rushed to the scene. Employees at the Dodge plant overturned six cars when several of their number refused to pay the six-cent fare, and conductors obeyed the company's order not to move. Policemen with drawn revolvers and mounted patrolmen were having difficulty tonight in preventing mob violence. At 9:30 o'clock, Police Commissioner Marquardt gave orders to arrest the crews who refused to move their cars. Officials of the street car company ordered the cars into barns as fast as possible.[135]

Meanwhile, on Friday, August 9, the Common Council adopted an ordinance introduced by Alderman John A. Kronk ordering five-cent fares on all expired DUR lines. It was signed by Mayor Marx but could not take effect until midnight, Monday, August 12.[136] Rioting continued throughout the weekend. DUR lawyers dashed into federal court on Monday morning, seeking an emergency order sustaining the one-cent fare increase. U.S. District Judge Arthur J. Tuttle refused, calling it a nasty mess that could only be resolved by President Wilson taking the controversy out of local political hands.[137] A few hours later, after the Kronk ordinance went into effect at midnight, the city secured a temporary injunction from Judge Harry J. Dingman in the Wayne County Circuit Court reversing six-cent fares. Having lost in both the state and federal courts, the DUR complied and the riots ended.[138] The DUR desperately telegraphed Taft and Walsh complaining that the War Labor Board's wage hike for motormen and conductors was costing the street railway company $2 million a year.

"Mr. Brooks pointed out that the Common Council not only refused to permit a higher fare so that additional revenue to meet the increases might be had, but enacted an ordinance reducing the fares, which the Labor Board had emphatically declared too low," said an industry magazine.

Mayor Pingree being put off a streetcar for refusing to pay five cents in 1895, a stunt repeated twenty-three years later by James Couzens in 1918. This drawing illustrated "A Comedy in Three Acts," *Detroit Free Press*, December 14, 1895, 1.

"Mr. Brooks said the company was endeavoring to maintain service so that the munitions factories would not be crippled, but warned that unless immediate relief was given the company would have to abandon service."[139]

Brooks retaliated directly against Couzens and Ford, ceasing construction on the nearly finished Ferndale Avenue extension that would serve the massive Ford Motor Company's Eagle shipbuilding plant on the Rouge River. Brooks claimed he was doing so because of reduced receipts.[140]

"All public statements to the contrary notwithstanding, this fare was not arbitrarily set up," said the *Michigan Manufacturer and Financial Record*. "It was put in effect only after long discussion and the refusal of the city to agree to any fare. Forthwith riot and the destruction of property by hoodlums and newsboys under the leadership of aspiring politicians ensued, and the railway company as the result of a midnight session of a court, was forced to return to a rate of fare which every public indication in this country shows to be insufficient for the maintenance of its service and its prosperity."

The editorial continued, directing its rage at Couzens.

> One prominent candidate for public office, whose millions do not seem to have given him sense, started the ball rolling by making a public show of his refusal to pay a fare which the railway company has indicated as being necessary to maintain its organization and its service. . . . A condition which renders it impossible for men to move to their work, which depreciates their ability to do a certain amount of work per day, which makes the capacity of factories ineffective and which shows an official determination to hinder Government production, is no less sabotage than is the usual form of proceeding against which the laws affecting sabotage have been directed. It is very easy for some of our gabblers to talk about prosecuting labor unionists for sabotage. How sadly shocking would they be were they to find the respected names of Couzens and Vernor and Kronk . . . attached to information issued by a federal grand jury for the same offenses.[141]

On appeal months later, the U.S. Supreme Court reversed Judge Tuttle, 6-3, directing him to decide if the ordinance cap on fares was confiscatory under the Fifth Amendment.[142] A month later, on February 7, 1919, Michigan's Supreme Court issued a two-paragraph per curiam opinion formally dissolving Judge Dingman's order, saying the federal court had primary jurisdiction by virtue of the DUR having filed there sooner.[143]

Judge Dingman's midnight order enforcing the Kronk ordinance had ended both the one-cent fare increase and the second most destructive and costly street railway riot in Detroit history. The inglorious episode also propelled Couzens ahead of all the other primary candidates: Judge William F. Connolly, who had Democratic Party backing, former Police Commissioner Gillespie of the Marx-Dodge-Oakman Republican machine, and Divie B. Duffield, a respected lawyer who had drafted the new city charter. Couzens defeated Connolly, 45,188-36,288, in the November election and became Detroit's new mayor.

CHAPTER 10

On Driving a Hard Bargain

Inaugural Address

In 1919, Henry Ford delivered 1,216,792 Model T automobiles and Mayor James J. Couzens delivered a fiery inaugural address to the Common Council in which he characterized streetcar service in Detroit as an intolerable disgrace. The mandatory municipal monopoly of street railways first adopted in 1915 at his suggestion had been fully incorporated into the new city charter, and he promised to fully comply. "Unless the Detroit United Railway agrees to reasonable terms by which the City takes over its city lines, I will be ready to adopt war measures," he declared. If necessary, he added, he would submit a purchase plan "every six months, until one was adopted."[1]

Couzens had concluded long before that the best course would have been for the city to build competing lines, deny everything to the Detroit United Railway (DUR) while waiting for the old franchises to expire, and then sit back and watch the new municipal lines crush the old company lines. Even so, against his deepest instinct and personal nature, he agreed to compromise, letting the Board of Street Railway Commissioners, whom Hutchins described as three amiable businessmen, persuade him that such a course would avoid a fight bad for Detroit. They were Francis C. McMath, Col. Sidney D. Waldon, former vice president of Packard Motors and the Cadillac Motor Car Company, and Abner E. Larned, president of an international maker of overalls based in Detroit, whom Couzens appointed to the vacant seats of Julius H. Haas and John F. Dodge, both of whom abruptly resigned following Couzens's election.

Couzens conferred informally with the DUR's Frank Brooks and consulted on a purchase price with Michael M. O'Shaughnessy, former San Francisco city engineer, who had supervised the building of its cable car system. Laboring under some excitement, negotiations for the purchase of the street railways opened on February 10, 1919. Meetings of the negotiators, always tense and sometimes bitter, were held nearly every day, generally in public at the city hall.

At a three-hour meeting on February 18, the city offered $29,683,936 if approved by voters on April 7. DUR directors refused. Instead, they privately adopted a minimum price of $33 million, enough to retire the bonded indebtedness of the company and its interurban subsidiaries. DUR negotiators, Brooks and Elliott G. Stevenson, nonetheless continued to argue for a higher price.

"At times the negotiators seemed to get farther and farther apart," Hutchins said. "Couzens tried, by browbeating Brooks and Stevenson and by calling them bad names, to win the glory of getting the company's properties for little or nothing. Twice by messenger and once by telephone he urged the chairman of the Board to relieve the situation by personally attending the meetings."[2]

A few days later, Hutchins said, the city learned that he and his wife were leaving for vacation in California. McMath called him at home. "First, saying that every word that should pass between the two would be reported to the mayor, he explained that the Board was making no headway with the company's representatives and that both the mayor and the commissioners thought it an inopportune time for Hutchins to go away—that he should remain at home to finish the deal."[3]

Brooks and Stevenson had come down to a figure that, although unsatisfactory, was not, Hutchins said, figuring the value of passenger and freight terminals and various other properties that would be retained by the DUR, greatly higher than the minimum fixed by his directors. Hutchins suggested a compromise to McMath.

> "That minimum, millions below the true value of the property," Hutchins added, "can be accepted or declined whether I am here or not. Anyhow, I am off for California tomorrow night."
>
> Two hours before train time the next evening, McMath telephoned that the chairman of the Board could depart in peace.[4]

On March 11, Couzens agreed to go to the voters on April 7, 1919, with a plan to buy the DUR for $31.5 million of which $15 million would be payable by July 21, 1919 and the remainder at 6 percent interest no later than December 31, 1931.[5] The voters would be asked to approve a $24 million bond issue to finance the down payment and to begin immediate construction of new municipal railway lines and other improvements. The board prevailed on Couzens to stay out of the campaign, arguing against stirring up the voters when the DUR had agreed to sell and all the Detroit newspapers were in favor. The compromise reached between McMath and Hutchins, however, was hollow. Hutchins later admitted that Brooks secretly led the DUR in joining "the opposing organizations in killing it so dead that nothing of the kind, he hoped, would ever come up again." Hutchins denied any personal participation and expressed regret, but he downplayed his brother-in-law's duplicity. "What effect the publicity he assisted in promoting had on a sea of publicity can only be surmised."[6]

"We are going to submit this price of $31,500,000 to the voters," Couzens said, making a sales pitch unworthy of Ford Motor Company's former vice president and general manager who remained a major stockholder and director. "If the people want to get control of the lines at once, all right; if not, we are willing to go on with the fight if it is the wish of the people we do so. It is the best we are able to do at the present time."[7]

Long-time alderman James Vernor objected to terms under which the DUR could continue to run interurban passengers and freight, saying it granted an irrevocable thirty-year interurban franchise to continue operating on the street railways Detroit was buying. Detroit Edison President Alex Dow was in favor. He had served under Mayor Pingree as manager of Detroit's municipally owned power plant in 1893. Dow knew that the growth of Detroit's industry was suffering because workers could not get to and from the factories.

"Rents are high and slum conditions are difficult to remedy because people must live where they can get transportation," he said. "And labor is discontented: what does an eight-hour day profit a laborer if he must spend two or three hours riding to and from work? I do not believe that a franchise favorable enough to the DUR to raise new money at a reasonable rate could get the necessary vote this year or any year in the near future. The best thing for the City of Detroit and the inhabitants thereof as a whole is always the best thing for the Edison Company. Whatever helps industry and trade helps us in the long run."[8]

In 1915, Henry Ford had personally endorsed Couzens's municipal ownership plan in an interview splashed across the top of the front page of the *Evening News*. "It is one of the safest business propositions I have ever heard of," Ford said. "I will gladly work under James Couzens in the street railway matter."[9] Ford's endorsement came on the day after Ford's board of directors accepted Couzens's resignation as general manager.[10] Therefore, it was an unwelcome surprise to him that strong opposition now came from the Ford Motor Company. Charles E. Sorensen, general manager of Henry Ford's Highland Park Plant, issued a loud protest, arguing that electric streetcars were out-of-date. The coming thing, he said, was Ford's gasoline-propelled streetcars. Hence, Sorensen argued, Detroit would be paying $31.5 million for electrical junk. "Mr. Sorenson takes a definite stance against the purchase of the DUR system on the ground that there is too much politics and too little science and commonsense involved," said the *Free Press*. "As a going concern and as a mode of conveyance representing the crest of modern transportation, he believes the D.U.R. system to be worth something but inasmuch as it is a system that will rapidly be superceded by more modern methods of transportation this D.U.R. system is in his mind, just so much junk going at a fancy price."[11]

During the last week before the election, Ford's campaign of interviews, handbills, and full-page newspaper advertisements persuaded thousands to vote against the two ballot proposals. The $24 million bond issue lost, 60,157-64,236. The purchase plan, needing a three-fifths majority, lost badly, 63,883-70,271.[12]

Neither Couzens nor the DUR would comment on the results for the press, but Couzens boiled with anger. "What Mr. Couzens said regarding Mr. Ford could not be presented in these polite columns," the *Detroit Saturday Night* reported a month later.[13]

Ford refused an invitation for his views on the street railway situation from the Board of Street Railway Commissioners. "It is my belief that the commission has taken upon itself a great responsibility in assuming that the recently submitted purchase plan was defeated because of statements made by Charles E. Sorensen, which would indicate that the people of Detroit are not capable of deciding matters of such importance for themselves," Ford replied by statement. "Repudiation by the voters of the railway plans as submitted makes it seem questionable in my mind whether or not you can claim to represent the people of the City of Detroit."[14]

In commenting on Ford's reply, the *Electric Railway Journal* told its readers what Couzens and everyone else in Detroit already knew. "There are some that professed to see in this a move by Mr. Ford against his old associate, Mayor Couzens. No one will probably ever know what the effect was of the agitation about the car on the election result, but there is no room left for guessing about the rebuke to the commission contained in Mr. Ford's letter."[15]

Ford gave an interview to a reporter for the *Electric Railway Journal* on April 9, 1919, in which he commented that the gasoline-powered streetcar he was developing "will be so light that its fuel consumption on rails will be extremely low, and furthermore it will not require heavy expense for track construction and up-keep. A light car meant frequent service. . . . From what he had seen and learned Mr. Ford ventured to prophecy that street railway traffic would be doubled at least if short headways and low graduated fares went hand in hand. It was up to the street railway men to see that the service was so good and so cheap that the owner of the automobile would use street railway service habitually instead of occasionally."[16]

Council President John C. Lodge said, "The people have had a fair proposition put up to them twice. It seems as if they are for municipal ownership in the abstract but when a concrete proposal comes before them, they balk at the price. What's the answer?"[17]

Why There's No Detroit Subway Today

When he was a second-term alderman in 1912, John Lodge proposed building a subway under Woodward Avenue.[18] A former reporter and city editor at the *Free Press*, he had served as secretary to Mayor George P. Codd and two years in the state house of representatives before being elected on the Common Council in 1909. Following his reelection, Lodge introduced a resolution adopted by the Common Council on February 27, 1912. It said:

> Whereas, it is apparent to all close observers that the street traffic on Woodward Avenue, during part of every day, has grown beyond the possibility of surface handling, and
>
> Whereas, all authorities agree that subways afford the best if not the only, method, of relief, it is
>
> Resolved, That this Council take steps as soon as possible to secure plans and estimates for a subway in Woodward Avenue.

Lodge's subway plan was referred to the Common Council's four-member Committee on Public Utilities, consisting of Aldermen Charles W. Burton, a lawyer, real estate developer, and son of Clarence M. Burton; Joseph E. Merritt; Maurice J. Keating; and John Harper. On March 12, they recommended inching ahead by asking the public works commissioner "to submit a supplemental estimate of $6,000 to cover the cost of preparing preliminary plans, specifications, profile, and cross-sections of a general subway system in the central section of the City and in Woodward, Michigan and Gratiot Avenues."

Their report was adopted, 33-0. Lodge was the only member of the Common Council following the issue because on April 16, 1912, he moved that the public works commissioner be directed to seek funding for the $6,000 study from the board of estimates, and on June 4, 1912, he moved to request that the public works commissioner direct the city engineer to proceed. Action, however, was postponed by its referral, again, to the Committee on Public Utilities, which held eight public hearings over the summer and fall before reporting back on January 7, 1913.

> The most serious problem confronting engineers in the study of the rapid transit situation in Boston, Chicago, New York, and Philadelphia had been the choice of routes. The general plan of Detroit renders

> this study unnecessary as far as the main thoroughfares are concerned, and the principal problems will be those of downtown loops and terminal stations. These should be so laid out as to serve the greatest area with the minimum cost of construction and operation and so as to most readily relieve the congestion of our streets within the half-mile circle during the rush hours, when it is estimated that upwards of 200,000 people pass the principal downtown corners. To thoroughly and permanently relieve the congestion now existing and daily increasing will require new rapid transit facilities on each of the six great thoroughfares leading out of the heart of downtown.

Such a vast subway system connecting to a new crosstown surface line along Grand Boulevard would render convenient service to the downtown business district from all remote parts of Detroit, they said. Recognizing that it was not financially feasible to build the complete system of subway and surface lines envisioned, they recommended beginning with downtown subway stations and terminals on Woodward Avenue. "In such a vast enterprise as this the absolute assurance that we are beginning right is of the utmost importance," they said. "Of the $6,000 allowed this committee by the Common Council and the Board of Estimates *less than $100 has been actually expended to date.* The work up to the present has been in the nature of an investigation as to the best method of proceeding with the preliminary work" (emphasis added). Therefore, they suggested entering into negotiations with consulting engineers and that the council president appoint three members to visit Boston, New York, and Philadelphia with the engineer hired to further investigate subway design and construction.

Their report was tabled without any further action until July 27, 1914, when the newly appointed Board of Street Railway Commissioners entered into an agreement with renowned Wall Street consulting engineers Barclay Parsons & Klapp to investigate downtown street railway traffic congestion and the possible construction of a subway. Heading the firm was William Barclay Parsons, who had designed and engineered New York City's subway system. It delivered a superb three-hundred-page report in January 1915 that began by noting what others had said before about Detroit.

> From a transportation standpoint, Detroit is a city of the semicircular type with its center substantially at the City Hall, its east and west diameter paralleling the Detroit River for a distance of about twelve miles, and a radius corresponding closely to Woodward Avenue extending north about seven miles from the river front. . . . The entire area covered by the city and suburbs, is, for traction purposes, practically level. The radial or hub-and-spoke system of streets formed by the principal avenues, such as Fort, Michigan, Grand River, Woodward, and Gratiot, which converge approximately to the City Hall, define the features of the city's general plan.[19]

Detroit, they said, had low average population density "caused by the prevalence of detached family residences, Detroit being peculiarly a city of individual homes. . . . A change in this condition is already noticeable, a substitution of flats and apartment houses having commenced, particularly in the older downtown residence districts. . . . This form of building activity has in other cities resulted in a congestion of population in limited areas, tending to greatly restrict the growth of outlying sections and to concentrate traffic along certain lines of travel."[20]

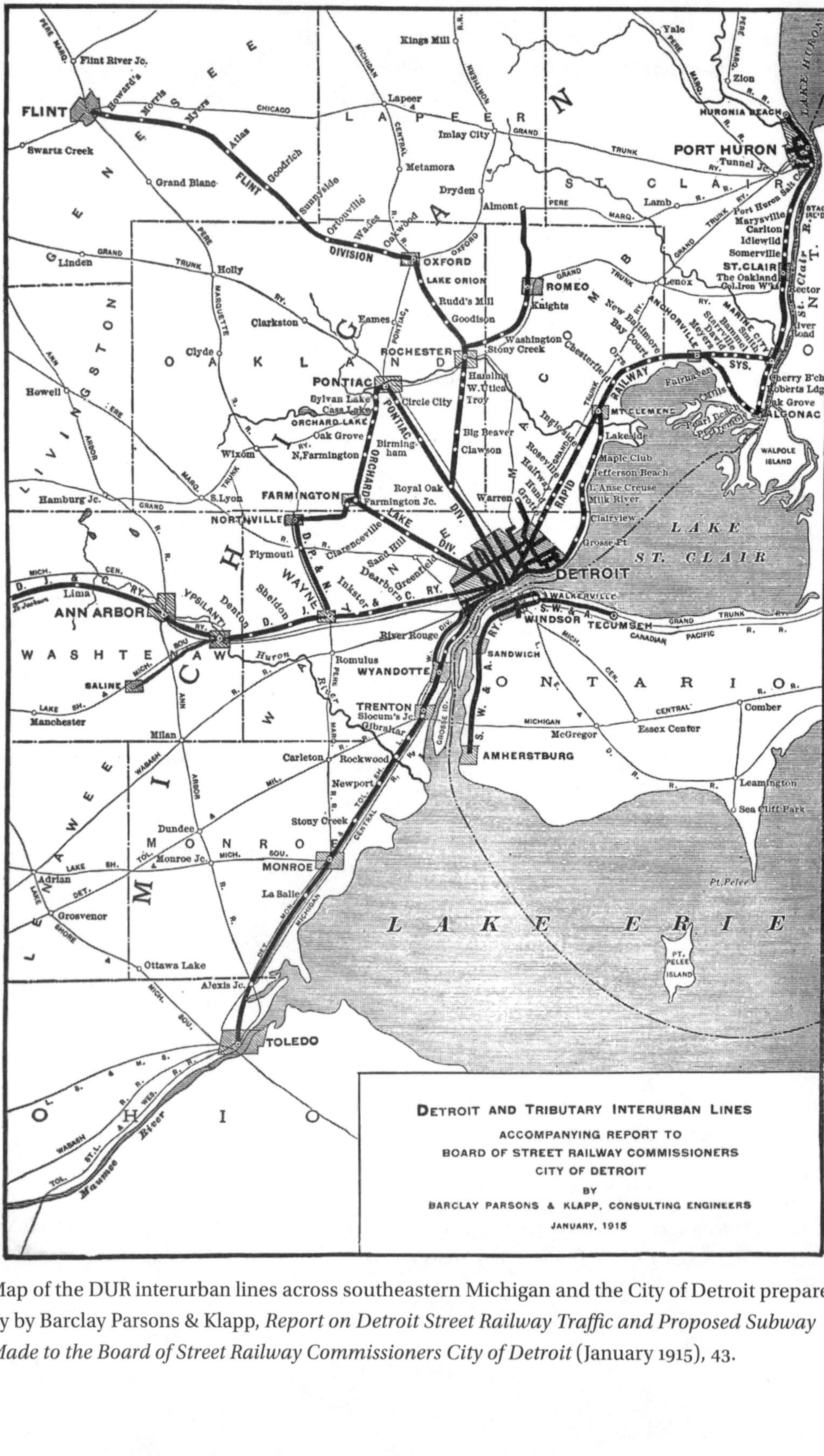

Map of the DUR interurban lines across southeastern Michigan and the City of Detroit prepared by by Barclay Parsons & Klapp, *Report on Detroit Street Railway Traffic and Proposed Subway Made to the Board of Street Railway Commissioners City of Detroit* (January 1915), 43.

Barclay Parsons & Klapp concluded, "In order, therefore, to make the street railways in Detroit, combined with a long subway on the heaviest traffic street, a financially self-supporting system, a material increase in fare over the whole city will be necessary." Eliminating the workingmen's fare and allowing citywide fare of at least five or six cents, they said, would be needed to pay for building such a long subway system.[21]

Building a short subway loop under Woodward Avenue south from Grand Circus Park would both relieve street traffic conditions and barely support itself, Barclay Parsons said. In his annual address to the Common Council on January 11, 1916, Mayor Marx endorsed the Barclay Parsons short subway plan.

> As a further means of relieving the congestion downtown, I believe your Honorable Body, and the Board of Street Railway Commissioners should give careful thought to the suggestion made in the traffic survey prepared by the latter, that the present surface lines on congested avenues within the half-mile circle, be dipped as a preliminary step towards the construction of a complete subway system. If immediate attention is given to this subject of congestion, and the officials of the Detroit United Railway manifest a desire to cooperate, I see no reason why relief may not be obtained within the next six or eight months.

Nobody did anything more and the problem of downtown congestion grew worse over the next two years. "One of our greatest troubles is that we have a New York concentration of business without New York's subways and elevated system to handle the people to and from their businesses," Street Railway Commissioner Waldon complained to the *Michigan Manufacturer and Financial Record* in March 1917.

> Our situation is not going to get better, but it is going to get worse with our continued growth of Detroit and the addition of more and more big buildings in the limited downtown area. . . . There are more people, more streetcars, more automobiles, more heavy trucks, and other vehicles and actually less street space in which to handle them. The streets have remained the same width, while the office buildings, hotels, and stores have been going skyward. Every foot of sidewalk and street in the downtown section is doing double the duty it did 10 years ago, and during that period there has grown up among us a common use of the motor car never anticipated in any "city planning scheme" that I have seen.[22]

Nothing else happened regarding a downtown Detroit subway until September 1919, when Couzens finally agreed to sell all of his stock to Henry Ford, and his Board of Street Railway Commissioners resigned en masse. Malcolm Bingay got the first part of the inside story handed to him in the Detroit Athletic Club (DAC), where he often went to exercise his elbow with Detroit's other movers and shakers in the Men's Tap Bar. As managing editor of the *Evening News* since 1909, one of the perks he likely enjoyed was a company-paid membership, entitling him to use of the club's members-only bar in its magnificent six-story neorenaissance building a block east of Grand Circus Park on the north side of Madison Avenue designed by Albert Kahn and opened in 1915. On long evenings like this, if he drank too much, the club's tight-lipped staff might discretely help Bing, as he was called, up to one of its well-appointed overnight rooms, bringing to him in the morning hot black coffee, clean undergarments, and his freshly pressed shirt, tie, pants, and jacket. In 1928, when the *News* fired him, he explained, "I was saying the right things in the wrong way and doing a lot of drinking."[23]

The DAC's history dates back to 1887, when the organization really was an athletic club, with a facility on Woodward Avenue south of the cultural center attracting Detroit's privileged younger men to its cinder running track, baseball diamonds, bowling alleys, and full gymnasium. The new building included an Olympic-size swimming pool, full-size basketball court and gymnasium, bowling alley, weight room, and lockers. Today, most of the 3,200 members join for the use of its dining rooms and bars shared with Detroit's other business and political leaders. Membership in the exclusive club, open to men and women both, costs several thousand dollars with healthy monthly dues, depending on age, and require nomination by six existing members, interviews, and screening by the board of directors.

Years later, writing for his book, *Detroit Is My Own Home Town*, Bingay remembered only that it was a summer evening. Necessary preceding events put the date of one of the greatest stories encompassing Detroit's political and automotive history as about September 15, 1919. Couzens, who had been mayor for less than a year, handed Bingay a slip of paper. "Here is a little present for you."

It was Henry Ford's personal check for $29,308,857.90. Bingay gasped, and then saw to whom the check was payable. Couzens laughed. "It was his way of letting me know that the story had broken."[24]

Couzens had quit the Ford Motor Company on October 12, 1915, in a showdown over an antiwar article Ford wanted published in the company magazine, *Ford Times*. Couzens had to approve everything, and this applied especially to articles in the *Ford Times*. Henry Ford had become increasingly vocal and highly critical of the war in Europe, taking a distinctly pacifist stance against loans to the allies and national war preparedness by the United States, which the country would not enter until two years later. The evening before, Couzens was asked to review final page proofs of the magazine. "You cannot publish this," Couzens told Charles A. Brownell, Ford's advertising manager. "These are Mr. Ford's personal views, not the views of the company. This is a company paper. He cannot use the *Ford Times* for his personal views. I will talk to Mr. Ford tomorrow."

Trouble between Ford and Couzens had been brewing for a while.

"I held up the *Times* because of your article in it about the war," Couzens told Mr. Ford at a ten o'clock meeting the next morning.

"You cannot stop anything here!" Ford snapped.

"Well, then . . . I will quit," Couzens replied, and he did, quickly arranging to leak his resignation decision to Detroit's newspaper offices.[25]

Couzens and his sister, Rosetta, still owned 10.5 percent of the Ford Motor Company, and he remained a director. Four years had passed before Edsel Ford came to his home at 610 Longfellow, a block south of Chicago Boulevard and a block west of Woodward Avenue in the Boston-Edison District, where they arranged the sale needed to close Ford's buyout of all other company shareholders. Their deal was for $30 million cash, of which $29,308,857.90 went to Couzens and $691,142.10 went to his sister.

Couzens talked with Bingay in the Men's Tap Bar until one o'clock in the morning. Bingay avoided explicitly mentioning if they were drinking, perhaps because Prohibition was in place. Michigan entered the Prohibition era earlier than any other state, but it was just about completely ignored by everyone. Bingay himself famously observed, "It was impossible to get a drink in Detroit unless you walked at least ten feet and told the busy bartender what you wanted in a voice loud enough for him to hear you above the uproar."[26]

A Michigan constitutional amendment prohibiting the sale of liquor, beer, and wine had been approved by a vote of 353,373-284,754 on November 7, 1916. Opponents in Detroit and the other major cities were overwhelmed by the outstate dry vote. Detroit was the first city in the United States with a population over 250,000 to legally go dry when the amendment took effect on May 1, 1918. National prohibition would not take effect under the Volstead Act until January 16, 1919. Early prohibition had a rocky legal start, with the Michigan Supreme Court overturning the 1916 referendum and the dry, rural, and Republican state legislature's attempt to adopt fixes while state, county, and city law enforcement were learning that stopping the flow of beer, wine, and liquor from Ohio and Ontario was a practical impossibility. Detroit was America's wettest city, according to Daniel Okrent's magnificent book, *Last Call: The Rise and Fall of Prohibition.* He handed the title to Detroit, the corrupt, booming blue-collar town known widely as "the City on a still."[27] During Prohibition, drinkers could choose from among twenty thousand speakeasies, about one for every thirty adults. The Board of Commerce estimated that the illegal alcohol business employed fifty thousand people, Detroit's second largest industry behind automobile manufacturing. The Detroit River played a big role, of course, as Canadian bootleggers assisted by Detroit's notorious Purple Gang smuggled alcohol freely across the border on trucks through the Windsor Tunnel and over the Ambassador Bridge, on freight cars through the railroad tunnel, and aboard high-speed powerboats.

The DAC responded to Prohibition by inventing its now famous cocktail, The Last Word. The recipe calls for equal parts gin, fresh-squeezed lime juice, green chartreuse, and maraschino liqueur. Although both Bingay and Couzens were well known at the DAC, as a private club counting among its members only Detroit's rich and powerful, there is no doubt they could and surely did share a few drinks as they talked.

"Never at any time did I find him in such a tender mood," Bingay wrote. "There, time and again, he expressed a wistful longing for the joys of intimate friendship that were denied him."

"Too many years of battling, I guess," Couzens explained. "I never learned to relax, to play as other boys and men learned. Every man's hand was against us in those days in the Ford factory. I learned to distrust and suspect everybody who came near me."

During their long evening together, Couzens told Bingay something else that would serve him well in the next few years.

"What are you going to do now?" Bingay asked. "Any more business ventures?"

"None! I'm through. I am going to put every cent I have into tax-exempt bonds so that I can be absolutely independent. If I own a share of stock in any company or corporation, my political enemies can say I have an ax to grind. This way I will be free from entanglements."[28]

Couzens was then tangling again with his Street Railway Commission, the Common Council, and the DUR. His new independence from Henry Ford would allow him to end the Thirty-Year War.

Earlier that summer of 1919, Couzens had reached a political conclusion about the city's street railways. It came to him when DUR motormen and conductors again demanded an increase in wages. They were getting 48 cents per hour and wanted 75 cents per hour. They asked Mayor

Couzens for his personal help in settling their labor dispute. Turnover since the first of the year, they complained, had been 1,500 men.

Having lost trust in Frank Brooks, Couzens sought out the assistant general manager, Ellsworth J. Burdick, who pleaded that the DUR needed across-the-board five-cent fares with one-cent transfers because the DUR was losing money. Couzens leaped into action. On May 26 at a special session, at his urging, the Common Council voted to audit DUR books. On June 6, the results were made public. It showed a small profit that Couzens realized could not support a wage hike without increased fares.[29] The union and the DUR reached a deadlock, and a strike began June 8, shutting down streetcar service across Detroit. Couzens went to court to force negotiations by seeking an injunction demanding service. Knowing as he did that in such cases nobody wins, Judge Adolph F. Marschner of the Wayne County Circuit Court strong-armed everybody into a deal.

The workers voted, 840-347, to accept 65 cents per hour. Unceremoniously putting an end to any hope for three-cent fares in Detroit, Couzens agreed to across-the-board five-cent fares with universal transfers for the next three months. Afterwards, the DUR agreed that a three-member arbitration panel would audit the books monthly and set fares for the next six-month period not higher than five cents with one-cent transfers except by agreement of the city. Judge Marschner retained jurisdiction.[30]

"I believe that the people of the city are more than compensated for the inconveniences to which they were put during the three-day tie-up by the overwhelming victory of the City," Lodge said. On the second day of the strike, however, Couzens had issued a statement.

> The moment has arrived to finish up our dealings with the Detroit United Railway. I reached that conclusion last night. That conclusion was confirmed when I left my farm at 5:55 this morning and came to town and saw how comfortably we were getting along without the Detroit United Railway. We will order the company off the non-franchise lines and put our own equipment on the tracks. By fall, we can have cars sufficient to have a fair-sized system of our own running, or to have forced the Detroit United Railway to turn over its property at junk prices. If the Council will cooperate, I am willing to let this end all relationship with the Detroit United Railway once and for all. We have been grasped by this lying corporation until it seems to me that they have made their final grasp.[31]

Couzens's own street railway commissioners turned against him. They had received a new report prepared by Barclay Parsons & Klapp in July.[32] The firm had recommended that Detroit enter into a cost-of-service franchise with the DUR based on the Taylor Plan that would require new crosstown extensions and the purchase of at least 300 new streetcars and 260 trailers at an estimated cost of $12,426,650. The new study addressed downtown traffic congestion in a city rapidly approaching one million residents. It recommended that Detroit itself finance a scaled-back subway consisting of two loops along Woodward Avenue and Fort Street at an estimated cost of $8.5 million.

On October 22, 1919, his street railway commissioners enthusiastically endorsed and submitted these recommendations for adoption by the Common Council over the stern protest of Mayor Couzens, who, instead, favored asking voters on April 5, 1920, for authority to borrow $15 million to start the piecemeal construction of a city-operated street railway system. "Well, gentlemen," Couzens said to them, "if that's your conviction, I'll have to ask for your resignations."[33]

Larned, McMath, and Waldon did so but in concert only after the Common Council defeated their report, 4-4, on November 4, 1919.[34] A week later, the full nine-member Common Council reconsidered and voted, 5-4, in favor of the subway plan but, needing seven votes, failed to override Mayor Couzens's subsequent veto. "As a responsible agent of the people, I feel it is my duty before presenting any proposition to them to analyze its every detail," Couzens said. "I have conscientiously tried to ascertain how the recommendations of the Board of Street Railway Commissioners would meet with the people's wishes, as indicated in their various votes upon railway settlement and fail to find where they agree in any instance."[35]

That put Couzens into lonely command of ending the Thirty-Year War. A street railway industry magazine said, "The Mayor had now become fully converted to the blackjack method of dealing with the Detroit Street Railway. . . . And he was willing to sacrifice something to put into effect a modification, which would bludgeon the Detroit United Railway into a sale of its property at a price so low that the people of the city would vote to accept it. . . . The idea of forcing a sale by the company to the City at salvage prices appealed too strongly to the City's chief executive to permit him to accept any other solution."[36]

CHAPTER 11

Nobody Stood Up

The Castator Ordinance and Closing the Belle Isle Bridge

On January 27, 1920, the Common Council unanimously agreed to put a $15 million bond issue proposal on the April 5 ballot to purchase expired lines and build strategically located new city-owned tracks, the piecemeal policy James J. Couzens was using under the *Fort Wayne* case to cripple and then buy pieces of the Detroit United Railway (DUR) at scrap value. Local newspapers called it the Castator ordinance because Mayor Couzens gave Alderman Fred W. Castator, a former streetcar conductor, the privilege of making its formal introduction to Detroit's Common Council.

Under the Castator ordinance, the city would take over the expired Woodward Avenue line from the Detroit River to Milwaukee Avenue and the Fort Street line from Artillery Avenue to Baldwin Avenue, covering twenty-one miles at an estimated purchase price of $850,000. In addition, the city would buy twenty-nine miles of other lines subject to the day-to-day agreement, the cost of which would be $1,370,000. If approved, Couzens promised to start building 103 miles of extensions, mostly crosstown, the day after the election at an estimated cost of $70,000 per mile, which he said would greatly relieve the congested downtown district without building an $8.5 million subway. The city would buy 400 streetcars at $10,000 each and 150 trailers at $5,000 each. Streetcar barns, tools, and equipment would cost another $1 million.

"Unquestionably Detroit is as badly a laid out city for a million folk today as she was designed for the two or three hundred thousand that was thought would be her maximum possible—up to ten or twelve years ago," said Edward Hungerford, a railway journalist of the 1920s. "Her ingenious plan of radiating streets, shooting out like spokes of a double wheel from her two civic centers downtown, was very good for a city whose homes and factories could be comprised within a radius of three miles or so. For one demanding a radius of six or seven or eight miles it is of little practical use; far inferior, in fact, to the straight checkerboard pattern of so many of our American cities. Yet her badly devised plan could be fairly taken by crosstown lines. . . . Now what has happened in regard to these crosstown lines?"[1]

Couzens would answer that for years the city had blocked the building of extensions, and especially crosstown lines, arising, in part, from jealous ward politics, but in greater measure as its only effective weapon in the Thirty-Year War. He was now going to build those 103 miles of badly needed extensions and crosstown lines, gaining both public favor and strategic advantage in advancing toward municipal ownership of the major lines serving Fort Street and Woodward, Jefferson, Grand River, Michigan, and Gratiot Avenues if not three-cent fares.

"The Mayor's . . . formula for smoothing out the long standing snarls in Detroit's traffic system and affording citizens their desired freedom from congestion at the heart of the city, is based on the idea of . . . affording the long-suffering industrial population an opportunity to travel on frequent north, south, east, and west crosstown . . . in order to move the hub of Detroit's traffic wheel," said an industry journal.[2]

Couzens also moved to protect his flank. "I have been watching the development of the gas streetcar, and recently I had a conference with Mr. Henry Ford, at which time he showed me several engines and plans for the car," Couzens said in January 7 correspondence to the Common Council. "In discussing the details with his engineers, I was assured that the gas streetcar could be built for a maximum of $5,000 per car, which would reduce the cost of car equipment 50 percent, or in other words, cut the cost down to about $2,000,000. The adoption of this system of transportation will obviate the necessity of electrically equipping the lines and of the building and equipping of power plants." Couzens took aldermen to inspect the new Ford gasoline streetcar at Sorenson's Dearborn tractor plant.[3]

Finally, to manage his new municipal ownership plan, Couzens appointed to the Board of Street Railway Commissioners Ralph B. Wilkinson, attorney;[4] William B. Mayo, chief engineer of the Ford Motor Company; and Griffith O. Ellis, publisher of the *American Boy* magazine,[5] whose wife was a member of the Scripps family, owners of the *Evening News*. Since his election in 1918, Couzens had learned well the judicious use of political appointments.

"This commission, once appointed, faded modestly into the background and left the Mayor free to handle the situation as he saw fit, unembarrassed by advice," said Harlow C. Clark in a long article for the *American Electric Railway Association* published in July 1920. "The essential difference between business and political methods in industry is well illustrated by the subsequent course of Mayor Couzens in putting over his $15 million public ownership plan."[6]

Frank Brooks announced that the DUR would fight the Mayor's "unfair and dishonest" methods by all legitimate means.

> Mayor Couzens now undertakes to force upon the people the so-called 'piecemeal' plan of acquiring a railway system, and proposes to create a second railway to engage in competition with this company. To accomplish this, the Mayor proposes to dismember and cripple our system and by coercion compel us to sell important parts of our system at less than the conceded value. For instance, he proclaims publicly that the cost of construction of our Woodward Avenue and Fort Street tracks is about $70,000 per mile (it was actually $100,000 per mile) and that he will force us to sell at $40,000 per mile.[7]

Now DUR attorney Elliot Stevenson submitted a desperate initiative petition for an ordinance referendum on granting a new franchise, a novel legal approach never before tested in Michigan,[8] while Mayor Couzens sent an animated film produced in favor of his proposal for screening by Detroit's theater audiences and distributed a series of beautifully colored maps showing what he proposed to immediately build under municipal ownership.[9]

Under the thirty-year ordinance submitted by Stevenson, the DUR offered to turn over all Detroit lines to a new company operating under the Taylor Plan required to spend $5 million per year for five years making needed line extensions. The new company also would be required to add 200 cars and 150 trailers by December 31, 1923, replacing all single cars with double cars and building fifty miles of extension lines per year. The DUR began a publicity campaign to get its proposal on the ballot under the slogan "Service at Cost." Mayor Couzens countered with his own slogan—"Service at Once."

The DUR initiative ordinance had been delivered to Corporation Counsel Clarence E. Wilcox for legal review on March 13. He said it was too late under the municipal charter to go before the voters on April 5. He flyspecked the ordinance, finding thirty-nine defects in its wording. The DUR desperately asked a three-judge panel of the Wayne County Circuit Court to order the ordinance onto the ballot anyway. Judges Arthur Webster, Henry A. Mandell, and Harry Dingman refused, agreeing with Wilcox that only if the Common Council failed to adopt the initiative ordinance within thirty days could it go before voters under the city charter, and thirty days had not yet expired.[10]

In its campaign against the Castator ordinance the DUR spent $500,000, aided in this decisive battle by street railway companies from across the country and by the street railway union.[11] A flood of literature clogged the Detroit post office, drawing attention from newspapers across the country. The *Evening Independent* of St. Petersburg, Florida, carried a syndicated report on March 23, 1920, quoting Mayor Couzens as saying that the DUR campaign produced a million pages of advertising and circulars, 250,000 song books and phonograph records mocking Couzens, and even Polish language cookbooks carrying company advertising. The DUR hired speakers, singers, and produced a motion picture provided to Detroit theaters.

Two former mayors, Philip Breitmeyer and William B. Thompson, joined former street railway commissioners Francis C. McMath, Sidney D. Waldon, and Abner E. Larned on another Committee of 57 in opposing the bond issue.[12] The Board of Commerce and a group of business leaders, led by Alvan Macauley and Henry B. Joy, both of the Packard Motor Car Company, joined in its fight. Mayor Couzens had support from the Federation of Labor and the widely circulated *Evening News* but opposition from the *Free Press*. "For years, he had been stepping on sacred toes," Jay Hayden, street railway commission secretary, recalled. "If he won this battle, it was clear that he would be even more firmly entrenched. The myriad of interests that he had thwarted moved as one in a supreme effort to stop this man."[13]

Having settled with Couzens, Henry Ford came out strongly in favor of municipal ownership,[14] and Detroit voters approved the Castator ordinance by a majority vote of more than three-fifths on April 5, 1920. The final tally was a remarkable 88,585-50,776.

The DUR responded with a flurry of lawsuits. "In commenting on the company's actions, Mayor Couzens stated that they were indicative of the desperation of the Detroit United Railway in the situation," said one industry newsletter.[15] It contested certification of the vote by the city election commission. DUR lawyer William M. Donnelly argued with a straight face that all of the ballots should be thrown out because they were printed on semitransparent paper and the routine tearing off of the corner of ballots exposed the voter's choice. A recount was taken, and the results were confirmed.

The DUR and others brought multiple lawsuits to restrain the $15 million bond issue, the decisions in which strengthened immeasurably the city's legal and political position as they came down from the courts one by one firmly against the DUR.[16]

Adding to the clamor, on April 17, 1920, DUR motormen and conductors demanded a raise from 65 cents to $1 per hour. The DUR appealed to Mayor Couzens and the Common Council for an increase in fares it needed to offer 75 cents per hour, which they referred to the Board of Street Railway Commissioners. The board passed it back, refusing to get involved. That prompted the DUR to abolish all transfers on May 31, and Mayor Couzens sued. Over the next few days, Couzens privately agreed to six-cent fares in closed-door settlement talks with Judge Ira W. Jayne of the Wayne County Circuit Court. "As in the case of a cut in wages, it was better politics to let the company initiate a higher passenger rate than to have to bear—later on—that onus himself," Jere Hutchins wrote.[17]

Couzens experienced all sorts of difficulties in getting municipal construction underway. The bonds voted in the referendum had to be sold, and Detroit investment brokers boycotted them. Couzens bought many of the bonds himself and used municipal funds to buy others. DUR lawyers argued that doing so was illegal, but he went ahead anyway and was sustained by the courts.[18] Steel railways were needed, and no major company submitted bids. Couzens arranged for the steel by making a personal plea to James A. Farrell, president of the U.S. Steel Corporation.

In July 1920, Henry Ford took his double-engine, eight-cylinder, 160-horsepower interurban streetcar capable of reaching a speed of eighty miles an hour out for a test drive along his recently purchased Detroit, Toledo, and Ironton Railroad between Dearborn and the Ohio River. "After only a few miles down the line a minor mechanical problem developed, thus aborting the trip," said Ford R. Bryan. "The car returned slowly on one engine while Henry returned to Detroit by automobile. Any further use of the gasoline railcar seems to be undocumented. Presumably, the car was soon scrapped, its demise unpublished."[19]

As promised, Couzens hired a contractor, the Department of Public Works issued permits, and on the day after the April 5 election, digging for the road foundation started at Charlevoix Street and Connors Road. This was quick work and good politics. Mayor Couzens drove the first spike in the construction of the new St. Jean Avenue line on August 24, 1920. The DUR, which had obtained permission in May 1919 to itself build a St. Jean extension suddenly sent construction crews. Mayor Couzens issued a cease and desist order with support from the Common Council. The DUR went to court protesting the city's unilateral revocation of consent.

New tracks of the new municipal lines had to cross old tracks of the DUR at St. Jean and Mack Streets. "As the law was then understood, the Detroit United Railway had the right to prevent this," Barnard wrote. "Consequently, there occurred another of those civic comedies with Couzens as script writer."[20]

At midnight on Saturday, January 8, 1921, under secret orders issued by Couzens, who was conveniently out of town, leaving Council President John C. Lodge as acting mayor, one hundred city workers, having stockpiled supplies nearby, converged at the intersection along with two hundred policemen. Under their protection, workers proceeded to cut the DUR rails. Not far away, a heavy wrecking train was idling on the DUR tracks. In the other direction, the DUR had stationed a snowplow. A large DUR truck was driven through the gang of men starting work and abandoned where it would obstruct the street.

DUR assistant general manager, Ellsworth Burdick, sprang out from a nearby drug store with a restraining order in his pocket obtained for him by company lawyers from Judge Dingman. Before Burdick could deliver his restraining order to anyone in charge, police arrested him and put him into a patrol wagon that sped over the drawbridge to a police station on Belle Isle. Behind them at midnight, the city drawbridge operator routinely opened the span, locked up, and went home. Although quickly released, Burdick spent the night on the island. By the next morning, when the drawbridge operator returned, the rail crossing had been finished, and Detroit's streetcars began running across the DUR lines.[21]

There was a legal uproar from DUR attorneys who said that the midnight crossing was "an abominable, damnable outrage."[22] They sought contempt of court proceedings against six city officials and threatened to sue for false imprisonment on behalf of Burdick. On February 4, Circuit Court Judges Ray Hart of Midland and Clayton C. Johnson of Coldwater, reassigned to hear the case, decided that even if Burdick did not succeed in making complete service of Judge Dingman's restraining order, it was due to the interference and conduct of city officials and employees. They enjoined the city against using the crossing but declined to order its removal pending further proceedings.[23]

By February 2, 1922, with the Belle Isle case stuck in eventually successful settlement negotiations under close court supervision, approximately six miles of lines were completed and municipal service started on the Charleviox and St. Jean lines with a five-cent fare on one-man, thirty-two passenger Birney safety streetcars.[24] The city kept streetcars on the east side of the contested intersection guarded by a watchman overnight to which passengers walked from west side streetcars. Several years before, the Common Council had prohibited the use of one-man streetcars as unsuitable for local traffic and reduced employment. The ordinance had to be amended. The beginning of service was marked by no public ceremony; Mayor Couzens and other city officials made a perfunctory inspection trip a few days after construction was completed.

Ouster Authority

One last desperate effort was made by the DUR in 1921 to win the Thirty-Year War. On January 10, it submitted another franchise ordinance initiative to the Common Council, having gathered all necessary petition signatures. It proposed that the city's new street railway lines be merged with those of the DUR in a new privately owned company operated on the Taylor cost-of-service plan. The DUR offered a number of attractive concessions to the public.

Couzens made a counterproposal to take over all of those DUR lines being operated under the day-to-day agreement. Judge Arthur J. Tuttle had dismissed one of the federal lawsuits against the bond issue, saying, however, that the 1920 ballot question gave the city no right to use the $15 million to purchase, condemn, or lease existing DUR lines but only to build its own street railway system. The city, he said, needed three-fifths approval under the state constitution to acquire any of the day-to-day lines.

Judge Tuttle's dismissal had been appealed to the U.S. Supreme Court. The DUR hired Charles Evans Hughes—then between his two appointments to the Supreme Court—to argue its case against the $15 million bond issue on procedural due process grounds under the Fourteenth Amendment to the U.S. Constitution. On February 28, 1921, Justice William R. Day, writing for a unanimous court,[25] said it would not depart from its earlier ruling against the DUR in the *Fort Wayne* case, which held that, where a street railway company operating under franchise granted for a definite time had enjoyed the full term, the city may require the company to remove its track within a reasonable time without impairing any contractual rights protected by the federal Constitution or depriving the company of its property without due process of law.

In the campaign that followed by the DUR for its Taylor Plan ordinance and by Couzens for his three-fifths ouster authority, the DUR issued a threat. If its proposal were not accepted, it would idle all streetcars. "We will not be intimidated," said Couzens.[26]

The *Evening News* reported that many prominent citizens opposed the DUR ordinance. "All businessmen know the DUR ordinance is unfair," the newspaper again quoted R. H. Fyfe on March 22, 1921. "In my opinion, it would not only be disastrous but suicidal for this great city to give the exclusive right of its streets to any organization whatsoever for transportation purposes, no matter what the organization promises to do, how generous and philanthropic it may be."[27]

The vote on April 4 overwhelmingly defeated the DUR initiative ordinance, 52,918-92,036. Couzens's proposal for using part of the $15 million bond issue to buy twenty-nine miles of DUR track being operated under the day-to-day agreement received well more than three-fifths approval, 96,539-50,704.

Municipal construction continued through a barrage of criticism over the quality of the roadbed, difficulty obtaining steel ties and rails, hiring of a $100,000 per year engineer, resident petitions, court actions, newspaper editorials, and complaints about the small, one-man Birney safety streetcars Couzens had put into use.

"Under present circumstances, municipal ownership and operation of the entire transportation system of Detroit seems inevitable—for better or for worse," said the *Electric Railway Journal*.

> Thus is the continuous political fight centering about the Detroit United Railway for more than twenty-five years apparently to be ended in the course of the next few years.
>
> The speed with which the municipal system is now being built and acquired is evidenced by the prospect of a mileage increased from 18 at the end of 1920 to 130 at the end of 1921. The project having gained such proportions, there is not an encouraging likelihood that the tide toward municipal ownership in Detroit will be stopped.[28]

Without transfers to Judge Woodward's radial streets—notably Woodward Avenue and Fort Street—the city's ability to provide service and its competitive posture were both weak. Couzens moved quickly. "Then came the city's next step, not unexpected, but a most serious one," Hutchins said. "Notice was given, under laws that had already been adjudicated, that the company must proceed at once to remove its tracks and overhead equipment from Woodward Avenue and Fort Street, two of the city's most important thoroughfares. The city planned to occupy these streets with tracks of its own. And this meant that the tracks on other streets would be ordered off one after another till none should be left, leaving the interurban tracks to dangle outside like so many broken cords."[29]

In July, the DUR had refused a $388,000 offer for the twenty-three miles of old street railway tracks and overhead wires, much of which city engineers said would need rebuilding.[30] Couzens followed with a threat, sending a new ouster ordinance to the Common Council. In August, it was adopted over opposition from affected businesses on Woodward Avenue and Fort Street that were unconvinced by the mayor's plan to lay temporary tracks and parallel railway lines one block each side of Woodward Avenue. They gathered sufficient petition signatures to force an ouster referendum onto the November ballot. If the voters approved, Mayor Couzens insisted that he would order the DUR to tear up its expired tracks, a weapon that no other mayor of Detroit had ever seriously considered using. An estimated fifty thousand riders used the two lines every day.

Stopping service on Woodward Avenue and Fort Street would be a financial catastrophe for DUR stockholders. Doing so would not only require the DUR to spend a large sum of money tearing up the tracks and restoring the streets, but it would destroy most of its valuable interurban service into downtown Detroit.

The *Wall Street Journal* pointed out that the DUR's interurban lines were "the largest and, perhaps, the most strategically situated in the country.... Freed of political bickering and expensive local campaigns the company, it is expected, will be in a more satisfactory position as a strictly interurban carrier." The keen financial mind of Mayor Couzens would not have failed to take note of what else the *Wall Street Journal* concluded. "There have been two weak points in Detroit United's financial structure—lack of comprehensive financing plan and 'absentee ownership.' Practically all stock is held outside of Detroit, much of it in Canada."[31]

In the election of November 8, 1921, the people stood by Mayor Couzens, reelecting and giving him full ouster authority by an overwhelming margin, 72,078-36,518.[32] They also gave him new weapons, approving a proposal permitting the Board of Street Railway Commissioners to operate gasoline motor buses and trackless electric trolley buses using overhead lines, 62,854-36,161.

Following the election, Couzens immediately acted on his right to take over at cost less depreciation all DUR tracks and streetcars being operated under the day-to-day agreement—except Woodward Avenue and Fort Street because of the immense leverage it gave him in negotiating over full municipal ownership. On December 12, 1921, Judge Clyde L. Webster of the Wayne County Circuit Court approved the purchase price determined by a board of arbitrators—$692,277 for 105 streetcars and 25 trailers payable to the DUR and $1,605,000 for twenty-nine and a half miles of railway tracks, poles, and overhead lines all payable to the Guaranty Trust Company of New York. Together with Detroit's new streetcars and construction of new street railways, administrative offices, and car yards, this consumed nearly all of the $15 million bond issue the people had voted. The city and the DUR agreed to share all of their lines with alternating streetcars and universal transfers. An end to the Thirty-Year War was nearing.

Couzens Seizes Victory Out of DUR Stockholder Turmoil

The DUR underwent a major shake-up at the board of directors meeting of May 25, 1921. Frank Brooks resigned as president claiming ill health.[33] His office remained vacant, the job filled by Allen

F. Edwards, DUR vice president. Wall Street capitalist Harrison Williams of the Central Union Trust Company, one of the DUR's principal financial backers, joined the board under pressure from worried bondholders in New York City. Williams was president of the North American Company of New Jersey, which owned a controlling interest in Detroit Edison.[34] He insisted on appointing to the board Alexander Dow, Detroit Edison president, and formed an executive committee consisting of himself as chairman, Hutchins, Dow, Edwards, and R. W. Martin, a director since early 1918 from New York City's prestigious banking firm Dillon, Read & Company.[35]

"I have been asked by Harrison Williams, New York, to serve with him as a director of the Detroit United Railway," Dow said in a statement issued following the meeting. "He and some friends of his have recently become interested in the Detroit United Railway. Mr. Williams suggested that I could be of help in dealing with the complications of our local street railway service, which he wants to see straightened out as quickly as possible."[36]

Dow and Edwards immediately stepped into the stalled negotiations that continued with Mayor Couzens over sale of the Woodward Avenue and Fort Street lines. Edwards, age forty-five, had come to work for the DUR in 1904 as purchasing agent and rose to vice president under Brooks, who had passed him over in naming his own son, Frank Brooks Jr., as general manager and heir apparent in January. Dow and Edwards, however, had made no progress since Couzens had put a firm offer of $388,000 on the table back in July.

"Mr. Dow used his best diplomacy with Mayor Couzens and that latter's associates to work out some plan that would stay their efforts," said Hutchins, "but the most he got for his pains was rather scant courtesy."[37]

The ouster ordinance approved by voters required the DUR to abandon service on Woodward Avenue and Fort Street within ten days of ballot certification by the Common Council and to remove all of its tracks, poles, and overhead wires within the next ninety days. The board of canvassers submitted its report for acceptance by the Common Council on November 15. Edwards announced that the DUR was prepared to suspend streetcar service on November 25. "It seems unfortunate that a satisfactory price for the lines to be ousted could not have been agreed upon," Edwards said in a press release. "The price of $388,000, which was named by the City as the amount they would be willing to pay for these lines, we considered in no way consistent with the value of the property proposed to be taken over, and have therefore declined to accept it."

With the deadline nearing, Hutchins said he stepped into the negotiations. "It was now thought that Chairman Hutchins should try his hand with Couzens," Hutchins wrote in his 1938 autobiography, which never mentioned the fact that New York bondholders had taken effective control of the DUR and put Harrison Williams on the board to replace him as chairman of a new executive committee.[38] Having made an appointment by telephone the evening before, he said, Hutchins appeared at 610 Longfellow at ten o'clock on a Sunday morning, probably November 13, 1921. The scene described by Hutchins is revealing. Mayor Couzens was well prepared, and Hutchins was ill advised to be there.

"Cordial greetings were exchanged in high good nature," Hutchins began. "Couzens was an artist in geniality. His handsome countenance, wreathed in smiles, was well worth looking at. On this occasion he was in his best form."

"Do you remember once 'bawling me out' in your office?"

"No," Hutchins said. "I do not."

"I went in with your auditor, Fullerton, to see about the collection of a coal bill."

"Are you . . . ?" Hutchins replied in surprise. "Are you the red-faced man who stuck his head through my door one day years ago to talk about coal bills?"

"I certainly am. And you bawled me out good and plenty."

Couzens had been working at the time for Alex Malcolmson's coal company, which supplied the street railway company's powerhouses with West Virginia coal, amounting to about two trainloads daily. The trains coming up from Virginia had to pass through the Hocking Valley coal district in Ohio. After the contract had been running for some time Hutchins discovered that the West Virginia coal was being exchanged for the Hocking Valley variety, 32 percent inferior in heat units, worth one-third less to the company and that much additional profit to Malcolmson.

"I do not suspect," said Hutchins, "that in your subordinate position you had anything to do with it but fraud seemed to have been attempted, and I had a right to make a fuss about it."

"Right you are," said Couzens.

The two men got down to business.

"Why shouldn't you lease our city lines in their entirety?" Hutchins asked.

"What's in your mind?" asked the mayor.

"That you can avoid further capital duplication by leasing and operating them at six per cent on their fair valuation, with the right to purchase outright at any time."

"Your company would be willing to lease to the City in some such way?"

"I am sure it would."[39]

Sessions to hammer out details began within a day or two. "In due course a valuation was tentatively agreed to that would return the company rentals amounting to about $2,000,000 annually," Hutchins said. "Then a large obstacle blocked progress." Hutchins wanted a clause in the lease guaranteeing that if the city failed, the DUR could repossess with the right to operate for a definite period of years. Hutchins was demanding what Tom Johnson failed to get for Richard Wilson before he sold to the failed Everett-Moore syndicate of Cleveland in 1898. Edward Moore was still an active DUR director with a long personal history with Hutchins.

"This made Couzens hot," Hutchins said. "It sounded to him too much like a franchise for the company. With no assurance that Couzens himself would continue long in office to administer them, to turn properties worth $40,000,000 over to the tender mercies of incoming and outgoing politicians, without some saving clause, would have been the height of folly."[40]

Hutchins made a play for more time at a meeting of the two negotiating teams on January 6, 1922. He took the lackluster position that the DUR's financial position precluded entering into another day-to-day lease arrangement pending necessary three-fifths voter approval for Detroit to legally operate all of the DUR's lines inside Detroit. Refusing to yield the initiative, Couzens upped the ante, demanding full municipal ownership. Unless the DUR came back with a satisfactory price, he would terminate negotiations and enforce the ouster ordinance, tearing up the DUR railway tracks on Woodward Avenue and Fort Street. Hutchins agreed to call a meeting of the DUR board of directors before coming back on January 12.

What happened next was an inevitable clash between the DUR's New York bondholders and Montreal stockholders. Major trouble had been brewing since the May 25 board meeting, when the

DUR board gave stockholders a 2.5 percent stock dividend in lieu of its usual quarterly 8 percent cash dividend. Worse, on August 30, 1921, the Michigan Public Utilities Commission had refused permission to award another 2.5 percent stock dividend, questioning both the DUR's good faith and its financial condition.[41] Stock dividends not only dilute the market value of individual shares and reduce individual cash dividends, but they also reduce the voting power of shareholders. Hutchins knew that he was playing a dangerous game with the Grey Nuns of Montreal.

"Vice president Ferguson, domiciled at Montreal, and keenly alive to the interests of the company, was put under fire by stockholders there who wanted their dividends, whatever else might happen," Hutchins said. "Their attitude was to cause trouble later on."[42]

The first public news of popular unrest among its Montreal stockholders surfaced in Detroit on January 5, 1922, when the *Free Press* reported a sharp drop in the price of DUR stock on the Montreal stock exchange. "This is not regarded as having anything to do with . . . the applications being made from two sources for proxies at the annual meeting next month," the newspaper said. "The generally weak undertone is probably the better explanation. So far as finances of the company are concerned, they are regarded as having worked into a better financial position lately."[43]

The outcome of a proxy war between the DUR's Montreal stockholders in favor of selling led by Charles Laurendeau and New York bondholders opposed to selling led by Harrison Williams was entirely predictable, but it caught Hutchins empty-handed and Couzens ready.[44] Laurendeau sent A. Avila Gingras, an ambitious, young Montreal stockbroker, to Detroit on January 12 to meet with Couzens. Couzens eagerly received him and listened to him.

"In private interviews, Gingras told Mayor Couzens among many other things what good fellows the stockholders were and how little in sympathy they were with Vice President Ferguson, their Montreal director, and with others of the management," Hutchins said. This was exactly what Couzens needed to know. "Couzens gave out a press interview attacking Ferguson as an unworthy person," Hutchins said. "He gave Gingras to understand that he was entirely in sympathy with the Montreal stockholders and he otherwise did and said what he could to stir up among the stockholders as big a rift as possible. All of this Gingras reported to his principals in Montreal to make them believe that with a change of directors all would be well. Gingras probably thought also that such a change might land a fat job for himself."[45]

Following his meeting with the mayor, Gingras appeared at the afternoon session of the city and DUR negotiating teams at Couzens's invitation. There, Gingras made a startling announcement. He told the gathering that he controlled proxies for more than 70,000 of the company's 153,750 outstanding shares.[46] "Mr. Gingras explained that while the interests he represented were heavy stockholders, they had kept hands off because they were not residents of Detroit," an industry journal said. "However, it was now considered necessary by them to take part in the company's affairs at this time because the property was apparently endangered."[47]

Attending for the city were Couzens; Wilcox; Ellis and Horace H. Esselstyn, street railway commissioners; Joseph S. Goodwin, municipal railway manager; and his assistant manager, Ross Schram. The DUR representatives were Edwards, Dow, Burdick, and Stevenson.[48] If Hutchins, too, was present, he sat silent as Edwards made two big mistakes negotiating with Couzens.[49]

With the annual meeting of stockholders less than three weeks away on February 7, Edwards objected to having Gingras present. "Edwards informed him that inasmuch as he is not a member of the director's committee, nor on the board, it would not be proper for him to take part in the conference," an industry journal said. Mayor Couzens was more than eager to let Gingras stay, but Gingras politely withdrew.[50] Couzens had achieved everything he needed.

Then, Edwards announced the DUR board's willingness to sell for $24.5 million. Couzens, who had already publicly said he was not in favor of paying more $20 million, politely explained that city officials had not completed their estimate. The exact price Detroit would be willing to pay was still undecided, he insisted.

On January 17, the *Montreal Gazette* interviewed DUR vice president A. J. Ferguson upon his return from the Detroit board meeting. "The recent reports," he said," were misleading . . . in that it was erroneously stated that Mayor Couzens had offered $20,000,000 for the property. . . . Mr. Ferguson went on to state that the shareholders of the company were being circularized in the above connection and that they will have placed before them a full and complete explanation of the situation at the forthcoming annual meeting, which takes place on Feb. 7."[51]

Ratcheting up the pressure on Montreal stockholders in apparent concert with Mayor Couzens, on January 24 a Detroit physician, Dr. Charles H. Lazowski, publicly announced his intention to seek a court order enforcing the ouster ordinance for the immediate removal of DUR tracks from Woodward Avenue and Fort Street. On January 30, his attorney, Carl J. Jankowski, obtained from Judge Harry J. Dingman an order to show cause by February 11 why the ouster ordinance should not be enforced.[52]

A few days before the annual meeting, Couzens took another big step toward driving down the price he would have to pay. Hutchins described what he did with some awe.

> One day late in the afternoon, while . . . a conference was in progress in a room in the City Hall, in through a private door stamped Mayor Couzens, red rims around his eyes and his flaming face violently contorted. Looking like one who might be either sick or extremely angry, he seized the rim of a chair, the knuckles of his hands showing white, and glaring at the railway chairman (who was sitting with Dow, Edwards, and Stevenson on the opposite side of the table), he turned loose a volume of unrestrained invective and abuse that suggested Pingree in his palmiest days.
>
> Disappointed because possession could not be gained by lease without raising a franchise question and wishing to widen a growing breach among the stockholders, he expressed wonder that any company would select as its responsible representative one so old as the chairman he faced, calling that representative a criminal and as many other hard names as he could think of. While this tirade, lasting some minutes, was going on, the chairman's mind turned lightly and reminiscently back half a century to the boys on the Texas prairies, to Tandy Walker, the half-breed Choctaw, to the outlaw Dallas in a Louisiana railroad camp, and to other men and scenes of older times, when such talk would necessarily have been brought to speedy conclusion.[53]

Seventy-one year old Hutchins was recalling, at least, the two gunfights in which he had engaged as a young man. "Now it was all part of a hard day's work," he said. "And all the while Couzens himself was playing a part."

Couzens had a final offer to deliver, ending the Thirty-Year War. "The city will pay $19,850,000 in cash for such of your properties as are needed for city service. Do you accept?"

"He knew very well the company itself would have to answer that question, and he knew also the sum offered was barely half the value," Hutchins said.[54]

A day or two later, Couzens apologized, blaming ill health and fatigue for his outburst, Hutchins said. Indeed, there were rumors that Couzens was suffering from migraine headaches. "The battle for municipal ownership and his nerve-racking ways to get things done just the way he wanted them done were taking their toll," said Bingay. "His headaches became so terrific that he was found several times collapsed on the floor of his office."[55]

The final step Couzens took was corporate political theater at its most dramatic. Couzens purchased a single share of stock from a shareholder named W. E. Cole, paying full par value of $100.[56] Less than two weeks before the annual meeting, he announced his intention to attend and vote his share with Gingras.

Having lost the proxy-gathering campaign to Gingras, Harrison Williams retained Wall Street financier Clarence Dillon to broker a truce. Dillon failed miserably. "New York interests, bankers, and the directors of the company have called a conference in New York for February 4 between themselves and the opposition interests headed by Gingras," the *Free Press* reported on February 1. "In an interview, Mr. Gingras said: 'I have been invited to attend this meeting but I have definitely decided not to do so. I will not consider a compromise of any kind but will remain in the fight to follow out my original plans.'"[57]

On February 7, Couzens took a front row seat at the DUR stockholder meeting. He listened to the discussion and then stood up and spoke. Unless the DUR agreed to sell all of its municipal lines, he would carry out his threat to tear up the tracks on Woodward Avenue and Fort Street under the ouster authority already approved by voters. Couzens told the assembled stockholders that he would pay $16.5 million exclusive of real estate—the forty-seven-acre Highland Park carhouse and shops had been a major obstacle.

"When the mayor appeared at the stockholders' meeting, he flatly told the owners of the D.U.R., however, that they would receive a better price for their lines during this month than they could ever hope to receive at any time in the future," the *Free Press* said. "This issue must be settled now, in February," he added.[58] Couzens had increased the pressure for agreement at his actual price of $19,850,000 while giving Hutchins and the new DUR board elected at the meeting much-needed wiggle room.

Hutchins told none of this in his book. All that he recalled was his own reelection. "At the ensuing annual meeting held in the company's general office building, and a rather lively affair, the complexion of the Board was radically changed," Hutchins said blandly.[59] Removed from the board were Williams, Dow, Martin, Donnelly, J. R. Nutt of Cleveland, and Senator Joseph M. Wilson of Quebec. Only by the keen legal advice of Stevenson was Hutchins prepared to invoke an obscure Michigan law intended to protect minority shareholders. Since 1885, Michigan's general corporation law had permitted cumulative voting under which shareholders could cast all or part of their votes for one candidate or distribute them among all or a few candidates as they saw fit, a tactic never used before in DUR elections.

Moore nominated just four candidates—Hutchins, Edwards, Ferguson, and himself. All were reelected. In his autobiography, Hutchins admitted that Gingras would have succeeded in ousting them without their surprise use of cumulative voting.[60] Holding proxies for more than 92,000 of the DUR's 150,000 shares, Gingras nominated and elected a controlling majority of seven French-Canadians, all residents of Montreal.[61]

Before the new board of directors met the next morning, Judge Laurendeau personally called on Hutchins, whose term of office as chairman of the board had expired. Laurendeau was a former Quebec Superior Court judge, Montreal city attorney, and leader of the French-Canadian majority that had gathered the proxies cast by Gingras. Laurendeau asked Hutchins to accept reelection. "This honor was not at all desired," Hutchins said. "But after arguments pro and con, declination would have seemed to indicate a lack of further interest."[62]

When the board gathered a few minutes later, Hutchins was reelected chairman, Edwards was replaced by Stevenson as acting president, and Burdick was named general manager.[63] Hutchins said Gingras was elected secretary and treasurer.[64]

The directors proceeded at once to discuss Couzens's offer to pay $19,850,000 for the Detroit lines. That question was already settled in their minds. "Couzens had talked in a kindly way to some of them," Hutchins said. "By accepting, he could be depended upon, they thought, to give aid in other ways, and they would be free to go along with the successful operation of the six hundred miles of interurbans that would be left."[65]

Stevenson objected that Couzens had since changed his offer. Instead of $19,850,000 cash, he would pay $2,770,000 down and $10,000,000 in twenty semi-annual installments of $500,000 each, the balance to be paid by December 31, 1931, at 6 percent interest. Detroit would be getting 273 miles of track, 10 car houses, and 1,029 streetcars, trailers, and service cars.

"This they thought would be as good, if not better than cash," Hutchins said.

"Would you not accept this offer?" asked one of the directors.

"I certainly would not—I'd see him blasted first," Hutchins replied. "It is not necessary to do so. Couzens's own commissions have reported knock-down values more than ten million dollars higher. His offer is wholly arbitrary. He thinks in millions and is keen for quick possession. There is nothing chivalric in his make-up. Stand for more and you will easily get a lot more."

Nobody stood.[66]

The new directors named a new negotiating team to iron out the details. They were Hutchins, Stevenson, Burdick, Gingras, and J. C. Butterworth, an Ottawa stockholder, the first time any Canadian stockholders were included in any meeting with Couzens and his street railway commissioners.[67] Couzens coldly never attended any of their meetings. He knew it was over, and both the DUR and city worked quickly.[68] The DUR kept fifteen acres at the rear of its Highland Park site and twelve acres at McGraw Street and Grand River Avenue. Otherwise, if approved by the voters, it was agreed that the city would buy all DUR lines in Detroit, Highland Park, Hamtramck, Springwells, and Warren Townships for $19,850,000, making it the largest municipality-owned transit system in the country with 373 miles of railway, 1,457 streetcars, and 4,000 employees effective at 12:01 A.M., May 15, 1922.

On the last day before the referendum on April 17, the *Evening News* again sought out then eighty-three-year-old R. H. Fyfe for his opinion. Fyfe confidently predicted that the people would approve. "[For] in the past the citizens of Detroit never failed to express themselves at the polls when their best interests were at stake," he said.[69] The vote was 55,669-12,243, an overwhelming majority.

Mayor Couzens hands the check to Jere Hutchins. Courtesy of the Research Library of Kenneth E. Schramm.

"Probably no one but Couzens could have won it," Barnard concluded. "Considering the stakes, the obstacles, and the bitterness of the opposition, he had, by his 'bull-headedness,' scored a victory that was unique in the annals of American politics in his or even later eras."[70]

Hutchins had jealous, off-hand personal praise. "About this time Couzens in a conversation with one of the company's general officers chuckled pridefully speaking of the millions that had been lopped off the purchase price by the dissension he had fostered."[71]

The *Civic Searchlight*, a well-regarded monthly publication of the Detroit Citizens League that had become the bible of the city's independent voter since its founding in 1912, asked, "Is this the end of the Thirty-Year War?"[72]

It was not. Mopping up litigation lingered.

The City of Detroit filed the last street railway lawsuit of the Thirty-Year War regarding allocation of outstanding general mortgage bonds covering all of the DUR lines in southeastern Michigan. Detroit feared that it might not get clear title because its purchase price was not enough to pay off $25 million owed to the DUR's 1,200 bondholders. The city sued to get a court order dividing the bonded debt between the street railway lines inside and outside of Detroit.

"It was a cause célèbre with a galaxy of legal counsel from Detroit and New York," Hutchins said.[73] On March 5, 1924, the Michigan Supreme Court unanimously affirmed a final decree entered in the Wayne County Circuit Court. In doing so, based on testimony from Hutchins, Judge Joseph Moynihan decided that the DUR lines acquired by Couzens were worth $43 million, the price Detroit should have paid ending the Thirty-Year War.[74]

CHAPTER 12

The Detroit Streetcar Parade

What happened to Detroit's streetcars after the Thirty-Year War is a much bigger story of the automobile industry, auto worker migration from the South, the Great Depression, the rise of the Ku Klux Klan in Detroit, systematic racial housing segregation, the political influence of public employee unions, World War II, the building of the interstate highway system, the beginning of white flight, and much more. More simply, however, as the city grew, riding the streetcar became less and less convenient to those families who lived outside of Grand Boulevard where the roads designed by Judge Woodward spread farther and farther apart. Even as Detroit's population peaked at 1,849,568 by 1950, ridership was declining annually until the entire street railway system was finally shut down in 1956.

On an overcast Sunday, April 8, 1956, the Highland Park High School's marching band led the Detroit Street Railway parade, playing "Auld Lang Syne" from seats on the back of an open truck. Following them was a red Ford Model T fire engine, a black Model T police wagon, and a long line of classic automobiles. Far behind rumbled twenty-four faded yellow and dull red DSR streetcars, carrying two thousand passengers taking a last ride on the Woodward Avenue railway line. Woodward Avenue streetcar service, which had begun at the Detroit River ninety-seven years ago, was ending at the Michigan State Fairgrounds.

Thousands of former residents from across southeastern Michigan brought their postwar children from suburban homes to the Sears, Roebuck & Co. department store in the City of Highland Park to see the streetcar parade. On the west side of Woodward Avenue, many of them stood in front of the sidewalk window displays of spring fashion. They had gone inside to shop each Labor Day weekend for school clothes, each spring for an Easter dress or a suit and shoes, and again each Christmas to see Santa Claus and the toy department. On the southwest corner of Sears Street and Woodward Avenue was an S.S. Kresge dime store, where they sometimes went after shopping trips to order Boston Coolers or hot dogs and icy mugs of root beer. The busy sidewalk scene was familiar to these families, who had steered their newly washed automobiles into the big Sears parking lot behind which stood Detroit's streetcar barns.

The Detroit Street Railway parade on Woodward Avenue in 1956. On the right is the now demolished Sears, Roebuck and Co. department store in Highland Park. On the left is the Administration Building of the Ford Motor Company. Courtesy of the Walter P. Reuther Library, Archives of Labor and Urban Affairs, Wayne State University.

Dominating the east side of Woodward Avenue was a red-brick, four-story office building and the historic 130-acre Highland Park industrial plant opened by the Ford Motor Company in 1910, highlighted by its huge power plant's five towering chimneys, water tower, and fifteen massive factory buildings, all designed by Albert Kahn and mostly abandoned for many years. In 1927, Henry Ford had moved most of its staggering sixty-two thousand daily workers far across Detroit to his River Rouge plant in Dearborn.

Mothers and fathers lined up at the curb with inattentive children who may have expected to see white-faced clowns with big red noses and black-faced jugglers on unicycles, American Legion marchers and Masonic Shriners wearing purple fezzes riding rumbling black and white motorcycles, howling police cars, blaring fire engines, and big, bright floats. This parade was boring them. Children begged their parents for nickels to buy cotton candy and balloons from the street vendors as they waited and waited for the parade to end.

Finally, the streetcars arrived, among them PCC No. 268, the last surviving streetcar today of the Detroit Street Railway clanging, clanging, and clanging like the song. Its electric motor hummed loudly. The scent of ozone reached the older spectators on the sidewalk and filled them with memories.[1] A few months after the parade ended, Detroit sold 186 of its PCC streetcars to Mexico City, which scrapped some for parts over the years. An 8.1 magnitude earthquake collapsed the roof over their carhouse in 1985, destroying all but the last. In 1981, the Michigan Transit Museum in Mount Clemens had reacquired PCC No. 268. It was undergoing restoration at the Selfridge Air National Base when heightened national security forced its eviction in 2012. Today, it sits in the backyard of the museum president on Gratiot Avenue in rural St. Clair County.

Detroit's last streetcar, PCC No. 268. Photo by Neil J. Lehto. Courtesy of the Michigan Transit Museum, Mount Clemens, Michigan.

Notes

Citations for most of the voluminous uses made of U.S. census reports, Journals of the Michigan State House of Representatives and Senate, State of Michigan corporate records, and meeting minutes of the Detroit Common Council have been omitted. The corporations division of the Michigan Department of Licensing and Regulatory Affairs maintains a free, online business entity search tool. A collection of the *Journal of the Common Council of the City of Detroit* is available for review by appointment only at the Detroit's City Clerk's archives and records office, 2 Woodward Avenue, Ste. 200, Detroit, Michigan; many but not all of the *Journals* through 1917 are available for free, online research at the Hathitrust Digital Library.

CHAPTER 1. BEFORE THE THIRTY-YEAR WAR

1. *California v. Central Pacific Railway Company*, 127 U.S. 1, 40 (1888).
2. *Slaughter-House Cases*, 83 U.S. 36 (1873) decided otherwise, 5-4, in one of the U.S. Supreme Court's most often criticized rulings under the privileges and immunities clause of the Fourteenth Amendment. In future cases, however, the majority's reasoning was rejected, and the dissenting side's opinions would prevail to protect individual rights against hostile state laws.
3. For example, in a case decided before adoption of the 1908 Michigan Constitution, the Michigan Supreme Court said, "The right of a municipality to refuse its consent to the use of its streets by a street railway is an *absolute* one, and its power in the first instance to impose conditions is *unlimited*" (emphasis added). *City of Monroe v. Detroit, Monroe & Toledo Short Line Railway*, 243 Mich. 315, 330 (1906). A judge stating a common law rule as absolute is rare because it so horrifies all the other judges to whom it is cited by lawyers making arguments in later cases.
4. Stanley I. Kutler, *Privilege and Creative Destruction: The Charles River Bridge Case* (New York: W. W. Norton 1978), 15. This book is truly a gem of historical constitutional law research and writing.
5. Kutler, *Privilege and Creative Destruction*, 7–8.
6. Ibid., 8.

7. Ibid., 13.
8. *Marbury v. Madison*, 5 U.S. 137 (1803); *Trustees of Dartmouth College v. Woodward*, 17 U.S. 518 (1819).
9. Kutler, *Privilege and Creative Destruction*, 19.
10. *Fletcher v. Peck*, 10 U.S. 87 (1810).
11. *Proprietors of the Charles River Bridge v. Proprietors of the Warren Bridge*, 24 Mass. 344 (1829).
12. The court heard two hours of argument on Saturday, January 21, and recessed until Monday, January 23, to hear more.
13. *Proprietors of the Charles River Bridge v. Proprietors of the Warren Bridge*, 36 U.S. 420 (1837).
14. *Proprietors of the Charles River Bridge v. Proprietors of the Warren Bridge*, 36 U.S. 465 (1837).
15. *Proprietors of the Charles River Bridge v. Proprietors of the Warren Bridge*, 36 U.S. 545–46 (1837).
16. *Proprietors of the Charles River Bridge v. Proprietors of the Warren Bridge*, 36 U.S. 646 (1837).
17. *Proprietors of the Charles River Bridge v. Proprietors of the Warren Bridge*, 36 U.S. 608 (1837).
18. Antoine de la Mothe Cadillac, "Description of the River of Detroit," in *Historical Collections: Collections and Researches Made by the Michigan Pioneer and Historical Society* (Lansing: Robert Smith Printing, 1904), 33:111. The particularly poetic translator went unidentified.
19. Cadillac used the French land measurement called the arpent—192.75 feet. Most of the farms he granted enjoyed one to three arpents of waterfront and stretched forty to sixty arpents inland.
20. Detroit historian Silas Farmer observed, "It is almost literally true that wherever a stream of water flowed, the Jesuits and French commandants followed its course." Silas Farmer, *The History of Detroit and Michigan or, The Metropolis Illustrated: A Chronological Cyclopaedia of the Past and Present*, 2nd ed. (Detroit: Silas Farmer and Company, 1889), 324.
21. Woodward was born in New York City in 1774. His parents named him Elias Brevoort Woodward, courting favor with his mother's wealthy uncle, Elias Brevoort. Woodward changed his popular name to Augustus after graduating from Columbia College in 1793, a choice evidently arising from his fresh education in the classic language, literature, and history of the Greek and Roman empires. Meaning "the revered one," his choosing of Augustus begs for psychological speculation, even more so because Elias Brevoort Woodward was the sort of person who would have made a detailed study of the life of Gaius Octavius Thurinus, who had changed his name to Caesar Augustus, the great Roman ruler.
22. Thomas McIntyre Cooley, *Michigan: A History of Governments* (Boston: Houghton, Mifflin, 1885), 149.
23. Many historical accounts personally blame Harvey.
24. On August 16, 1901, a brass tablet was erected on the west wall of what Silas Farmer called the Palms Building on the northeast corner of Jefferson Avenue and Shelby Street. Silas Farmer, "Historic Tablets and Memorials," in *The Bi-centenary of the Founding of City of Detroit, 1701–1901: Being the Official Report of the Celebration of July 24, 25, 26, 1901* (Detroit: Common Council, 1902), 294. Helen E. Keep and M. Agnes Burton, *Guide to Detroit* (Detroit: Conover Press, 1916), 95. The inscription on the tablet was as follows: "This tablet marks the starting point of the notable fire of June 11, 1805, which is commemorated in the City Seal. That fire destroyed every house save one in the ancient town of Detroit. It obliterated old lot lines and narrow streets, and secured the wide avenues and public squares of the present day." There is a Palms Building on Woodward Avenue across from Comerica Park. That was not where the tablet was erected. Its whereabouts today are unknown.
25. Hull and his wife, Sarah, brought along only their son and two of their seven daughters. Other daughters were married and living elsewhere. Part of the household was a seventeen-year-old African

American slave named Tillo.

26. Some earlier historians misunderstood the legislative authority of the governor and judges. Griswold did not have a vote on legislation as secretary of the territorial government under the Northwest Ordinance of 1787, which said, in pertinent part: "Sec. 5. *The governor and judges, or a majority of them,* shall adopt and publish in the district such laws of the original States, criminal and civil, as may be necessary and best suited to the circumstances of the district, and report them to Congress from time to time: which laws shall be in force in the district until the organization of the General Assembly therein, unless disapproved of by Congress; but afterwards the Legislature shall have authority to alter them as they shall think fit" (emphasis added).
27. Friend Palmer, a cousin of U.S. Senator Thomas W. Palmer, wrote, "He laid out this city after Michigan's first organization as a territorial government, under the direction of Governor Hull and Judge Woodward; the plan was designed by the latter, to which Mr. Smith, as a scientific man, was much opposed; he considered it visionary, and ill-adapted for the purposes for which it was intended." Palmer offered no reference for his report of Smith's opinion. Friend Palmer, *Early Days in Detroit* (Detroit: Hunt & June, 1906), 920.
28. Governor Hull to Secretary Madison August 3, 1805, in *Historical Collections,* 31:524–25. Many years later, such a plan was found at the State Department. "First Official Plan Made of Detroit after 1805 Fire Found in State Department Archives," *Detroit Free Press,* April 12, 1909, 5. The *Democratic Press and Michigan Intelligencer* was first published in 1831. It was renamed the *Daily Free Press* in 1835 and the *Detroit Free Press* in 1866. Henceforth, it will be referred to as the *Free Press.*
29. Augustus B. Woodward, "Protest of Judge Woodward against the Sale of Certain Lands, June 1, 1818," in *Historical Collections: Collections and Researches Made by the Pioneer Society and Historical Society,* 2nd ed., vol. 12 (Lansing: Wynkoop Hallenbeck Crawford, 1908), 473. Many historians have quoted Woodward's remarkable tract without explaining his cryptic reference to lakes Cuinissuque and Arabasca as among the cross-continental connected bodies of water upon which Detroit had a prime location. While some early eighteenth-century geographers referred to today's Athapescow Lake in the northwest corner of Saskatchewan as Arabasca Lake, unless Woodward was taking some personal license in renaming Lake Champlain, as he was wont to do, a source for Cuinissuque has defied both geographical and etymological research. In 1946, Malcolm Bingay, a Detroit newspaperman, who never let the facts stand in the way of a good story, identified Cuinisuque—he dropped the second "s"—with Winnipeg generally and Arabasca with Winnipegosis, a village near Lake Winnipeg, Manitoba. Malcolm W. Bingay, *Detroit Is My Own Home Town* (New York: Bobbs-Merrill, 1946), 215.
30. John Gentle, "On the Evils Which Have Proved Fatal to Republics," *Aurora (Philadelphia) General Advertiser,* February 6, 18, 21, and 25, 1807, cited in Marie Heyden, "Justice Woodward and the Michigan Territory," *Michigan History,* Spring 1967. Excerpts of the anonymous columns were reproduced in Farmer, *History of Detroit,* 26, 96–97, and 855–58. Detroit had no locally published newspaper until 1817. Among the three Pennsylvania newspapers, William Duane, publisher of the *Aurora,* may have had a few Detroit subscribers, but he had many more in Washington, D.C., where there were readers Duane and Gentle were seeking to influence.
31. The huge stone referred to by Gentle stood in Campus Martius at the intersection of Monroe Street and Woodward Avenue until it was buried out of sight and paved over many years later.
32. Woodward sent an explanation to James Madison on March 14, 1807. "It is not true that thirty days

and thirty nights were employed in taking observations," he said. "A meridian line, from which all the others were run, was taken from one solar observation, and one sidereal observation on the night of the same day, within fourteen or fifteen hours from the first. The wit is unquestionably handsome, and appropriate; but it is not true that any delays were occasioned by the precision." To James Madison from Augustus Woodward, March 14, 1807, Founders Online, National Archives: RG 59-Territorial Papers—TP, Michigan, http://founders.archives.gov.

33. The motto inscribed on the Detroit seal officially adopted in 1827 is attributed to Father Gabriel Richard. Surveying the destruction of his church and the town's other three hundred buildings, including homes, sheds, shops, and barns, many stories say he was heard to sigh, "Speramus Meliora. Resurget Cineribus."
34. The first meetings of the governor and judges were held at the urgently rebuilt Smyth's Tavern on Woodward Avenue near Woodbridge Street. Farmer, *History of Detroit*, 95.
35. Hull was acting on concerns expressed by Madison in correspondence to him dated July 23, 1805. *The Territorial Papers of the United States*, vol. 10, *The Territory of Michigan, 1805–1820*, ed. Clarence Edwin Carter (Washington, DC: United States Government Printing Office, 1942), 22.
36. Woodward and Hull were referring to the fact that the bastard children of Detroit's settlers had no common law right of inheritance from their French fathers or native Indian mothers.
37. Jefferson forwarded their report to the U.S. Congress on December 23, 1805. "Land Titles in the Michigan Territory, No. 112, 9th Congress, 1st Sess.," in *American State Papers: Documents, Legislative and Executive, of the Congress of the United States in Relation to the Public Lands*, ed. Walter Lowri, vol. 1 (Washington, DC: Duff Green, 1834), 229–31.
38. 2 Stat. 398, April 21, 1806.
39. An undated city-published monograph, *The First 300 Years: Detroit Water and Sewerage Department*, ed. Michael Daisy (http://detroitmi.gov/), DWSD publicist, proudly but wrongly described L'Enfant as an African American, the consequence, he explained in a telephone interview, of his confused reading of a revisionist history written by C. L. Lewis for a February 1966 article in *Negro Digest* (*Black World*). Lewis claimed that Benjamin Banneker, a freed Negro, who had assisted in surveying the District of Columbia, salvaged the plan after President Washington dismissed L'Enfant.
40. Farmer described the notebook now held by the Detroit Public Library's Burton Historical Collection: "That the plan was suggested by Judge Woodward is evidenced by the fact that seven pages of his Private Memorandum Book, commenced March 29, 1802, are occupied with a map of the city of Washington cut into sections. Anyone who looks at this book, and examines the old plan of 1806, could be convinced that Woodward made it from suggestions afforded by the plan of Washington. . . . Our old French city thus has features in its plan, which perpetuates remembrances of the capitals of its earliest and its latest Government." Farmer, *History of Detroit*, 28.
41. John W. Reps, "Planning in the Wilderness: Detroit, 1805–1830," *Town Planning Review* 24, no. 4 (1955): 240.
42. Farmer, *History of Detroit*, 53.
43. Clarence Burton wrote a splendidly detailed introduction to his compilation of the land board's minutes. Clarence M. Burton, *Governor and Judges Journal: Proceedings of the Land Board of Detroit*, ed. M. Agnes Burton ([Detroit], 1915), 3–10.
44. One of the Detroit area's best-known streets, John R, begins in downtown today and ends twenty

miles north in the City of Rochester Hills's Bloomer Park. John R. Williams was Detroit's first mayor under the municipal charter of 1824.

45. Burton, *Governor and Judges Journal*, 7.
46. Augustus B. Woodward and Frederick Bates, "Allotment of Lands after the Detroit Fire of 1805," in *Historical Collections*, 31:574–83.
47. Catherine Cangany, *Frontier Seaport: Detroit's Transformation into an Atlantic Entrepôt* (Chicago: University of Chicago Press, 2014), 147.
48. Bates left for Pittsburgh in late November 1806, to attend to the estate of his brother, Tarleton Bates, who had been killed in a duel. From there he carried a lengthy report on Detroit's Land Board to Washington, D.C., where President Jefferson prevailed on him in February 1807 to resign his post in Detroit and accept the position of secretary and land recorder for the Louisiana Territory in St. Louis.
49. Farmer, *History of Detroit*, 48.
50. In his first annual report to the Common Council on February 20, 1883, Farmer said, "The ordinance of 1843 under which, by the courtesy of your honorable body, I was appointed City Historiographer, makes it my duty to present an annual report. I do not find that my predecessors conformed to the ordinance, but a desire to further the interests of the city leads me to present a few facts of a practical historic character." Farmer submitted a 172-page report.
51. Farmer, *History of Detroit*, 948.
52. Ibid. His remark had an obvious double meaning. James Witherell had been appointed in 1808 to replace Bates. Woodward and Witherell, a physician, became fierce political enemies.
53. Under the Northwest Ordinance, the territorial governor served a three-year term and the secretary a four-year term unless sooner revoked, unlike the three judges who served indefinitely during good behavior. Jefferson reappointed Hull and replaced Griswold with Reuben Atwater. Correspondence sent to Jefferson by Detroit attorney Harris H. Hickman on January 9, 1808, had accused Griswold of plotting a political coup with John Gentle, John Harvey, postmaster James Abbott, and Mr. Jones, a hatter. Hickman suggested that it was Griswold who actually wrote the series of eighteen newspaper articles critical of Hull and Woodward that had been published in the *Pittsburgh Commonwealth* and other newspapers, usually attributed to Gentle.
54. Burton, *Governor and Judges Journal*, 9.
55. Woodward joined Detroit's first Masonic Lodge, Zion Lodge #1, on September 5, 1808, receiving the Entered Apprentice degree. He passed the Fellowcraft degree on October 3, 1808, and earned full membership as a Master Mason on October 14, 1809, according to the lodge's bound minute book reviewed by Richard H. Sands, "Judge Augustus Woodward: A Freemason and Founder of the First Complete Public Education System in America," *Bonisteel Masonic Library*, http://www.bonisteelml.org/Judge_Woodward.htm. This tends to suggest that the alleged influence of Freemasonry on the design of Detroit that has been remarked upon over the years is wrong.
56. To James Madison from Augustus Woodward, July 18, 1807, Founders Online, National Archives, http://founders.archives.gov.
57. Burton, *Governor and Judges Journal*.
58. Today, the 8,640 acres actually surveyed are still called the "10,000-acre wilderness tract" in Wayne County land records.
59. Burton, *Governor and Judges Journal*, 67.

60. The U.S. Congress never voted upon Woodward's layout of Detroit. "The original plan fell into the hands of Aaron Greeley, surveyor, in whose house it was seen in a broken window, keeping out the weather and in whose hands it disappeared." Clarence M. Burton, *The Building of Detroit* ([Detroit?], 1912), 25. This book is a little gem of Detroit early history.
61. Burton, *Governor and Judges Journal*, 50.
62. "Circus" is Latin for circle or ring.
63. Woodward, "Protest of Judge Woodward," 477–78.
64. Farmer, *History of Detroit*, 28.
65. Clarence M. Burton, William Stocking, and Gordon K. Miller, *The City of Detroit, Michigan, 1701–1922* (Detroit: S. J. Clarke, 1922), 1:312.
66. Eight Mile Road served as the east-west baseline for the later land survey of Michigan undertaken by the federal government. The system used to do so originated under the Land Ordinance Act, passed by the Continental Congress at Thomas Jefferson's urging, in 1785. Jefferson was an architect, and he had a decided predisposition for straight lines and right angles. The law said: "A surveyor of each state shall be appointed by Congress to divide the said territory into townships of six miles square by lines running due north and south, and others crossing at right angles. . . . The plats of the townships shall be marked out by subdivisions of one mile square." *Journal of Continental Congress* 28 (May 20, 1785): 375. The surveyor's first task was to establish the points from which land would be measured. A line from Michigan's east to west lakeshores was the baseline. This became Eight Mile Road. Today, it is a county line completely across the state and, after jumping over Lake Michigan, is the state line between Wisconsin and Illinois. The north-south line—called the meridian—ran approximately through Jackson and St. Ignace. These two lines, the baseline and the meridian, define the boundaries of townships that appear as a part of real estate descriptions of almost all Michigan land transactions. The system did not apply in areas where the U.S. Congress had recognized private claims. Earlier, after the fire of 1805, Woodward had, indeed, placed his instruments and astronomical devices on the summit of a huge stone in the center of Campus Martius at the junction of Woodward and Monroe Street in order to determine true north. It was from this point of origin that Michigan's official survey was begun. Today it is marked by a medallion embedded in the stone sidewalk at the western point of the diamond surrounding Woodward Fountain. Campus Martius at that time was low and marshy, undesirable for building. Over the years, Detroit raised it considerably with hundreds of yards of earth.
67. Farmer, *History of Detroit*, 889. Judge Woodward foresaw what was going to happen under his plan for Detroit. When advertising his Michigan real estate for sale in the *Detroit Gazette* on August 16, 1825, he offered to accept payment in five equal installments over nine months but "after completion of the Grand Clinton Canal [Erie Canal] an advance of thirty-four per centum will be expected on all of the real property."
68. Malcolm J. Rohrbough, *The Land Office Business: The Settlement and Administration of American Public Lands, 1789–1837* (Oxford: Oxford University Press, 1968), 221–49.
69. Article 12, section 3 of the Michigan Constitution of 1835.
70. "Navigable waters" referred to, at least, lighthouses, harbors, piers, buoys, and dredging.
71. "The quibbling about the word *establish* in Article One, Section Eight of the Constitution—some argued that Congress had the power to build roads and others retorted that it might only *establish*

rights of way—masked a far deeper problem. Neither congressmen nor voters thought in national terms" (emphasis added). John R. Stilgoe, *Common Landscape of America, 1580 to 1845* (New Haven: Yale University Press, 1982), 109.

72. Joseph Story, *Commentaries on the Constitution of the United States*, 4th ed. (Boston: Little, Brown and Company, 1873).
73. Joseph Story, *Commentaries on the* Constitution, 161.
74. Joseph Story, *Commentaries on the Constitution*, 163–64. The tension in Justice Story's thinking, however, is illustrated by what he said about the limited power of Congress to make appropriations for internal improvements. "But it has been contended that the constitution is not confined to mere appropriations of money; but authorizes congress directly to undertake and carry on a system of internal improvements for the general welfare; whenever such improvements fall within the scope of any of the enumerated powers. Congress may not, indeed, engage in such undertakings merely because they are internal improvements for the general welfare, unless they fall with the scope of the enumerated powers. The distinction between this power, and the power of appropriation is, that in the latter, congress may appropriate to any purpose, which is for the common defense or general welfare; but in the former, they can engage in such undertakings only, as are means, or incidents to its enumerated powers." Story, *Commentaries on the Constitution*, 161.
75. David Walker Howe, *What Hath God Wrought: The Transformation of America, 1815–1848* (Oxford: Oxford University Press, 2007), 213. See E. F. Albertsworth, "Advisory Functions in the Supreme Court," *Georgetown Law Journal* 23, no. 4 (May 1935): 643–70; "The Advisory Opinion and the United States Supreme Court," *Fordham Law Review* 5, no. 1 (January 1936): 94–114. This simple correspondence between a justice and the president is mischaracterized as an advisory opinion not only because at least two of the justices otherwise had expressly refused to participate but because the so-called advisory opinion was delivered privately to President Monroe. "If this letter . . . was intended in any sense official, it received no such treatment by Monroe," Donald G. Morgan said. "The action was unorthodox then, and today would be deemed highly exceptionable." Donald G. Morgan, *Justice William Johnson: The First Dissenter* (Columbia: University of South Carolina Press, 1954), 124.
76. The banking case Justice Johnson referred to was *McCulloch v. Maryland*, 17 U.S. 316 (1819), a landmark U.S. Supreme Court decision. The state of Maryland had attempted to impose a tax on all notes of banks not chartered in Maryland. Though the law, by its language, was generally applicable to all banks not chartered in Maryland, the Second Bank of the United States was the only out-of-state bank then doing business in Maryland, and the law was recognized in the court's opinion as having specifically targeted the U.S. Bank. The court struck down the Maryland tax, saying the necessary and proper clause allowed the federal government to pass laws not among the Constitution's list of express powers.
77. The undated letter is among the Monroe Papers in the Library of Congress. Morgan, *Justice William Johnson*, 123–24.
78. President James Buchanan vetoed a bill appropriating $55,000 for dredging the shipping channel through the St. Clair Flats on February 1, 1860. He did so based on constitutional objections against local internal improvements. "The truth is that most of these improvements are in a great degree local in their character," Buchanan said, "and for the especial benefit of corporations or individuals in their vicinity, though they may have an odor of nationality on the principle that whatever benefits any

part indirectly benefits the whole." James Buchanan, "Veto Message, February 1, 1860," *The American Presidency Project*, http://www.presidency.ucsb.edu/ws/?pid=68392.

79. Cooley, *Michigan*, 280.
80. Susan Fino, "Perspectives: Federal Jurisprudence, State Autonomy: De Tocqueville or Disney? The Rehnquist Court's Idea of Federalism," *Albany Law Review* 66 (2003): 765, 769.
81. Peter L. Rousseau, "Jacksonian Monetary Policy, Specie Flows, and the Panic of 1837," *Journal of Economic History* 62 (2002): 457–88.
82. "Public wagon roads" was the popular description adopted by state and federal governments to describe the earliest roads between cities constructed by cutting the trees and brush for wagons beginning in the late 1700s. Still on the books more than one hundred years later in Michigan is section 1 of Act No. 283 of the Public Acts of 1909. It says: "There is hereby created and established a state highway department, which shall be charged with the giving of instruction in the art of building, improving and repairing *public wagon roads* and bridges, collecting reports from township and county highway commissioners, overseers of highways and superintendents and commissioners of streets in villages and cities, and with the distribution of any state reward for improving the *public wagon roads*, that this legislature or any future session may provide for, or any funds that may be given to the state for such purposes by the United States government" (emphasis added). The original bill creating Michigan's State Highway Department was adopted in 1905: Act No. 146 of the Public Acts of 1905.
83. Constitution of 1850, art. 14 § 9. An excellent summary of the state railroad debacle can be found in Hannah Emily Keith, *An Historical Sketch of Internal Improvements in Michigan, 1836–1846* (Ann Arbor: Michigan Political Science Association, 1900).
84. Cooley, *Michigan*, 291. The Michigan Supreme Court had to repeatedly scold the legislature against authorizing municipalities to engage in works of internal improvement. *People ex rel. Bay City v. State Treasurer*, 23 Mich. 499 (1871) and *People ex rel. Hubbard v. Springwells*, 25 Mich. 153 (1872). The supreme court was called upon to and did serially reject enforcement of bond issues made under legislation authorizing municipal pledges of credit in aid of railroad construction. *People v. Township of Salem*, 20 Mich. 452 (1870); *Bay City v. State Treasurer*, 23 Mich. 499 (1871); *Thomas v. Port Huron*, 27 Mich. 320 (1873). See also *Port Huron v. McCall*, 46 Mich. 565 (1881); *Pierson Township v. Town Board of Reynolds*, 49 Mich. 224 (1882). The U.S. Supreme Court held to the contrary in *Township of Pine Grove v. Talcott*, 86 U.S. 666 (1874) and *Taylor v. Ypsilanti*, 105 U.S. 60 (1882). The Michigan Supreme Court, nonetheless, reaffirmed its decisions in *Dodge v. Van Buren Circuit Judge*, 118 Mich. 189 (1898).
85. *Laws of the Territory of Michigan*, vol. 2 (Lansing: W. B. George & Company, 1874), 214. A town meeting at Bronson's Hotel on June 4, 1822, at which Augustus B. Woodward presided, unanimously adopted a resolution "to promote the enterprise of George Deming and his associates to supply the city of Detroit with water, and it will be agreeable to us that the legislative authority should give him an *exclusive privilege* for a certain number of years, under equitable conditions" (emphasis added). Friend Palmer, *Early Days in Detroit* (Detroit: Hunt & June, 1906), 254–55. Attorney Henry J. Hunt had researched and favorably reported on the city's authority to grant exclusive rights.
86. A penstock was a household-sized reservoir constructed of wood designed to fill with water between uses and needed because the waterworks plant operated during limited hours.
87. Davis was a retail merchant, banking, and real estate investor, described as "a stout man of medium

height and blond complexion, magnetic and pushing, and somewhat eccentric in his ways." Davis organized and was financially ruined in his failed Gibraltar and Flat Rock canal project in which he may have swindled Daniel Webster of $2,500. Palmer, *Early Days in Detroit*, 960. Hathon was a surveyor and mapmaker.

88. Rufus Wells sold his rights to Eurotas P. Hastings, who joined Lyon, Davis, and Hathon as incorporators of the Detroit Hydraulic Company. Hastings was a well-regarded banker, who served Detroit in many roles, including recorder's court judge and federal court commissioner.

CHAPTER 2. THE HENDRIE STREETCAR ERA

1. During and immediately after the war, U.S. officials and pro-Union writers most often referred to the Civil War as the War of the Rebellion. *The War of the Rebellion: A Compilation of the Official Records of the Union and Confederate Armies* (Washington, DC: U.S. Government Printing Office, 1880–1901).
2. Detroit covered 12.7 square miles, roughly bounded by what today would be 25th Street on the west and Mt. Elliott Avenue on the east. The northern boundary generally followed the railroad tracks of the Michigan Central and Grand Trunk Railroads, Milwaukee, Dubois, Leland, and Elmwood Streets, and Gratiot Avenue.
3. Mayor William C. Duncan signed the ordinance on November 24, 1862, the official effective date. Section 21 of the ordinance said: "The powers and privileges conferred by the provisions of this ordinance shall be limited to thirty years from and after the date of its passage." The consent granted for the use of city streets to operate streetcars, therefore, would expire at midnight on November 23, 1892.
4. Eben North Willcox signed the articles of incorporation for "The Detroit City Railway" on May 9, 1863 with a double "l" in his name. In subsequent street railway company litigation and in the Compiled Ordinances of Detroit of 1912, overly zealous proofreaders used a single "l." U.S. Census takers never correctly recorded both his first and last names. The 1885 edition of *The Detroit Blue Book*, a studiously fact-checked directory, included among the city's social elite a Mr. E. N. Willcox, his wife, two daughters, and a son, residents of 442 Brush Street. One early history book wrongly reported his name as Wilson. Clarence M. Burton, *Compendium of History and Biography of the City of Detroit and Wayne County, Michigan* (Chicago: Henry Taylor, 1909), 126.
5. In the printing of the statute, the word "tram" was misprinted "train." *Street Railway of Grand Rapids v. West Side Railway*, 48 Mich. 433 (1882). Detroit's streetcars were never popularly referred to as trams. Newspaper headline writers and reporters sometimes called them trolleys. Mostly, they were called streetcars and will be so called throughout here.
6. The others were J. W. Kelsey, John J. Harris, John H. Wiggins, Amos B. Merritt, and John L. Lawrence. A book published in 1907 agreed that Willcox and Rice were the principal investors but added Charles Fargo, an American Express agent, and Frank Phelps, Detroit Baseball Club catcher. Robert B. Ross, *The Early Bench and Bar of Detroit from 1805 to the End of 1850* (Detroit: Richard P. Joy and Clarence M. Burton, 1907), 221. Obviously, Willcox, who was better known in Detroit as a stock promoter than as a lawyer, had been dealing with many possible investors in his speculative scheme.
7. Moore was political secretary to U.S. Senator James McMillan between 1889 and 1903, an officer of the Union Trust and the Security Trust from 1904 to 1914 and director of the Detroit Museum of Art from

1914 to 1917.

8. Charles Moore, "Municipal Ownership of Street Railways in Detroit," *Quarterly Journal of Economics* 13(1899): 453–54.
9. Section 21 of the ordinance said, in pertinent part: "Provided further, that if said grantees, or their assigns, cannot procure the requisite amount of rail of the Philadelphia or other suitable pattern, to build said railways, within the time specified, with a suitable and competent force, then the time shall be extended, until such rail can be obtained, and laid with a suitable and competent force."

   What the Willcox investors and the City intended by the "Philadelphia pattern" is unclear. Many different shapes were then being used in Philadelphia to address the installation, maintenance, and operating problems of railway and wheel design. What was actually used in Detroit consisted merely of a flat rail, probably not the "Philadelphia pattern."
10. The filing recited that the street railway company was being organized under the Tram-Railway Act, Laws of 1855, p. 338 as amended by the Laws of 1861, p. 11. It required such companies to file articles of association with the secretary of state that, among other things, limited its term of existence to thirty years. The second of the articles of association filed with the secretary of state specifically provided that "the term of existence of said company shall be thirty years from and after the date of these articles, *viz*, May 9th, a.d. 1863." Therefore, its corporate life would expire at midnight, May 8, 1893, six months after its franchise from Detroit would expire.
11. The new Syracuse investors were Thomas T. Davis, Austin Myers, James J. Belden, Nathan Randall, L. Harris Hiscock, and Frank Hiscock. Catlin said they bought stock as well as bonds. George B. Catlin, *The Story of Detroit* (Chicago: R. R. Donnelley and Sons, 1923), 574. Willcox was never active in the management of the company and sold all of his stock by the 1870s.
12. On September 26, 1864, the *Free Press* reported that former Adrian Mayor Benjamin Folsom had become a major owner of the railway and was serving as its general manager. "Change in the City Railway Office," *Detroit Free Press*, September 26, 1864, 1. Little more about him could be found. In 1866, Folsom obtained a patent for a snow, ice, and mud scraper that attached to streetcars. Otherwise, he appears in no other early history of Detroit streetcars.
13. The federal tax on all railway, steamboat, and ferry revenues dated back to 1862. Uniformly across the country, street railway fares were five cents. The U.S. Congress adopted legislation specifically allowing the 2.5 percent duty to be passed along as a one-cent fare hike on March 3, 1865. *Statutes at Large*, vol. 13, ed. George P. Sanger (Boston: Little, Brown, 1866), 38th Congress, Session II, Chapter 78, p. 485. The 2.5 percent duty amounted to one-eighth of a cent. Street railway companies eagerly kept the additional seven-eighths of a penny bonus.
14. The ordinance was otherwise amended many more times, repealing the company's exclusive rights to some roads for nonuse, extending the deadline for completing others, and specifically adding others. One interesting change reduced the fare to one cent for passengers traveling to the Elmwood or Mount Elliot Cemeteries on the Jefferson Avenue line.
15. The name change arose from an unusual special act of the state legislature, Act No. 330, adopted on March 6, 1871. The company did not file amended articles incorporating the change until February 3, 1882. The earliest franchise from Springwells Township among Detroit's records is dated June 17, 1880. Otherwise, there are no records of the originally named company having obtained the consent to operate in Springwells Township before 1871, which could explain the legislative name change:

its owners were, perhaps, aligning the names by which they had been operating in Springwells Township with that they used in Detroit. Between 1857 and 1885, the western border of the city of Detroit lay along Twenty-Fifth Street. Portions of Springwells Township were annexed to Detroit on five different occasions. In 1906, Detroit annexed the villages of Delray and Woodmere. Thomas Klug, "Railway Cars, Bricks and Salt: The Industrial History of Southwest Detroit before Auto," unpublished typewritten manuscript, November 5, 1999, http://www.motorcities.org/pdf/Southwest_Det_Industry_TKLUG.pdf.

16. *Detroit Advertiser and Tribune*, April 21, 1866. Evidently, the owners of the remaining eighty-seven shares refused to participate in the trust arrangement. One earlier book erroneously said Hendrie and McMillan came in as trustees when the company's capital stock was increased to $500,000 in 1867. Robert B. Ross and George B. Catlin, *Landmarks of Detroit: A History of the City*, rev. Clarence M. Burton (Detroit: Evening News Association, 1898), 544. All other accounts never mention the stock trust or wrongly tie Hendrie's lease arrangement to an increase in capital stock from $100,000 to $500,000 in 1866. E.g., Jack E. Schramm and William H. Henning, *Detroit's Street Railways*, vol. 1, *City Lines 1863–1922* (Chicago: Central Electric Railfans' Association, 1978), 14. Actually, the capital stock was not increased to $500,000 until July 14, 1877, when Hendrie and McMillan signed amended articles of association, which specifically described them as trustees for 1,123 shares.
17. In 1872, Hendrie alone was personally sued as lessee for wrongful death arising from a streetcar accident. Hendrie won. *James Kelly v. George Hendrie*, 26 Mich. 255 (1872).
18. Miller and Hendrie had married sisters, Catherine and Sarah Trowbridge, respectively.
19. *Detroit United Railway v. Michigan*, 242 U.S. 238 (1916) reversing *People v. Detroit United Railway*, 125 N.W. 700 (1910) affirmed on rehearing, *People v. Detroit United Railway*, 162 Mich. 460 (1910). See also *City of Detroit v. Detroit United Railway*, 173 Mich. 314 (1912).
20. Graeme O'Geran, *A History of the Detroit Street Railways* (Detroit: Conover Press, 1931), 26. This book was his 1930 dissertation submitted for a doctor of philosophy in economics from the University of Michigan. His telling of events is often unreliable, and his understanding of them is frequently wrong. A book review published by the *National Municipal Review* in May 1932 said, "Based almost exclusively upon newspaper sources, the reader will wish that the book were mature and interesting. The appendix of fifteen charts and tables contains some useful exhibits and the bibliography is poorly prepared." For the early years (1862–99), O'Geran primarily relied on a curious five-volume set of mimeographed typescripts of Detroit newspaper articles bound together by Geo. A. Drake & Company, 103 Woodward Avenue, Detroit, Michigan, and now held by the Bentley Historical Library of the University of Michigan. This time-costly retyping and mimeographing of several hundred newspaper articles suggests that multiple copies were intended to be made in a well-financed and well-organized effort, but no other copies of the five-volume set seem to have survived. All of its articles are dated between 1862 and 1899 with significant and inexplicable omissions, including the entire 1891 street railway strike. The Bentley Library acquired the five-volume set from the university's Engineering Department transportation library sometime in the 1970s. For the later years (1900–22), O'Geran said he relied upon a seven-volume "Newspaper Scrap Book of Detroit United Railway" without saying from where they came to him. Elsewhere, he credited University of Michigan engineering professor Henry E. Riggs with providing the loan of valuable documents. Riggs may have been the source of the "Newspaper Scrap Book." O'Geran never cited the journals of Common

Council meetings or state corporate records. He interviewed few of the major players. He joined the economics faculty of Syracuse University in 1928 where he had a thirty-one-year teaching career. He died at age ninety-seven in 1989, leaving to the university a large autograph collection, including those of the first forty-one presidents, Henry Ford, and Thomas Edison.

21. Kenneth T. Jackson, *Crabgrass Frontier: The Suburbanization of the United States* (New York: Oxford University Press, 1985), 113.
22. Its articles of incorporation were not filed with the secretary of state until May 1, 1869.
23. The company had obtained thirty-year consent to operate, again over the veto of Mayor Hugh Moffat, on June 16, 1875. Thomas Cox was appointed manager, and by October cars were running from the post office at Griswold and Larned along State, Cass, Ledyard, and Third Streets north to Holden Road. By February 1874, the company had eight Cleveland-built streetcars carrying one thousand passengers a day.
24. By the time the original seven-year lease expired on May 1, 1873, Hendrie was described as one of the largest stockholders by the *Detroit Advertiser and Tribune* on June 17, 1873, which otherwise said nothing regarding renewal. Several years later, on January 20, 1876, the *Detroit Advertiser and Tribune* briefly mentioned that Hendrie had obtained an eight-year lease. By June 20, 1888, the company had 3,851 shares outstanding, according to amended articles of association that increased capital stock to $1 million.
25. Jacob was chairman of the Committee on Liquor Bonds, which on May 18, 1879, recommended his among sixty other liquor bonds unanimously approved that evening by the Common Council.
26. "Their Work Is Done," *Detroit Free Press*, November 23, 1889, 8.
27. "State Notes," *Marshall Statesmen*, April 10, 1896, 3.
28. "Jacob Was Discharged," *Detroit Free Press*, May 17, 1896, 12.
29. The storefront was located at 268–72 Rivard Street. The farm was located along the south side of Jefferson Avenue, east of Fox Creek, in Grosse Pointe Township, an area that George Hendrie had co-owned and developed.
30. Jacob died of heart disease in his Detroit home, 272 Rivard Street. He was sixty-five years old. He was cremated, and his ashes were buried in the family plot at the Elmwood Cemetery. The *Evening News* was remarkably kind, saying, "when retired from public life there was no better known man in Detroit. . . . His chief characteristics that made him locally famous were a dogged tenacity . . . and unlimited energy and willingness to fight. In his public career, he was probably second only to Governor Pingree in point of picturesqueness. . . . *He left a large estate*" (emphasis added). *Detroit in Nineteen Hundred and One: A Chronological Record of Events* (Detroit: The Evening News Association 1902), 48.
31. *The People ex rel. The City of Detroit v. The Fort Street & Elmwood Street Railway Co.*, 41 Mich. 413, 414 (1879).
32. The Detroit and Grand Trunk Junction Street Railway Company had been purchased by the Congress and Baker Street Railway Company on September 17, 1875, all of the stock of which was formally exchanged share for share with the Detroit City Railway on June 26, 1882.
33. In his annual address to the Common Council on January 14, 1879, Mayor George C. Langdon bitterly complained that despite all the damage street railway companies caused to public roads, state law exempted them from the real and personal property taxes paid to the city by all other industrial and commercial businesses. Mayor Langdon said that Detroit's seven streetcar companies paid only an

annual license fee generating revenues of only $1,112.50. They also paid a state tax of 0.5 percent on their capital stock totaling $1,852.29, none of which was returned to the city. "This appears to me to be discrimination in favor of such companies as against all other classes and kinds of business enterprise and property," he said. "The authority to organize such companies may originate in the statutes of the State, but the privilege of operating when organized is derived from the City of Detroit, and a more valuable franchise than that of using the public streets and avenues of the city can scarcely be named."

34. The new expiration date of November 14, 1909, was a result of ordinance language providing that "the ordinance passed November 24, 1862, and the amendment thereto, are hereby extended and limited to thirty years from *this date*" (emphasis added). The ordinance was adopted by the Common Council, 22-4, and signed by Mayor Langdon on November 14, 1879.
35. Section 22 of the Street-Railway Act imposed an annual 0.5 percent annual state tax on the capital stock of railroad corporations in lieu of personal property taxes. Section 31 said later amendments would not apply to existing corporations unless the corporations were specially named. When section 22 was repealed by a new General Property Tax Act, the Detroit City Railroad was not specifically named. It was on this ground that the company filed suit.
36. *Detroit City Railway Company v. Guthard*, 114 U.S. 133 (1885).
37. *City of Detroit v. Detroit City Railway Company*, 76 Mich. 421 (1888).
38. O'Geran, *History of the Detroit Street Railways*, 45–46.
39. The original grant by the city in 1868 was to "Nathaniel Prouty, Moses F. Dickinson, William B. Wesson, Harvey King, James P. Mansfield, their associates, successors, and assigns, organized in a corporation under the laws of the State of Michigan." Joseph W. Dailey and his brother, Charles M. Dailey, purchased a controlling interest in the spring of 1871.
40. The Daileys increased capital stock in the Grand River Street Railway Company to $100,000 in a filing made with the secretary of state on August 27, 1888, likely in connection with their sale to Miller.
41. Shareholders of the new company were George Hendrie, William McMillan, William K. Muir, Sidney D. Miller, Sidney T. Miller, William K. Anderson, and Cameron Currie. They each bought forty $100 shares for a total of $28,000, leaving 9,720 shares available for sale by other major investors.
42. "Aretus A. Wilder," *Vintage Machinery*, http://vintagemachinery.org/mfgindex/detail.aspx?id=2215.
43. Schramm and Henning, *Detroit's Street Railways*, vol. 1, *City Lines 1863–1922*, 22.
44. The Dix Avenue Railway Company never made any corporate filing with the secretary of state. The Detroit Electric Railway Company made its corporate filing on May 17, 1886.
45. These were powered by the heat of mixing water and caustic soda.
46. George W. Hilton, *The Cable Car in America: A New Treatise upon Cable or Rope Traction as Applied to the Working of Street and Other Railways*, rev. ed. (San Diego: Howell-North Books, 1982), 48, 82, 150.
47. Schramm and Henning, *Detroit's Street Railways*, vol. 1, *City Lines 1863–1922*, 38. O'Geran, *History of the Detroit Street Railways*, 34.
48. Schramm and Henning, *Detroit's Street Railways*, vol. 1, *City Lines 1863–1922*, 76.

CHAPTER 3. BEGINNING OF THE THIRTY-YEAR WAR

1. *Heffron v. Detroit City Railway*, 92 Mich. 406 (1892).
2. *Heffron v. Detroit City Railway*, 92 Mich. 409 (1892).
3. *Heffron v. Detroit City Railway*, 92 Mich. 411 (1892).
4. Following the death of his first wife, Muir married George Hendrie's sister, Christine.
5. McMillan's oldest son, William, played an active role in the company's subsequent history, according to an article in the *Michigan State Gazette*, March 1907. Otherwise, nothing is known about his role in the company.
6. "George Hendrie Capitalist, Dies Saturday Night," *Detroit Free Press*, December 21, 1913, 1. Detroit's early historians and biographers, Farmer, Ross and Catlin, and Burton, joined in competition with the social registers, which served to introduce the aspiring elite to those who did not need their names in the *Blue Book*, which remained a popular index of Detroit's social elites until the late 1970s when readership of local society news faded. In some cases, it is apparent that Burton's biographical notes from his 1922 publication, for example, were written by either the subject themselves, a close friend, or family member. The cliché-ridden entry for Hendrie's son Strathearn, for example, includes this over-the-edge self-congratulatory description of his business career: "His judgment was notably sound and his discrimination keen. He had the ability to correlate seemingly diverse interests into a unified and harmonious whole and to bring about important results in the achievement of a given purpose in business. His cooperation was therefore eagerly sought in the management and control of large concerns, and his labors were crowned with a notable measure of success."
7. The Great Western Railway took financial control of the Detroit and Milwaukee in 1860 after it defaulted on debt payments. In 1878, Great Western purchased it outright and refinanced its debts. The reorganized company was called the Detroit, Grand Haven & Milwaukee Railroad.
8. Contrary to what was actually installed, section 3 of the ordinance awarding a franchise to the Detroit City Railway required "the gauge of the track shall be at least four feet eight and one-half inches, and so as to accommodate the most common width of carriage wheels."
9. *Record of Service of Michigan Volunteers in the Civil War 1861–1865*, State Archives of Michigan. Orson B. Curtis, *History of the Twenty-Fourth Michigan of the Iron Brigade* (Detroit: Winn & Hammond, 1891). This is a fascinating, highly detailed, and well-written history of the Detroit and Wayne County regiment's illustrious role in the Civil War. Gaffele's Company F saw action in the Battle of Dabney's Mill, Virginia, on February 7, 1865, after which the Twenty-Fourth Infantry was sent to Springfield, Illinois. The regiment returned home to Detroit and mustered out on June 30, 1865.
10. Detroit's Hendrie Avenue was so named before 1900 as indicated in a lawsuit trying to block street paving decided by the Michigan Supreme Court on June 2, 1911. *Brady v. City of Detroit*, 166 Mich. 252 (1911).
11. The Hammond Building was among the first in Detroit offering steam heat, a hydraulic elevator, and lighting by Edison incandescent bulbs as well as natural gas when it opened in 1890 at Woodward Avenue and Fort, Congress, and Griswold Streets. The building was demolished in 1956 to make way for the fourteen-story headquarters of the First National Bank of Detroit that was acquired by JP Morgan Chase & Company in 2004. The building was named for George H. Hammond, a pioneer in refrigerated railcars and wholesale and retail products, with a meatpacking plant in Indiana, where

the town was renamed in his honor when he died in 1886 just as construction work was getting started on his new building in Detroit.

12. Hendrie and four partners built an electric double-track street railway along Woodward Avenue north from Detroit to Pontiac beginning in 1900, buying up franchise and right-of-way privileges that were held by the Detroit and Birmingham Plank Road Company and Oakland Railway Company.
13. Judge Charles Moran's second wife, Justine McCormick, had ten children, one of whom, William B. Moran, was born May 24, 1844. He graduated from the Fordham University Law School in 1866. He was a founder of the Peninsular Stove Company and an original shareholder of the Detroit Electric Light and Power Company, among many other businesses. William B. Moran's sole child, Katherine, married Strathearn Hendrie.
14. *Moran v. Moran*, 106 Mich. 8 (1895). How the sale to Hendrie of the Grand Marais parcel could possibly have been a bona fide deal between two socially prominent cousins and one of their close friends during the mentally ill cousin's divorce tickles the legal imagination. Undoubtedly, there was much more untold to the story by the court opinion.
15. "Senator McMillan was a very rich and very successful man," said Clarence Burton. "He was above vulgar dishonesty. He was industrious in his public capacity, and had no doubt done the state some service. And yet he was the highest type of that most dangerous product of our political institution—the plutocrat. In the service of public corporations, he corrupted and poisoned the well-springs of good government." Geoffrey G. Drutchas, "Gray Eminence in a Gilded Age: The Forgotten Career of Senator James McMillan of Michigan," *Michigan Historical Review* 28, no. 2 (Fall 2002): 111. Drutchas cited "James McMillan, *Clarence M. Burton Scrapbook*, 68:136." That citation and attribution to Burton is misleading because Drutchas was actually quoting from a newspaper clipping Burton had pasted into his scrapbook. Rather than Burton's opinion, it was a quote from the editorial page of a newspaper, probably the *Detroit Journal*.
16. Thomas P. Somma, "The McMillan Memorial Fountain: A Short History of a Lost Monument," *Washington History* 14, no. 2 (fall/winter 2002/2003): 96–107. Eric Fidler, "Historic Fountains Rot Away in a Local National Park," *Greater Greater Washington*, September 29, 2011, http://greatergreaterwashington.org/post/12213/historic-fountains-rot-away-in-a-local-national-park/. In 1915, Charles Moore wrote an effusively flattering biographical sketch of James McMillan. His unintentionally ironic closing sentence said: "Proverbially republics are ungrateful; but in the fair city of Washington, in a park named in his honor, the people whom he so faithfully served and who loyally returned him to the Senate, are erecting no statue of bronze or of marble to pass with the fashion of the day, but a fountain of living water, the one kind of monument which through the ages has proved an imperishable memorial." Charles Moore, "James M'Millan, United States Senator from Michigan," *Michigan Historical Collections* 39 (1915): 173, 186.

CHAPTER 4. THE PROGRESSIVE ERA

1. Schwarz used a popular photograph of Pingree in staging his work.
2. On May 16, 1902, the *Evening News* objected, arguing that the "position placed the back of the statue to those using the park seats—those that Mr. Pingree called the common people. While alive that was not the Governor's position. . . . Near the upper end of Washington Boulevard, facing Park Street and

the Grand Circus, would be a much better position, even from an artistic view." *Detroit in Nineteen Hundred and Two: A Chronological Record of Events* (Detroit: The Evening News Association, 1903), 47.

3. In June 1984, a construction company hired to spruce up Grand Circus Park turned its sandblasters on the Pingree sculpture and two others, the Russell Alexander Alger Memorial Fountain and Mayor William Cotter Maybury, who succeeded Pingree. When the dust settled, all three pieces were badly pitted by what they did. Carol Forsythe, objects conservator of the Detroit Institute of Arts, said the drastic cleaning was like "taking a metal bristle brush or steel wool and removing the whole top layer of the sculpture. You lose all trace of small, intricate work." Giorgio Gikas, a sculptural restoration master metalworker who had emigrated from Athens, Greece, volunteered to restore them.
4. A much prideful Pingree entered his height as 5 feet 10¾ inches on his passport application for a family trip to Europe in 1888. His forehead, chin, and face he described as full, his nose straight, and his hair light brown, slightly grey.
5. The actual details of Pingree's release back to the Union army are murky. Col. John S. Bersey of the Detroit Light Guard, a state military unit during Pingree's service as governor, identified the soldier he stepped in for as Private John Phelps of the First Vermont Heavy Artillery. Bersey may have personally interviewed Pingree. John S. Bersey, *Cyclopedia of Michigan: Historical and Biographical* (New York: Western Publishing and Engraving, 1900), 74–75. Bersey's first-person account of Pingree's escape, however, is unverifiable among federal Civil War records. Theodore S. Peck, *Revised Roster of Vermont Volunteers and Lists of Vermonters Who Served in the Army and Navy of the United States during the War of the Rebellion, 1861–66* (Montpelier, VT: Watchman Publishing, 1892). One of the three men named Phelps who fought in the Civil War from the First Vermont Heavy Artillery was General John W. Phelps, who distinguished himself in battle at New Orleans and who had resigned over the army's treatment of slaves in 1862. Neither of the other two was recorded as a prisoner of the Confederate army. Some biographers wrongly describe the prison camp from which Pingree escaped as located at Milan, Georgia. Others said it was West Pulaski, Georgia. See, e.g., "The Hon. Hazen S. Pingree (Deceased)," *The Successful American*, August 1901.
6. Farmer, *History of Detroit*, 1148.
7. Alderman John Christian Jacob was the sole vote against his appointment on August 8, 1893.
8. Henry P. Baldwin was elected Republican governor of Michigan in 1868, serving until 1873. He was appointed to the U.S. Senate in 1879–81.
9. Pharmacist James Vernor created Vernor's ginger ale in 1866, one of the oldest soft drinks. The legendary story is that he had been working on a medicinal tonic of vanilla and spices with the addition of ginger before he went to fight in the Civil War. Upon his return, he opened the oak barrel containing this base mixture and was surprised by its zesty, sweet, gingery flavor when added to soda water.
10. Melvin G. Holli, *Reform in Detroit: Hazen S. Pingree and Urban Politics* (Westport, CT: Greenwood Press, 1981), 8.
11. In 1895, Detroit published a 262-page book, *Laws Enacted by the Legislature of 1895 Affecting the Municipality of Detroit* (Detroit: James H. Stone & Company, 1895).
12. A few years before, it had been even worse. In 1881, the state legislature required the city to have both a separately elected ten-member Board of Councilmen and a thirty-two-member Board of Aldermen.

When the smaller board was abolished in 1887, the aldermen began calling their body the Common Council. The state created sixteen wards lined up alongside each other stretching from the river to the city's northern boundary, much like the old French ribbon farms. Such an arrangement benefited the old French landowners more than their tenant residents.

13. The Democratic candidate for mayor in 1883 was president of a wholesale wine and liquor company. Republicans called the Democratic convention at which Marvin H. Chamberlain was nominated "the liquor dealers' convention." In 1897, the *Free Press* counted ten saloonkeepers among the city's aldermen elected to the Common Council. Olivier Zunz, *The Changing Face of Inequality: Urbanization, Industrial Development and Immigration in Detroit, 1880–1920* (Chicago: University of Chicago Press, 1982), 109.
14. Larry Engelmann, "Old Saloon Days in Michigan," *Michigan History Magazine* 61 (1977): 127.
15. Father Kolasinski's congregation split into two warring Poletown camps that fought violently for many years following his removal. He kept his exuberantly ornamented Gothic Prussian-designed St. Albertus Catholic Church, which opened in 1885 and officially closed in 1980. It was sold by the Archdiocese of Detroit to the Polish American Historic Site Association for $100. Infrequent masses continue to be celebrated there. "Poletown Saints," *Metro Times*, October 6, 2010.
16. "Legislation was purchased for cash—generally deposited in the legislator's coat, hung by prearrangement in his office while he was busy with aldermanic affairs on the floor of the Common Council." Leo Donovan, "Detroit: City of Conflict," in *Politics and People: The Ordeal of Self-Government in America*, ed. Robert S. Allen (New York: Arno Press, 1947), 152.
17. Melvin G. Holli, *The American Mayor: The Best and the Worst Big-City Leaders* (University Park: Pennsylvania State University Press, 1999), 38.
18. "Rout of the Ring!" *Detroit Evening News*, January 15, 1890, 1.
19. "Street Car Facilities. Mayor Pingree Elaborates the Views Expressed in His Inaugural Address. Cameron Currie Gives His Opinions on the Present Management," *Detroit Free Press*, January 17, 1890.
20. Paul D. Carrington, "The Constitutional Law Scholarship of Thomas McIntyre Cooley," *American Journal of Legal History* 41, no. 3 (1997): 368–99.
21. Oliver Wendell Holmes Jr., *The Common Law* (Mineola, NY: Dover Publications, Inc. 1991), 1.
22. The name "Burned-Over" was coined in 1950 by historian Whitney Cross, who was inspired by the social and intellectual history of upper western New York from 1800 to 1850, an area so heavily evangelized during antebellum revivalism that there was no unconverted population. Whitney R. Cross, *The Burned-Over District: The Social and Intellectual History of Enthusiastic Religion in Western New York, 1800–1850* (Ithaca, NY: Cornell University Press, 1982).
23. *Clark v. City of Des Moines*, 19 Iowa 199 (1865); *City of Clinton v. Cedar Rapids and Missouri River Railroad Company*, 24 Iowa 455, 475 (1868), *Merrill v. Monticello*, 138 U.S. 673 (1891). In *City of Clinton* he famously wrote, "Municipal corporations owe their origin to, and derive their powers and rights wholly from, the legislature. It breathes into them the breath of life, without which they cannot exist. As it creates, so may it destroy. If it may destroy, it may abridge and control. Unless there is some constitutional limitation . . . the legislature might, by a single act, if can so suppose it capable of so great a folly and so great a wrong, sweep from existence all of the municipal corporations in the State, the *corporation* could not prevent it. We know of no limitation on this right so far as the corporations themselves are concerned. They are, so to phrase it, the mere tenants at will of the legislature."

24. *Stetson v. Kemp*, 13 Mass. 272 (1816).
25. John Forrest Dillon, *Commentaries on the Law of Municipal Corporations*, 5th ed. (Boston, Mass.: Little, Brown and Company, 1911), 154.
26. *People ex. rel. Leroy v. Hurlbut*, 24 Mich. 44 (1871). Quo warranto is Latin for "by what warrant?" In this case, the supreme court was being asked to direct the state attorney general to require that Hurlbut show by what authority he exercised the office of sewer and water commissioner in Detroit. Only the attorney general, who enjoyed wide discretion, could bring such a case.
27. In Michigan, the phrase "ripper legislation" was applied to local bills ripping away, for example, the authority of municipal government in the appointment of officials to manage local parks, public works, and police.
28. *People ex. rel. Leroy v. Hurlbut*, at 107. Quoted in Carrington, "The Constitutional Law Scholarship of Thomas McIntyre Cooley," 379.
29. Joan C. Williams, "The Constitutional Vulnerability of American Local Government: The Politics of City Status in American Law," *Wisconsin Law Review* 83 (1986): 83–153. Professor Williams described Dillon as "an academic ally of the robber barons of the Gilded Age" (Ibid., 90). She argued that Dillon postured his judicial opinions in pursuit of a Wall Street legal career, which he did get with his appointment in 1878 as general counsel of the United Pacific Railroad. "He clearly designed his life to join the corporate elite by serving as their spokesman," she claimed (Ibid., 92).
30. *People ex rel. the Detroit and Howell Railroad Company v. Township Board of Salem*, 20 Mich. 452 (1870).
31. The Tenth Amendment of the U.S. Constitution is sometimes cited as a source of local self-government protection. David J. Barron, "The Promise of Cooley's City: Traces of Local Constitutionalism," *University of Pennsylvania Law Review* 147 (1999): 487–612; Amasa M. Eaton, "The Right to Local Self-Government," *Harvard Law Review* 13 (1900): 441–54.
32. It says: "In June 1885, the legislature passed the state's first 10-hour employment law, but employers and employees could by contract evade the statute. When the lumber mill owners in Saginaw insisted on continuing the 11- or 12 hour workday, the workers who were paid by the day struck. Their slogan was 'Ten hours or no sawdust.' The strike, which became violent, grew into Michigan's largest of the century. A few years later, Governor John T. Rich, referring to strikes of the era said: 'It is hardly consistent to condemn labor organizations for taking the law into their own hands unless some lawful and practicable method is provided for the protection of their interests.' Protection against unfair working conditions for which the Saginaw lumber mill workers went on strike did not become reality until the next century, when laws regulating hours, wages, and working conditions we take for granted were adopted." The era was commemorated by a Michigan Legal Milestone placed in Saginaw in 1988. "Michigan Legal Milestones: 9. Ten Hours or No Sawdust," *State Bar of Michigan*, https://www.michbar.org/programs/milestone/milestones_tenhoursornosawdust.
33. "The Work Goes On," *Detroit Free Press*, April 19, 1891, 19.
34. "Three More Laid Off," *Detroit Evening News*, April 13, 1891, 1. The *Detroit Evening News* published a daily newspaper beginning in 1873 under James E. Scripps under a variety of names, including the *Sunday News* and *Detroit and Tribune News*. Henceforth, here it will be referred to only as the *Evening News*. Its circulation grew dramatically under Scripps's son-in-law, George G. Booth, beginning at the turn of the century by targeting home delivery to all of Detroit's sprawling neighborhoods. Its editorial

position regarding street railways consistently favored Detroit's working-class families during the strike and later.

35. Ibid.
36. "Notes," *Detroit Free Press*, April 22, 1891, 2.
37. "Can It Be Possible? Is Detroit to Have Rapid Transit in the Near Future," *Detroit Free Press*, April 22, 1891, 6.
38. "To Extent the Strike," *Detroit Free Press*, April 23, 1891, 2.
39. "Street Car Strike," *Detroit Free Press*, April 22, 1891, 2.
40. Harry Barnard, *Independent Man: The Life of Senator James Couzens* (Detroit: Wayne State University Press, 2002), 26. Barnard cited no source.
41. "BLOODSHED," *Detroit Free Press*, April 23, 1891, 1.
42. Ibid.
43. Ibid.
44. "Hazen Pingree: Quite Possibly Detroit's Finest Mayor," *Detroit Evening News*, January 6, 2013.
45. Holli, *Reform in Detroit*, 39.
46. "BLOODSHED," *Detroit Free Press*, April 23, 1891, 2.
47. "More Bloodshed: Riotous Scenes at the Foot of Woodward Avenue," *Detroit Free Press*, April 24, 1891, 1.
48. O'Geran specifically cited only articles in the *Free Press*, published between April 18 and 25, 1891. O'Geran, *History of the Detroit Street Railways*, 78–87.
49. Bingay, *Detroit Is My Own Home Town*, 236. His newspaper career began in 1901 as a printer's devil at the *Evening News*. When he was twenty-one, he was made sports editor, and at twenty-four, city editor. Five years later, he was managing editor, a post he held until 1928 when he was fired. After a year toiling as a public relations flak (as Bingay might have called them), he was hired as managing editor of the *Free Press*, a post he held when a story on an American Legion parade won five *Free Press* reporters the Pulitzer Prize. He wrote a daily column called "Good Morning" and a sports column under the nom de plume of "Iffy the Dopester" who still appears every so often in the *Free Press* sports pages today.
50. "More Bloodshed: Riotous Scenes at the Foot of Woodward Avenue," *Detroit Free Press*, April 24, 1891, 1.
51. Ibid.
52. "Woodward Avenue: Mayor Addresses the Populace from His Dog Cart," *Detroit Free Press*, April 24, 1891, 1.
53. "Hendrie Didn't Shoot: He Pulled a Revolver, However, and Scared a Striker," *Detroit Free Press*, April 24, 1891, 2.
54. Richard Jules Oestreicher, *Solidarity and Fragmentation: Working People and Class Consciousness in Detroit, 1875–1900* (Urbana: University of Illinois Press, 1989), 234–36.
55. Bingay, *Detroit Is My Own Home Town*, 236. Bingay's account, written freestyle of what actually happened, was directly refuted by a *Free Press* report on April 24, 1891. It said policeman succeeded in stopping the crowd from shoving the streetcar any closer than thirty to forty feet beyond the end of the tracks toward the Detroit River dock. "Hendrie Didn't Shoot: He Pulled a Revolver, However, and Scared a Striker," *Detroit Free Press*, April 24, 1891, 2. Dickinson served as postmaster general

from January 1888 until Cleveland's term ended in 1889, when he returned to the practice of law in Detroit. Railroad workers went on strike soon after Dickinson took office, interrupting the nation's mail delivery. Dickinson refused to call in federal forces to break the strike but reworked distribution routes so that mail delivery remained unaffected. Dickinson also applied civil service hiring rules to the post office upon Cleveland's request, cutting the effect patronage had on his department. A Dickinson speech the following day may be some indication of the inflammatory tone Bingay said he took on Thursday. "Mr. Dickinson declared that the very best way to *serve* the City Railway, if the latter is antagonistic, which however, the speaker did not believe or assert, would be by making attacks on the railway property," the *Free Press* reported (emphasis added). "Monster Meeting," *Detroit Free Press*, April 25, 1891, 2. This apparently prompted criticism from Dickinson, and the newspaper published a rambling clarification on its editorial page on Sunday. "The sense in which the reporter used the word 'serve' was in its proper one of 'to labor in the interest of' and the context shows this very plainly. . . . The use of the word 'serve' in the report, which aimed merely to give the substance of Mr. Dickinson's strong and admirable speech—a speech conceived in the right spirit and which had great weight with the men—has led to some misconception through the attaching of the meaning 'deal with' to the word 'serve.' This latter was a meaning which could not possibly be attached to Mr. Dickinson's remarks, and it was not the intention of the report to convey it. The strikers' cause has no truer friend than Mr. Dickinson, but is also an earnest advocate of law and order." *Detroit Free Press*, April 26, 1891, 4.

56. Holli, *Reform in Detroit*, 39.
57. Strathearn Hendrie took up arms again as a U.S. Navy ensign aboard the SS *Yosemite*, an auxiliary cruiser, which grounded the Spanish transporter SS *Antonio Lopez* off San Juan, Puerto Rico, during the Spanish-American War, on June 28, 1898. The *Yosemite* stood off nearby and avoided fire from the Spanish forts and two Spanish gunboats, until it was relieved on July 15. Meanwhile, the Spanish were able to finish salvaging nearly the entire cargo before the much more heavily armed SS *New Orleans* quickly polished off the cargo ship with twenty incendiary shells. Upon his return, he was greeted by his Grosse Pointe hometown as a war hero. Among others serving on the *Yosemite* were his younger brother George Trowbridge Hendrie and University of Michigan Engineering School Dean Mortimer E. Cooley.
58. "Notes of the Day," *Detroit Free Press*, 2.
59. "Jefferson Avenue," *Detroit Free Press*, April 25, 1891, 1.
60. "The Blockade Still Continues on City and Grand River Lines," *The Detroit Evening News*, April 24, 1891, 1.
61. Ibid.
62. W. J. Law and W. A. Taylor represented the employees on the five-member arbitration committee while Hendrie sent George Jerome and Michael J. Dee, editor of the *Evening News*. Together, they selected Rev. Dr. C. R. Henderson of the Woodward Avenue Baptist Church as their fifth member.
63. "The Common Council: Various Aldermen Warmed the Ears of the City Railway," *Detroit Free Press*, April 25, 1891, 2.
64. Miller died in 1904, many years before publication of Catlin's book. It is a tribute to the influence of Miller's family and his reputation that Catlin, who was librarian of the *Evening News*, did not specifically name him.

65. Catlin, *The Story of Detroit*, 618.
66. Hazen S. Pingree, *Facts and Opinions; or, Dangers that Beset Us* (Detroit: F. B. Dickerson, 1895), 37. John J. Speed had served on the Wayne County Circuit Court from 1882 to 1886. Detroit had two chief legal officers. The city attorney was elected for a two-year term. The city counselor was appointed by the mayor subject to confirmation by the Common Council for a three-year term.
67. *Detroit Evening News*, April 23, 1891, 2.

CHAPTER 5. FROM THE STREETS TO THE HALLWAYS

1. Holli, *Reform in Detroit*, 41.
2. Pingree, *Facts and Opinions*, 30.
3. Jere C. Hutchins, *A Personal Story* (Norwood, MA: Plimpton Press, 1938), 182.
4. Ibid.
5. Hutchins, *A Personal Story*, 181.
6. Ibid., 208–9.
7. The articles of association they filed to operate in Detroit and its neighboring communities capitalized the company at $500,000. They bought ninety shares each. Strathearn Hendrie would be described as general manager of the Wyandotte and Detroit River Railway Company organized the following year by Charles Swift to operate on these same routes.
8. Swift had a remarkable career. His street railway investments spread as far as the Philippines where he won a franchise to operate street railways in Manila under Governor-General William Howard Taft.
9. Sold in strips of eight, they were variously labeled and referred to as either "workingmen's" or "workingman's" tickets by the city, the company, and subsequent state and federal court cases.
10. Detroit kept local time—sun time—until 1900 when the Common Council attempted to switch to central standard time, moving city hall clocks twenty-eight minutes ahead. Detroit's corporation counsel rendered a legal opinion that unless otherwise specified in the ordinance, the mention of a time meant standard time, the legal time set by state government. Residents, nonetheless, disagreed over the matter until a citywide vote confirming the change in 1905. Meanwhile, "workingmen's fare" tickets issued by the streetcar companies described both sun time and standard time to avoid arguments with riders because the operative time standard was not specified by applicable ordinances. The U.S. Congress did not adopt standard time zones based on those used by railroads until the Standard Time Act of 1918. The Interstate Commerce Commission had authority to make local adjustments until 1966 when the responsibility for doing so was transferred to the Department of Transportation.
11. Pingree, *Facts and Opinions*, 205.
12. Woodward Avenue's influential residents opposed overhead lines. The six-month delay was intended to give them time to judge the relative merits of cable versus overhead electric cars.
13. "One Franchise Granted," Detroit Free Press, July 1, 1891, 8.
14. Ibid.
15. "Paying a High Price," *Detroit Free Press*, July 1, 1891.
16. "One Franchise Granted," Detroit Free Press, July 1, 1891, 8.
17. Pingree, *Facts and Opinions*, 205–7.

18. Section 3 of the amending ordinance said: "This ordinance shall take effect when the Detroit *City* Railway Company shall file with the City Clerk an acceptance thereof in writing, provided such written acceptance shall be filed, within 30 days after the date of passage of this ordinance" (emphasis added). The amendment changed *City* to *Street.*
19. "Who Owns Detroit? An Answer Found in Yesterday's Common Council Proceedings," *Detroit Free Press*, July 2, 1891, 9. Charles Swift's franchise petition for the Detroit Suburban Railway Company owned by Strathearn Hendrie, however, did not come up for a third reading.
20. Burton, *Compendium of History and Biography of the City of Detroit and Wayne County*, 409–10.
21. Pingree, *Facts and Opinions*, 51.
22. "The Mayor Aroused: Red Hot Argument in His Office," *Detroit Evening News*, July 3, 1891, 1.
23. Samuel Williston, "History of the Law of Business Corporations before 1800," *Harvard Law Review* 2 (1888): 105–24.
24. *Dartmouth College v. Woodward*, 17 U.S. 518, 636 (1819).
25. Ibid.
26. "The Mayor Aroused," *Detroit Evening News*, July 3, 1891, 1; "Resented by the People Prominent Citizens United in a Call for a Mass Meeting Monday Night," *Detroit Free Press*, July 4, 1891, 8.
27. Pingree, *Facts and Opinions*, 53–54.
28. "The Voice of the People," *Detroit Free Press*, July 7, 1891, 4.
29. "Riotous! Great Uproar in the Common Council," *Detroit Evening News*, July 8, 1891, 1.
30. Holli, *Reform in Detroit*, 41.
31. *Detroit Free Press*, July 8, 1891, 4.
32. "Riotous: Great Uproar in the Common Council," *Detroit Evening News*, July 8, 1891, 1. Holli, *Reform in Detroit*, 42.
33. Ibid.
34. "The Mayor's Veto," *Detroit Free Press*, July 8, 1891, 4.
35. "THE OCTOPUS SOLD," *Detroit Free Press*, July 24, 1891, 1.
36. None of Detroit's newspapers or earlier historians noted that Hendrie had not sold his suburban streetcar lines serving Dearborn, Highland Park, Hamtramck, Grosse Pointe, and elsewhere outside city limits or the still pending ordinance for streetcar service to Wyandotte.
37. Contrary to the original articles of association filed on September 2, 1891, most accounts wrongly add a possessory apostrophe to Citizens.
38. Preferred stockholders own a higher claim on the assets and earnings than common stockholders. They generally are given a right to dividends that must be paid before any dividends to common stockholders, but they usually have no voting rights. The exchange of Hendrie's common stock and bonds for preferred stock in the new company would have been ideally suited to and explain the subsequent off-stage role played by the Hendrie family.
39. Mulliken resigned a few months later, according to "Detroit, Mich.," *Street Railway Journal* 7, no. 12 (December 1891): 702.
40. Hoyt Post, Calvin K. Brandon, and Hibbard Baker had originally obtained consent to operate street railways in the Township of Grosse Pointe on April 11, 1887. It set forth no expiration date. Post's franchise was acquired by the Hendrie family's Detroit Suburban Railway Company, which was sold to Waller for $900,000. "Detroit, Mich.," *Street Railway Journal* 8, no. 12 (December 1892): 773.

Years later, U.S. District Judge Charles C. Simons rejected arguments that the consent was perpetual. *Security Trust Company v. Village of Grosse Pointe*, 32 F.2d 706 (E.D. Mich. 1929).

41. George Catlin's otherwise badly garbled account of events in 1891 said: "All the inside of the transaction was never clearly known, but rumors were afloat to the effect that the stock held by D. M. Ferry, M. S. Smith, and Simon J. Murphy amounted to $50,000 each; that the McMillans held $100,000; H. B. Ledyard, $25,000; W. C. Colburn, $25,000; H. M. Campbell, $25,000, while J. D. Hawks and others held $175,000 in blocks of $10,000 and less. It was asserted that the new company held altogether $550,000 of stock while the old Hendrie interest still held $450,000." Catlin, *The Story of Detroit*, 623. Catlin's figures likely were drawn from *Evening News* files. They are generally consistent with a later report in the *Free Press*. "IT IS SOLD! The Deal in Street Car Lines Finally Completed," *Detroit Free Press*, September 2, 1894, 1.
42. "Sidney D. Miller: He Will Hereafter Devote His Attention to Law and Banking," *Detroit Free Press*, July 24, 1891, 1.
43. "THE OCTOPUS SOLD," *Detroit Free Press*, July 24, 1891, 1.
44. Furthermore, defending against enforcement of the revocation clause would be more complicated for Hendrie by section 24 of the original ordinance that automatically made such a transfer. It said: "*Whenever the* said grantees, their successors or *assigns*, shall *have organized* themselves into *a body* politic and *corporate*, under the Act of the Legislature of the State of Michigan, *all the powers and privileges granted* and conferred to and upon them *by this ordinance shall be* given, granted, and *duly vested in said corporation without any* further action, *consent*, permission, or authority *of the Common Council* whatever" (emphasis added).
45. The city and the Citizens Street Railway Company entered into a settlement approved on October 14, 1892, allowing for double tracks between Grand River and Michigan Avenues with a connecting third track extending to Jefferson Avenue and Atwater Street.
46. Pingree, *Facts and Opinions*, 56. The old Larned Street hall where the July rally had been held was a converted skating rink.

CHAPTER 6. THE LAWYERS BATTLE

1. Socialist Party candidate Frederick G. Dienzer joined the two Democratic Party nominees, William G. Thompson and John D. Miner, in the lopsided loss to Pingree.
2. Jacob's tight grip on the reins of power before Pingree's reelection is demonstrated by the fact that he was not only chairperson of the Election Commission siding against one of the nominated candidates trying to get on the November ballot in this election, but he was also chairman of the Wayne County Board of Supervisors, roles that today's statutory incompatible office law would prohibit. *Shield v. Jacob*, 88 Mich. 164 (1891).
3. Casgrain was a lame duck. He had lost his bid for reelection, 15,801-8,723, to Frank A. Rasch, who played no public role in the pending street railway litigation.
4. Jake Sharp obtained the Broadway Avenue street railway franchise in New York City from the "Boodle Board of Aldermen" in 1884. Several aldermen were convicted of bribery and several others fled to Canada. New York courts decided that the fact that the perpetual franchise was obtained by bribery did not impair its validity.

5. Rather than a flat flange, groove rails had a cupped flange below the surface of the road, creating no obstruction to other vehicles. The groove, however, filled with dirt and other refuse and in winter caked up with ice. Pingree spent several hundred dollars from the city budget taking aldermen and public works commissioners to see groove rail demonstrations in Buffalo, New York.
6. His was not an exact reading of the original 1862 ordinance, which gave greater leeway in favor of the streetcar company to a judge having to decide a court case over streetcar rail design. A judge normally defers to legislative discretion in deciding cases challenging police power regulations. The Detroit City Railway's ordinance actually reserved only "the right to make such further rules, orders, or regulations as may, from time to time, be deemed necessary to protect the interest, safety, welfare or accommodation of the public in relation to said railways." Missing was the phrase "by the Common Council" from deciding what was necessary to protect "the City and public." The fuller wording wrongly quoted by Mayor Pingree was added to later ordinances.
7. Delos F. Wilcox, *Municipal Franchises: A Description of the Terms and Conditions upon which Private Corporations Enjoy Special Privileges in the Streets of American Cities* (New York: Engineering News Publishing Company, 1910), 349–50. His book is an unrecognized classic of municipal franchise public policy and law. Raised in rural southern Michigan's Ida Township, Wilcox graduated from the University of Michigan. He earned a PhD in political science from Columbia University in 1896. Wilcox led various civic organizations in Cleveland and Grand Rapids and the Detroit Municipal League, predecessor of the Detroit Citizens League and its influential publication called *Civic Searchlight* of which R. H. Fyfe was a former president. In 1907, Wilcox was appointed to head New York City's franchise bureau and later was deputy commissioner of water supply, gas, and electricity.
8. Hutchins, *A Personal Story*, 129–30.
9. Daniel B. Klein and John Majewski, "Plank Road Fever in Antebellum American: New York State Origins," *New York History* 75 (January 1994): 39–65. They describe the building of the Salina-Central Square Plank Road by George Geddes, started in 1844 and completed in 1846.
10. Laws of Michigan, No. CXIII, approved March 22, 1837.
11. The State of Michigan had negligible bonded interest bearing debt of less than $600,000 as of June 30, 1889, all arising from Civil War borrowing, according to *Poor's Manual of the Railroads of the United States* (New York: H. V. & H. W. Poor, 1900).
12. Farmer, *History of Detroit*, 926.
13. *Erin Township v. Detroit & Erin Plank Road Company*, 115 Mich. 465 (1898). See also *Detroit & Plank Road Company v. Macomb Circuit Judge*, 109 Mich. 371 (1896). The court rejected a challenge by the plank road company to the township's authority to enforce Plank Road Act regulations on Gratiot Avenue, a former military road.
14. "President's Annual Address," in *The Michigan Engineer* (Battle Creek, MI: Review and Herald Publishing Company 1901), 8. The original source of this story appears lost.
15. *City of Detroit v. Detroit & Howell Plank Road Company*, 43 Mich. 140, 147–49 (1880).
16. *City of Detroit v. Detroit & Howell Plank Road Company*, 43 Mich. 140, 149 (1880).
17. Holli, *Reform in Detroit*, 32.
18. *Village of Highland Park v. Detroit & Birmingham Plank Road Company*, 95 Mich. 489, 490 (1893).
19. *Attorney General v. Detroit & Saline Plank Road Company*, 97 Mich. 589, 592 (1893).
20. "Dickinson's Position," *Detroit Evening News*, March 11, 1892, 1.

21. Ibid.
22. "Almost Unanimous Don M. Dickinson and Alfred Russell Retained by the Council," *Detroit Free Press*, February 3, 1892, 5.
23. "A Mixture: The Case of Alfred Russell," *Detroit Evening News*, March 16, 1892, 1; "Hired Away!," *Detroit Free Press*, March 16, 1892, 1.
24. Holli, *Reform in Detroit*, 46.
25. Ibid.
26. Ibid.
27. Pingree, *Facts and Opinions*, 56.
28. "The Hanchett Case: Mr. McMillan Did Not Urge His Appointment," *Detroit Evening News*, February 27, 1893, 3.
29. In correspondence to the Common Council explaining his bill for legal services in November 1893, Kent said, "The suit was begun in March 1892, by the City Counselor in accordance with the advice of Alfred Russell and Don M. Dickinson. It was only in consequence of their retirement from the case that I was retained."
30. Why Speed named the out-of-state corporation as a defendant is puzzling. As a mortgage holder, it had no immediate rights that Detroit needed litigated. Therefore, while the trust company might have been allowed to intervene, it was not a necessary party to deciding when the franchise expired. Speed's relationship with Pingree deteriorated to the point that on July 25, 1893, Pingree sought his removal. "Since his appointment said Speed has by public utterance placed the matters of the greatest importance to the City, now in litigation, in jeopardy, by, it seems to me, most unwise and uncalled for interviews in the public press," Pingree said. "While admitting the ultimate success of the present litigation, he questions the policy of the City, the motives of the officials, and advocates the interests of the defendants." Speed twice successfully defended his office in the Michigan Supreme Court: *Speed v. Common Council of the City of Detroit*, 97 Mich. 198 (1893) and *Speed v. Common Council of the City of Detroit*, 98 Mich. 360 (1894). Speed could not be forced to leave Detroit City Hall until 1896 when his three-year term expired. He ended up doing legal work for Detroit's street railway companies among other private and public clients.
31. William Livingstone, *Livingstone's History of the Republican Party*, vol. 1, (Detroit, 1900), 539.
32. A preliminary ruling by Judge Taft carefully noted that the order of publication had erroneously named "The Washington Trust Company" instead of "The Washington Trust Company of New York." He pointed out that service by publication against it under an incomplete name could be regarded as invalid. Moreover, he said, any nonresident defendant served by publication could have had the pro confesso order set aside upon payment of costs. *City of Detroit v. Detroit City Railway Company*, 54 F. 1, 9–10 (E.D. Mich. 1893). Judge Taft also pointed out that the order for publication drafted by Speed erroneously named as defendant "The City Railway" instead of "The Detroit City Railway." Consequently, attorneys for the Washington Trust Company of New York subjected themselves to Detroit's taking of the pro confesso order upon firm legal ground.
33. The street railway companies played hardball outside of the courtroom, too. The *Free Press* reported that while the case was pending they refused to pay $60,000 in property taxes and $36,939 in charges for paving and cleaning railway tracks. "Will the Fight Go On? The Company Is Pretty Heavily in Debt to the City," *Detroit Free Press*, October 4, 1894, 5.

34. Quoted in Schramm and Henning, *Detroit's Street Railways*, vol. 1, *City Lines 1863–1922*, 38.
35. Swan was the son of Scottish-Irish parents who moved to the Michigan Territory in 1835. He attended Detroit public schools and several years of classes at the University of Michigan before leaving to work with two uncles on steamboats paddling the San Joaquin and Sacramento Rivers while studying law in California. Swan returned to Detroit, joined the offices of attorney Henry M. Duffield, and was admitted to the practice of law in 1867. Three years later, Swan was appointed assistant U.S. attorney for the Eastern District of Michigan, where he served for seven years. He left for the private practice of maritime law for several years before President Benjamin Harrison appointed him to the U.S. District Court for the Eastern District of Michigan in 1891. Duffield would make his career representing the street railway companies against the city.
36. Act Aug. 13, 1888 (25 Stat. 433) allowed any defendant in a state court living outside the forum state to remove a case into the circuit court for the United States if "it shall be made to appear to such circuit court that from prejudice or local influence he will not be able to obtain justice in such state court."
37. Ch. 137, 18 Stat. 470.
38. Taft's unique federal public service career spanned forty-eight years beginning in 1882 as a tax collector for the Internal Revenue Service and ending in 1930 with his retirement as chief justice of the U.S. Supreme Court. During the intervening years, he served as U.S. solicitor general, judge of the Sixth Circuit Court of Appeals, governor-general of the Philippines, secretary of war, and president. Severens was born in Rockingham, Vermont, in 1825, the son of a farmer, studied law in the office of the U.S. attorney of Vermont and was admitted to the bar in 1859. He moved to Three Rivers, Michigan, in 1860, and served as prosecuting attorney for St. Joseph County for five years before moving to private practice in Kalamazoo and mounting several unsuccessful election campaigns for the Michigan State Senate, Michigan Supreme Court, and U.S. Congress as a Republican. President Grover Cleveland rewarded him with an appointment to the U.S. District Court for the Western District of Michigan in 1886. Severens took an active part only in deciding against Detroit's remand motion on January 5, 1893. Otherwise, he signed none of the later court opinions in the case. Severens was sick at home in Grand Rapids, unable to attend the hearing on Detroit's motion to dismiss on March 15, 1893, after which Judge Taft immediately proceeded to hear arguments on the legal merits of the case, which continued for two more days. "The City Railway Case," *Detroit Free Press*, March 16, 1893, 9; "Hearing in Progress," *Detroit Free Press*, March 17, 1893, 9; "Finally Submitted," *Detroit Free Press*, March 18, 1893, 2. As the circuit judge, Taft's opinion was decisive over even vigorous dissent by both district judges. Even if he had participated, therefore, Judge Severens could not have changed the result.
39. Illustrative of an imbalance of financial resources between the two sides, the two lawyers representing Detroit, Kent and Hanchett, who initially got assistance from City Attorney Speed, were paid $20,965.43 and $15,500, respectively, between March 1892 and October 1894. At the defense table sat Ashley Pond and Otto Kirchner, who argued on behalf of the various street railway companies. Sidney T. Miller represented his father and the other cotrustee for bonds issued by the Detroit City Railway Company. John T. Donnelly, Duffield, and Frederick A. Baker III represented the Washington Trust Company of New York, trustee for the mortgage bonds issued by the Detroit Citizens Street Railway Company.
40. He did so despite Alderman Griggs's warning in a minority report protesting the hiring of outside

counsel delivered to the Common Council on December 15, 1891: "On the other hand . . . the companies would carry it up, and before the end could be reached the *aid of the United States Court would be invoked in behalf of non-resident stock and bond holders* and the result would be litigation lasting at least six years and a decided uncertainty as to whether or not the city would be victorious in the end" (emphasis added).

41. Members of the Common Council, at least, would know that he was referring to then U.S. senator James McMillan.
42. *City of Detroit v. Detroit City Railway Company*, 54 F. 1 (E.D. Mich. 1893).
43. In *Geist v. Detroit City Railway Company*, 91 Mich. 446, 448–49 (1892) the Michigan Supreme Court overturned a jury verdict against the company in a negligence case involving the collision of a streetcar and hearse because the plaintiff's attorney made a closing argument in which he referred to the defendant as "the unfortunate city railway, whether driven through the streets by the mob or driving along its usual course."
44. *City of Detroit v. Detroit City Railway Company*, 54 F. 18 (E.D. Mich. 1893).
45. *City of Detroit v. Detroit City Railway Company*, 54 F. 20–21 (E.D. Mich. 1893).
46. *City of Detroit v. Detroit City Railway Company*, 55 F. 569 (E.D. Mich. 1893).
47. *City of Detroit v. Detroit City Railway Company*, 55 F. 575 (E.D. Mich. 1893).
48. "Big Boodle: Mayor Pingree Says It Was Offered Him," *Detroit Evening News*, January 21, 1893, 1.
49. *City of Detroit v. Detroit City Railway Company*, 56 F. 867 (E.D. Mich. 1893).
50. *City of Detroit v. Detroit City Railway Company*, 60 F. 161 (E.D. Mich. 1894).
51. "The opinion of the circuit judge, in my judgment, in its reasoning and conclusions, is so utterly subversive of the principles of equity that I am unwilling, by my silence, to sanction an apparent assent to what seems to me to be a most inequitable result," Judge Swan wrote. *City of Detroit v. Detroit City Railway Company*, 56 F. 867, 895.
52. *City of Detroit v. Detroit City Railway Company*, 60 F. at 174–75 (E.D. Mich. 1894).
53. Doris Kearns Goodwin, *The Bully Pulpit: Theodore Roosevelt, William Howard Taft, and the Golden Age of Journalism* (New York: Simon & Schuster, 2013), 214–15.
54. *City of Detroit v. Detroit City Railway Company*, 56 F. 873–74 (E.D. Mich. 1893).
55. *City of Detroit v. Detroit City Railway Company*, 56 F. 876 (E.D. Mich. 1893).
56. *City of Detroit v. Detroit City Railway Company*, 56 F. 881–86 (E.D. Mich. 1893).
57. *Kent County Agricultural Society v. Houseman*, 81 Mich. 609 (1890).
58. *City of Detroit v. Detroit City Railway Company*, 56 F. 890 (E.D. Mich. 1893).
59. *City of Detroit v. Detroit City Railway Company*, 56 F. 908 (E.D. Mich. 1893).
60. *City of Detroit v. Detroit City Railway Company*, 56 F. 892 (E.D. Mich. 1893).
61. "Detroit Troubles," *Street Railway Review* 3, no. 6 (June 15, 1893): 333.
62. Par value has no relationship to market value. The par value of a share of stock is the dollar amount stated in the corporate charter below which the company cannot sell so investors can be confident that nobody else will receive a more favorable issue price. The articles of association of the Detroit Citizens Street Railway Company had set capital stock as $4 million: forty thousand shares at $100 each.
63. O'Geran, *History of the Detroit Street Railways*, 119. Pingree complained that the Detroit Citizens Street Railway Company mortgaged its lines for "$7 million on a real investment of less than $3

million." He observed that lenders obviously had been persuaded "that the franchise, aside from the investment under which they are operating, is worth more than $4 million." Pingree, *Facts and Opinions*, 65.

64. Pingree, *Facts and Opinions*, 63.
65. Beginning in 1934, Woodward Avenue was widened. Most of the buildings and homes along the east side had to be demolished. The Woodward Avenue Baptist Church lost forty-six feet across the front and its 208-foot stone tower. The Central United Methodist and the St. John's Episcopal suffered a similar fate. A spectacular five-alarm fire destroyed the Woodward Avenue Baptist Church on August 3, 1986.
66. Pingree, *Facts and Opinions*, 63.
67. Holli, *Reform in Detroit*, 53. "The Boycott," *Detroit Evening News*, March 8, 1893, 1. Webster's letter of resignation received by the Common Council explained to the contrary that he was being sent by his employer to the Pacific Coast for four to six weeks.
68. Holli, *Reform in Detroit*, 53.
69. Pingree, *Facts and Opinions*, 62.
70. On March 26, 1894, the *Free Press* reported, "Miss Gertrude Pingree, age 27, daughter of Mayor Pingree, died about 1 o'clock this morning at the family residence of empyema. She had been failing in health for some time and several weeks ago, a southern trip was taken by the family in hope of building up her constitution but without any benefit. Miss Pingree was a young lady of charming character and her untimely death will excite the sympathies of the whole community for her bereaved parents." Gertrude was not twenty-seven years old. She was born in 1874, according to a handwritten notation made on her father's 1888 passport application. The next day's issue of the *Free Press* did correct its error.
71. "Funeral of Gertrude Pingree," *Detroit Free Press*, March 29, 1894, 5.
72. Pingree, *Facts and Opinions*, 62–63.
73. His nine-year tenure in Detroit was abruptly cut short in 1901 by reports in the *Evening News* that Dr. MacLaurin had been carrying on an extensive mail-order hair remedy business. "MacLaurin's Little SideLine," *Detroit Evening News*, May 21, 1901, 1. The *Brooklyn Daily Eagle* reported on May 9, 1901, that Dr. MacLaurin had resigned to accept a position in Rochester, New York. "Some of the congregation have expressed objections to the doctor being a part owner of a British Columbia gold mine, saying that this is too worldly for a Baptist pastor," the *Daily Eagle* said. "He, however, defends this on the ground that it is a clean and legitimate business." "Dr. MacLaurin Declines Brooklyn Call," *Brooklyn Daily Eagle*, May 9, 1901, 20.
74. On June 27, 1901, her casket was moved to the Welch family mausoleum in the Woodlawn Cemetery in preparation for Mayor Pingree's burial there. Both were again moved on July 23, 1903, to a beautiful marble mausoleum with a gorgeous stained-glass window of an apple tree just a short drive from the front entrance to Woodlawn Cemetery.
75. The U.S. Census completed April 21, 1910, reported that he and a second wife, Nan, a Michigan native, were living at 409 Cadillac Avenue with a twenty-seven-year-old female servant.
76. *Pingree v. Pingree*, 170 Mich. 36 (1912).
77. *Detroit City Railway v. City of Detroit*, 154 U.S. 500 (1894). Only the U.S. Sixth Circuit Court of Appeals had jurisdiction to review Judge Taft's opinion in a removal case from which no further appeal was

possible.

78. "There are bondholders who are anxious to sell and stockholders that feel the same way. Then there are stockholders that want to fight and bondholders that want to fight. They are suspicious of each other and there is bad feeling all around," said City Controller Charles W. Moore. "Mr. Moore Has Figures: The Controller Is Doing Some Street Car Work," *Detroit Free Press*, May 9, 1894, 5.
79. "Refuse the Ordinance: Directors of the Citizens Co. Acted Yesterday," *Detroit Free Press*, May 8, 1984, 1.
80. Judge's Taft's opinion regarding the Congress and Baker Street Railway Company and the Cass Avenue Railway Company on January 31, 1894, strongly urged settlement. "I have given three months to the defendant railway company for a compliance with the decree, because, if the tracks are to be removed, that is not an unreasonable time for the purpose. Moreover, it will afford some opportunity for an adjustment of this controversy, which it is hoped will result either in a new grant to the defendant company, reasonable in its terms, or the sale of the plant on an appraised value to any new company who may operate the old lines. *In expressing such a hope, I assure that the municipal authorities will be influenced by considerations of municipal honor, and will not, for the immediate pecuniary benefit accruing to the City or the public, take unconscionable advantage of the position in which this decree put the street railway company; and that it will be seen to be, as it certainly is, for the ultimate benefit and reputation for integrity and fair dealing of the City of Detroit that a compromise be made with the company, enabling it to secure an adequate return for the large cash investments which it has made, in entire good faith*" (emphasis added). *City of Detroit v. Detroit City Railway Company*, 60 F. 161, 175 (E.D. Mich. 1894). Mayor Pingree specifically quoted Judge Taft's admonition word-for-word in a message to the Common Council at its meeting on March 13, 1894.
81. "Refuse the Ordinance: Directors the Citizens Co. Acted Yesterday," *Detroit Free Press*, May 8, 1894, 1. Many stock promoters in the late 1800s inflated their claims about a company's assets and profitability, selling its stocks and bonds in excess of the company's actual value. To do so, they would exchange property with a new corporation in return for stock at par value. On the balance sheet, the property would be booked as the corporation's only capital, and because legal capital was fixed to par value, the value of the property would be likewise inflated on the books. While the promoter had $10,000 in stock and the corporation had $5,000 worth of assets they would be valued at $10,000 on company financial statements.
82. In an 1895 speech to the Detroit Chamber of Commerce, Pingree described "a communication to the Common Council in which I stated that the stockholders of the Detroit Citizens Street Railway Company had held a meeting for the purpose of raising $75,000 to bribe your mayor. . . . Did it occur to the Chamber of Commerce that the raising of such a sum for such a purpose was a graver menace to corporate capital than the ravings of the anarchist and that it is such criminal acts as convey the direst threat to business interests?" Hazen S. Pingree, "Address Made before the Chamber of Commerce of Detroit during the Fourth Term Mayoralty Campaign," November 2, 1895.
83. Nevins owned the Plainfield Street Railway in New Jersey. It had only nine miles of railway with twenty passenger cars in 1889. Consequently, Currie and Nevins appear to have been stalking horses disguising their actual buyer.
84. The Orme Wilson and Company Storehouse in Loudon, Tennessee, that Wilson built with his silent partner, James Chambers Orme, was added to the National Registry of Historic Places in 1980. Slaves were believed to have been chained in the building's basement, unshackled to load and unload

Tennessee River barges.

85. Richard Thornton Wilson applied for a pardon from London on June 4, 1865. His request came recommended by Governor William G. Brownlow of Tennessee, who, without further explanation, said, "Mr. Wilson was lenient toward Union men, and on this ground I advise his pardon." President Andrew Johnson granted his pardon on August 15, 1865. Case Files of Applications from Former Confederates for Presidential Pardons ("Amnesty Papers") 1865–1867, (National Archives Microfilm Publication M1003, 73 rolls), Records of the Adjutant General's Office, 1780s–1917, Record Group 94, National Archives, Washington, DC.
86. "Wilson Death Puts Many in Mourning," *New York Times*, November 27, 1910. Brett Duval Fromson, "Confederates Among Us," *New York Times*, April 15, 2007. Daniel E. Sutherland, *The Confederate Carpetbagger* (Baton Rouge: Louisiana State University Press, 1988), 125. *The Confederate Veteran*, published in Nashville from 1897 to 1932 for the Civil War's Confederate army veterans, said that when Wilson returned to Richmond from England he carried with him proceeds from the sale of Confederate government cotton in Europe and when he went north, he used this money to establish his investment banking company (April 1911, 158).
87. Among them was a particularly elusive business partner, most often referred to in Detroit and elsewhere as Major J. M. Edwards. He could not be identified in Civil War records. It seems likely that James M. Edwards began his career with Wilson in the Confederate army, perhaps in its engineer corp. Together they attended the annual dinner of the Confederate Veterans Camp of New York. "Cheers for the Flag," *New York Times*, January 19, 1896, 3. Edwards was a master builder of railroads, overseeing for Wilson construction of the Yazoo and Mississippi Valley Railway between Memphis and New Orleans in the 1880s and the Yonkers Street Railway in 1894. Wilson sent him to manage the Mathieson Alkali Works, Saltville, Georgia, until 1917, when he retired. Born in 1849, he died on May 24, 1920.
88. The *New York Times* said on May 25, 1912, that his probate estate alone was valued at $16,072,470.69 by an appraisal filed in connection with the administration of his will.
89. Currie and Ferry briefly served on the new board of the directors. "IT IS SOLD!"
90. "Detroit Street Railroad Deal: R.T. Wilson & Co. and J.M. Edwards of New York the Purchasers," *New York Times*, September 2, 1894; "75 Cents Per Dollar: Former Street Car Man Says It Was the Price Paid," *Detroit Free Press*, September 6, 1894, 1. "Not More Than Three Millions," *Detroit Free Press*, September 7, 1894, 5.
91. Hutchins, *A Personal Story*, 164–65.
92. *Detroit Citizens Street Railway Company v. City of Detroit*, 64 F. 628 (6th Cir. 1894). Lurton and Taft sat together on the U.S. Sixth Circuit Court of Appeals. President Taft would later appoint Lurton to the U.S. Supreme Court.
93. *Detroit Citizens Street Railway Company v. City of Detroit*, 64 F. 646 (6th Cir. 1894).
94. *Detroit Citizens Street Railway Company v. City of Detroit*, 64 F. 632 (6th Cir. 1894).
95. *Detroit Citizens Street Railway Company v. City of Detroit*, 64 F. 647 (6th Cir. 1894).
96. Lurton was born in Newport, Kentucky, on February 26, 1844, and raised in Clarksville, Tennessee. He attended the Douglas University in Chicago in 1860 but eagerly joined the Confederate army at the outbreak of the Civil War. Discharged for a lung infection, he soon reenlisted and was captured by Union soldiers. He escaped but was recaptured and released on parole by President Abraham

Lincoln just before the war ended. Lurton resumed his studies and graduated from Cumberland University Law School in 1867. He returned to Clarksville and began the practice of law. In 1875, at the age of thirty-one, he was appointed by the governor of Tennessee to the Sixth Chancery Division of Tennessee and became the youngest chancellor in the history of the state. He resigned after three years and resumed the private practice of law, serving as president of the Farmers and Mechanics National Bank in Clarksville, Tennessee, from which he earned a reputation as a financier. Lurton was elected to the Tennessee Supreme Court in 1886 and became its chief judge in 1893. Later that year, President Grover Cleveland appointed Lurton to the U.S. Court of Appeals for the Sixth Circuit, where he served for sixteen years. President William H. Taft nominated Lurton to the U.S. Supreme Court on December 20, 1909. The Senate confirmed the appointment on January 3, 1910. Lurton served on the Supreme Court for four years. He died on July 12, 1914, at the age of seventy.

97. *Greenlaw v. Pittit*, 11 S.W. 357 (1889).
98. Maury Klein, *History of the Louisville & Nashville Railroad* (Lexington: University Press of Kentucky, 2003).
99. On October 28, 1893, Ellis filed a complaint in the Wayne County Circuit Court seeking an accounting from Mayor Pingree of funds he used for "entertainment, feasts, and trips on palace cars over the country." "Conspiracy Charged: Attorney General Ellis Informs against Mayor Pingree," *Detroit Free Press*, October 29, 1893, 1. The Michigan Supreme Court dismissed the case on technical grounds two years later. *Ellis, Attorney General v. City of Detroit*, 107 Mich. 92 (1895).
100. *City of Detroit v. Ellis*, 103 Mich. 612 (1895).
101. Hutchins, *A Personal Story*, 127–28. "To Clear the Avenue: Instructions to the Marshal of Highland Park," *Detroit Free Press*, November 6, 1894, 2.
102. Mayor Pingree called a special meeting of the Common Council on October 15, 1894, overcoming, 29-0, legal objections that had earlier blocked putting such an advisory question on the ballot. On March 13, 1894, Pingree told the Common Council that he had abandoned municipal ownership of tracks because the city lacked legal authority to do so under the charter. The proposition submitted to voters was in abbreviated form:

    City ownership of street railway tracks. Yes ☐
    City ownership of street railway tracks. No ☐

103. Hutchins, *A Personal Story*, 7. Historical and genealogical researchers have found no definitive record.
104. "A Horrid Tragedy," *Port Gibson Herald and Correspondent*, September 12, 1851.
105. Schramm and Henning, *Detroit's Street Railways*, vol. 1, *City Lines 1863–1922*, 71.
106. "Their Franchise Revoked: Suburban Railway Co. May Lose Some of Their Rights," *Detroit Free Press*, September 19, 1894, 5; "To Clear the Avenue: Instructions to the Marshal of Highland Park," *Detroit Free Press*, November 6, 1894, 2.
107. The stately three-story brick home built in 1875 is depicted in a pen-and-ink drawing in Farmer, *History of Detroit*, 437. Katherine Whitney McGregor purchased the home in 1903 as a place for homeless, crippled, and backward children. She donated the land to Highland Park in 1918, stipulating that it be replaced as soon as possible with a new library building costing at least $255,000. The magnificent Beaux Arts–style McGregor Public Library opened in 1926. It was closed and boarded-up in 2002, when the State of Michigan put the city government into financial receivership.
108. The Highland Park Railway Company had received a franchise from the Township of Greenfield to

provide three-rail electric streetcar railway service on Woodward Avenue from Baltimore Avenue to Puritan Street on October 17, 1885. A small portion of Greenfield Township along either side of Woodward Avenue later incorporated as the Village of Highland Park.

109. Hutchins, *A Personal Story*, 128–29.
110. Ibid., 129–30.
111. The rally described by Hutchins actually was three months later on January 26, 1895. It arose from pending state legislation to strip Mayor Pingree of his appointive power over several important boards and commissions. "Twas Plain: The Feeling against Dr. Duncan McLeod Shown Last Night at the Mass Meeting," *Detroit Free Press*, January 27, 1895, 1.
112. Hutchins, *A Personal Story*, 130–31.
113. Ibid., 131–32.
114. Ibid.
115. Ibid., 132–33.
116. When the company filed articles of association dated December 10, 1894, Moore dropped out, and Charles L. Pack and Charles W. Wason of Cleveland had been added as a minority stockholders. A member of the Pack forestry family, Charles lived in Cleveland, managing the wealth he had accumulated from Michigan. Wason was a purchasing agent and engineer for the East Cleveland Railway Company in 1877 where Wason became interested in using electricity to power street railways. He was put in charge of electrifying the company's lines, and this project developed into the first electric railroad for public use in the United States. Subsequently, Wason rose through the ranks to become the president or director of a number of other railway, electric, and telephone companies. From 1909 until his death in 1918, Wason amassed a remarkable collection of more than nine thousand books, periodicals, manuscripts, documents, drawings, maps, and other materials on China that he bequeathed to Cornell University.
117. Pack and Everett had "revised, enlarged and improved" upon a franchise ordinance originally proposed to the Common Council on October 13, 1891, from Homer Warren, Stevens, Snow, C. A. Newcomb, E. W. Voight, John M. Nicol, Frederick Marvin, and Fremont Woodruff, according to an article from the *Evening News* republished in 1922. Delos F. Wilcox and M. M. O'Shaughnessy, *Municipal Railways in the United States and Canada* (Chicago: Public Ownership League of America, 1922), 18. Warren pursued getting a franchise for service along Warren Avenue west to the city limits several times between 1891 and 1894 without ever getting a hearing before the Common Council. Among his many prospective investors was R. H. Fyfe.
118. "A New One: Latest Street Car Sensation on the Tapis for To-Night," *Detroit Free Press*, November 20, 1894, 1. (Tapis is an archaic description for the council chamber's table coverings.)
119. "IT IS LAW! Final Action on the Street Railway Ordinance," *Detroit Free Press*, December 5, 1894, 1. An opinion piece headlined "Municipal Reform in Typical American Cities: The Fight Against Corruption in Detroit" published by the *New York Times* on August 17, 1903, said, "Pingree's use of questionable instruments was further illustrated in one of the phases of the long fight he made against the Citizens Street Car Company. When in 1894 a new company was formed to parallel the lines of the old company, Pingree encouraged the new owners, as it proposed to give eight tickets for a quarter while the established rate was five cents. The man who financed the new company found it necessary to use money in the Council and Pingree knew it, but he never made any effort to bring to punishment

either the street car men or the Aldermen who took the bribe."

120. The filing made with the secretary of state on December 10, 1895, used all capital letters in article 1 of the articles of association. "The name by which this corporation shall be known in law, is, THE DETROIT RAILWAY."
121. Tom Loftin Johnson and Elizabeth J. Hauser, *My Story* (New York: B. W. Huebsch, 1911), 91. Albert Johnson's financial stake in the Detroit Citizens Street Railway Company, if any, never was disclosed either by Wilson or Tom Johnson. He was never again mentioned in any historical account regarding Detroit's street railways.
122. Ibid., 92.
123. Hutchins, *A Personal Story*, 133.
124. Ibid., 133–34.
125. Ibid., 134. Hutchins purchased fifteen electric street cars from the Nassau Electric Railroad of Brooklyn, which had suffered the collapse of its powerhouse. Johnson and R. T. Wilson were actively interested in the Nassau street railway company.
126. Arthur E. DeMatteo, "Cleveland's A.B. DuPont: Engineer, Reformer, Visionary," *Northeast Ohio Journal of History* 1, no. 1 (fall 2002), http://blogs.uakron.edu/nojh/.
127. Hutchins, *A Personal Story*, 138.
128. Ibid.
129. "Hot, Red Gore: What the Johnson-Pack Lawsuit Is For," *Detroit Evening News*, June 3, 1896, 1. Holli, *Reform in Detroit*, 103.
130. Johnson and Hauser, *My Story*, 92–94.
131. Paul Leake, "The Street Railway Situation in Detroit," in *Proceedings of the Buffalo Conference for Good City Government and the Sixteenth Annual Meeting of the National Municipal League*, ed. Clinton Rogers Woodruff ([Philadelphia]: National Municipal League, 1910), 121–22.

CHAPTER 7. COMPETITIVE FIGHT REALLY BEGINS

1. Holli, *Reform in Detroit*, 104.
2. Hutchins, *A Personal Story*, 141.
3. Holli, *Reform in Detroit*, 105.
4. "Hotter than Ever: The Street Railway Fight at Lansing Yesterday: House Committee Held a Session in the Evening," *Detroit Free Press*, July 17, 1895, 3.
5. "ROUND ONE! Won by the Detroit Railway in Its Fight at Lansing," *Detroit Free Press*, April 18, 1895, 1.
6. "KILLED IT! Legislators Experience a Sudden Change of Heart," *Detroit Free Press*, April 19, 1895, 1.
7. *Journal of the House of Representatives of the State of Michigan*, vol. 2, (Lansing: Robert Smith & Company, 1895), 1518–19. The *Detroit Free Press* wrongly reported the tally as 41-51. "KILLED IT!."
8. Hutchins, *A Personal Story*, 141.
9. Holli, *Reform in Detroit*, 105.
10. "KILLED IT!. On May 14, by unanimous consent, the state senate indefinitely postponed taking any action on Senate Bill No. 319.
11. "No More Concessions: Mayor Pingree Thinks the Citizens' Company Has Enough," *Detroit Free Press*, April 20, 1895, 5.

12. In 1867, this section was strengthened against municipalities by the state legislature, which provided that "after such consent shall have been given and accepted by the corporation to which the same is granted, such authorities shall make no regulations or conditions whereby the rights or franchises so granted shall be destroyed or unreasonably impaired." Act No. 35 of the Public Acts of 1867.
13. *Detroit Citizens Street Railway Company v. City of Detroit*, 110 Mich. 384 (1896).
14. George I. Reed, *Bench and Bar of Michigan: A Volume of History and Biography* (Chicago: Century Publishing and Engraving, 1897), 387.
15. *Detroit Citizens Street Railway Company v. City of Detroit*, 110 Mich. 394–95 (1896).
16. Of course, Judge Montgomery could have explained that the express language of the statute merely barred rivals from operating streetcars on another's railways as opposed to entire streets. Such a narrow reading is plausible, but it would have been contrary to how both street railway companies and Detroit officials had always more broadly interpreted them.
17. *Detroit Citizens Street Railway Company v. City of Detroit*, 110 Mich. 398 (1896).
18. *Detroit Citizens Street Railway Company v. City of Detroit*, 110 Mich. 393–94 (1896).
19. The U.S. Supreme Court affirmed. *Detroit Citizens Street Railway v. Detroit Railway*, 171 U.S. 48 (1898). The unanimous opinion concluded by saying, "Easements in the public streets for a limited time are different, and have different consequences, from those given in perpetuity. Those reserved from monopoly are different, and have different consequences, from those fixed in monopoly. Consequently those given in perpetuity and in monopoly must have, for their authority, explicit permission, or, if inferred from other powers, it is not enough that the authority is convenient to them, but it must be indispensable to them" (Ibid., 55). The U.S. Supreme Court was unwilling to overturn the Michigan Supreme Court's narrow reading of the Street-Railway Act.
20. Clarence Burton may have met Jere Hutchins at these ceremonies. Among Burton's vast collection of books donated to the Detroit Public Library was William Benson Scott, *Street Railways of Detroit; a compilation of the state laws, city and suburban ordinances and franchises and court decisions, granting and relating to the rights of street railway corporations of Detroit, Michigan* (New York: Knickerbocker Press, 1895). The book was personally signed for Burton by Hutchins on July 10, 1895. It has sadly gone missing from Burton library shelves since I found the dedication.
21. Wilcox, *Municipal Franchises*, 352.
22. Johnson and Hauser, *My Story*, 95–96.
23. Ibid., 96–97.
24. O'Geran, *History of the Detroit Street Railways*, 143.
25. "No Transfers! One of Tom Johnson's New Rules Goes into Effect Today," *Detroit Free Press*, November 21, 1895, 1. O'Geran, *History of the Detroit Street Railways*, 149.
26. Hutchins, *A Personal Story*, 154.
27. A popular old song, "Johnny, Get Your Gun," from 1886, included a verse:

    I looked ole Satan in de eye,
    Johnny, get your gun, get your gun,
    Said he, "I'll want you by-an'-by,"
    Johnny, get your gun, get your gun;
    Fetch me up an alderman,
    Johnny, get your gun, get your gun,

Put him in my frying pan,
Johnny, get your gun, get your gun.

28. "WHOA, BILL! The Street Car Horse Has Heard It the Last Time. The Last Horse Car," *Detroit Evening News*, November 10, 1895, 5; "Last Horse Car," *Detroit Free Press*, November 10, 1895, 23.
29. "Nickel or Walk: Tom L. Johnson Sprung His Five-Cent Bluff Yesterday," *Detroit Free Press*, November 25, 1895, 1.
30. "Against Tom Johnson," *Detroit Free Press*, November 24, 1895, 7. The petition asked the Common Council to prevail on the Detroit Railway Company to build streetcar lines on Larned or Woodbridge Streets to compete with Johnson's Jefferson Avenue line.
31. "BOYCOTT IS ON: Five-Cent Fare Order Being Rebuked by the Citizens," *Detroit Free Press*, November 26, 1895, 1; Holli, *Reform in Detroit*, 107.
32. Holli, *Reform in Detroit*, 107–8.
33. "No Thirty-Year Franchise," *Detroit Free Press*, November 22, 1895, 4.
34. "No Let Up: The Mayor Wants the War to Go On," *Detroit Evening News*, November 25, 1895, 1.
35. "All Kick: Lively Day on the Street Cars," *Detroit Evening News*, November 25, 1895, 1.
36. Hutchins, *A Personal Story*, 141.
37. "PUT THEM OFF: Conductor Ballard Claims That He Paid the Mayor's Street Car Fare," *Detroit Free Press*, December 15, 1895, 1.
38. "PAID NO FARE! Mayor Pingree Carried Out an Oft-Repeated Threat," *Detroit Free Press*, December 14, 1895, 1.
39. Holli, *Reform in Detroit*, 109–10.
40. Hazen S. Pingree, *Seventh Annual Message of Hazen S. Pingree, Mayor of Detroit to the Common Council* (Detroit: The Thos. Smith Press 1896), 3–4.
41. This is but one of many different stories told of the first horseless carriage to drive Detroit streets. The famous quote appears in a clipping hand-dated and noted 3/7/96 *Det. Journal*. Neither its date nor its publication by the *Detroit Journal* could be verified. Many accounts erroneously reference a one-paragraph article on the back page of the *Free Press* on March 7, 1896. See, e.g., Arthur M. Woodford, *This Is Detroit, 1701–2001* (Detroit: Wayne State University Press, 2001), 89–90. The twelve-page issue of the *Free Press* published on March 7, 1896, however, contains nothing about King's horseless carriage. Later *Free Press* articles raise additional doubt. "A Novel Motor Carriage," *Detroit Free Press*, August 16, 1896, 5, said, "A good many people have been rather startled for a day or two past by seeing a wagon come tearing along the street at a lively rate, dodging people and teams. . . . Detroit has now come to the front with a motor carriage. It is in its roughest form, the horseless wagon that has attracted so much attention during the last day or two, and is the invention of Charles B. King of this city." One article, "Journal Tells of Old Detroit Auto," *Detroit Free Press*, September 12, 1915, D3, said a periodical, *Cycle Age* 1, no. 9, published in Detroit on April 16, 1896, described King's horseless carriage in phrases identical to those generally attributed to the *Detroit Journal*.
42. O'Geran, *History of the Detroit Street Railways*, 146. A few months earlier, on May 19, 1896, Henry W. Campbell, Calvin K. Brandon, Bethune Duffield, Samuel A. Plumer, and George Dorr had filed articles of association for an unrelated street railway company they called the Detroit Electric Railway Company. It never obtained consent to operate from the City of Detroit. In choosing a legal name for the new company, therefore, the "T" was capitalized in *The* Detroit Electric Railway Company.

43. McNairy was a paint manufacturer and Cleveland capitalist. A former Detroit city attorney and businessman, Corliss had been a street railway investor for many years. He participated in organizing the Highland Park Railway Company in 1886. In 1894, he won a seat in the U.S. Congress, serving three terms.
44. "Reported Purchase by R. T. Wilson," *New York Times*, July 14, 1896, 2.
45. Section 2 of article 19A of the State Constitution of 1850 said: "No railroad corporation shall consolidate its stock, property, or franchises with any other railroad corporation owning a parallel or competing line; and in no case shall any consolidation take place except upon public notice given of at least sixty days to all stockholders, in such manner as shall be provided by law."
46. Johnson and Hauser, *My Story*, 94.
47. Pingree won his nomination for governor on the fourth ballot at the August 6 Republican Party convention in Grand Rapids. "Pingree . . . built up a strong machine in Detroit and Wayne County, and by his anti-corporation speeches gained a great personal following among the farmers and poorer classes of people throughout the State. The following was successfully organized by Albert Pack, President of The Detroit Railway, the first three-cent-a-mile railway in the United States." "Pingree for Governor," *New York Times*, August 7, 1896, 3.
48. Holli, *Reform in Detroit*, 111–12. "He'll Resign: Mr. Pingree May Throw up the Office of Governor," *Detroit Free Press*, January 7, 1897, 1.
49. Holli, *Reform in Detroit*, 112.
50. "Ping's Goal," *Detroit Evening News*, December 10, 1896.
51. The Fort Wayne and Elmwood Railway Company had reorganized and on July 1, 1892, transferred all of its rights and property to the Fort Wayne and Belle Isle Railway Company, which obtained a new thirty-year franchise from the city in 1896.
52. *Attorney General ex rel. Moreland v. Common Council of the City of Detroit*, 112 Mich. 145 (1897). Lawyers Frederick A. Baker III and John J. Speed represented the attorney general. Moreland was implicated in ongoing concrete contractor fraud and bribery. He was removed as public works commissioner by the Common Council and fled ahead of his prosecution to Mexico. "Scandal in Detroit Now," *New York Times*, June 26, 1903, 3.
53. Maybury's election was a defeat for Governor Pingree, who had handpicked Great Lakes ship commander Captain Albert E. Stewart as his successor. Pingree viewed Maybury as a corrupt baby-kisser who was in Johnson's pocket. At a Stewart campaign rally in an old auditorium on Congress Street, Pingree lashed out against Maybury, announcing, "Gentleman, all I gotta say is that what Detroit needs is a man for mayor who will tell those public utilities to kiss something besides babies." Quoted in Bingay, *Detroit Is My Own Home Town*, 240.
54. City of Detroit, *Journal of the Common Council from January 13, 1903, to January 12, 1904, Inclusive* (Detroit: Thos. Smith, 1904), 564.
55. "New Funeral Car: Used Yesterday at the Obsequies of George Sheldon," *Detroit Free Press*, June 18, 1897, 5.

CHAPTER 8. THREE-CENT FARES OR MUNICIPAL OWNERSHIP

1. O'Geran, *History of the Detroit Street Railways*, 162. "Will Let Them Wait," *Detroit Free Press*, December 14, 1898, 4.
2. "Returned! Vice-President Hutchins' Ordinance Sent Back—No Thanks," *Detroit Free Press*, December 14, 1898. O'Geran, *History of the Detroit Street Railways*, 161–63.
3. Hutchins, *A Personal Story*, 150.
4. "Detroit Street-Railway Ownership," *Western Electrician* 24, no. 15 (April 15, 1899): 210.
5. McLeod was not related to and was misidentified by Professor Eugene C. Murdock, *Tom Johnson of Cleveland* (Dayton: Wright State University Press, 1994), 47, as Alex McLeod, Mayor Pingree's former secretary. Murdock was a professor of history at Marietta College in Ohio. He is best remembered on campus today as a rabid baseball fan with an enormous collection of baseball monographs, serials, photographs, scrapbooks, and programs, covering the years 1905–76, as well as some minor league programs and photographs. Also included within the collection are oral history tapes of early twentieth-century major league players he recorded filling a remarkable sixty-nine feet of storage boxes at the Cleveland Public Library.
6. Tom Johnson had visited Detroit and Lansing while the bill was pending in the state legislature. Among other things, the *Free Press* reported that Johnson, his brother, Albert, and DuPont "took a trolley ride to Pontiac as the guests of George and Strathearn Hendrie. Mr. Hutchins stated afterwards that the trip had no significance as bearing upon the local street railway situation or any possible change in the ownership of the Pontiac line." "Pingree Did Not Talk to Tom Johnson," *Detroit Free Press*, March 11, 1899, 2.
7. Senators Frank A. Lyon of Hillsdale and George F. Monaghan of Detroit voted against adoption.
8. "Detroit Street Railways," *New York Times*, April 23, 1899, 13, said that "it has been shown conclusively that the erasures found in the McLeod bill were made before passage by either House." The reference to erasures went otherwise unexplained.
9. The untidy drafting of the legislative title of the McLeod Act was much broader than its actual language. It said, "An Act to authorize the *City of Detroit* to construct, acquire, maintain, and operate Street Railways and to construct extensions thereof" (emphasis added).
10. Section 1 of the McLeod Act made successors to the original appointees, however, subject to nomination by the mayor and confirmation by the Common Council. The Pingree legislation had neatly sidestepped Maybury.
11. Despite his earlier refusal to take on the franchise extension litigation, Dickinson widely was believed to be Governor Pingree's first choice. Democrats favored appointing William B. Thompson, city treasurer, who emerged as a fierce opponent of Pingree's municipal ownership legislation.
12. "Municipal Ownership of Street Railways in Detroit," *Literary Digest* 18, no. 15 (April 15, 1899): 420–21.
13. "Pingree Night School: His Option Is Really Held by Tom Johnson," *Detroit Free Press*, April 11, 1899, 3.
14. In 1897, Wilson had organized a $7 million holding company in the State of Virginia he called the Citizens Traction Company, which owned all of the stock of his Detroit railway companies, the Detroit Citizens Street Railway Company, the Detroit Electric Railway Company, and the Detroit, Fort Wayne and Belle Isle Railway. The Citizens Traction Company prepared blanket mortgages disposing of all of its Detroit stock to the Metropolitan Railway Company organized to deal with Governor Pingree's

commission, according to *Poor's Manual of the Railroads of the United States.* One purpose of forming the Virginia holding company and the Metropolitan Railway Company might have been to organize Wilson's legal position against profit-sharing claims by Johnson.

15. In 1880, Hutchins married Anna Brooks. Frank Brooks was her younger brother. Hutchins and Frank Brooks became lifelong friends and street railway associates. Anna Hutchins died of typhoid fever in 1901. Hutchins married Sarah Russel in 1903.
16. *Railway World* (Philadelphia: Railway World Publishing Company, 1899), 376.
17. "The Cleveland Situation," *Street Railway Journal*, October 5, 1907, 532.
18. Hutchins, *A Personal Story*, 151.
19. Holli, *Reform in Detroit*, 119.
20. "Detroit Street-Railway Ownership," *Western Electrician* 24, no. 18 (May 6, 1899): 259.
21. "Pingree Discusses Municipal Ownership," *New York Times*, January 27, 1900.
22. Bemis was educated at Amherst College and Johns Hopkins University, receiving his PhD in 1885 in history and economics. Before Kansas State, he had taught economics at Amherst, Vanderbilt, and the University of Chicago, from which he had to leave because of his radical political and economic views. He favored municipal ownership of public utilities and street railways. Bemis wrote prolifically about local government, tax policy, municipal ownership of utilities, working conditions, labor strikes, trade unions, socialism, religion, and social problems.
23. Gilbert Wilkes of Detroit was assigned to appraising the overhead electrical construction, including the poles and foundations. George Dingwall of Detroit was assigned to appraising the real estate. Albert Albrecht was assigned to appraising the powerhouses and shops. James D. Hawks, former manager of the Detroit Citizens Street Railway Company, was assigned to appraising the track construction, including the foundations, railroad pavement, rails, and bond wires. An accountant for the Detroit Citizens Street Railway Company, E. B. Hutchinson, was assigned to gathering and organizing four years of net earnings data from the four street railway companies needed by Professor Bemis to appraise franchise rights.
24. Johnson and Hauser, *My Story*, 96. Neither Pingree nor anyone else ever disclosed who had offered the $300,000 sweeter. Nobody except Johnson had any financial reason to do so. Johnson had publicly agreed that the company would buy and deliver back to the Pingree commission $400,000 in bonds.
25. Holli, *Reform in Detroit*, 118. The Street Railway Commission reportedly offered to issue $16 million in bonds for Johnson to sell at par value. "Johnson agreed, so far as he was concerned, saying that he had not a dollar's interest in the road, but adding that Wilson would not enter upon such a proposition," according to "Detroit Street-Railway Ownership," *Western Electrician* 24, no. 19 (May 13, 1899): 271.
26. *Attorney General v. Pingree*, 120 Mich. 550, 569–71 (1899). Not only was the supreme court's legal reasoning roundly criticized but also its letting political hostility to municipal ownership influence the outcome. Thomas W. Brown, "The Detroit Street Railway Decision," *American Law Review* 33 (1899): 853.
27. *Bird v. Common Council of the City of Detroit*, 148 Mich. 71 (1907).
28. Governor Pingree had offered to add two Democratic Party members to the Street Railway Commission, so buying up all the shares among themselves made no good political sense because doing so suggested that they were positioning themselves to earn a personal financial windfall if the

deal was approved.

29. Edward L. Bemis, "Detroit's Effort to Own Her Street Railways," *Municipal Affairs*, vol. 3, 1899, 486–87.
30. Hazen S. Pingree, Three-Cent Fares, Nos. 1–14, July 13–29, 1899, Bentley Historical Library, University of Michigan, Ann Arbor, MI.
31. "Indignation Still Runs High against the Johnson-Pingree Scheme," *Detroit Free Press*, July 15, 1899, 1.
32. Pingree, Three-Cent Fares.
33. Ibid.
34. "The Blow That Almost Killed Pingree," *Detroit Free Press*, July 16, 1899.
35. "Plan with Johnson's Detroit Street Car Negotiations Broken Off," *Logansport Pharos-Tribune*, July 18, 1899, 10.
36. "To enforce this ordinance would be an act not of regulation but of spoliation," Judge Swan wrote. "The police power includes the general management as regards the protection of life and property and the accommodation of the public, but the Legislature itself could not affect the fares agreed upon. It might be for the welfare of the public that the fares should be abolished altogether, but that would be confiscation and could not be tolerated." "Against Three-Cent Fares," *New York Times*, March 20, 1900, 1. The U.S. Supreme Court affirmed. *Detroit v. Detroit Citizens Street Railway Company*, 184 U.S. 368 (1902).
37. *Detroit Citizens Street Railway Company v. Common Council of the City of Detroit*, 125 Mich. 673, 703–5 (1901).
38. Pack and Everett had a grandiose plan for a street railway system stretching from Buffalo to Cleveland to Chicago. They would soon learn that supplying electricity beyond twenty miles from their power stations was impractical.
39. "Strife among Street Railway Owners," *San Francisco Call*, December 27, 1900, 2.
40. Johnson boasted that "the public did not know that I had agreed to reduce the cost to the City by such share of the purchase price as would come to me as my profit. It would have been useless to tell this. Nobody would have believed it." Johnson and Hauser, *My Story*, 96. His claim, however, does not bear scrutiny.
41. Ibid., 106.
42. Eugene C. Murdock, *Tom Johnson of Cleveland* (Dayton, OH: Wright State University Press, 1994), 50. "Brooklyn Trolley Deal: R. T. Wilson Sells His Nassau Stock and Old Stories Are Revived," *New York Times*, September 20, 1898.
43. Schramm and Henning, *Detroit's Street Railways*, vol. 1, *City Lines 1863–1922*, 85.
44. "Tom Johnson's Big Suit," *New York Times*, December 27, 1900, 5; "Mr. Johnson's Suit Settled," *New York Times*, December 29, 1900. In 1956, Virgil V. McNitt, a New England newspaper publisher who had worked at the *Cleveland Press* during Johnson's years as mayor (1901–9), said the settlement was $800,000. V. V. McNitt, "Idol of the People," *Michigan Alumnus Quarterly Review* 63, no. 10 (December 8, 1956), 157. McNitt failed to note the source of this conclusion. A more recent biography said Johnson sold his shares in the Detroit Citizens Street Railway Company for $16,800. Kevin O'Connell, *Tom Johnson: The Life and Times of Cleveland's Greatest Mayor* (Cleveland: Green Road Press, 2001), 22. O'Connell provided no reference. In a telephone interview, moreover, he was unaware that the sale he reported may have been part of a bigger settlement with Wilson. O'Connell said he had discarded his research materials and could not recall the source of his information.

45. Johnson was an enigmatic municipal politician of the Progressive Era. A biographical essay describing him as an advocate of three-cent street railway fares published by the *Successful American* in August 1901 was reversed at his apparent insistence in November 1901. The correction said, "Neither did Mr. Johnson, as stated, advocate and secure three-center fares for the people of Cleveland. Mr. Johnson, as we all know, is a very able and capable man, who is playing the game of politics for all it is worth, and should be given credit for his great success in reaching the masses; but, as we are advised, he had always advocated five cent fare on all roads in which he is interested." "Tom L. Johnson Not a Three-Cent Fare Man," *Successful American* 4, no. 5, November 1901, 626.
46. Hutchins, *A Personal Story*, 165–66.
47. Ibid., 166.
48. The $130 million Everett-Moore syndicate failed on January 3, 1902, and all of its assets were taken over by a committee of Cleveland bankers. Hutchins was named by them to replace Everett as president and general manager of the Detroit United Railway.
49. Everett and Moore had formed their Everett-Moore syndicate in 1894. Together they controlled more than 1,200 miles of electric street railways and many telephone companies in Ohio and Michigan.
50. Van Cortlandt served on the DUR board of directors until February 18, 1918, when he committed suicide by cutting his throat with a silver-handled razor in the bathtub of his four-hundred-acre farm in Mount Kisco, New York, leaving an estate estimated at $7 million. "Consults Pastor before Suicide," *New York Times*, February 19, 1918.
51. *Detroit in Nineteen Hundred: A Chronological Record of Events, Both Local and State during the Closing Year of the Twentieth Century*, ed. S. B. McCracken (Detroit: Evening News Association, 1901), 9.
52. Section 8 of article 5 of the Michigan Constitution of 1850 required the governor to deliver a message to the state legislature upon leaving office. "He shall give to the Legislature, and at the close of his official term, to the next Legislature, information by message of the condition of the State, and recommend such measures to them as he shall deem expedient." The Michigan Constitution of 1963 removed the requirement for an exaugural address. "While the exaugural message is somewhat unusual," said a 1961 report by the Citizens Research Council of Michigan, which tallied six other states doing so, "it appears to offer no serious disadvantages and could be helpful to the extent that the governor may use it as an occasion to make recommendations in the light of experience at a time when more immediate political considerations would ordinarily be less pressing." *A Comparative Analysis of the Michigan Constitution, Volume 1, Article VI* (Detroit: Citizens Research Council of Michigan, October 1961), 50.
53. "Pingree Says Farewell," *New York Times*, January 4, 1901, 5. The newspaper used just four lines at the end of the column-long article for the inaugural address of the new governor, Aaron T. Bliss, saying, "Gov. Bliss, in his message, urged on the legislators the advisability of economy in all appropriations and suggested a short session of the Legislature in the interest of economy."
54. When Hazen Pingree died, his estate subject to probate was valued at $301,310 with debts of $6,252. Most of the estate consisted of stock in his shoe factory. *The Corunna Journal*, March 13, 1902.
55. "Eli Ransom Sutton, '91/, '92, LL. M. '92," *Michigan Alumnus* 41, no. 8 (November 24, 1934): 128.
56. He was also a promoter of the Detroit and Flint and the Grand Rapids, Holland & Lake Michigan Railways, a large part of which was bought by the Hendrie family on March 28, 1902. "Railway

Transfers," *New York Times*, March 29, 1902, 5. Andrews fraudulently dipped into bonds issued to finance construction of the Grand Rapids, Holland & Lake Michigan Railway. Of the $1.5 million bonds, Andrews had used at least $396,000 for his own purposes, placing $105,000 with the State Bank for a loan of $95,000, $80,000 with the Dime Bank for a loan of $60,000, $70,000 with the First National Bank for a loan of $45,000, $71,000 with the Preston National Bank for a loan of $50,000, and $50,000 to A. L. Stephens to purchase a fashionable mansion on Woodward Avenue. See also *Union Trust Company v. Preston National Bank*, 144 Mich. 106 (1906). Andrews was vice president and largest shareholder of the Preston National Bank.

57. "Frank Chester Andrews," *Successful American* 4, no. 2, August 1901, 460.
58. "A Plunger's Downfall: The Amalgamated Slump Caught a Prominent Detroit Speculator," *Michigan Miner*, March 1, 1902.
59. Case arranged with Andrews for a second $45,000 certified check to be deposited and wired to New York through the State Savings Bank. Dividing payment between two checks and adding an extra $5,000 kicker suggests Case's complicity in the check-kiting scheme.
60. *First National Bank v. Currie*, 147 Mich. 72 (1907). Currie was a member of the board of directors of the Detroit Clearing House Association, which met daily at 12:15 p.m. to exchange checks between banks. It should have been obvious to him what Andrews was doing especially because the members agreed among themselves on February 7 not to present the $662,000 through the clearinghouse. Currie asked the First National Bank to extend the time for payment on the $50,000 check his firm had endorsed while he and Andrews scrambled for the next three days before the First National Bank deposited it directly at the City Savings Bank.
61. City Savings Bank cashier Henry R. Andrews, who was unrelated, had been elected school board treasurer April 18, 1900, upon his promise to pay 2.5 percent interest on deposits. The position made him ex-officio treasurer of the Library Commission. *Board of Education of Detroit v. Union Trust Company*, 136 Mich. 454 (1904).
62. "Bank Director Ruined," *New York Times*, February 28, 1903, 2.
63. At a preliminary court hearing on April 26, Frank Pingree admitted, "last July the directors discovered that the bank was holding some of Frank C. Andrews's paper, which they had not approved. Pingree said he talked the discovery over with Frank C. Andrews. . . . After a heated argument Andrews finally agreed to sell his real estate and straighten out the affair. Mr. Pingree said that Andrews told him they could sell the City Savings Bank by fall as there were two banks that wanted to buy it." "Pingree Tells His Story," *Des Moines Leader*, April 27, 1902, 1.
64. "Frank C. Pingree Passes from Life," *Detroit Free Press*, April 3, 1910, 21.
65. "'Get-Rich-Quick' Andrews Dies of Paralysis at 47," *Detroit Free Press*, December 13, 1918, 3.
66. "Frank C. Andrews Dead," *New York Times*, December 13, 1918, 15.
67. Case was born in Flint on November 26, 1876. He worked at the Commercial National Bank as a messenger and clerk from 1895 to 1899 when he came to work for Cameron Currie.
68. The Panic of 1907 was a financial crisis that occurred when the New York Stock Exchange fell almost 50 percent from its peak the previous year. There were numerous runs on New York banks and trust companies. The panic eventually spread throughout the nation when many state and local banks and businesses entered bankruptcy. The panic was triggered by a failed attempt in October 1907 to corner the market on stock of the United Copper Company.

69. One of many lawsuits arising was Charles L. Freer's suit for recovery of $52,000 worth of stock he had loaned to Currie a short time before the firm went into receivership. Some years later, the case was so well known that the plaintiff-wife in a divorce case cited the physician-husband's gambling as grounds for divorce. The Michigan Supreme Court responded by saying, "There is some foundation in the charge that defendant was a gambler. While culpable and an evidence of moral instability, we are not prepared to hold that, as proven, it amounted to a cause of divorce. He was in no sense a professional gambler, but is shown to have at times manifested a weakness for attending horse races and investing disastrously in his judgment as to the comparative speed of the competing horses. If his defense depended upon his denials and explanations in that connection, there would be little hope for him. He is also shown to have sought to increase his financial resources by investment in stocks through the brokerage firm of Cameron Currie & Company, which failed disastrously, and he stated at the time that he had lost everything. While this venture is to be deprecated as evidence of a gambling inclination and *poor judgment*, the courts have not yet gone so far as to hold such conduct ground for divorce" (emphasis added). *Cadieux v. Cadieux*, 180 Mich. 99, 105 (1914).
70. *Austin v. Hayden*, 171 Mich. 38, 56 (1912). See also *Austin v. Hayden*, 176 Mich. 331 (1913); *People's State Bank v. Miller*, 185 Mich. 565 (1915).
71. Case and six clerks and telegraph operators were indicted for criminal fraud and conversion. "Detroit Brokers Indicted," *Urbana Courier-Herald*, June 3, 1909, 5. Currie was also criminally charged. "Brokers to Be Arrested," *New York Times*, January 30, 1909, 2. Wayne County Prosecutor Philip T. VanZile dismissed all of the conspiracy charges pending against Currie on December 2, 1910, following a questionable ruling denying admissibility of certain evidence. "Conspiracy Charges Fail," *New York Times*, December 3, 1910, 5.
72. *Matter of Cameron Currie*, 23 Am. B. R. 539 (E.D. Mich. 1910). See also 20 Am. B. R. 790.
73. Jane Schermerhorn, "Moving Day Jolts Yondotega Tradition: X-Way Ousts Exclusive Club," The Yondotega Club, *Discuss Detroit*, http://www.atdetroit.net/forum/messages/76017/83687.html?1159238206.

CHAPTER 9. EVERY MAYOR HAD A THREE-CENT FARE PLAN

1. Codd was elected after serving just two years on the Common Council from 1902 to 1904. His father had served on the Common Council from 1865 to 1870. Codd graduated from the University of Michigan in 1891 where he was captain of the baseball team for a record-setting four years.
2. Hutchins, *A Personal Story*, 186.
3. The Michigan State Bar Association was organized on February 22, 1890, in Detroit. Duffield was elected its first president on June 2, 1890. The Michigan Supreme Court did not create today's State Bar of Michigan until 1935.
4. Hutchins, *A Personal Story*, 187.
5. Ibid., 188.
6. Ibid., 194.
7. Committee of Fifty on Street Railway Questions, "Minutes of the Fifth Meeting of the Committee of Fifty held at the Common Council Chambers in the City of Detroit," June 7, 1909, Bentley Historical Library, University of Michigan, Ann Arbor, MI. Delos F. Wilcox, "The Control of Public Service

Corporations in Detroit," *Annals of the American Academy of Political and Social Science* 31 (May 1908): 42–58. The DUR annual report published in December 1903 boldly asserted: "A peculiarity of this three-cent franchise is that it covers every line in the City, the three-cent franchise providing that upon expiration of any other franchise, this company has the right to streets occupied by the company whose franchise expires. The worst that could be done to the Detroit United, therefore, is to compel it to charge the rates of fare above given on any of the streets occupied by tracks under the high fare franchise, at any time they may expire." "General Investment News: Detroit United Ry.," *Commercial & Financial Chronicle* 78, no. 2010, January 2, 1904, 47. The DUR report created barely a stir in Detroit. "We'll See When the Time Comes," *Detroit Evening News*, December 21, 1903, 2. "Some Rights in Streets," *Detroit Free Press*, December 23, 1903, 10. A summary of the incredible 350 separate streetcar franchises granted to 50 companies by the City of Detroit since 1862 can be found in Frederick Barcroft, *Report and Appraisal of the Detroit United Railway (City Lines), Detroit, Michigan, October 1, 1909* (Detroit: J. Mack Printing House, 1909), 203–19.

8. Ibid.
9. Doyle was a manufacturer of cooperage stock who invested in real estate, including the Majestic Building. He served as Michigan bank commissioner from 1911 to 1915. He was killed in a streetcar accident on January 6, 1919.
10. Hutchins, *A Personal Story*, 196.
11. Ibid., 199.
12. "To Announce Personnel: The Citizens' Anti-Franchise Committee Named Monday," *Detroit Free Press*, October 21, 1906, 4.
13. "Anti-Franchise Fight Gives Eleven Arguments Against and Plan Rally," *Detroit Free Press*, October 25, 1906, 8.
14. Hutchins, *A Personal Story*, 199.
15. Allan L. Benson, "The Detroit United Railway Company Bribing Detroit Newspapers to Get Its Street Railway Franchises Extended," *Arena* 36, no. 204 (November 1906): 553.
16. Hutchins, *A Personal Story*, 199.
17. "Any Time, Tom, Says Frazer," *Detroit Free Press*, October 30, 1906, 1.
18. Hutchins, *A Personal Story*, 200. In 1916, according to minutes of the DUR board of directors on May 31, 1916, Hutchins's annual pay was $30,000. Jere C. Hutchins Papers, 1902–1942, Burton Historical Collection, Detroit Public Library.
19. "Tom Johnson's Hand Exposed: Codd Says Magnate Fears Detroit Will Get Lower Fares than Cleveland," *Detroit Free Press*, October 31, 1906, 10.
20. Hutchins, *A Personal Story*, 216.
21. Carton principally represented the Buick Motor Company's William C. Durant. His railroad clients included the Pere Marquette Railroad.
22. The delegates were overwhelmingly Republican with only eight Democrats. "But while on several important questions the convention was very closely divided, the regular party lines were not in evidence," said John A. Fairlie in the article "The Michigan Constitutional Convention," *Michigan Law Review*, May 1908, 533–51. "To some extent the convention could be separated into a radical and a conservative group; but a middle group held the balance of power and the final result was at least acceptable to all the members of the convention" (Ibid., 534). Fairlie was a University of Michigan law

professor and a delegate himself.

23. Article 8, section 23 of Michigan's Constitution of 1908 said: "Subject to the provisions of this constitution, any city or village may acquire, own and operate, either within or without its corporate limits, public utilities for supplying water, light, heat, power and transportation to the municipality and the inhabitants thereof; and may also sell and deliver heat, power and light without its corporate limits to an amount not to exceed 25 percent of that furnished by it within the corporate limits and may also sell and deliver water outside of its limits in such amount as may be determined by the legislative body of the city or village; and may operate transportation lines without the municipality within such limits as may be prescribed by law; Provided That the right to own or operate transportation facilities shall not extend to any city or village of less than 25,000 inhabitants."
24. Article 8, section 20 of Michigan's Constitution of 1908 said: "The legislature shall provide by general law for the incorporation of cities and by a general law for the incorporation of villages; such general laws shall limit their rate of taxation for municipal purposes, and restrict their power of borrowing money and contracting debts."
25. As approved by the voters in 1908, article 8, section 21 said: "Under such general laws, the electors of each city shall have power and authority to frame, adopt and amend its charter, and, through its regularly constituted authority, to pass all laws and ordinances relating to its municipal concerns, subject to the Constitution and general laws of this state."
26. Delos F. Wilcox, "The Street Railway Crisis in Detroit," *The Economic World* 10, no. 17 (October 23, 1915): 528.
27. *Kuhn v. Common Council of the City of Detroit*, 164 Mich. 369, 388 (1911): "The contrary construction of piecemeal amendment would be out of harmony with the scheme of home rule law proposed by the Constitution and the statute would make the confusion intended to be remedied by 'general laws' worse confounded."
28. Glinnan was arrested July 26, 1912, for taking a $1,000 cash bribe from an undercover private detective, William J. Burns, who recorded the entire episode on a dictograph. Burns had been secretly brought in by Mayor Thompson regarding a request from the Wabash Railroad to vacate Seventh Street for construction of new freight sheds. Glinnan was reelected and acquitted a sensational trial on October 29, 1914.
29. *Attorney General ex. rel. Vernor v. Common Council of Detroit*, 168 Mich. 249 (1912). See also *Attorney General ex. rel McRae v. Thompson*, 168 Mich. 511 (1912); *Gallup v. City of Saginaw*, 170 Mich. 195 (1912).
30. *Attorney General ex. rel. Vernor v. Common Council of Detroit*, 168 Mich. 252 (1912).
31. William G. Deacon, "Detroit Politics Halt Development," *Public Service*, 12, no. 4 (April 1912): 125.
32. Act No. 5 of the Public Acts of 1913. The bill was named for Republican Senator Leonard D. Verdier of Grand Rapids. He served in the state house of representatives in 1909–10 and 1911–12 and as senator in 1913–14 and 1915–16. He was born in Grand Rapids on October 19, 1877. He graduated from the Literary Department of the University of Michigan in 1899 and from the Law Department in 1901.
33. *Attorney General ex. rel. Barbour v. Lindsay*, 178 Mich. 524 (1914).
34. Paul Leake, "The Detroit Referendum: An Unexpected and Remarkable Result of the Vote on the Street Railway Proposition," *Moody's Magazine*, December 1906, 90.
35. Wilcox, "Control of Public Service Corporations in Detroit," 44.
36. Ibid., 43.

37. "City to Fight to Last Ditch," *Detroit Free Press*, July 26, 1907, 12.
38. "Federal Interference in Detroit," *The Public* 10, no. 487, August 3, 1907, 419.
39. *City of Detroit v. Guaranty Trust Company of New York*, 168 F. 608, 609 (6th Cir. 1909). "May Re-Enact Hally Ordinance," *Detroit Free Press*, April 7, 1908, 5.
40. *City of Detroit v. Guaranty Trust Company of New York*, 168 F. 608 (6th Cir. 1909).
41. Hutchins, *A Personal Story*, 217–18. "For several months past it has been difficult for street railways to sell bonds for improvements, and directors of . . . Detroit United concluded to omit dividends for the time being until the investment situation has become clearer. Officials . . . believe that the interest of the stockholders will be best served by following this course." "Toledo Railways and Light: Stock Selling below Price at Which It Was Underwritten—Three-Cent Fare Agitation," *Wall Street Journal*, October 17, 1907, 6.
42. Hutchins, *A Personal Story*, 218–19.
43. Hutchins, *A Personal Story*, 219. Stock-jobbing is the rapid buying and selling of securities with the intent of generating quick profits.
44. "Detroit Municipal Policy and Montreal D.U.R. Holdings," *Detroit Free Press*, October 18, 1907, 4.
45. Hutchins, *A Personal Story*, 220.
46. Ford R. Bryan, "Gasoline Rail Car," *Dearborn Historian* 26, no. 2 (1986); Ford R. Bryan, *Beyond the Model T: The Other Ventures of Henry Ford* (Detroit: Wayne State University Press, 1997), 71. Montreal was the home of a Roman Catholic order of nuns organized in 1739, today called the Grey Nuns of the Sacred Heart. The easy pejorative reference Bryan made to the DUR's Montreal stockholders (misspelled "Gray") may have arisen in Detroit's upper financial and social circles considering the long history of Canadian ownership of Detroit's street railways dating back to the early days of Hendrie, McMillan, and Muir. In 1910, the *Free Press* said the religious order was "famous in Canada, where they are reputed to be of great wealth, being large property owners and workers among the poor." "In Picturesque Habits 600 Nuns Gather," *Detroit Free Press*, July 6, 1910, 3.
47. Barcroft had been a member of the American Institute of Architects since 1902, the educational and professional standards of which for admission to membership were, in those early years, left to state chapters.
48. *Public Service* magazine reported in April 1912 that the cost of Barcroft's report was $30,000. William G. Deacon, "Detroit Politics Halts Development," *Public Service* 12, no. 4 (April 1912): 125, 128. In May 1912, the Committee of Fifty sought payment of another $1,200 owed to nine engineers whom it said Barcroft never paid. In addition, Barcroft arranged for publication of his report by the J. Mack Printing House at a cost of $5,700 to the City of Detroit. Barcroft, *Report and Appraisal of the Detroit United Railway*. Barcroft sent copies of the book throughout the street railway engineering industry.
49. Hutchins, *A Personal Story*, 225.
50. "The Appraised Values of the Electric Street Railway of Detroit, Mich.," *Engineering-Contracting* 34, no. 1 (July 6, 1910): 16.
51. O'Geran, *Detroit Street Railways*, 225–26.
52. "Brooks Rails at Barcroft's Figures on D.U.R. Valuation," *Detroit Evening News*, November 5, 1909, 1.
53. *Statement of Frederick T. Barcroft in Answer to Request to Appear Before Board of Arbitration Detroit in re: Barcroft Appraisal of the United Railway Properties*, April 21, 1910, 3, Burton Historical Collection, Detroit Public Library, Detroit, MI.

54. "Detroit Situation," *Electric Railway Journal* 35, no. 19 (May 7, 1910): 843.
55. O'Geran, *Detroit Street Railways*, 227.
56. Hutchins, *A Personal Story*, 226.
57. Ibid., 206–7.
58. Ibid., 207–8.
59. *Proprietors of Charles River Bridge v. Proprietors of Warren Bridge*, 36 U.S. 430, 439 (1837).
60. Fred A. Baker III, *Duration of Municipal Street Grants* (Detroit: Record Printing Company, 1910), 30.
61. *Detroit Citizens Street Railway Company v. Detroit Railway*, 171 U.S. 48, 55 (1898).
62. Baker, *Duration of Municipal Street Grants*, 33.
63. Franchises originally granted to the Fort Wayne and Elmwood Street Railway Company expiring in 1910 were the subject of a subsequent Common Council resolution adopted on July 19, 1910, demanding an additional $200 per day, which the DUR refused to pay and was the subject of decisive litigation.
64. Baker, *Duration of Municipal Street Grants*, 111–12.
65. Hutchins, *A Personal Story*, 234.
66. Ibid., 235.
67. Ibid.
68. Ibid., 235–37.
69. Ibid., 237. Root would, indeed, successfully defend his legal opinion in the U.S. Supreme Court five years later. *Detroit United Railway v. Michigan*, 242 U.S. 238 (1916) reversing *People v. Detroit United Railway*, 125 N.W. 700 (1910) affirmed on rehearing, *People v. Detroit United Railway*, 162 Mich. 460 (1910). "Detroit Company Wins Fare Case," *Electric Railway Journal* 48, no. 25 (December 16, 1916): 1271.
70. Hutchins, *A Personal Story*, 237–38.
71. Ibid., 238.
72. Ibid., 238–39.
73. Ibid.
74. Deacon, "Detroit Politics Halts Development," 126.
75. "A Word of Explanation Re Street Car Question," *Detroit Free Press*, December 7, 1911, 4.
76. Deacon, "Detroit Politics Halts Development," 126.
77. Ibid.
78. *City of Detroit v. Detroit City Railway*, 172 Mich. 136, 145 (1912).
79. Ejectment was a civil action under the common law of England by which to recover title or possession of land.
80. *City of Detroit v. Detroit United Railway*, 172 Mich. 136, 159 (1912).
81. *City of Detroit v. Detroit United Railway*, 172 Mich. 136, 153 (1912).
82. *Detroit United Railway v. Detroit*, 229 U.S. 39 (1913).
83. *City of Detroit v. Detroit United Railway*, 172 Mich. 136, 154–55 (1912).
84. Baker never did get to personally argue his theory. Charles D. Joslyn, Hinton E. Spalding, William L. Carpenter, and John C. Donnelly represented the DUR.
85. *City of Detroit v. Detroit United Railway*, 172 Mich. 136, 149 (1912).
86. *City of Detroit v. Detroit United Railway*, 172 Mich. 136, 156 (1912).

87. *City of Detroit v. Detroit United Railway*, 172 Mich. 136, 158 (1912).
88. Hutchins, *A Personal Story*, 239.
89. *Detroit United Railway v. Detroit*, 229 U.S. 39 (1913).
90. "Detroit's Municipal Ownership Amendments Carried," *Electric Railway Journal* 41, no. 16 (April 19, 1913): 731–32.
91. Barnard, *Independent Man*, 38.
92. "History of Children's Hospital of Michigan," Walter P. Reuther Library, Wayne State University, May 20, 2013, http://reuther.wayne.edu/node/10265.
93. Ibid., 90. All but 10 percent of Ford employees—those under age twenty-two—benefited from the wage hike as the factory changed from two nine-hour shifts to three eight-hour shifts. "We believe," said Mr. Ford, "in making 20,000 men prosperous and contented rather than follow the plan of making a few slave drivers in our establishment multi-millionaires." Ibid., 93.
94. Barnard, *Independent Man*, 92–93.
95. Hutchins, *A Personal Story*, 242.
96. O'Geran, *History of the Detroit Street Railways*, 274.
97. Ibid., 270.
98. Hutchins, *A Personal Story*, 243.
99. Barnard, *Independent Man*, 85.
100. Ibid., 244.
101. "What the Labor Leaders Found in Europe," *Public Service* 17 (December 1914): 167–69.
102. Hutchins, *A Personal Story*, 244. Harry Barnard—born Harry Kletzy in Pueblo, Colorado, in 1906—inexplicably rewrote part of this conversation even while citing what was reported by Hutchins in his autobiography. Barnard, *Independent Man*, 103.
103. "President Hutchins Replies to Detroit Commission," *Electric Railway Journal* 43, no. 23 (June 6, 1914): 1296–97.
104. Ibid.
105. Hutchins, *A Personal Story*, 245.
106. Ibid.
107. Ibid., 246.
108. "Buying the D.U.R.," *Detroit Evening News*, April 3, 1915, 1. The *Evening News* said the annual statement reported $1,615,000 treasury securities. In his book, Hutchins curiously called the sum "fourteen hundred thousand." He used the same phrase to describe the price paid for the DUR lighting plant and street railways in Windsor. Hutchins, *A Personal Story*, 247 and 280. Actually, bonds totaling $1,715,000 were being held by the DUR's treasury. "The Detroit Purchase," *Electric Railway Journal* 45, no. 19 (May 8, 1915): 901.
109. Hutchins, *A Personal Story*, 247–49.
110. Ibid., 247–48.
111. An accountant hired by the commission found bonded debt of $4.1 million against the DUR's Flint, Pontiac, and Orchard Lake divisions that also was included in the $24.9 million. "Detroit Purchase Negotiations," *Electric Railway Journal* 45, no. 15 (April 10, 1915): 725.
112. "Nov. 2 Is Day Set for Vote on Purchase of D.U.R. System," *Detroit Evening News*, August 24, 1915, 1. O'Geran, *History of the Detroit Street Railways*, 278–79.

113. Hutchins, *A Personal Story*, 250. A disastrous $4 million fire in 1951 destroyed most of Michigan's archived records.
114. "Huge Crowd Hears Car Commissioners Outline Their Plans," *Detroit Evening News*, October 31, 1915, 1.
115. O'Geran, *History of the Detroit Street Railways*, 283.
116. Hutchins, *A Personal Story*, 251.
117. Ibid., 260–61.
118. Ibid., 262.
119. Ibid., 267. The 2,359-member employee union sought the firing of all 260 female conductors hired by the company in arbitration before the National War Labor Board, a demand they dropped after the first day of hearings on December 13, 1918. In 1917, a state constitutional amendment granting suffrage to Michigan women lost by a one hundred thousand majority. Three years later, the same proposition carried by a majority of two hundred thousand votes.
120. "The Official Announcement by President Frank W. Brooks," *Electric Railway Service* (December 7, 1917), 5. The *Electric Railway Service* was a newsletter published and distributed on streetcars by the DUR.
121. "Skip-stop" was a service pattern that reduced electric power consumption, lessened travel times, and increased capacity by having streetcars make only some of the designated stops along a route. On December 21, 1917, the Federal Fuel Administration ordered the DUR to resume skip-stops and to reduce streetcar illumination by 50 percent to conserve coal. James Couzens was one of the three members of the Wayne County committee issuing the order.
122. "Five-Cent Fares in Detroit," *Electric Railway Journal* 50, no. 23 (December 8, 1917): 1053–54.
123. Employees assigned to a "split-run" shift would work two- to four-hour periods in the early morning, mid-day, and late afternoon. Streetcar motormen and conductors bitterly resented the unpaid split between runs that provided significant cost savings to the DUR.
124. O'Geran, *History of the Detroit Street Railways*, 320.
125. Hutchins, *A Personal Story*, 268.
126. Barnard, *Independent Man*, 114.
127. *In re Employees v. Detroit United Railway Company*, National War Labor Board, Docket No. 32, July 31, 1918.
128. Ibid.
129. "Couzens to Test Right of D.U.R. to Raise Fares," *Detroit Free Press*, August 8, 1918, 1. "Couzens' Fare Test Case On," *Detroit Evening News*, August 8, 1918, 1.
130. "Mayoral Race Lacking in Pep," *Detroit Free Press*, August 4, 1918, 5. Barnard, *Independent Man*, 115. "Thirty-Year Controversy Brought to an End," *Electric Railway Journal* 59, no. 20 (May 20, 1922): 839. "Couzens and the M.O. as Seen from the Outside," *Detroit Evening News*, May 22, 1922, 20.
131. "Arrest D.U.R. Conductors If 6c is Charged: Candidate Couzens Carries Out Intention as Planned," *Detroit Free Press*, August 9, 1918, 1. Barnard, *Independent Man*, 115. O'Geran, *History of the Detroit Street Railways*, 202. Barnard broadly cited Detroit papers from August 14, 1918. They do not support his reference. O'Geran cited the *Evening News*, May 22, 1922. Each tells slightly different versions of the exchange between Couzens and the conductor. Hutchins and Bingay told a much abbreviated story. Hutchins, *A Personal Story*, 270. Bingay, *Detroit Is My Own Home Town*, 122. Diligent searching found no newspaper photographs of the incident. The following weekend, the Broadway Strand

Theater's newsreel showed James Couzens being ejected from a streetcar for refusing to pay the six-cent fare. It was screened at a host of movie theaters the following week. "How to Keep Cool Pictured in Free Press Film Edition," *Detroit Free Press*, August 12, 1918, 2.

132. "Tumult and Shouting," *Electric Railway Journal* 52, no. 7 (August 17, 1918): 311.
133. Barnard, *Independent Man*, 116.
134. Ibid., 126.
135. "Overturn Cars in Detroit: Passengers Refuse to Pay Six-cent Fares and Start Several Riots," *New York Times*, August 11, 1918.
136. "Ordinance Fixing Fares at 5c Takes Effect Tuesday," *Detroit Free Press*, August 12, 1918, 3.
137. "D.U.R. Take Fare Case to the U.S. Supreme Court," *Michigan Manufacturers and Financial Record* 22, no. 7 (August 17, 1918): 17.
138. "The Law Steps In," *Detroit Free Press*, August 14, 1918, 4; "Brooks Says D.U.R. Kept Within Law," *Detroit Evening News*, August 14, 1918, 5.
139. "Tumult and Shouting," 311.
140. "Construction News," *Electric Railway Journal* 52, no. 9 (August 31, 1918): 397.
141. "Teasing the Goose That Lays the Golden Egg," *Michigan Manufacturer and Financial Record* 22, no. 7 (August 17, 1918): 26. "The whole city of Detroit, members of the council, city administration, politicians seeking office who advised the people not to pay the new fares, managers of the D.U.R., and the car-riding public, ought to be heartily ashamed of themselves." "Shameful Conduct," *Detroit Free Press*, August 12, 1918, 4.
142. *Detroit United Railway v. City of Detroit*, 248 U.S. 429 (1919). Justices Oliver Wendell Holmes Jr. and Louis D. Brandeis concurred in the dissenting opinion written by Justice John H. Clarke, who quoted from an earlier Holmes dissent in *Denver v. Denver Union Water Company*, 246 U.S. 178 (1918) that said: "We must assume that the Water Company may be required, within a reasonable time, to remove its pipes from the streets. *Detroit United Railway v. Detroit*, 229 U.S. 39. . . . In view of that right of the city, which, if exercised, would make the company's whole plant valueless as such, the question recurs whether the fixing of any rate by the city could be said to confiscate property on the ground that the return was too low. . . . The ordinance of the city could mean no more than that the company must accept the city's rates or stop—and as it could be stopped by the city out and out, the general principle is that it could be stopped unless a certain price should be paid." Delos F. Wilcox, "Rate Regulations Where Franchises Have Expired," *American City* 20, no. 3 (March 1919): 216.
143. *Detroit United Railway v. Dingman*, 204 Mich. 543 (1919). Per curiam is Latin for "by the court." It describes a decision of an appeals court in which no judge is identified as its author.

CHAPTER 10. ON DRIVING A HARD BARGAIN

1. "How Is Mayor to Get D.U.R.: Citizens and City Hall Hum with Speculation over 'War Measures,'" *Detroit Free Press*, January 16, 1919, 8. "The Mayor's First Official Utterance," *Detroit Free Press*, January 16, 1919, 4. Barnard, *Independent Man*, 114. O'Geran, *History of the Detroit Street Railways*, 200–201.
2. Hutchins, *A Personal Story*, 271.
3. Ibid., 273.
4. Ibid.

5. "Detroit Purchase Arranged," *Electric Railway Journal* 53, no. 11 (March 15, 1919): 533–34; "Detroit M. O. Vote April 7," *Electric Railway Journal* 53, no. 12 (March 22, 1919): 614.
6. *Hutchins* at 274. "Analyzing the 'D.U.R. Myth,'" *Michigan Manufacturer and Financial Record* 23, no. 13 (March 29, 1919): 5–6, 16–18.
7. "Detroit M.O. Vote April 7," *Electric Railway Journal* 53, no. 12 (March 22, 1919): 614. Barnard, *Independent Man*, 126. O'Geran, *History of the Detroit Street Railways*, 296.
8. O'Geran, *History of the Detroit Street Railways*, 306–7. "Dow Supports Purchase Plan," *Detroit Evening News*, April 1, 1919, 19. Dow's latter statement may be the genesis of the famous often misquoted remark of former General Motors President Charles E. Wilson during a hearing on his nomination by President Dwight D. Eisenhower as secretary of defense in 1952.
9. "Ford Indorses Purchase Plan: 'One of the Safest Business Propositions I Ever Heard of,' Says Motor Car King," *Detroit Evening News*, October 13, 1915, 1. Barnard, *Independent Man*, 127.
10. "Resignation of Couzens Is Accepted," *Detroit Evening News*, October 13, 1915, 1. The two headlines were side by side on the front page.
11. "Why Buy the D.U.R.? Ford Man Asks," *Detroit Free Press*, April 4, 1919, 8; "Cities Hidden D.U.R. Price," *Detroit Free Press*, April 6, 1919, 13; "Says New Can Is Not 'Dream,'" *Detroit Free Press*, April 7, 1919, 5.
12. "Detroit Refuses to Pay the Price," *Electric Railway Journal* 53, no. 15 (April 12, 1919): 739–40.
13. Barnard, *Independent Man*, 127. "Senator Couzens Metamorphosis from Business Man to Politician," *Detroit Saturday Night*, December 30, 1922.
14. "Detroit Conference May 9," *Electric Railway Journal* 53, no. 18 (May 3, 1919): 885.
15. Ibid.
16. "An Optimistic Talk on Street Railways by Henry Ford," *Electric Railway Journal* 53, no. 15 (April 12, 1919): 738.
17. O'Geran, *History of the Detroit Street Railway*, 308.
18. In early 1906, Mayor Codd was widely but wrongly reported to have joined with Frank C. Andrews, the notorious bank fraud convict, in promoting an $8.3 million downtown subway with two hundred miles of new surface lines to be financed by Prendergast & Rawson of New York City. *Wall Street Journal*, February 26, 1906, 2; "Detroit Letter," *Moody's Magazine*, March 1906, 485; "Detroit Roads," *Railroad Gazette* 40, no. 10 (March 9, 1906): 78; "Detroit, Mich," *Electrical World* 47, no. 10 (March 10, 1906): 540; "The Proposed Codd-Andrews Subway," *Detroit Evening News*, January 26, 1906, 5; "Figure New 3-Cent Line Would Pay," *Detroit Evening News*, March 13, 1906, 1; "Codd's Ordinance to Go to Council within a Month," *Detroit Evening News*, March 26, 1906, 1. Codd had, indeed, floated a vague subway plan. "Subway Project: Now Codd Has Gigantic Plan to Help Him to Second Term," *Detroit Free Press*, February 27, 1906, 10. The thoroughly confusing episode, however, was muddied even further when a Detroit attorney named Frank D. Andrus came forward seeking a street railway franchise for what he called the People's Subway & Transit Company. "Withholds Backers: F.D. Andrus Won't Say Who Is Behind the Street Railway Plan," *Detroit Free Press*, April 12, 1906, 3. A skeptical committee of the Common Council refused to take up his scheme, and it died within weeks. O'Geran, *History of the Detroit Street Railways*, 206–9.
19. Barclay Parsons & Klapp, *Report on Detroit Street Railway Traffic and Proposed Subway Made to Board of Street Railway Commissioners City of Detroit* (January 1915): 5.
20. Ibid., 7.

21. Ibid., 24.
22. "Solution of Parking Problem," *Michigan Manufacturer and Financial Record* 19, no. 14 (March 31, 1917): 6.
23. Malcolm W. Bingay, *Of Me I Sing* (Indianapolis, IN: Bobbs-Merrill Company 1949), 240.
24. Bingay, *Detroit Is My Own Home Town*, 124.
25. Barnard, *Independent Man*, 6.
26. Daniel Okrent, *Last Call: The Rise and Fall of Prohibition* (New York: Simon & Schuster, 2010), 129.
27. Ibid., 256–59.
28. Bingay, *Detroit Is My Own Home Town*, 125.
29. "Fare Raise Unavoidable," *Detroit Free Press*, June 4, 1919, 4.
30. Due in most part to the growing city's population in the postwar period, monthly audits for July, August, and September showed that the company was earning net income instead of suffering net loss. On December 26, the DUR waived its claim for the one-cent transfer charge, and the arbitration proceeding was dismissed. "Request for Transfer Charge Withdrawn," *Electric Railway Journal* 55, no. 1 (January 3, 1920): 75.
31. Barnard, *Independent Man*, 128. "Urges City Ownership: Detroit Mayor Proposes Municipal Lines to End Car Strike," *New York Times*, June 10, 1919, 13.
32. Barclay Parsons & Klapp had submitted a second report on December 1, 1917, updating what it had concluded in 1915. The second engineering study also recommended building sixty-five miles of downtown subways, elevated lines on Woodward, Michigan, Gratiot, and Forest Avenues, and crosstown extensions further out in the city. It said Detroit should finance and build the system, and regulate fares at cost of service, while the DUR should operate it. They warned that without a fare increase, no improvements could be financed. The money generated by a fare hike would be equally divided between the city and the DUR, with the city's share used to pay off the debt. Eventually, the city could use its share to acquire the DUR. The study concluded that any outright purchase of the DUR before that time would make it impossible for Detroit to finance the building of a rapid transit system.
33. Barnard, *Independent Man*, 129.
34. "Detroit Rejects the Tayler Plan," *Electric Railway Journal* 54, no. 19 (November 8, 1919): 872.
35. "Detroit Council Persistent," *Electric Railway Journal* 54, no. 20 (December 13, 1919): 951; "Detroit's Mayor Sustained," *Electric Railway Journal* 54, no. 21 (December 20, 1919): 1013.
36. Harlow C. Clark, "Politics and Population: The Detroit Muddle, the Reasons for It, and the Prospects for a Final Satisfactory Settlement, A Municipal Ownership Plan that has Transferred the Odium of Bad Service from the Company to the Politician," *AERA* 8, no. 12 (July 1920): 1289–90.

CHAPTER 11. NOBODY STOOD UP

1. Edward Hungerford, "Detroit Muddles Along," *Electric Railway Journal* 56, no. 4 (July 24, 1920): 164.
2. "New System Approved," *Electric Railway Journal* 55, no. 3 (January 17, 1920): 169–70.
3. "City Officials View 'Gas' Car," *Detroit Free Press*, March 9, 1920, 15.
4. Wilkinson resigned in August 1921. Couzens appointed Horace H. Esselstyn, civil engineer and former Detroit public works commissioner to fill the vacancy.

5. *American Boy* was a monthly magazine for juvenile boys published from 1899 to 1941 with a circulation reaching five hundred thousand in 1929.
6. Clark, "Politics and Population," 1292–93.
7. "Railway Makes Counter Franchise Bid," *Electric Railway Journal* 55, no. 12 (March 20, 1920): 615.
8. The Street-Railway Act's requirement for municipal consent did not expressly describe how it should be done. Consequently, courts would look elsewhere in state law and in the municipal charter. No other statue applied. Detroit's charter embraced the adoption of ordinances by initiative. Wilcox, *Municipal Franchises*, 722–23, argued in favor in allowing everyone—all men and women—to vote on franchises. The U.S. Supreme Court upheld a public right of initiative against the State of Arizona in a recent constitutional challenge. *Arizona State Legislature v. Arizona Independent Redistricting Commission*, 576 U.S. (2015).
9. Clark, "Politics and Population," 1293.
10. Clark, "Politics and Population," 1293; "Large Detroit Registration," *Electric Railway Journal* 55, no. 13 (March 27, 1920): 664–65; "In Its Concluding Phase," *Electric Railway Journal* 55, no. 14 (April 3, 1920): 718. O'Geran, *History of the Detroit Street Railways*, 337.
11. "Detroit's Battle on in Earnest," *Electrical Railway Journal* 55, no. 10 (March 10, 1920): 486; "Mayor to Blame, Says D.U.R. Head," *Detroit Free Press*, March 30, 1920, 10.
12. "Large Detroit Registration," 664.
13. Barnard, *Independent Man*, 129–30.
14. "City Officials View 'Gas' Car," 15. Barnard, *Independent Man*, 130.
15. "Railway Will Contest Detroit Election," *Electric Railway Journal* 55, no. 16 (April 17, 1920): 823–24.
16. See, e.g., *Detroit United Railway v. City of Detroit*, 255 U.S. 171 (1921); *VanBaalen v. City of Detroit*, 217 Mich. 883 (1921); *Detroit United Railway v. Wayne County Judge*, 212 Mich. 230 (1920).
17. Hutchins, *A Personal Story*, 280.
18. Wayne County Circuit Judge Henry A. Mandell's refusal to enjoin sale of the railway bonds to the Detroit Sinking Fund Commission was affirmed as moot because Couzens had succeeded in rearranging for their purchase elsewhere. *Detroit United Railway v. City of Detroit*, 214 Mich. 170 (1921).
19. Bryan, *Beyond the Model T*, 73. Bryan's great-great-grandfather Samuel Ford was brother to Henry Ford's grandfather John Ford. He worked for the Ford Company from 1941 to 1974 and published numerous articles and eight Ford-related books.
20. Barnard, *Independent Man*, 131.
21. "Detroit Lays Tracks, Evades Injunction," *New York Times*, January 10, 1921; "Coup d'État by Municipal Line," *Electric Railway Journal* 57, no. 3 (January 15, 1921): 151.
22. "Calls M.O. Car Coup 'Outrage': Tactic Employed in Crossing D.U.R. Tracks 'Damnable,' Declares Stevenson," *Detroit Free Press*, January 27, 1921, 1.
23. "Municipal Railway Crossing Illegal," *Electric Railway Journal* 57, no. 7 (February 12, 1921): 325.
24. The so-called one-man safety car invented by Charles O. Birney and Joseph M. Bosenbury introduced the use of pneumatically balanced and interlocking doors. If any door was stuck open, a passenger or other object blocked the door, the motors could not be started. The controls also included an early application of the deadman, a device that removed power from the motors if the handle was released for any reason. The car would then coast to a stop.

25. *Detroit United Railway v. City of Detroit*, 255 U.S. 171 (1921).
26. Barnard, *Independent Man*, 132.
27. O'Geran, *History of the Detroit Street Railways*, 350.
28. "A Dangerous Precedent in the Making," *Electric Railway Journal* 57, no. 25 (June 18, 1921): 1111.
29. Hutchins, *A Personal Story*, 282.
30. "$17,000 a Mile Offered by Municipal Line for Private Property," *Electric Railway Journal* 58, no. 4 (July 23, 1921): 146.
31. *Wall Street Journal*, August 16, 1921, quoted in "Financial Authority Points Out D.U.R. Weak Spots," *Electric Railway Journal* 58, no. 4 (August 20, 1921): 295. "Financial Authority Points Out D.U.R.'s Weak Spots," *Electric Railway Journal* 58, no. 8 (August 20, 1921): 295.
32. Couzens only needed simple majority approval of the initiative referendum on his ouster ordinance.
33. The illness suffered by Brooks, age fifty-seven, may have been tuberculosis from its vague description by Hutchins. "As soon as he was able to travel, Mrs. Brooks and he went to the Riviera," Hutchins said. "It was hoped—but hoped in vain—that a few months in the mild climate of that region would restore him. They returned to Detroit and not long afterwards Frank Brooks died—died as he had lived—as courageous, as loyal, and as sweet a soul as ever fought the battle of life." Hutchins, *A Personal Story*, 279.
34. By the end of the Roaring Twenties, he would be described as one of the richest men in the United States. "Smithsonian May Get Jewel of a Villa," *New York Times*, May 19, 1984.
35. "Detroit United Railway," *United States Investor* 32, no. 23 (June 4, 1921): 1184; "New Interests in Detroit United," *Electric Railway Journal* 57, no. 23 (June 4, 1921): 1061; "Dow Aids Detroit Traction," *New York Times*, May 28, 1921; "D.U.R. in Charge of Administrative Committee," *Electric Railway Journal* 67, no. 24 (June 11, 1921): 1094.
36. "New Interests in Detroit United," *Electric Railway Journal* 57, no. 23 (June 4, 1921): 1061.
37. Hutchins, *A Personal Story*, 282.
38. His autobiography described the executive committee as consisting of "Chairman Hutchins, President Edwards, and Director Alex Dow." Hutchins, *A Personal Story*, 281. "About four years or more previous to its publication this story was written, a bit now and then, at home, and away, during a period of considerable time and wholly from memory," Hutchins wrote in a foreword to the book. "It may be a shade lacking in chronological and factual accuracy and in the use of proper names." Ibid., ix.
39. Ibid., 283–84.
40. Ibid., 285.
41. *In the Matter of the Application of the Detroit United Railway*, Case No. D-1117, Michigan Public Utilities Commission, May 18, 1921, August 30, 1921, and December 1, 1921. After the first stock dividend, the DUR had 153,750 shares outstanding of 250,000 authorized. "Michigan Commission Charges Bad Faith," *Electric Railway Journal* 58, no. 11 (September 10, 1921): 418; "Stock Dividend Refused," *Electric Railway Journal* 58, no. 24 (December 10, 1921): 1045.
42. Hutchins, *A Personal Story*, 281.
43. "D.U.R. Stock Breaks Sharply in Montreal," *Detroit Free Press*, January 5, 1922, 12.
44. A financial news weekly published in New York City reported that Ferguson, DUR vice president, was furiously soliciting proxies on behalf of existing management and that Brueau & Company, a

Montreal brokerage, was seeking proxies on behalf of large stockholders. "Fight for Control," *Financial World* 37, no. 2 (January 9, 1922): 70.

45. Hutchins, *A Personal Story*, 285–86.
46. "Mayor Grants Truce to D.U.R.," *Detroit Free Press*, January 13, 1922, 2.
47. "Ouster Delayed," *Electric Railway Journal* 59, no. 3 (January 21, 1922): 131.
48. The *Free Press* reported that Moore was also present: "Mayor Grants Truce to D.U.R."
49. "Leasing Plan Causes Split," *Electric Railway Journal* 59, no. 2 (January 14, 1922): 85; "Ouster Delayed," 131.
50. "Ouster Delayed," 131.
51. "Full Statement of Detroit Matters to Be Made at Annual Meeting," *Electric Railway Journal* 59, no. 4 (January 28, 1922): 165.
52. "Action Put Off on Car Ouster," *Detroit Free Press*, January 25, 1922, 4. "Ouster Delay Reason Asked," *Detroit Free Press*, January 31, 1922, 5. Raising a suspicion of involvement by Couzens, Jankowski never obtained service of process on Mayor Couzens or any of the other city officials named as defendants before the DUR annual meeting, and the case was dismissed a couple of weeks later. "Purchase Outlook Improved," *Electric Railway Journal* 59, no. 8 (February 25, 1922): 327.
53. Hutchins, *A Personal Story*, 286–87.
54. Ibid., 287.
55. Bingay, *Detroit Is My Own Home Town*, 123.
56. "Mayor Will Sit in With D.U.R.," *Detroit Free Press*, January 26, 1922, 5.
57. "News from Canada Dominion: Gingras to Fight D.U.R. Compromise; Montreal Stockholder Refuses to Attend Meeting," *Detroit Free Press*, February 1, 1922, 14.
58. "D.U.R. and City to Talk Sale: Committee Representing Company to Confer with Mayor Thursday," *Detroit Free Press*, February 14, 1922, 4.
59. Hutchins, *A Personal Story*, 287.
60. Ibid.
61. They were Gingras, Laurendeau, P. A. Boivin, J. Ovide Desmasais, Montreal suburban bus operator, Honore Blouin, J. B. Gill, and Louis A. Gosselin. "Detroit Meeting Eventful," *Electric Railway Journal* 59, no. 6 (February 11, 1922): 246.
62. Hutchins, *A Personal Story*, 287–88.
63. "Burdick Made Head of D.U.R.," *Detroit Free Press*, February 9, 1922, 5.
64. Hutchins, *A Personal Story*, 288. Contemporaneous news reports at the time reported that Albert E. Peters was elected secretary. The position of treasurer was left vacant. "Detroit United Ry.—New Directors & Officers," *Commercial and Financial Chronicle*, February 11, 1922, 626. Gingras was not elected treasurer until a subsequent meeting of the stockholders and directors held on March 11, 1922. "People Will Decide," *Electric Railway Journal* 59, no. 11 (March 18, 1922): 488.
65. Hutchins, *A Personal Story*, 288.
66. Ibid., 288–89.
67. "D.U.R. and City to Talk Sale," 4.
68. "City Matures Traction Plan: Railway Body to Lay D.U.R. Purchase Before Couzens Saturday," *Detroit Free Press*, February 18, 1922, 1.
69. O'Geran, *History of the Detroit Street Railways*, 361.

70. Barnard, *Independent Man*, 133.
71. Hutchins, *A Personal Story*, 289.
72. "People to Own and Run D.U.R.," *Civic Searchlight* 9, no. 4 (April 1922): 2.
73. Hutchins, *A Personal Story*, 295.
74. *City of Detroit v. Detroit United Railway*, 226 Mich. 354 (1924).

CHAPTER 12. THE DETROIT STREETCAR PARADE

1. The St. Louis Car Company delivered PCC 268 to Detroit in 1949. A street railway industry committee called the Presidents' Conference Committee had designed and engineered the PCC streetcar.

Bibliography

Bak, Richard. *Detroit 1900–1930*. Charleston, SC: Arcadia Publishing, 1999.

———. *Detroitland: A Collection of Movers, Shakers, Lost Souls, and History Makers from Detroit's Past*. Detroit: Wayne State University Press, 2011.

Baker, Frederick A., III. *Duration of Municipal Street Grants*. Detroit: Record Printing Company, 1910.

Barnard, Harry. *Independent Man: The Life of Senator James Couzens*. Detroit: Wayne State University Press, 2002.

Base, Miroslav. "The Development of Detroit 1701–1920: A Planning History." Unpublished manuscript, Division of International Urban Studies, Center for Urban Studies, Wayne State University, July 1970.

Baut, Donald V. "Track 'n' Trolley." *Dearborn Historian* 11 (winter 1971): 3–22.

Bingay, Malcolm W. *Detroit Is My Own Home Town*. Indianapolis, IN: The Bobbs-Merrill Company, 1946.

———. *Of Me I Sing*. Indianapolis, IN: The Bobbs-Merrill Company 1949.

Bluestone, Daniel M. "Detroit's City Beautiful and the Problem of Commerce." *Journal of the Society of Architectural Historians* 47, no. 3 (September 1988): 245–62.

Blume, William Wirt. "Legislation on the American Frontier: Adoption of Laws by Governor and Judges: Northwest Territory 1788–1798; Indiana Territory 1800–1804; Michigan Territory." *Michigan Law Review* 60, no. 3 (January 1962): 317–72.

Booth, Henry J. *Treatise on the Law of Street Railways: Embracing Surface, Sub-Surface and Elevated Roads, whether Operated by Animal Power, Electricity, Cable or Steam Motor*. Philadelphia: T. & J. W. Johnson, 1892.

Boyle, Kevin, and Victoria Getis. *Muddy Boots and Ragged Aprons: Images of Working-Class Detroit, 1900–1930*. Detroit: Wayne State University Press, 1997.

Bragg, Amy Elliott. *Hidden History of Detroit*. Charleston, SC: History Press, 2011.

Bryan, Ford R. *Beyond the Model T: The Other Ventures of Henry Ford*. Detroit: Wayne State University Press, 1997.

Bureau of Labor, State of Michigan. *Ninth Annual Report*. Lansing: Robert Smith, 1892.

Burton, Clarence M. "Augustus Brevoort Woodward." In *Historical Collections: Collections and Researches*

Made by the Michigan Pioneer and Historical Society, 29:638–64. Lansing: Wynkoop Hallenbeck Crawford, 1901.

———. *The Building of Detroit*. [Detroit?], 1912.

———. *Cadillac's Village, or Detroit under Cadillac: With List of Property Owners and a History of the Settlement, 1701 to 1710*. Detroit: C. M. Burton, 1896.

———. *Compendium of History and Biography of the City of Detroit and Wayne County, Michigan*. Chicago, Henry Taylor, 1909.

———. *Governor and Judges Journal: Proceedings of the Land Board of Detroit*. Ed. M. Agnes Burton. [Detroit], 1915.

———. *History of Detroit, 1780–1850: Financial and Commercial; Report of Historiographer*. Detroit: C. M. Burton, 1917.

Burton, Clarence M., William Stocking, and Gordon K. Miller. *The City of Detroit, Michigan, 1701–1922*. Detroit: S. J. Clarke, 1922.

Cangany, Catherine. *Frontier Seaport: Detroit's Transformation into an Atlantic Entrepôt*. Chicago: University of Chicago Press, 2014.

Carter, Clarence Edwin, ed. *The Territorial Papers of the United States*. Vol. 10, *The Territory of Michigan, 1805–1820*. Washington, DC: United States Government Printing Office, 1942.

Catlin, George B. *The Story of Detroit*. Chicago: R. R. Donnelley and Sons, 1923.

Cavin, Ruth. *Trolleys: Riding and Remembering the Electric Interurban Railways*. New York, Hawthorn Books, 1976.

Clark, Harlow C. "Politics and Population: The Detroit Muddle, the Reasons for It, and the Prospects for a Final Satisfactory Settlement, a Municipal Ownership Plan That Has Transferred the Odium of Bad Service from the Company to the Politician." *AERA* 8, no. 12 (July 1920): 1269–1304.

Cooley, Thomas McIntyre. *Michigan: A History of Governments*. Boston: Houghton, Mifflin, 1885.

Craig, W. H. "From Georgia Cabin to $40,000,000 Fortune." *Atlanta Journal Magazine*, June 10, 1923, 13 and 22.

Cyphers, Christopher J. *The National Civic Federation and the Making of a New Liberalism, 1900–1915*. Westport, CT: Praeger, 2002.

Dahlheimer, Harry. *Public Transportation in Detroit*. Detroit: Wayne University Press, 1951.

Davis, Robert Scott. "The Georgia Odyssey of the Confederate Gold." *Georgia Historical Quarterly* 86, no. 4 (2002): 569–86.

Deacon, William G. "Detroit Politics Halts Development." *Public Service* 12, no. 4 (April 1912): 125–28.

DeMatteo, Arthur E. "The Downfall of a Progressive: Mayor Tom L. Johnson and the Cleveland Streetcar Strike of 1908." *Ohio History* 104 (1998): 24–41.

Drutchas, Geoffrey G. "Gray Eminence in a Gilded Age: The Forgotten Career of Senator James McMillan of Michigan." *Michigan Historical Review* 28, no. 2 (fall 2002): 78–113.

Dunbar, Willis Frederick, and George S. May. *Michigan: A History of the Wolverine State*. 3rd rev. ed. Grand Rapids, MI: William B. Eerdmans, 1995.

Ely, Richard Theodore, and George Ray Wicker. *Elementary Principles of Economics*. New York City: Macmillan, 1909.

Faber, Don. *The Boy Governor: Stevens T. Mason and the Birth of Michigan Politics*. Ann Arbor: University of Michigan Press, 2012.

Farmer, Silas, ed. *The Bi-Centenary of the Founding of the City of Detroit, 1701–1901: Being the Official Report of the Celebration of July 24, 25, 26, 1901*. Detroit: C. M. Rousseau & Sons, 1902.

———. "Historic Tablets and Memorials." In *The Bi-Centenary of the Founding of City of Detroit, 1701–1901: Being the Official Report of the Celebration of July 24, 25, 26, 1901*, ed. Silas Farmer, 288–96. Detroit: C. M. Rousseau & Sons, 1902.

———. *The History of Detroit and Michigan or, The Metropolis Illustrated: A Chronological Cyclopaedia of the Past and Present*. 2nd ed. Detroit: Silas Farmer and Company, 1889.

Fishman, Robert, ed. *The American Planning Tradition: Culture and Policy*. Washington, DC: Woodrow Wilson Center Press, 2000.

Fuller, George N., ed. *Historic Michigan: Land of the Great Lakes*. Vol. 2. Dayton: National Historical Association, 1966.

Gay, Cheri Y. *Detroit Then and Now*. San Diego: Thunder Bay Press, 2001.

Goddard, Stephen B. *Getting There: The Epic Struggle between Road and Rail in the American Century*. Chicago: University of Chicago Press, 1996.

Golden, Brian M. *Farmington Junction: A Trolley History*. Farmington, MI, 1999.

Goodwin, Doris Kearns. *The Bully Pulpit: Theodore Roosevelt, William Howard Taft, and the Golden Age of Journalism*. New York: Simon & Schuster, 2013.

The Government of the City of Detroit and Wayne County, Michigan, 1701 to 1907. Detroit: Mannausa & Wieber, 1907.

Greer, David Alan. "Revolutionary, Federalist, Republican: The Early Life and Reputations of William Hull." PhD diss., Texas Christian University, 2007.

Hamlin, Marie Caroline Watson. *Legends of Le Détroit*. 2nd ed. Detroit: Thorndike Nourse, 1884.

Haney, Lewis Henry. *A Congressional History of Railways in the United States, 1850–1887, Bulletin of the University of Wisconsin*, no. 342. Madison: University of Wisconsin, 1910.

Hathaway, Ellen C. *History of Highland Park*. Highland Park: Board of Education, 1957.

Heyden, Marie. "Justice Woodward and the Michigan Territory." *Michigan History*, Spring 1967, 43–55.

Hilton, George W. *The Cable Car in America: A New Treatise upon Cable or Rope Traction as Applied to the Working of Street and Other Railways*. Rev. ed. San Diego: Howell-North Books, 1982.

Historical Collections: Collections and Researches Made by the Michigan Pioneer and Historical Society. Vol. 31. Lansing: Wynkoop Hallenbeck Crawford, 1902.

Holli, Melvin G. *The American Mayor: The Best and the Worst Big-City Leaders*. University Park: Pennsylvania State University Press, 1999.

———. *Reform in Detroit: Hazen S. Pingree and Urban Politics*. Westport, CT: Greenwood Press, 1981.

Hooker, Clarence. *Life in the Shadows of the Crystal Palace, 1910–1927: Ford Workers in the Model T Era*. Bowling Green, OH: Bowling Green State University Popular Press, 1997.

Horwitz, Morton J. *The Transformation of American Law, 1780–1860*. Cambridge, MA: Harvard University Press, 1977.

Howe, Daniel Walker. *What Hath God Wrought: The Transformation of America, 1815–1848*. Oxford: Oxford University Press, 2007.

Hulbert, Archer Butler. *Historic Highways of America*. Vol. 10, *The Cumberland Road*. Cleveland: Arthur H. Clark Company, 1904.

Hutchins, Jere C. *A Personal Story*. Norwood, MA: Plimpton Press, 1938.

Jackson, Kenneth T. *Crabgrass Frontier: The Suburbanization of the United States*. New York: Oxford University Press, 1985.

Jaffe, Eric. *The King's Best Highway: The Lost History of the Boston Post Road, the Route That Made America*. New York: Scribner, 2010.

James, Sheryl. "A Street Called Woodward." *Michigan History*, May 1, 2002, 42–53.

Jenkins, W. C. "Problems in Municipal Economics." *National Magazine*, April 1909, 104–11.

Johnson, Malcolm B. *Red, White, and Bluebloods in Frontier Florida*. Tallahassee: Rotary Clubs of Tallahassee, 1976.

Johnson, Tom Loftin, and Elizabeth J. Hauser. *My Story*. New York: B. W. Huebsch, 1911.

Johnston's Detroit City Directory. Detroit: James Dale Johnston & Company, 1861.

Judson, Adoniram B. "History and Course of the Epizootic among Horses upon the North American Continent in 1872–73." In *Public Health Reports and Papers: Presented at the Meetings of the American Public Health Association, 1873*, 88–109. New York: Hurd and Houghton, 1875.

Klein, Daniel B., and John Majewski. "Plank Road Fever in Antebellum American: New York State Origins." *New York History* 75 (January 1994): 39–65.

Klein, Maury. *History of the Louisville & Nashville Railroad*. Lexington: University Press of Kentucky, 2003.

Kozora, Kathryn. *Detroit's East Riverfront: People and Places of Yesterday*. Detroit: City of Detroit Recreation Department, 1982.

Kutler, Stanley I. *Privilege and Creative Destruction: The Charles River Bridge Case*. New York: W. W. Norton, 1978.

"Land Titles in the Michigan Territory, No. 112, 9th Congress, 1st Sess." In *American State Papers: Documents, Legislative and Executive, of the Congress of the United States in Relation to the Public Lands*, ed. Walter Lowrie, 1:229–31. Washington, DC: Duff Green, 1834.

Larson, John Lauritz. *Internal Improvement: National Public Works and the Promise of Popular Government in the Early United States*. Chapel Hill: University of North Carolina Press, 2001.

Leake, Paul. *History of Detroit: A Chronicle of Its Progress, Its Industries, and the People of the Fair City of the Straits*. Vol. 1. Chicago: Lewis Publishing, 1912.

———. "The Street Railway Situation in Detroit." In *Proceedings of the Buffalo Conference for Good City Government and the Sixteenth Annual Meeting of the National Municipal League*, ed. Clinton Rogers Woodruff, 120–41. [Philadelphia]: National Municipal League, 1910.

Leary, Margaret A. *Giving It All Away: The Story of William W. Cook and His Michigan Law Quadrangle*. Ann Arbor: University of Michigan Press, 2011.

———. "William W. Cook and Detroit Street Railways, 1891–1894." *Chronicle of the Historical Society of Michigan* 29, no. 4 (2007): 21–23.

Livingstone, William. *Livingstone's History of the Republican Party*. Vol. 1. Detroit, 1900.

Lovett, William P. "Pingree of Detroit—Demagogue or Statesman?" *National Municipal Review* 8, no. 9 (November 1919): 595–97.

Martelle, Scott. *Detroit: A Biography*. Chicago: Chicago Review Press, 2012.

McCracken, S. B., ed. *Detroit in Nineteen Hundred: A Chronological Record of Events, Both Local and State during the Closing Year of the Century*. Detroit: Evening News Association, 1901.

McNitt, V. V. "Idol of the People." *Michigan Alumnus Quarterly Review* 63, no. 10 (December 8, 1956): 152–58.

Meacham, Jon. *American Lion: Andrew Jackson in the White House*. New York: Random House, 2009.

Meyer, Katherine Mattingly, and Martin C. P. McElroy, eds. *Detroit Architecture: A.I.A. Guide*. Rev. ed. Detroit: Wayne State University Press, 1980.

Middleton, William D. *The Interurban Era*. Milwaukee: Kalmbach, 1961.

Miller, John Anderson. *Fares, Please! A Popular History of Trolleys, Horse-Cars, Street-Cars, Buses, Elevateds, and Subways*. New York: Dover, 1941.

Moore, Charles. "Augustus Brevoort Woodward: A Citizen of Two Cities." *Records of the Columbia Historical Society* 4 (1901): 114–27.

———. "The Beginnings of Territorial Government in Michigan." In *Historical Collections: Collections and Researches Made by the Michigan Pioneer and Historical Society*, 31:510. Lansing: Wynkoop Hallenbeck Crawford, 1902.

———. *Governor, Judge and Priest: Detroit 1805–1815*. New York: DeVinne Press 1891.

———. "Municipal Ownership of Street Railways in Detroit." *Quarterly Journal of Economics* 13 (1899): 453–64.

Moran, J. Bell. *The Moran Family: 200 Years in Detroit*. Detroit: Alved of Detroit, 1949.

Morgan, Donald G. *Justice William Johnson: The First Dissenter*. Columbia: University of South Carolina Press, 1954.

Murdock, Eugene C. *Tom Johnson of Cleveland*. Dayton: Wright State University Press, 1994.

Myers, Gustavus. *The History of the Public Franchises in New York City (Boroughs of Manhattan and the Bronx*. New York: Reform Club Committee on City Affairs, 1900.

Nimmo, Harry M. *The Men of '05: Some Pen Pictures and a Few Other Things Concerning One Hundred or More Gentlemen Connected with the First All-Republican Government of Michigan*. Detroit, 1905.

Oestreicher, Richard Jules. *Solidarity and Fragmentation: Working People and Class Consciousness in Detroit, 1875–1900*. Urbana: University of Illinois Press, 1989.

O'Geran, Graeme. *A History of the Detroit Street Railways*. Detroit: Conover Press, 1931.

Okrent, Daniel. *Last Call: The Rise and Fall of Prohibition*. New York: Scribner, 2010.

Orton, Lawrence D. *Polish Detroit and the Kolasinski Affair*. Detroit: Wayne State University Press, 1981.

Owen, Wilfred. *Transportation for Cities: The Role of Federal Policy*. Washington, DC: Brookings Institution, 1976.

Palmer, Friend. *Early Days in Detroit*. Detroit: Hunt & June, 1906.

Parkins, Almon Ernest. *The Historical Geography of Detroit*. Chicago: University of Chicago Libraries, 1918.

Parkman, Francis. *A Half Century of Conflict*. Boston: Little, Brown, 1897.

Parsons, Frank. *The Bondage of Cities*. Philadelphia: C. F. Taylor, 1900.

Pickens, Buford L. "Early City Plans for Detroit: A Projected American Metropolis." *Art Quarterly* 6 (1943): 34–51.

Pingree, Hazen S. *Facts and Opinions; or, Dangers That Beset Us*. Detroit: F. B. Dickerson, 1895.

Poremba, David Lee. *Detroit: 1860–1899*. Charleston, SC: Arcadia, 1998.

———. *Detroit: A Motor City History*. Charleston, SC: Arcadia, 2001.

———, ed. *Detroit in Its World Setting: A Three-Hundred Year Chronology, 1701–2001*. Detroit: Wayne State University Press, 2001.

Powell, Lyman P. *Historic Towns of the Western States*. New York: G. P. Putnam's Sons, 1901.

Pratt, Mason D., and C. A. Alden. *Street-Railway Roadbed*. New York: John Wiley & Sons, 1898.

Remini, Robert V. *Henry Clay: Statesman for the Union*. New York: W. W. Norton, 1991.

Report of the Committee of the House of Representatives to Whom Was Referred the Message of the President of the United States of December 23, 1805, Transmitting a Report from the Governor and Presiding Judge of the Territory of Michigan Relative to the State of That Territory, March 18, 1806.

Reps, John W. "Planning in the Wilderness: Detroit, 1805–1830." *Town Planning Review* 25, no. 4 (1955): 240–50.

Rips, Rae Elizabeth, ed. *Detroit in Its World Setting: A 250-Year Chronology 1701–1951*. Detroit: Detroit Public Library, 1953.

Rohrbough, Malcolm J. *The Land Office Business: The Settlement and Administration of American Public Lands, 1789–1837*. Oxford: Oxford University Press, 1968.

Ronnick, Valerie Michele. "From Rome to Detroit: Augustus Woodward and the Campus Martius." In *Detroit and Rome: Building on the Past*, ed. Melanie Grunow Sobocinski, 12–16. Dearborn: University of Michigan-Dearborn, 2005.

Ross, Robert B. *The Early Bench and Bar of Detroit from 1805 to the End of 1850*. Detroit: Richard P. Joy and Clarence M. Burton, 1907.

Ross, Robert B., and George B. Catlin. *Landmarks of Detroit: A History of the City*. Rev. Clarence M. Burton. Detroit: Evening News Association, 1898.

Scheiber, Harry N. "The Transportation Revolution and American Law: Constitutionalism and Public Policy." In *Transportation and the Early Nation: Papers Presented at an Indiana American Revolution Bicentennial Symposium*, 20. Indianapolis: Indiana Historical Society, 1982.

Schramm, Jack E., and William H. Henning. *Detroit's Street Railways*. Vol. 1, *City Lines 1863–1922*. Chicago: Central Electric Railfans' Association, 1978.

Schramm, Jack E., William H. Henning, and Thomas J. Dworman. *Detroit's Street Railways*. Vol. 2, *City Lines 1922–1956*. Chicago: Central Electric Railfans' Association, 1980.

Schramm, Kenneth. *Detroit's Street Railways*. Charleston, SC: Arcadia, 2006.

Scott, William Benson. *Street Railways of Detroit; a Compilation of the State Laws, City and Suburban Ordinances and Franchises and Court Decisions, Granting and Relating to the Rights of Street Railway Corporations of Detroit, Michigan*. New York: Knickerbocker Press, 1895.

Sheldon, E. M. *The Early History of Michigan: From the First Settlement to 1815*. New York: A. S. Barnes, 1856.

Smith, Michael O. "The City as State: Franchises, Politics, and Transit Development in Detroit 1863–1879." *Michigan Historical Review* 23, no. 1 (1997): 1–32.

Southeastern Michigan Council of Governments. *Historical Population and Employment by Minor Civil Division, Southeast Michigan: Population, 1900–2000; Employment, 1970–2000*. Detroit: SEMCOG, 2002.

Stilgoe, John R. *Common Landscape of America, 1580 to 1845*. New Haven: Yale University Press, 1982.

Stocking, William, and Gordon K. Miller. *The City of Detroit, Michigan, 1701–1922*. Detroit: S. J. Clark, 1922.

Sutherland, Daniel E. *The Confederate Carpetbaggers*. Baton Rouge: Louisiana State University Press, 1988.

Tucker, Patrick M., and Laurel E. Heyman. "Welcome to Hard Times: Two French Merchants and Militiamen in the Detroit River Region during the War of 1812." *Michigan Historical Review* 38 (2012): 53–81.

Warner, Sam Bass, Jr. *Streetcar Suburbs: The Process of Growth in Boston, 1870–1900*. 2nd ed. Cambridge, MA: Harvard University Press, 1978.

Warren, Charles. "The Charles River Bridge Case." *The Green Bag* 20, no. 6 (1908): 284–96.

———. "The Charles River Bridge Case, Part II." *The Green Bag* 20, no. 7 (1908): 346–54.

Wilcox, Delos F. "The Control of Public Service Corporations in Detroit." *Annals of the American Academy of Political and Social Science* 31 (May 1908): 42–58.

———. *Municipal Franchises: A Description of the Terms and Conditions upon Which Private Corporations Enjoy Special Privileges in the Streets of American Cities.* New York: Engineering News Publishing, 1910.

Wilcox, Delos F., and M. M. O'Shaughnessy. *Municipal Railways in the United State and Canada.* Chicago: Public Ownership League of America, 1922.

Williston, Samuel. "History of the Law of Business Corporations before 1800." *Harvard Law Review* 2 (1888): 105–24.

Wood, Charles W. "He Had Millions, but Wanted a Job." *Collier's*, August 5, 1922, 9.

Woodford, Arthur M. *Detroit and Its Banks: The Story of Detroit Bank & Trust.* Detroit: Wayne State University Press, 1974.

———. *This Is Detroit, 1701–2001.* Detroit: Wayne State University Press, 2001.

Woodward, Augustus B. "Protest of Judge Woodward against the Sale of Certain Lands, June 1, 1818." In *Historical Collections: Collections and Researches Made by the Pioneer Society and Historical Society*, 2nd ed., 12:473. Lansing: Wynkoop Hallenbeck Crawford, 1908.

Youngstrand, C. O., ed. *A Gallery of Pen Sketches in Black and White of Our Michigan Friends "As We See 'Em."* Detroit: Wm. Graham Printing, 1905.

Zunz, Olivier. *The Changing Face of Inequality: Urbanization, Industrial Development, and Immigration in Detroit, 1880–1920.* Chicago: University of Chicago Press, 1982.

Index

*Page numbers in **boldface** refer to illustrations.*

E

F

V

W

Y